the food & wine lover's guide
to melbourne
& surrounds

Hardie Grant Books

the food & wine lover's guide to melbourne & surrounds

Introduction by
Stephanie Alexander

Melbourne Geelong **Bellarine** Mornington
Peninsula **Yarra Valley** Dandenong Ranges
Nagambie and Strathbogie Ranges Phillip Island
Ballarat Macedon Ranges **Daylesford**

This book is an initiative of
Melbourne & Surrounds Marketing Inc.

First published in 2006 by
Hardie Grant Books
85 High Street
Prahran, Victoria, 3141
Australia

Copyright © in text: Stephanie Alexander,
Allan Campion, Michele Curtis,
Claude Forell, Michael Harden

Copyright © in images: David Hannah,
Simon Griffiths, Adrian Lander, Mark Roper

For a full list of picture credits see p.322

All rights reserved. No part of this publication
may be reproduced, stored in a retrieval
system of transmitted in any form by any
means, electronic, mechanical, photocopying,
recording or otherwise, without the prior
written consent of the publishers and
copyright holders.

National Library of Australia
cataloguing-in-publication data

The food and wine lover's guide
to Melbourne and surrounds.

ISBN 1 74066 373 X.

1. Restaurants -
    Victoria - Melbourne Region.
2. Dinners and dining -
    Victoria - Melbourne Region.
3. Food industry and trade -
    Victoria - Melbourne Region.
4. Wineries - Victoria - Melbourne Region.
I. Campion, Allan.

647.959451

Design and typesetting by Pfisterer + Freeman

Prepress by Publishing Prepress (Port Melbourne)

Printed in China by SNP Leefung

Acknowledgements

Melbourne is blessed with many fabulous food and wine experiences, showcasing the fresh, quality produce sourced from its surrounding regions. Literally right on Melbourne's doorstep is an abundance of culinary adventures and great places to explore, all within an easy drive and all offering their own special experiences. This is unique among Australian cities, and something that makes Melbourne a truly great destination and ideal springboard for lovers of food & wine.

As sponsor of this unique publication, **Melbourne and Surrounds Marketing Inc.** would like to thank Hardie Grant Books for sharing our vision, partnering us, and providing the expertise to make this book a reality.

Also, our very special thanks to the writers, Stephanie Alexander for her introduction, Claude Forell, Michael Harden, Allan Campion and Michelle Curtis, for telling the story of each region in glowing words. Thanks too to photographers Simon Griffiths, David Hannah, Adrian Lander and Mark Roper who have stunningly captured the visual delights of our regions. These writers and photographers have roamed every corner of our regions and handpicked the features that make each region unique.

We also hope this book will inspire you, our readers, on your own culinary journeys. We hope you will explore Melbourne and Surrounds, **The Food & Wine Lover's Guide** in hand, and discover for yourself some fabulous food and wine. There are passionate people to meet, regional produce to be tasted and wines to be savoured. We promise a warm welcome will await you at each special destination!

Contributors

Writers

Stephanie Alexander

Stephanie Alexander is a cook, restaurateur, food writer and champion of the quality and diversity of Australian food. She ran the internationally acclaimed Melbourne restaurant Stephanie's for twenty-one years from 1976. In 1994 she was awarded an Order of Australia for her services to the hospitality industry and to tourism. Stephanie is the author of numerous books including *Stephanie's Seasons*, *Cooking and Travelling in South-West France* (co-author) and the bestselling food bible *The Cook's Companion*. She is a regular contributor to the Melbourne *Age* and the *Sydney Morning Herald*.

Allan Campion and Michele Curtis

Allan Campion and Michele Curtis live, breathe and write about food. Professional chefs and award-winning writers, they are major contributors to the Australian food scene with more than twenty books to their credit, as well as regular newspaper and magazine features. They are also food consultants, host culinary tours, cooking classes and demonstrations, and are partners in Ludo, The Good Food Store in bayside Melbourne. Allan and Michele's books include the annual *Foodies' Guide to Melbourne* and *The Seasonal Produce Diary*, as well as the award-winning *Every Day in the Kitchen* and their latest cookbook *Food With Friends*.

Claude Forell

Claude Forell was the founding editor of *The Age Good Food Guide*, an editor of *The Age* Epicure section and a regular restaurant reviewer for more than twenty-five years. Now a freelance food and travel writer, he has also been associated with *The Age* as a staff writer, European correspondent, columnist and contributor for more than fifty years. He and his partner, Joy Durston, who is co-ordinator of Daylesford Macedon Produce, have a property at Glenlyon, near Daylesford.

Michael Harden

Michael Harden has specialised in food writing for the last six years. He reviews restaurants and writes food and travel stories for the *Sunday Magazine* (supplement to the *Sunday Herald-Sun* and the *Sunday Telegraph*) and for the *Melbourne Weekly*. Michael is a regular contributor to the *Herald-Sun* 'City Style' pages and writes for *The Age Good Food Guide*, *The Age Cheap Eats* and *Australian Gourmet Traveller Restaurant Guide*. Michael is also the author of *Celebrazione!*, and a co-author of the Wyndham Estate *Seasons Plate Cookbook*.

Photographers

Simon Griffiths

Simon Griffiths is a leading Melbourne-based photographer whose work appears regularly in magazines such as *Australian Gourmet Traveller*, *Vogue Living* and *Australian Country Style*. He has also been the photographer for numerous food, wine, and travel books, including *The Food and Wine Lover's Guide to the Great Ocean Road* and *Food and Wine Lover's Guide to Melbourne's Bays and Peninsulas*; *Salute*; *Cooking and Travelling in South-West France*; and *Under the Olive Tree*.

David Hannah

Originally from Scotland, Hannah first came to Australia in 1990 to look around and to take a few photos. After a few years travelling in Asia and Europe, including a stint as a photojournalist, he returned to study and work with some of Australia's top photographers. David is based in Melbourne, but with clients including Tourism Victoria and Tourism Australia, he works on advertising and editorial assignments in Australia and throughout the world. He is also a regular contributor to *Gourmet Traveller Wine* magazine

Adrian Lander

Adrian Lander trained as a chef in England, then discovered a passion for photography while working in Austria. Now based in Australia and specialising in food and wine photography, Adrian's work has featured in numerous national and international magazines, and books including *Red and White* by Max Allen, *Chalk and Cheese* by Will Studd, *Celebrazione*! the story of the De Bortoli family in Australia, and the Wyndham Estate *Seasons Plate Cookbook*.

Mark Roper

Mark Roper hails from London where he specialised in editorial portraits and travel. Since arriving in Melbourne six years ago he has been kept busy shooting numerous advertising campaigns as well as for food, interiors and travel magazines including *Delicious*, *Vogue Entertaining*, *Vogue Living*, *Interiors*, *Good Taste*, *Vive*, *Condé Nast Traveller UK*, and *Qantas* magazine.

melbourne & surrounds

nagambie and strathbogie ranges

Rushworth
Violet Town
Bendigo
Nagambie
Euroa
Heathcote
Maldon
Castlemaine

macedon ranges

Seymour
Malmsbury
Tallarook
Kyneton
Broadford

yarra valley

daylesford

Clunes
Lancefield
Kilmore
Hepburn Springs
Woodend
Romsey
Wandong
Daylesford
Mt Macedon
Heathcote Junction

ballarat

Creswick
Macedon
Wallan
Gisborne
Whittlesea

melbourne

Ballarat
Mernda
St Andrews
Yarra Glen
Buninyong
Mount Helen
Healesville
Coldstream
Bacchus Marsh
Melton
Lilydale

dandenong ranges

MELBOURNE
Olinda
Monbulk
Werribee
Dandenong

geelong

bellarine

Portarlington
Frankston
Cranbourne
Geelong
Mornington
Kooweerup

mornington peninsula

Queenscliff
Tyabb
Barwon Heads
Mount Martha
Point Lonsdale
Dromana
Hastings
Torquay
Portsea
Sorrento
Red Hill
Rosebud

phillip island

Anglesea
Flinders
Cowes
Newhaven
San Remo
Wonthaggi

A sample of the rich and varied produce that helps make Melbourne and surrounds a delight for food and wine lovers.

Introduction

Stephanie Alexander

Melbourne is the vibrant capital of Victoria. It is my hometown and reminds me just a little of Paris. Both are cities that thrive on good talk and good food, both have a certain briskness possibly connected with their similar breezy climates, and both have a sense of neighbourhood. Increasingly suburbs and neighbourhoods are developing their own personalities, and their residents are often very loyal. As in Paris I am still discovering *quartiers* I know little about. Whenever I do stray into a new neighbourhood in Melbourne there are interesting food discoveries to be made.

Every Melbourne food lover has benefited from the contribution made by our migrants over the last fifty years. Sydney Road, Brunswick is the home of Middle Eastern specialities, Johnson Street Fitzroy is where one heads for fresh or dried *chorizo*, bagels come from East Caulfield, borscht from Acland Street, Italian specialities are to be found in Brunswick and Carlton, and for anyone living in a suburb that is home to an Asian population, be it Abbotsford, Footscray, Springvale or Box Hill, a bundle of just-picked greens for stir-frying, a takeaway roast duck, a jar of dried shrimp, or a drinking coconut will be available seven days a week.

It would be foolish to suggest that some suburbs are not more affluent than others, but by and large, the food supply is egalitarian. Shopping strips still include a fruit and vegetable shop of the old-fashioned variety. These same shopping strips almost always have a friendly butcher, but less often a fresh fish shop. Inner-suburban Melburnians mostly live close to a large, fresh-food market, and the steady growth of interest in sustainable agriculture is reflected in the growth of the organic sections of these markets.

Melburnians love good coffee. Our Italian migrants introduced us to espresso in the early sixties and right away it became very fashionable to meet for coffee in 'coffee lounges'. There are plenty of places where tea is also taken seriously – such as Brunswick Street in Fitzroy. We have teahouses in arcades, kiosks at the end of piers and jetties, and coffee shops in galleries and public spaces, and we have plenty of picnic tables in our parks.

And then there are our restaurants. Our chefs are skilled and are exploring their own style. The wine industry grows and grows. Melbourne food is firmly planted in the minds of the world's foodies as a must-see phenomenon and culinary tourism grows in importance with every passing year. At all price levels, the restaurants represent an extraordinary range of ethnic traditions and styles both in the city and suburbs. The neighbourhood restaurant is an important place and most neighbourhoods have at least one gem. We don't usually travel too far during the week to eat. And it is simplicity itself to assemble a picnic from any one of a number of specialist food and bread shops and head for the Moonlight Cinema in the Botanic Gardens, or a concert at the Myer Music Bowl.

Our three million inhabitants mean a city that is exciting but not over-crowded. In a few minutes I can be in the centre of the city with all the bustle of up-to-the minute commerce and in as few minutes I can be in parkland or walking along the river.

Thirty years ago if one travelled outside of Melbourne the experience was very hit-and-miss. Rarely was one tempted to dawdle through country towns, or happen upon an interesting restaurant or friendly hostelry. Accommodation was in lacklustre motels with paper-thin walls or in neglected and sad hotel rooms. My own childhood was spent more than forty years ago on the Mornington Peninsula, and my parents who loved to be with friends around a table, would rush to any restaurant that opened its doors. Most lasted one season only as the return-to-school exodus at the end of January meant there were simply no more visitors.

How things have changed. Tourism is acknowledged as vitally important to the state's economy and it is booming. A weekend at any one of the destinations mentioned in this book now promises good food including a wide range of local specialities, excellent wine, delightful accommodation, probably a museum or art gallery with surprisingly rich collections, possibly a literary festival or a weekend celebrating spring wildflowers, a nut harvest or grape vintage or a sporting event. Winemakers have in many cases blazed the trail. Where wineries have flourished with their cellar-door tastings, so also have bed and breakfast establishments with character and charm, small private hotels and guesthouses. More and more couples have decided on a sea or tree change and have opened or revived kiosks, cafés, restaurants, or produce stores that are supported by both visitors and locals. Many of these entrepreneurial ventures have become the hub of the community and noticeboards and announcements tell of a rich and varied community life where one can take classes in almost anything, go bushwalking or horse-riding, call on all manner of local expertise, and where children are offered an astonishing range of activities. The message is that life is good and business is brisk in these towns.

Many of these regional centres take pride in their environmental awareness and support farmers' markets as well as businesses that are deemed to be environmentally friendly. Dedicated people have developed and promoted the markets and the food trails so that visitors can experience local cheese, or fruit or honey, or venison. I have yet to visit a farmers' market and come away without a bulging basket.

I holiday each year in a small town on the Bellarine peninsula and never fail to gasp with delight at the first viewing of our magnificent coastline along the Great Ocean Road. And who could not be entranced by the purple, pink and white expanse of lavender in bloom at Lavendula at Daylesford? I accompanied a busload of inner-city kids on a mushroom hunt in the Macedon Ranges last year and we did gather plenty of mushrooms but just as importantly the kids revelled in the unfamiliar and beautiful bushland.

Lifestyle has almost become a dirty word, linked as it usually is with acquiring new material possessions. But the benefit of a few days lived at a slower pace – away from one's own pressing domestic chores – strolling down a different street, walking in scented bushland, picnicking beside a river, or enjoying the vista of blue hills, breathing in clear air, enjoying a glass of local wine, and dawdling on quiet roads, adds immeasurable quality to life and allows us to return to the everyday recharged, and inspired to do it again very soon.

Turning the pages of this book will be sure to stir the reader to get out there and experience some of the fabulous wine, food and scenery that Melbourne and regional Victoria has to offer. Do it very soon!

Stephanie

contents

Introduction by Stephanie Alexander

1	Melbourne
34	Mornington Peninsula
66	Phillip Island
86	Yarra Valley
114	Dandenong Ranges
138	Nagambie and Strathbogie Ranges
158	Macedon Ranges
188	Daylesford
218	Ballarat
242	Bellarine
272	Geelong
298	Directory
318	Index
322	Photo credits

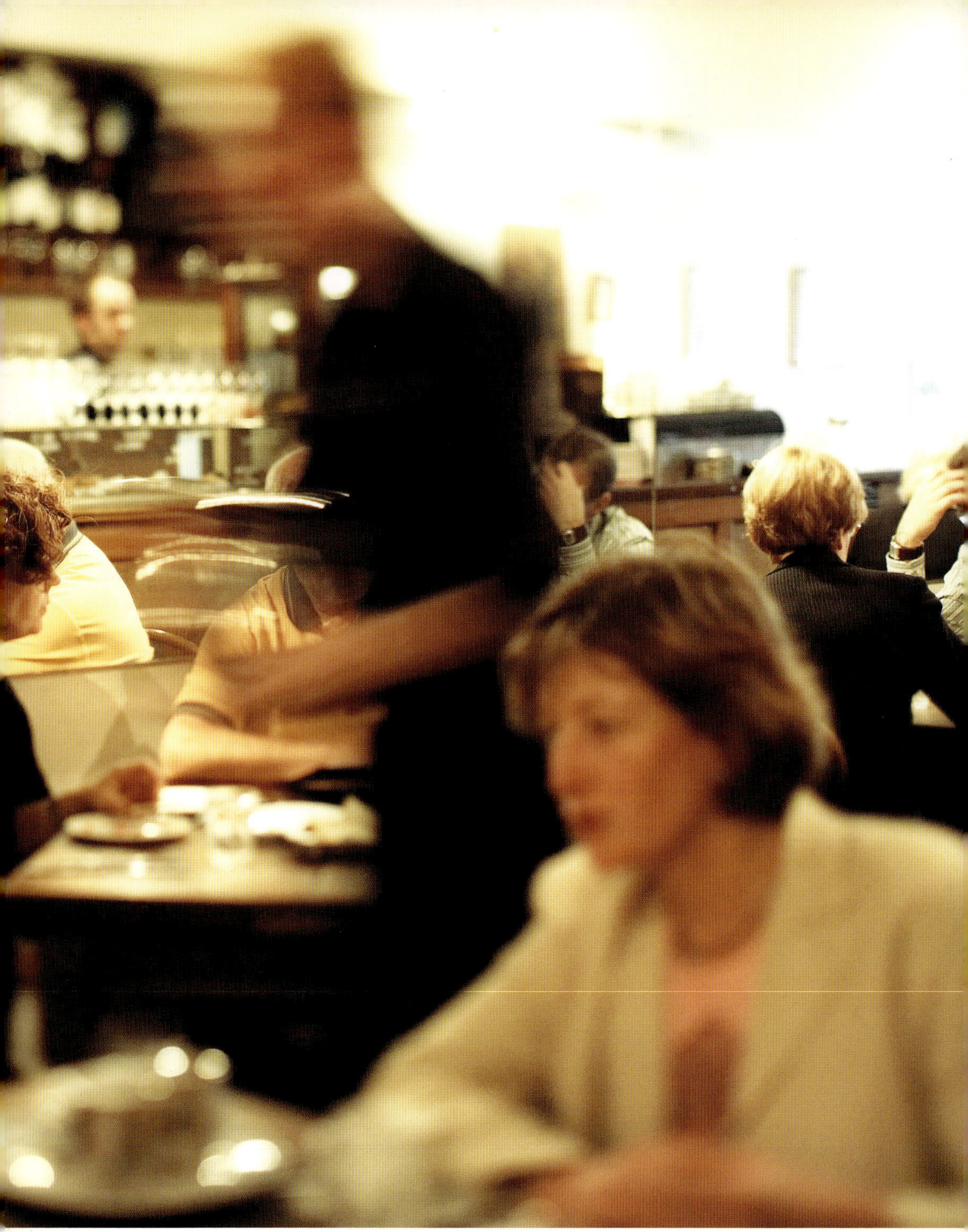

melbourne

michael harden

melbourne

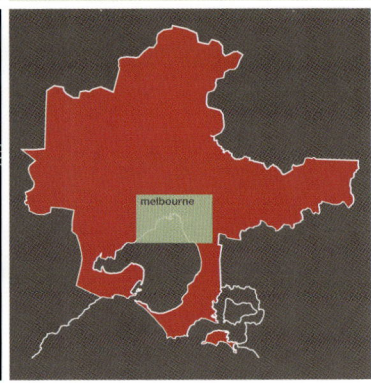

Fitzroy Nth		Alphington				
Flemington	Parkville	Clifton Hill				
Footscray	Fitzroy		Kew			
	Carlton	Collingwood				
	• Victoria Market	Abbotsford				
Yarraville	MELBOURNE					
		Richmond	Hawthorn	Camberwell		
	South Melbourne		Kooyong			
Port Melbourne	South Yarra					
	Albert Park	Prahran	Toorak			
			Armadale			
Williamstown	Middle Park					
	St Kilda	St Kilda East	Malvern			
PORT PHILLIP	Elwood	Caulfield				

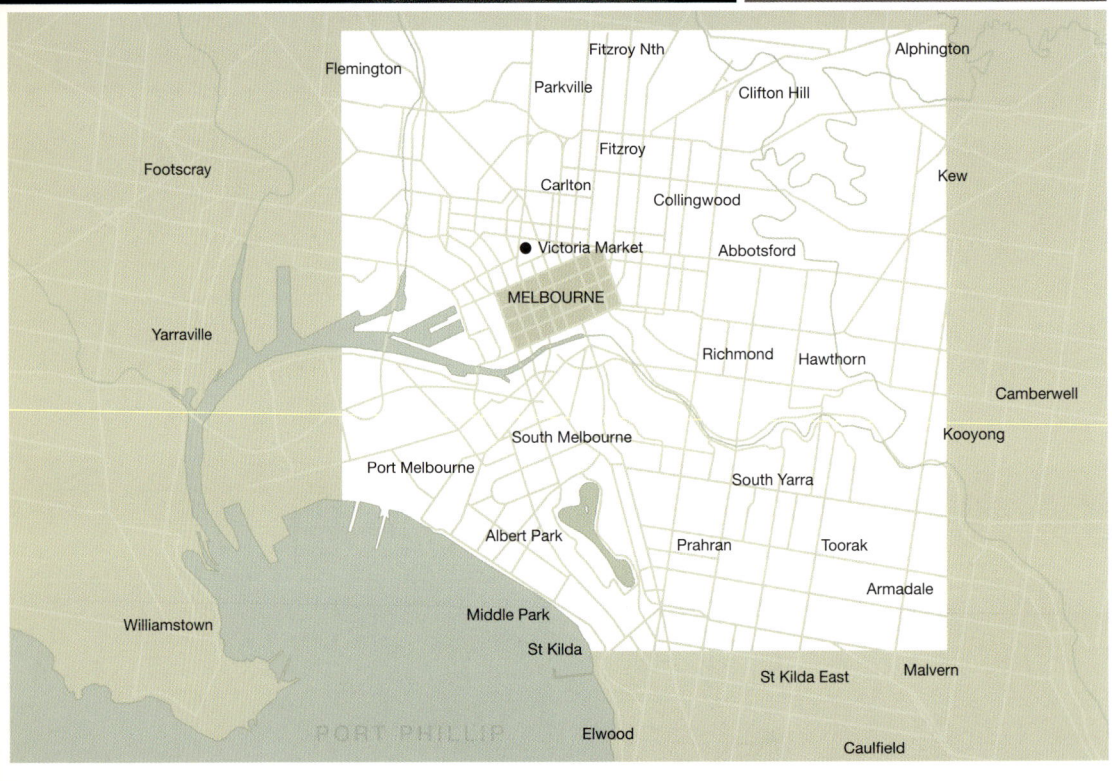

Melbourne is a city obsessed with food and wine ... the opening of a new restaurant is acceptable water cooler conversation and the standard of coffee is cause for civic pride

Above
Stocking up at the 'Vic Market'.

Opposite
The city skyline along the Yarra River.

There are more than a dozen sizeable food and wine events held across the city every year and the biggest, the Melbourne Food and Wine Festival, pulls in 270 000 people. Melbourne is the kind of place where it is perfectly reasonable to drive across town to buy renowned sausages or to get into a heated debate about the merits of different pizza bases. It is a city obsessed with food and mad about wine, but go exploring and you'll soon discover that it has every reason to be.

Melbourne has a remarkably strong and diverse restaurant, bar and café culture. Eating out is a constantly interesting and surprising experience whether you're grabbing a quick bowl of hot and sour soup in Chinatown, washing down tapas with sherry in a laneway bar or mopping up a tagine with Turkish bread on the waterfront. Melbourne's restaurant scene has nurtured and attracted some truly brilliant chefs, but in terms of a chicken-and-egg scenario – what came first, the chefs or the scene – you could argue that Melbourne's food culture owes as much to the accessibility of brilliant produce and a constant stream of migrants as it does to the people who cook so skilfully today.

Great ingredients inspire great cooking and this is perhaps where Melbourne's real strength as a food and wine destination begins – easy access to wonderful produce. A lucky geographical position has the city surrounded by fertile farming regions with a wide variety of soil types and climates that are capable of producing an enviable array of ingredients, while its close proximity to the sea has meant fresh seafood is always available. The added bonus of having some of the country's best winemaking regions on the doorstep – and a population that loves a drink – has helped wine become a constant on the Melbourne scene.

Waves of immigrants – Chinese, Italian, Greek, Lebanese, Vietnamese, Ethiopian – and a population increasingly open-minded and receptive to new flavours have also had a huge effect on the food fabric of Melbourne. Each wave of immigrants has brought with it both people who understand and cook the cuisine of the 'old country' alongside a ready-built customer base of fellow immigrants who want real rather than assimilated versions of the food they

Right
A busy lunchtime in one of Melbourne's café hubs, Hardware Lane.

Opposite
Late afternoon at Albert Park Lake.

know. The food culture of the city cannot help but become richer and more diverse for it. With its many produce markets providing fertile ground for new ingredients and ideas to take root in the general population, Melbourne has become a city with a broad and knowledgeable palate.

So arrive hungry, take a deep breath and plunge in – it's a deep, delicious and constantly surprising pool.

Foodstores and producers

It is easy to find good produce in Melbourne. The food markets – both large and small – that are scattered across the city are the most obvious sources of ingredients but certainly can't claim a monopoly on all the best ingredients. Across Melbourne, often in the most unlikely and unassuming places, you can find little stores that are baking fantastic bread, selling incredibly fresh and varied seafood, pampering cheese, making chocolate or specialising in Portuguese, Japanese or Lebanese groceries and ingredients. There are treasures everywhere waiting to be found and, in Melbourne, you never have to dig too deep before discovering produce-gold.

The Queen Victoria Market should be the first port of call for anybody wanting to know what makes the city's food heart thump. Officially operating since 1878, the Queen Vic is the largest open-air market in the southern hemisphere. It sprawls over 7 hectares of the CBD's north-west and attracts more than a million and a half visitors every year. But facts and figures only tell part of the story and to really understand why the Queen Vic Market has become part of Melbourne's soul (and why there was such a vehement public outcry in the 1970s when developers began laying plans to dismantle it) you need to visit the market on a Saturday when the place is heaving with locals of every age, colour and creed.

Walking into the Meat Hall by the Elizabeth Street entrance, you are immediately assailed by the incredible noise and energy – not to mention the smell – of the place. Butchers, fishmongers and chicken specialists shout out

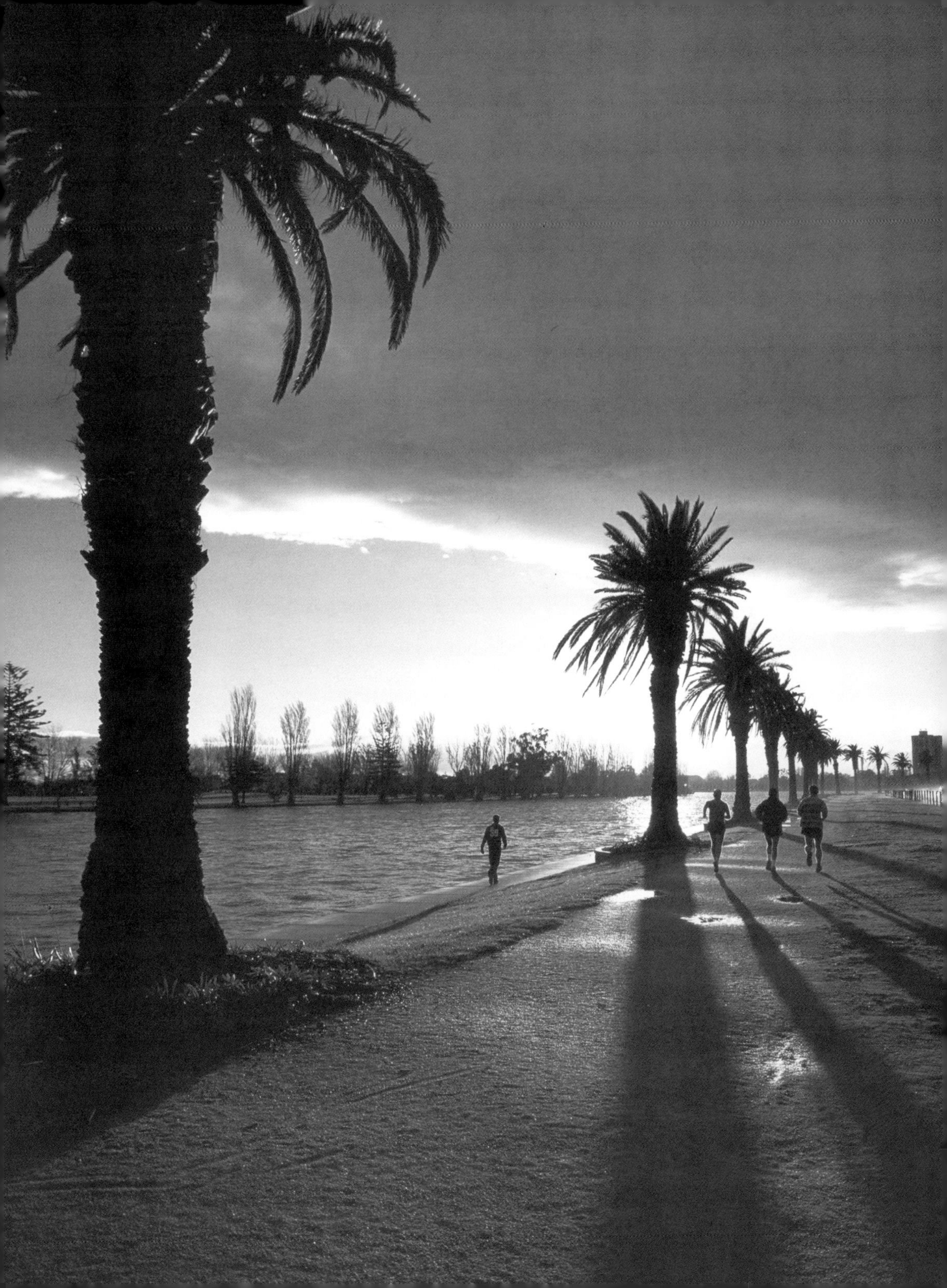

to the bag-toting, trolley-pushing crowds, enticing them with special deals on the amazing variety of produce heaped up in the glass cases that line the aisles.

Further in you'll discover the more sedate but no less vibrant art deco style of the Deli Hall with its marble counters filled with an unbelievable range of cheese, meat, bread, coffee, game, pasta, olives, nuts, honey, eggs, pickles, jam and dried fruit. Look for the Polish Deli with its amazing variety of smallgoods from black pudding to smoked eel, or the incredible array of cheese and butter at Curds and Whey and discover the Chicken Pantry's remarkable selection of poultry, eggs and game meat, much of it free-range and hormone-free.

For fruit and vegetables, head outside to the 'sheds' (vast open-sided structures) where mounds of farm-fresh produce – everything from humble spuds and pumpkin to Asian greens and fresh water chestnuts – stretch away in every direction. Those interested in organic produce should head to I Shed while mushroom lovers should pay particular attention to Cameron Russell's Stall 83 where, in the cooler months, a knee-weakening range of wild and exotic mushrooms, many of them hand-picked by Cameron, are on display.

The famed Queen Victoria Market is part of Melbourne's soul, renowned for the quality and diversity of its produce.

In any other city, the scope and size of the Queen Victoria Market would be more than enough to satisfy the marketing population's needs, but for Melburnians it seems, too many markets are barely enough.

Over in the west, the **Footscray Market** provides one of the best culinary adventures in town, particularly when you fossick amongst the fishmongers, discovering strange seafood bounty you've never seen before. A brilliant multi-cultural blend of stalls – from Ethiopian to Italian to Vietnamese –

With its many produce markets providing fertile ground for new ingredients and ideas to take root in the general population, Melbourne has become a city with a broad and knowledgeable palate

This page and opposite
The Queen Vic is a showcase for the city's multicultural food scene, a melting pot of nationalities and an ever-changing kaleidoscope of farm-fresh produce.

not only provides good ingredients but also some obvious hints as to why Melbourne's food scene is so diverse. While in this neighbourhood, pay a visit to the nearby Little Saigon Market where the frenetic atmosphere and an incredible range of Asian produce and exotic fruit provides what is arguably Melbourne's closest thing to the real Vietnamese McCoy.

An altogether different experience awaits you at the **Prahran Market**. The oldest continuously running market in Australia, the Prahran Market has come a long way since it was moved from an overcrowded patch of land to its present site in 1864 where it has become the neatest and most genteel of all Melbourne's markets. Luckily all the order and matching aprons does not equate with sterility and stuffiness and some of the best market produce – from organic meat and vegetables to fantastic seafood and a remarkable range of deli and dry goods – alongside the most knowledgeable stall owners are found here.

South Melbourne, Preston, Dandenong and Camberwell also have their own well-attended markets but the newest sign of Melbourne's addiction comes from the relatively recent appearance in the city of monthly farmers' markets. These markets (at the Collingwood Children's Farm and next to the Veg Out Community Gardens in St Kilda to name just two) attract farmers and producers into the city to talk about and sell their produce direct to city consumers in an old-fashioned, plastic bag-free environment. The produce reflects the seasons (so don't expect to pick up tomatoes in winter) but the range of fruit and vegetables, honey, eggs, smoked meat, artisan cheese, olive oil, jams and preserves is snapped up by an ever-increasing crowd, lured by a desire to discover where their ingredients came from and how they were treated. While not strictly organic, the farmers' markets favour smaller producers who keep their use of chemicals and sprays to a minimum. The pretty outdoor settings – particularly the one beside the Yarra at the Collingwood Children's Farm – and the crowds of dedicated

Meat, poultry, game, smallgoods and seafood of all descriptions entice locals and visitors to the Queen Vic.

food fans make these markets a unique, cosy and comforting environment for any food and wine lover.

Of course the markets are an ideal place to start for any food hound but to really make like a Melburnian you also have to gather a list of specialty shops where you buy particular items.

In some cities it might seem slightly ridiculous to cross town to buy sausages, but those cities won't have sausages as good as the ones made by Andrew Vourvahakis in the back room of his shiny butcher shop in Anderson Street, Yarraville. Andrew, who is always on for a chat about his not-so-humble snags, has been anointed Sausage King a couple of times and when you taste his cheese kranskys made from pork and beef-shoulder you'll be willing to genuflect too. His frankfurts are equally good and there is a constantly changing selection of other flavours like Sicilian pork and Greek lamb.

For traditional European smallgoods you need to cross back to the other side of town and visit **Prahran Continental Butcher** in Chapel Street. This is a place where the leg ham is smoked over apple wood, the liverwurst is made from chicken livers and the range of European specialities runs from weisswurst to black pudding. Even better, there is a grill in the store so you can do your shopping while chomping on a freshly cooked continental sausage in a roll piled with sauerkraut and mustard.

Largo Butchers in Brunswick Street, Fitzroy, is another place of meat pilgrimage with regular pilgrims including some of the best chefs in town. Brothers Roger and Simon Ongarato make brilliant prosciutto and pancetta (alongside a wide range of other continental smallgoods), intensely flavoured, rich-coloured Italian meats that have been patted and rubbed, hung for at least six months and generally mollycoddled before you buy them. Well-aged meat is outstanding here (especially the beef) and you can also find rabbit, chicken and, occasionally, goat.

Not far from Largo, in Fitzroy's Johnston Street, is a little piece of Portuguese and Spanish food heaven. **Casa Iberica** is one of the city's true gems and the moment you smell the shop's chorizo-scented air and hear owner Alice De Sousa chatting in Spanish to many of her long-time customers is the moment you become addicted to the place. There is a treasure trove of olives, sherry vinegar, smoked paprika, rice, olive oil, paella pans and drinking chocolate to be found on the shelves in the dimly lit shop but the main action happens in the glass-fronted deli case. The dried chorizo here is the best in town and you can also get fantastic jamon, black pudding, bacalao and an impressive selection of Spanish and Portuguese cheese. If all the delicious treasure is making you feel faint, treat yourself to a sweet, fortifying, custard-filled Portuguese tart.

A couple of suburbs away in North Carlton is **Canal's**, arguably the best seafood store in Melbourne. Occupying the same unassuming shopfront in Nicholson Street since 1931, Canal's is easy to miss but if you are disoriented, look for the crowd that, on busy weekends, can actually spill out onto the street. The reason for the regular crush is the Canal family's dedication to the freshest fish and shellfish and the attention to detail. They'll shuck oysters, fillet fish and clean calamari for you and there is always somebody available to tell you the best way to handle your soft shell crab, whole snapper or smoked trout.

Melbourne is mad about food and mad about wine, but go exploring and you'll soon discover that it has every reason to be

Above
Melbourne's Colonial Tramcar Restaurant whooshes past.

From left to right
Melbourne's Chinatown; classic Italian cooking at Enoteca Silena in North Carlton; yum cha at the award-winning David's in Prahran; and European fare at the European in Spring Street, Melbourne.

Any food-obsessed city worth its salt must be able to produce good bread and Melbourne has a terrific range of small bakeries dishing up a wide range of excellent loaves.

St Kilda's **Baker D. Chirico** is not only one of the smartest-looking bakeries in town – all pared-back, designer-rustic style – but Daniel Chirico is a true artisan who specialises in sourdough and turns out loaves and baguettes with remarkable flavour and a wonderful crispy–chewy crust.

In Ripponlea, the **Firebrand Bakery** has been doing its sourdough thing for years and makes one of the best, chewy casalingas in town alongside breads made with soda and potato. Nearby, **Frank's Elsternwick Bakery** in Glenhuntly Road specialises in old-fashioned rye bread and is the best place in town for fresh baked pretzels.

On the north side of the river, the **Gertrude Street Organic Bakery** grinds its wholemeal flour fresh every day, uses mostly natural yeasts and bakes bread that is moist, chewy and hugely flavoured. The hours and the loaves – from amazing fruit loaf to black olive bread – are limited so grab what you can when you can.

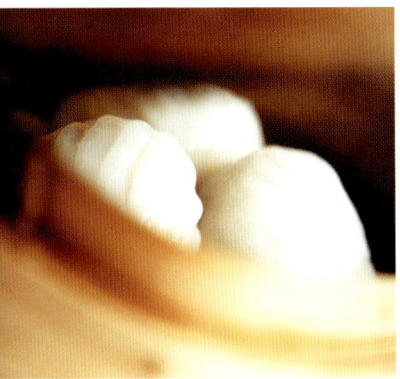

Brunswick Street's **Babka** is another north-side bakery worth a visit. Babka includes a very popular café with an Eastern European lean (think borscht and dumplings) and a great range of bread. The baguette and ficelle are particularly fine here, as are chewy rye loaves and the cute, currant-speckled shoo fly buns.

If you're not interested in tracking down produce from one end of town to the other, Melbourne has a couple of not-to-be-missed, one-stop,

Right and opposite
Richmond Hill Café and Larder, started by food doyenne Stephanie Alexander, and its cheese room, stacked with local and imported specialist and artisan-made cheeses.

bells-and-whistles gourmet food destinations. These are the type of places where you not only find shelves full of exotic products you never knew you needed but they are also almost bound to stock that obscure ingredient that you can't find anywhere else.

The Essential Ingredient is at the back of the Prahran Market, a perfect addition to the Market's excellent produce and one of the nicest shopping experiences a food and wine lover could hope to have. The Essential is a true food superstore offering amazing ranges of vinegar and oils from all over the world, seemingly endless lines of antipasto ingredients, herbs and spices, preserves, dressings and capers alongside a superb range of cookbooks and kitchenware. Chefs, restaurateurs, home cooks and the food curious come here both for specific purposes ('must pick up some more saffron syrup') and for inspiration ('why didn't I think of Iranian fairy floss before?'). It is one of Melbourne's finest food resources.

Simon Johnson has two stores (in Fitzroy and Toorak) that pack a lot of what Simon believes to be the best in the world – from oil to chocolate to anchovies – into a reasonably contained space. Charming staff will make you a coffee to keep you alert while browsing. Perhaps the stores' best features are their dedicated cheese rooms that stock an unusual range of local and imported cheese.

Another top cheese destination is the cheese room at the **Richmond Hill Café and Larder**. The purpose-built humidity and temperature-controlled room allows the cheese to mature at an ideal rate and the range includes European, British and Australian cheeses mainly from smaller dairies and artisan makers. Regular classes are held to unravel the mysteries of the tricky world of cheese.

From the Middle Eastern foodstores in Brunswick to the Italian stores on Lygon Street, the Jewish delis on Carlisle Street and the Asian supermarkets of Richmond, Melbourne always has more and then some more to offer. Start poking around now – it'll take a while before you reach the end.

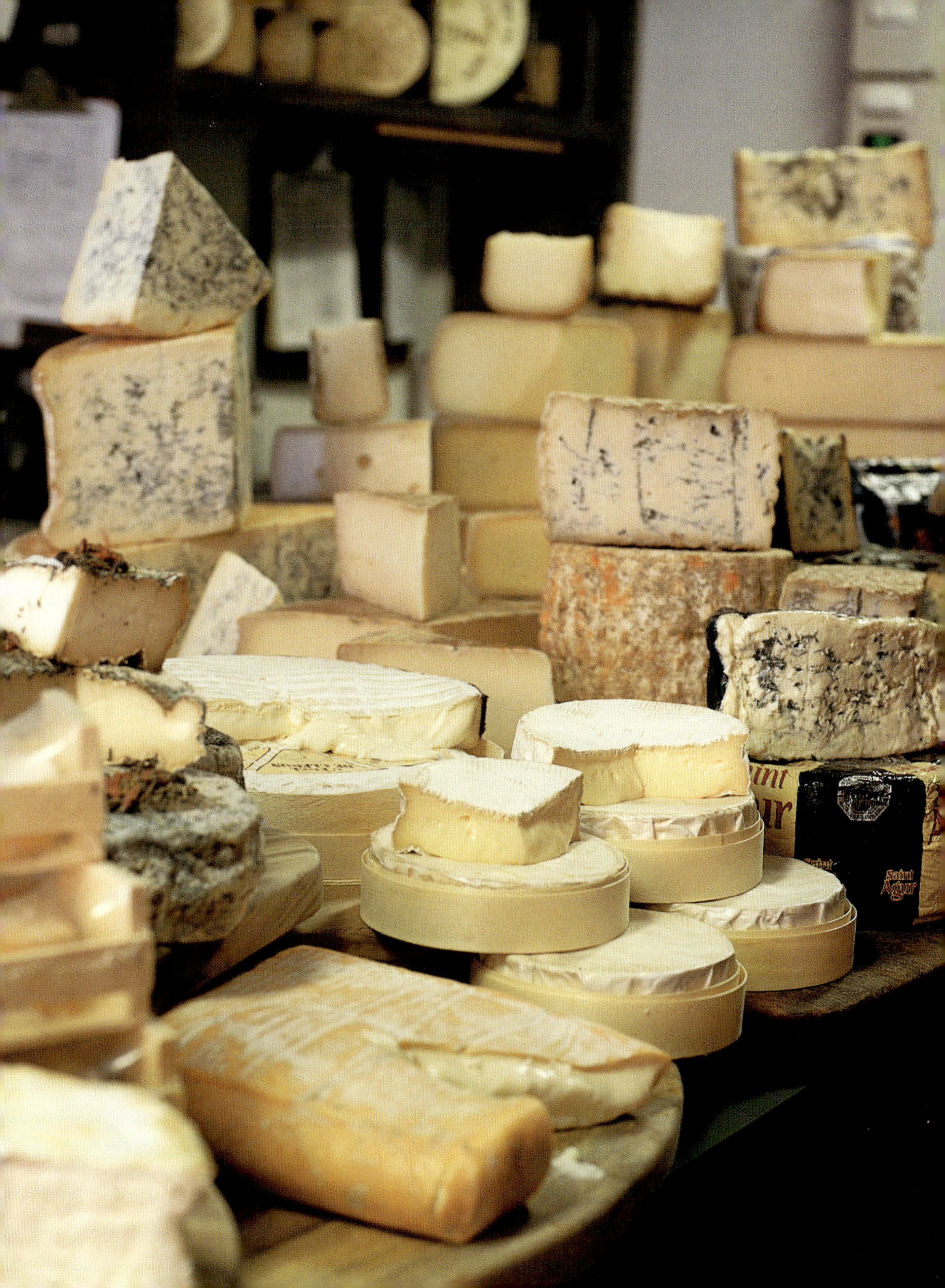
Saint
Agur

Bread and butter pudding

Phillippa Grogan,
Phillippa's, Armadale

125 ml milk
250 ml cream
½ vanilla pod or 1 tsp vanilla essence
2 eggs
75 g sugar
1½–2 croissants or 160 g slices of good stale bread *
rum-soaked raisins, or chopped chocolate pieces grated nutmeg
butter (to butter dish)

*Try chocolate sour cherry loaf, pain d'epice (for a gingerbread pudding), or any stale plain, good bread.

Heat milk, cream and vanilla pod. Whisk eggs and sugar together. Whisk milk into egg and sugar.

Butter a 750-ml dish and layer thin slices of croissant or other suitable stale bread.

Sprinkle with rum-soaked raisins or chopped chocolate pieces. Soak puddings with the above mix for at least 30 minutes, preferably longer. Sprinkle with grated nutmeg. Bake at 120°C until cooked (about 1 hour).

Serves 4

Phillippa Grogan, Phillippa's

Phillippa Grogan has some hardcore attitudes when it comes to making bread. Her uncompromising stance on technique and flavour caused many of the bakers she interviewed for her brand-new bakery to walk out of the interview the moment they understood how she wanted her bread made.

'I have some very firm ideas about what is 'cheating' when it comes to bread,' says Phillippa. 'If you add sugar, malt, Vitamin C or soy flour to bread then I consider that cheating. More than one or two per cent yeast in the bread is cheating too. We use only flour, water, salt and yeast. It is harder to make bread the way we do, but we know it will taste better.'

Before opening her Armadale shopfront business in 1994, Phillippa worked in London for nine years, mainly at Sally Clarke's where she not only discovered the traditional baking methods used in all **Phillippa's** bread today but also found Andrew O'Hara, a New Zealand baker equally interested in artisan bread-making techniques. Phillippa's original plan was to open her own business in London but too many difficulties led to a return to Melbourne where she opened her bakery just six months after her plane touched down.

Andrew O'Hara had gone home to New Zealand and was planning a return to London but came via Melbourne on the ruse of doing some stopgap work at Phillippa's. Phillippa says that once Andrew started producing the bread at Phillippa's it 'took off' and because 'it is very hard to keep a good baker' she married him.

Phillippa's bread has become one of the best-known brands in Melbourne and is stocked in small and large foodstores, supermarkets and gourmet joints across the state. The original shopfront remains in Armadale but the bakery moved to a larger warehouse space in Richmond several years ago to cope with ever-increasing demand. Despite the move, rising demand and an increased range of goods (including spiced nuts, jams and preserves, tarts, biscuits and pastries), Phillippa and Andrew still won't 'cheat' and continue

Above and opposite top
Phillippa's breads and gourmet provisions.

Opposite below
Phillippa Grogan at her original shop and café in Armadale.

making the bread in the same, labour intensive and time-consuming way they have always done. All the Phillippa's range – made from rye, spelt, white and organic flour – has low amounts of yeast that mean the dough takes longer to prove, resulting in more intense flavours and better textures.
It is amazing that despite the quantity in which Phillippa's bread is now made, it still tastes and looks so handmade.

Phillippa's bakery has become something of a Melbourne institution, producing handmade breads, biscuits, pastries and flans of exceptional quality.

Phillippa's addiction to the artisan life is perhaps best demonstrated by her regular stalls at two of Melbourne's farmers' markets. She says she loves the markets ('I wouldn't do it if I didn't') and being able to rise to the challenge of putting her product before a crowd that is 'specific and fussy about what they eat'. She likes to test out any of her new products on the people who are most particular about the products they buy. It is nice to see that more than a decade after she opened her bakery, Phillippa still enjoys the challenge of making things difficult for herself.

Winestores

Melbourne is fertile territory for wine lovers. With the most relaxed licensing laws in the country, a climate conducive to sheltering indoors over a bottle of red or two, a market culture that encourages people to try new things and Australia's biggest market for imported wine, the city has developed a well-educated and inquisitive wine-buying public with some extremely good wine stores, bars and restaurant wine lists to match.

Melbourne has not escaped the phenomenon of enormous price-warring chains able to sell liquor at rock-bottom prices and many independent wine retailers are under pressure. Some have been forced out of the market but others have understood that to survive they have to be more than just a bottleshop. Realising that they cannot compete in terms of price with the big chains, many independents are focussing on the niche market of wine buyers who are interested in learning about wine and who consider wine buying an experience rather than just another shopping trip. It seems the boring old suburban bottleshop is becoming an endangered species.

The **Prince Wine Store** in South Melbourne is a fine place to witness a wine retailer adapting beautifully to this new, more competitive climate. An extension of the wine store at the Prince Hotel in St Kilda, South Melbourne's Prince Wine Store is arguably the best wine shop of its kind in Australia in terms of the breadth and quality of its stock, the education courses it offers and the level of knowledge amongst its well-trained staff.

It is a large place, but not overwhelmingly so and an edgy fit-out – all slatted wood and concrete – includes a central, glass-enclosed 'pod' where shoppers are encouraged to flick through an extensive selection of wine books and magazines over a coffee. There are tastings every weekend, monthly wine courses for beginners, amateur experts and professionals (including the internationally recognised Wine and Spirit Education Trust course) and regular wine dinners that highlight particular producers. It is the kind of well-run, well-connected place where, if you can't find the specific wine you are after, they will usually be able to track it down for you within two days.

If you're just there to buy a bottle of wine for dinner that night though, the Prince Wine Store is a great place to shop. There is a 50/50 mix of international and Australian wine and an impressive range of cognac,

The City Wine Shop in Spring Street, Melbourne, is one of the new-wave wine bars offering Melburnians and visitors fine wine and simple, well-prepared food.

Armagnac, single malt and blended whiskey. The logical layout has an ever-changing selection of excellent value-for-money wines at the front, shelves in the middle where varietals from all over the world are grouped in one place (Australian sangiovese sitting alongside great Chianti) and then, further back, a selection of rare and brilliant wine bound to make any cork dork go weak at the knees. It is reassuring to know that all the wine – whether you're spending $20 or $200 – has been chosen according to the store's policy of value for money. Make sure you talk to the staff and tell them what you're eating – they give good advice whether you're contemplating fish and chips or sashimi-grade tuna.

Just around the corner from the Prince Wine Store is another excellent wineshop filling a different niche. **Cloudwine** specialises in small, boutique wineries from across Australia and, according to co-owner Jacinta Plazzer, is biased towards places 'where the owners spend more time in the vineyard than anywhere else'.

Originally an internet business started by three people who grew up in the country and spent their spare time visiting little wineries, Cloudwine now has

Five seriously good wine lists

- France-Soir, South Yarra
- Charcoal Grill On the Hill, Kew
- Cookie, City
- Melbourne Supper Club, City
- Circa, The Prince, St Kilda

two stores (South Melbourne and Camberwell) and is a good place to taste what is going on with Australian wine beyond the big players. While all the major wine-producing regions in Australia get a look in, the South Australian and Victorian sections are the largest in the shop and there are wines here from a number of off-the-radar producers that you won't find in any other retail outlets.

If you've got a thirst for Italian wine, **Enoteca Sileno** in North Carlton is the place to cure what ails you. The bottleshop section of this stylish Italo-centric

Australia's biggest market for imported wine, Melbourne has developed a well-educated and inquisitive wine-buying public with some extremely good wine stores, bars and restaurant wine lists to match

Zucchini flower and anchovy tarts

Andrew McConnell, Circa, The Prince, St Kilda

2 sheets puff pastry
200 g ricotta cheese
2 tbsp grated parmesan
3 tbsp cream
12 anchovies
12 zucchini flowers
12 basil leaves
black pepper and sea salt

Cut the puff pastry into small rectangles 3 cm by 5 cm. Transfer the pastries onto a lightly buttered baking tray.

Whip the ricotta cheese with the parmesan and cream, add salt to taste. Top each tart with a tablespoon of ricotta cheese. Spread the ricotta across the surface of the tart leaving a small band of pastry exposed around the edge. Lay an anchovy and basil leaf on the ricotta and finally lay the zucchini flower running the length of the tart. Bake in the oven for 10 minutes at 180°C or until golden.

When cooked dust with a little cracked black pepper and sea salt.

Makes 12

Opposite above and centre
John Portelli at Enoteca Silena in North Carlton. The enoteca combines superb Italian produce, an impressive range of Italian wines and the sleek Vino Bar.

Opposite below
Brigitte Haffner and James Broadway at Gertrude Street Enoteca, Fitzroy.

complex has a room dedicated to Barolo and Barbaresco, a whole wall of grappa and is a good place to have all your preconceived ideas about the worthlessness of Frascati shattered.

Started as in importing business by Gino Di Santo in 1953, **Enoteca Sileno** has gained a well-earned reputation as treasure trove of superb Italian produce – parmesan, oil, pasta, vinegar, sugo and so on – and an increasingly good range of exclusively imported Italian wine. Since moving into the Rising Sun Hotel building on Nicholson Street, Enoteca Sileno now boasts a sleek 'vino bar' where you can try a wide variety of Italian regional cuisine (highlighting products from their produce range) over a glass of ten-year-old Barolo or a bottle of crispy dry, thirst-quenching Frascati.

Enoteca holds regular tastings in its Barolo room and, according to manager (and Gino Di Santo's son-in-law) John Portelli, the fact that they import all the wine here themselves means that you won't find these producers anywhere else. As well as that, because they cut out the middleman, prices are very reasonable.

'All the wine we bring here is chosen by us to match the food we serve both in the produce shop and the Vino Bar,' says John. 'It is important to taste food from a particular region with wine that comes from the same region as the dish, just as they do in Italy.'

With more boring old bottleshops morphing into winestores with attached bars, restaurants and education facilities, wine lovers have never been so spoilt for choice as they are in Melbourne now.

Gertrude Street Enoteca

In recent years, Gertrude Street in Fitzroy has become one of Melbourne's most interesting food and wine hubs. The mix of shops on the once seedy strip includes superstar pizza joint **Ladro**, **Gertrude Street Organic Bakery**, **Books For Cooks**, **Organic Gertrude**, **Yelza** and, most recently **Gertrude Street Enoteca**.

Owned by former architect and President of the Australian Slow Food movement, James Broadway, chef and cooking writer Brigitte Hafner and their friend Rosa Mitchell, Gertrude Street Enoteca faithfully captures the spirit of the traditional Italian enoteca – a casual place with a bit of food where you can go to drink, buy and talk about wine – but does it in a quintessentially Melbourne fashion.

James (or Jamie as he is widely known) fell in love with the idea of opening an enoteca in Melbourne over many trips to Italy for his wine-importing

> Brigitte is a big fan of artisan produce and her simple food reflects her preference for the handmade and organic

business. He found the typical suburban bottle shop with its museum-like air depressing and thought the whole experience of buying wine could be much improved with a convivial atmosphere, music, the smell of coffee in the air and the opportunity to sit down with a glass of wine. When the shopfront in Gertrude Street with its little courtyard out the back and the light-filled front room became available the three partners knew immediately that this was the right shop in the right neighbourhood for the kind of business they wanted to do.

Gertrude Street Enoteca is a casually stylish place that is hard to define. It doesn't fall neatly into any of the usual boxes – café, bar, wine shop – but cleverly amalgamates all three. There is no menu and the blackboard over the bar is more likely to contain poetry or a recipe on how to roast a duck than list what food is available. Brigitte is a big fan of artisan produce and the simple food she prepares – panini at lunch time, cheese and antipasto at night and whatever else she finds that is in season and interesting – reflects her preference for the handmade and organic.

The selection of wine in Enoteca's middle room, with its floor-to-ceiling shelves and glass cases full of cognac, is always changing and reflects Jamie's passions and biases.

'I guess you could call me a benchmarker,' he says. 'I like to find the people who are hitting the nail on the head in some way with whatever wine they are making. It doesn't matter to me what the wine costs – it could be $20, it could be $80 it could be $200 – as long as it is doing something right.'

He says that he likes handmade wines that 'haven't been fiddled with too much', made by people serious about the world of wine and 'with an interest in benchmarking'.

According to Jamie and Brigitte, people have understood the concept of what they are trying to do very quickly, though they're not sure whether it is to do with the neighbourhood or whether Melbourne wine lovers are looking for an experience (and a panini) to go with their wine buying. Jamie sees a day when all the old bottleshops embrace the enoteca idea and the suburbs will be full of people sitting around chatting about wine. Pop into the Gertrude Street Enoteca some time and you'll agree that it's not such a bad idea.

Five great city laneway restaurants

- Mo Vida – authentic tapas and Spanish sherry in Hosier Lane
- Syracuse – superb wine list and a romantic setting in Bank Place
- Yu-u – great yakatori in a hidden basement location off Flinders Lane
- Vue de Monde – masterfully worked food and edgy attitude off Little Collins Street.
- Supper Inn – crispy suckling pig in this bustling late-night Cantonese place on Celestial Avenue.

Eating Out

It is difficult – if not impossible – to define the dining scene in Melbourne. It is a scene of such breadth and diversity that no box is large enough or the right shape for everything to fit. While this is not such good news for writers trying to succinctly capture the qualities of Melbourne's dining scene, it is the best news possible for food and wine lovers wanting to add some exceptional and exciting dining experiences to their list.

There are a few generalisations you can make about Melbourne's cafés and restaurants. For starters, the quality of ingredients is always pretty high because Melbourne is not only blessed with a strong market culture but is surrounded by farming regions that pump out a remarkable range of good fresh ingredients. Add a conveniently situated ocean full of seafood and you have a fine starting point for a solid dining scene.

Markets have played an important role in the development of Melbourne's eating culture, not only by an easily accessible supply of ingredients but also by educating the public about the joys of eating fresh, top quality produce.

Ask any chef where they shop and you will inevitably hear about the fruit and veggie stall at the Queen Victoria Market where they always get their salad leaves and herbs, or another at the South Melbourne Market where they believe you can get the best potatoes, or the deli at Prahran where they treat their cheese with respect.

Increasingly, the best chefs in Melbourne are also discovering the small, artisan producers from the regions surrounding Melbourne, sourcing rare-breed black pigs or salmon roe from the Yarra Valley, rhubarb from Nagambie or rabbits from Gippsland. Often these ingredients are name-checked on restaurant menus, which further educates the public about what they are eating. One of the undeniable assets of a strong dining culture is a

> The food was kept simple and cheap but was made using quality ingredients, breakfast was served all day and a high standard of coffee was rigorously maintained

well-informed public that forces chefs to keep raising the bar. Melbourne's diners are a very well-informed mob who are very particular about their produce.

Another generalisation about Melbourne's restaurants is that they lean towards a more casual, informal style of eating. While there are still a few top-notch, fine dining experiences to be had – places like **Jacques Reymond** in Windsor and **Grossi Florentino** and the **Flower Drum** in the city – Melbourne is no longer a hub of the Big Night Out dining experience.

Part of the reason for this was the economic wobbles experienced by Victoria in the 1980s that drained money out of the top end of the market. Some fine dining establishments closed leaving a pool of people with outstanding food knowledge and service skills looking around for something else to do. These people began to move into the café scene, keeping the casual café approach but upping the ante in terms of food and service.

Marios in Brunswick Street, Fitzroy, was one of the pioneers of the new-style Melbourne café and, as proof that it hit the right nail on the head, is still going strong after twenty years. Owners Mario DePasquale and Mario Maccarone had both worked in formal restaurants but wanted to open the type of place they longed to eat in but couldn't find. The food was kept simple and cheap but was made using quality ingredients, breakfast was served all day and a high standard of coffee was rigorously maintained. The café also opened late but what really set Marios apart was the exceptional service, courtesy of a solid core of funky-looking waistcoated waiters. It was the most visible sign that café culture was finally being taken seriously.

Marios has had a fleet of imitators but remains one of the best examples of the quintessential Melbourne-style café.

Around the same time one of Melbourne's defining dining styles also emerged – the chic Italian café. Maurice Terzini's uber-stylish **Caffe e Cucina**, which opened in Chapel Street in the late 1980s, was the blueprint for the look and approach that continues to be a recognisably Melburnian style – linen-draped tables, dark wood panelling, bentwood chairs, dim lighting, wooden blinds and traditional Italian dishes made with authentic, first-class ingredients. This style of café thrived on the growing numbers of Melburnians wanting to eat quality food in a less formal manner and fed off the city's strong Italian influence. People understood the concept of these new cafés because, after a history of Italian immigration stretching back for a century, dishes like Spaghetti Bolognese had been adopted as something of a national dish. The added style and quality of these new places struck a chord with the Melbourne dining scene and are now an established feature of the city. Those wanting to try this uniquely Melbourne blend should make a booking at **Becco** or **Il Bacaro** in the city, or St Kilda's **Melbourne Wine Room** or **Café Di Stasio**.

Perhaps an even more important factor in Melbourne's shift towards an informal style of eating comes from the fact that going out for a meal, drink or coffee is just something that Melbourne dwellers do. A cooler climate with distinct seasons plays a big part in why eating out is as much a part of the Melbourne lifestyle as going to the footy, or breathing. When the skies are grey and the wind is icy popping into a cosy bar for a glass of red or huddling with friends over the warmth of a fortifying pasta or a bowl of hot and sour soup seems like a very sensible thing to do.

The Melburnian love of casual dining crosses many cultural boundaries. The apparently unstoppable love affair with designer pizza is one example and Fitzroy's **Ladro** with its buzzy dining room, fabulous service, fantastic wood-fired pizza courtesy of chef Rita Macali and constant waiting list for tables shows that variations on the Italian theme still have plenty of life in them yet.

Across the river in South Yarra, the **Ay Oriental Tea House** is putting a new spin on the way people consume Chinese food. Owner David Zhou has taken an old pub, given it a colourful and stylish makeover that manages to straddle 1920s Shanghai and 1960s pop art, and begun serving yum cha all day. There is an extensive list of teas (all of which can be purchased in the tea shop at the front of the building), a good wine list and a menu of tea-based cocktails. The Teahouse has a wonderful flexibility and you feel as comfortable coming in here for a pot of tea and a couple of steamed buns as you do ordering a bottle of wine and making a meal of it.

David, who also owns a couple of tea shops and an excellent a la carte Shanghaiese restaurant called **David's**, had originally planned to go back to his native Shanghai to get some ideas for his latest venture but he ran out of time. He was forced, he says, to 'believe in his own vision' and has created a unique 'European/Oriental/Aussie' business that now has people from Shanghai coming in to take photos (and possibly the idea) to show back in China.

Over at Docklands, Middle Eastern flavours are being given the casual treatment at **Mecca Bah**. Co-owner and executive chef Cath Claringbold came to love the taste of sumac, labne and harissa while working under the godfather of modern Middle Eastern food in Melbourne, Greg Malouf. She presents a more formal version of her Middle Eastern food at Southgate's **Mecca**, but at this waterfront café and bar the approach is relaxed with a menu full of dishes designed to share and a constant stream of Turkish pizza coming out of the wood-fired oven.

The distinctive flavour of the Ay Oriental Tea House in Prahran, serving Shanghaiese and Cantonese-style food and exotic teas.

One of the other renowned Middle Eastern dining experiences in Melbourne, aside from a trawl up and down the Turkish and Lebanese shops and cafés on Sydney Road, is at **Abla's** in Carlton. Now well into its third decade, Abla's may look homey and unassuming but owner Abla Ahmad's delicious take on Lebanese home cooking has been enormously influential on the Melbourne dining scene. Abla's has changed little over the years so eating here gives you both an excellent dining experience and a glimpse at the roots of Melbourne's robust modern Middle Eastern dining culture.

It is difficult – if not impossible – to define the dining scene in Melbourne. It is a scene of such breadth and diversity that no box is large enough or the right shape for everything to fit

The European in Spring Street, Melbourne, is known for its old world ambience, excellent coffee and well-stocked cellar of European wines.

The ever-increasing move to casual dining and the absence of a busy crowd of top-end dining in Melbourne does not mean that there is no innovative cooking happening. On the contrary, there are some enormously talented chefs working in the city who constantly push the boundaries to maintain Melbourne's reputation as an edgy and exciting place to eat.

Chefs like Geoff Lindsay at **Pearl**, Shannon Bennett at **Vue de Monde**, Teage Ezard at **ezard** and Andrew McConnell at **Circa** have little in common in terms of cooking styles and influences but do share a bond in terms of a fanatical devotion to artisan produce, a rigorous technical approach to their food and an understanding of the origins and philosophies of the cuisines from which they take inspiration.

Andrew McConnell is executive chef at St Kilda's **Circa, The Prince**, and with his partner Pascale Gomes-McNabb, owns a restaurant in Carlton called **Mrs Jones**. Melbourne born and bred, Andrew is a chef who has worked and travelled extensively overseas (including stints in restaurants in Hong Kong and Shanghai and a couple of years as a tour chef for pop stars like Madonna), leans towards European techniques in his cooking, and is a complete fanatic when it comes to the quality of his ingredients. His experiences overseas have helped him appreciate the freedom the Melbourne dining scene offers.

'I believe Melbourne is one of the most exciting places to cook professionally in the world mainly because we don't have any rules or any real history,' he says. 'There is an openness from the public to diversification and experimentation and it is exciting because there is nobody around like there is in Europe looking at what you are doing and saying, oh you can't do that.'

Andrew believes that Melbourne does not possess a particular style of eating ('unless you consider diversity a style') but looking at the unique and thoughtful way he combines ingredients and his commitment to sourcing the best ingredients he can find from the city's surrounding regions, you could say that Andrew McConnell is cooking a particular Melbourne style of food.

'I like to think that it is my own interpretation of Melbourne,' explains Andrew. 'After travelling extensively and living in and learning about the cultures that influence our food here, I have combined those experiences with what I learnt growing up in Melbourne. I'm not trying to reinvent the wheel, though. It is more personal than anything. I'm really just a Melbourne boy.'

'Many chefs here look outside of Melbourne for inspiration but I am very proud of what we have here and the resources we have. It is great to be interested in what is going on outside of Melbourne but we have to realise

EUROPEAN

From right
Con Christopoulos, and the typical dark wood panelling, stylish fittings and imported wines of his café, the European.

that we are a big and smart enough dining culture to start looking at what we've got, where we are now and where we can push it.'

Of course the best way to understand and to see which direction the Melbourne dining scene is being pushed is to get out there and eat. It is a job well suited to any true food and wine lover.

Con Christopoulos, restaurateur

Con Christopoulos reckons that Melbourne is best summed up by three things – dark wood, red wine and espresso. Looking at the Melbourne restaurant scene – particularly in the CBD where Con has helped set the tone and feel of countless cafés, bars and restaurants – his summary seems pretty accurate. But then again, as owner (with a series of partners) of six highly successful eating and drinking venues in the city, he is in a pretty unique position to observe (and even sway) how Melburnians eat and drink.

Con originally wanted to be a physiotherapist but fell into and in love with restaurants instead. He ended up owning a couple of places with his family before going overseas for the first time, but it was only after a year of seeing how things were done in South America and Europe that he opened a café that really made a difference to the way things were done in his home town.

Café Segovia in Block Place was one of the first eating places in Melbourne to popularise the city's laneways, offering wine by the glass, excellent music, a moody European vibe and well-cooked simple food. He had Segovia for three years and then sold it and went to Europe for a year, 'making notes and taking photos and sitting in good cafés for hours to see how they were doing things'.

Shortly after returning to Melbourne he and two partners opened two places at the same time – a serious wine and food bar called **Syracuse** and a menu-less espresso bar called **Degraves** – both in city laneways and both with Con's now trademark look, using recycled and antique materials to make them appear as if they had been around forever. The laneways were chosen not only because they were the cheaper option at the time but also because of the 'quirky, European feel' they had.

Con no longer owns Syracuse but has the **European** in Spring Street (popular with the politicians who work across the road in the Parliament building) with the very popular late-night venue the **Melbourne Supper Club** upstairs and the designer bottleshop and café **City Wine Shop** next door. He also has another café in Flinders Lane called **Journal** and a bustling little Italian bistro in the legal precinct called **Benito's** and a share in **Pelican**, a vibey, architect-designed café and tapas bar in St Kilda.

Most of his places have a reputation for first-rate wine lists that are largely – or in the case of The European, exclusively – made up of European wines, terrific coffee and good service.

Con says that his inspiration came not only from Europe but also from Melbourne – the weather, the markets and the attitude of the Italian cafés in Lygon Street. 'People might knock Lygon Street for its lack of quality,' he says, 'but what it gave us was an attitude. My first cappuccino in Melbourne was in Lygon Street. We used to wag school and walk to Café L'Alba and spend the day playing money machines, eating mortadella rolls and drinking cappuccino. It was heaven.'

By creating such successful businesses, Con's attitude is now a Melbourne attitude. Spend some time in any of his businesses and you can see that that is a good thing for the city.

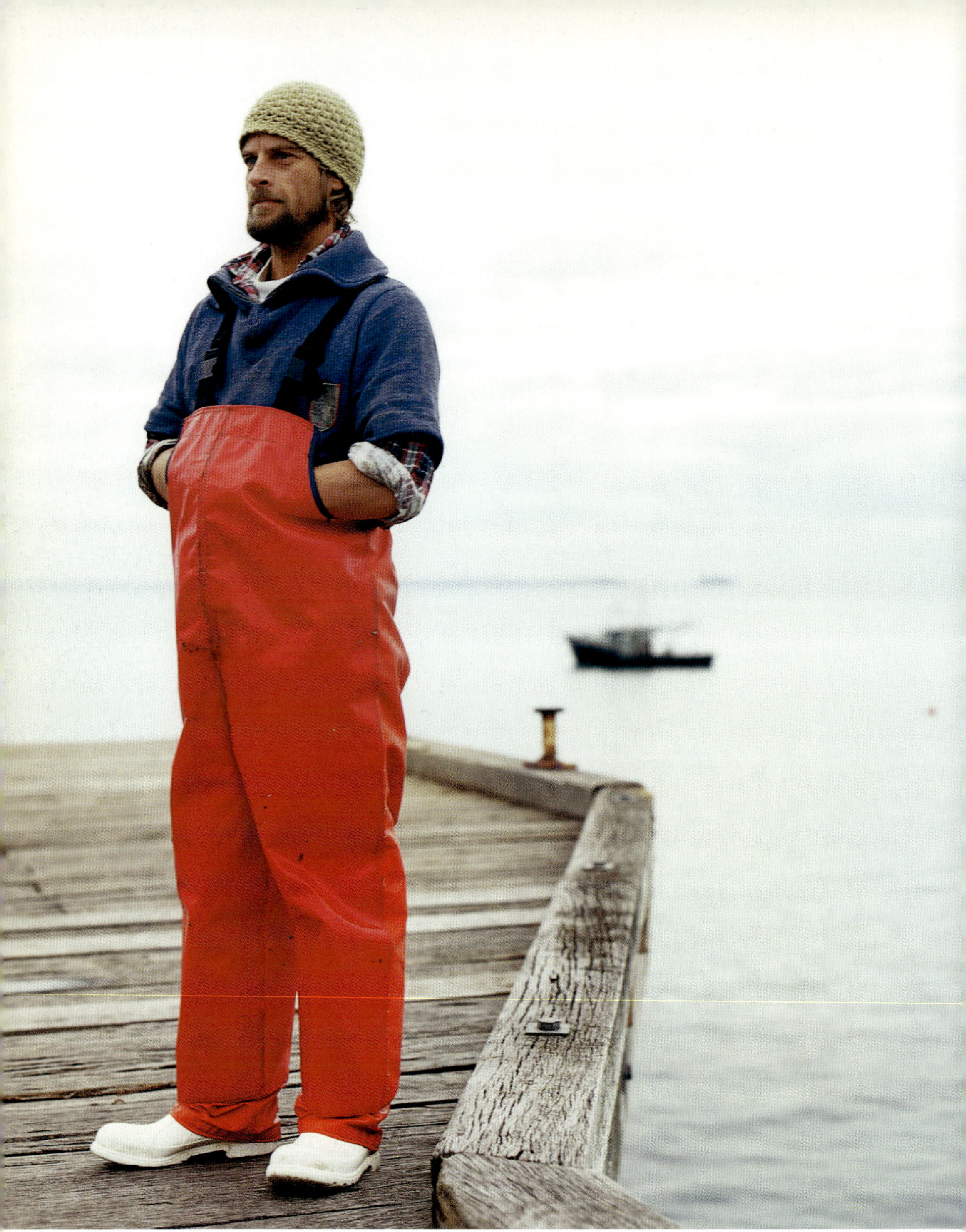

mornington peninsula

michael harden

mornington peninsula

The influx of people from food and wine-mad Melbourne has transformed a sleepy rural area to a creative hothouse of increasingly excellent cool-climate wines, specialist crops, artisan produce and restaurants

Boathouses nestled in the trees along the peninsula foreshore.

The Mornington Peninsula has undergone enormous changes in the last decade or so. The amazingly beautiful region, surrounded by the waters of Port Phillip Bay, Bass Strait and Westernport Bay, has always been popular with holiday-makers attracted by a combination of coast and countryside, lush forests of pine and eucalyptus, sweeping hills, sandy bay beaches and dramatic ocean views. But as the roads have been improved and the commute from Melbourne reduced to an hour, more and more city folk have opted for a sea change, turning their weekenders into permanent residences.

This influx of people from food and wine-mad Melbourne has transformed a sleepy rural area of small-scale cattle farms, horse studs, fledgling wine industry, vegetable growers and orchards to a creative hothouse of increasingly excellent cool-climate wine, specialist crops, artisan produce and restaurants run by chefs committed to creating a regional cuisine.

Ask any long-term resident about the changes and you will get a mixture of regret at the loss of a slower-paced rural lifestyle and pride at the quality and amazing diversity that their relatively small landmass is able to produce. But as the Peninsula's reputation as a unique food and wine region grows and the quality of the produce, wine and restaurants expands, there is a growing understanding that the area is simply refining its natural strengths and recognising its true potential.

Historically, the current changes are more of a logical progression than a dramatic shift. The original inhabitants, the Bunurong people, hunted and gathered food in the bush and on the shore, leaving huge piles of shells as evidence of their taste for seafood. Only 50 years after explorer Matthew Flinders landed at Bird Rock near Mornington in 1802, the Mornington Peninsula witnessed a flurry of activity as settlers felled timber for an insatiable Melbourne market, established crops of wheat and oats, grazed cattle, planted orchards of cherry, pear, apple and quince trees and fished the surrounding waters for crayfish and mussels, snapper and shark. There were even small vineyards planted in the late 19th century, though the erratic

Above and opposite
The quaint boathouses typical of the peninsula and a fishing dinghy.

climate and even more erratic wine market meant that these attempts were long abandoned by the 1970s, when the first disaffected city folk with long pockets and winemaking dreams began planting the hinterland with vineyards. So the Mornington Peninsula has always been something of a food bowl, but it has only been during the last couple of decades that people have begun to refine what they are planting to suit the vagaries of a maritime climate.

Vineyards and wineries have been the most noticeable evidence of this considered approach with chardonnay and pinot noir emerging as the Mornington Peninsula's signature wine strengths. But the existence of farms and orchards specialising in strawberries, cherries, chestnuts, avocados, organic vegetables, olives and apples and small artisan businesses specialising in local meat, making cheese and brewing beer make the Mornington Peninsula a particularly exciting destination for any food and wine lover.

Foodstores and producers

The best way to explore the Mornington Peninsula's incredible variety and quality of produce is to get in the car and get lost. While much of the best produce is found around the hilly, pine and eucalypt forested areas of Red Hill and Main Ridge there are home-grown treasures to be found from one end of the Peninsula to the other, from the hinterland to the seaside, and mostly away from the main roads.

For those who can't live without a map there are some decent guides like the Mornington Peninsula Gourmet Food Map and Get Fresh at the Farm Gate. But how much better is it to follow your nose, feast your eyes on the scenery and discover the roadside stalls selling pumpkins and eggs or the pick-your-own cherry farm yourself? The small dirt roads winding through beautiful bush not only offer some wonderful food experiences but also provide the perfect way to experience the most serene and secluded parts of the Mornington Peninsula.

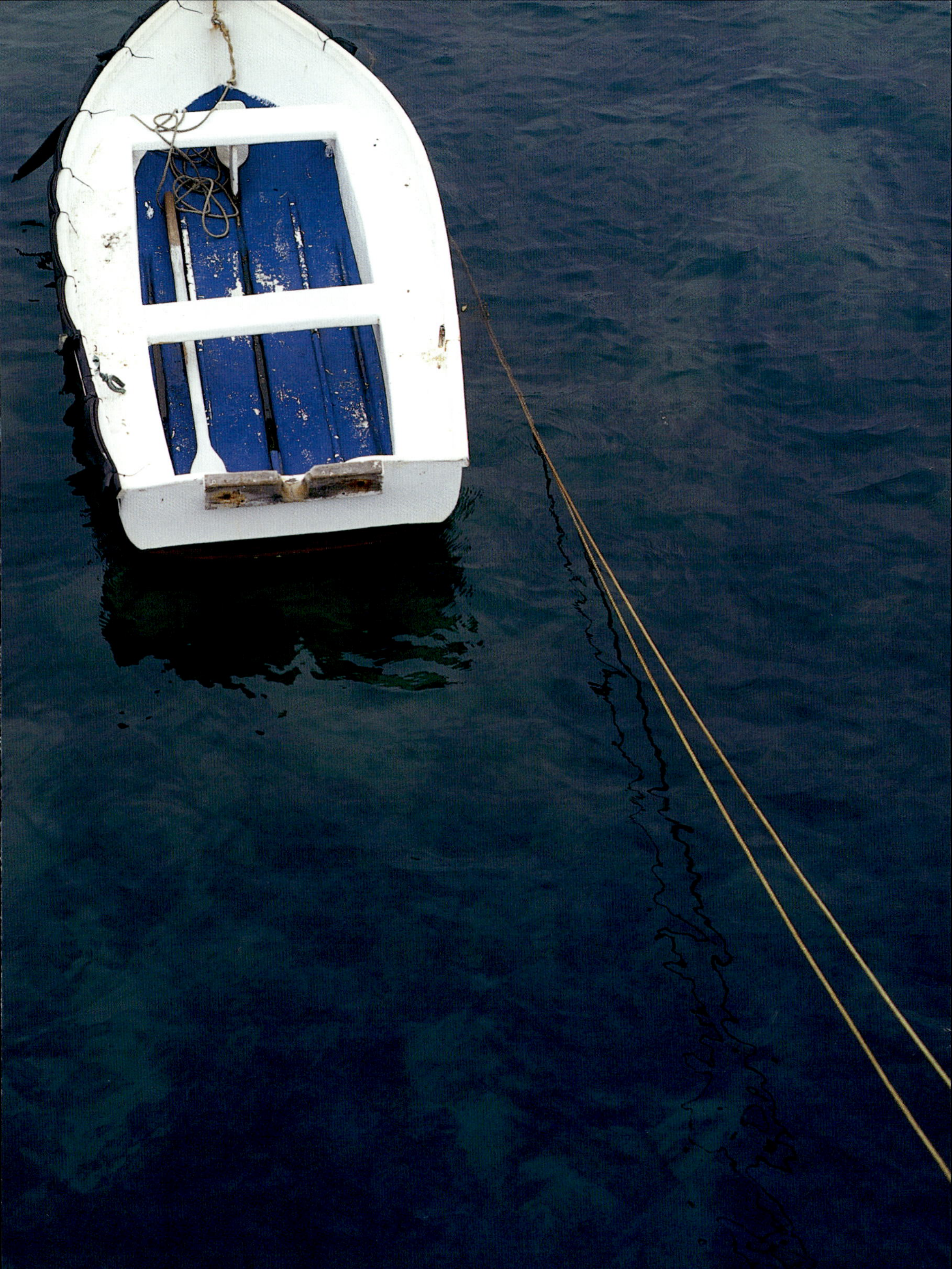

Five terrific farm-gate products

- Organic honey and honeycomb from Bungower Park, Derril Rd, Moorooduc

- Free-range eggs from Summerhill Farm, Barkers Rd, Main Ridge

- Olive oil from Summerfields, Hunts Rd, Bittern

- Organic vegetables from Bryant's, Old Cape Shank Rd, Rosebud

- Blueberries from Drum Drum Blueberry Farm, Davos St, Main Ridge

Opposite
'Harry' Harris sells his just-from-the-water mussels from Flinders Pier, as well as to restaurants.

If you like all your free-range eggs (and fruit and vegetables and jams and preserves) in one basket there are markets held just about every Saturday. The biggest and busiest of these is the 30-year-old **Red Hill Community Market**. The sprawling mass of colour and movement with the creed 'make it, bake it, grow it or breed it' explodes early on the first Saturday of the month and shows just how abundant the region is, no matter what the season.

A series of Mornington Peninsula-centric food stores are also good places to get a quick local produce fix. The **Red Hill Cool Stores**, set up in a former apple-packing shed, combines local arts and crafts with a good selection of jam, pickles, cheese, olive oil, wine and a small selection of seasonal fresh produce. It is also the perfect place to get the low-down on what is happening with local produce and where to find the best stuff. Close by, the **Red Hill Cellars** masquerades as a regular supermarket but has a great range of local goodies including fresh produce and a wall of wine dedicated to the best of the local drops. If you're on the Port Phillip Bay coast, Rosebud's **The Tasting Station** stocks an extensive range of the peninsula's finest from cheese and wine through to jams, pickles and olive oil. But for the fully fledged produce forager, the best thing to do is get on the road and go direct to the source.

Flinders, on the southern coast of Westernport Bay, has retained an old-fashioned fishing village air despite being increasingly colonised by burnt-out city slickers. Down at the Flinders jetty, recreational fishermen cast hand lines from the weathered timber wharf, regularly pulling in flipping fish and ink-squirting squid against a backdrop of bobbing fishing boats. In such a picture-perfect setting, it seems almost too good to be true that you can stroll out onto the jetty and buy mussels that have been pulled from the water less than a kilometre away. It is, as Michael 'Harry' Harris, operator of **Flinders Shellfish**, says 'a simple luxury that you can't do much anymore'.

Harris has been farming mussels off Flinders since 1992 before he 'bought a piece of water' off Flinders and established his own business in 2000. He does a roaring trade from his boat that is moored at the jetty every weekend (except in early spring when the new 'crop' is still growing), and also supplies 150 kg of his plump, juicy mussels per month to restaurants across the Mornington Peninsula. If you don't know much about cooking mussels, Harry has more than one recipe up his sleeve to show you just how good truly fresh shellfish can be.

Harry's mussel laksa

'Harry' Harris,
Flinders Shellfish, Flinders

1 tbsp oil
1 onion, finely sliced
3 cloves fresh garlic, crushed
1 tsp fresh ginger, finely grated
2 tsp of red curry paste
1 x 400 g can coconut milk
1 x 400 g can peeled tomatoes, optional
1 bunch bok choy
2 kg of Harry's mussels, rinsed and debearded
Mornington Peninsula chardonnay
coriander to garnish

Heat oil in heavy-based fry pan; brown onion, garlic and ginger. Then add curry paste to pan, gradually add coconut milk on low heat until the desired taste of the curry is obtained. A can of peeled tomatoes added after the curry paste will greatly enhance the flavour. Bok choy can be added, for texture and colour before serving. Whilst the curry is simmering place the cleaned mussels into a saucepan, generously splash with white wine, replace lid, bring to boil, simmer until mussels are open.

Give mussels a stir or shake whilst cooking to help pop open. Once open, tip most of the mussel juice out, serve into bowls, spoon laksa over mussels and garnish with fresh coriander.

Serves 4

Right
Gourmet provisions from Red Hill Coolstores. Quality, locally grazed Mornington Peninsula meat.

Opposite
Fruit picking at Ellisfield Farm.

If you're after fruits of the land rather than of the sea, you should head to the winding, tree-lined roads and dirt tracks of Main Ridge and Red Hill. Not only is the area home to many of the Mornington Peninsula's better-known wineries, but there is also brilliant fruit of the non-grape variety. Orchards of apple and cherry trees were established here in the very early days of European settlement, taking advantage of the higher inland altitude and cooler temperatures that mean the fruit ripens more slowly and the flavours become more intense.

Bite into one of the fat, red, sun-warmed strawberries from **Sunny Ridge Strawberry Farm** and you understand the climatic advantage immediately. Big, juicy, firm and almost unbelievably sweet, the strawberries from Sunny Ridge put the bland, chalky supermarket versions to shame. It is little wonder that Mornington Peninsula strawberries are becoming a brand in their own right.

Established as a mixed fruit and vegetable farm in 1964 by the Gallace family, Sunny Ridge now produces more than 3 million punnets of strawberries per year, making it Australia's largest strawberry producer. But even with the tourist facilities that were built in 1997 to cope with the increasing crowds who flocked to pick their own strawberries (and raspberries and cherries), Sunny Ridge doesn't feel like a heaving strawberry factory. On sunny days when the fields next to the shop and factory buildings are filled with people picking strawberries and the shop is full of people buying jam or sparkling strawberry wine and eating the house-made strawberry ice cream, the place still has a modest, home-made, farm-gate feel.

This relaxed pace is evident at most of the U-pick and farm-gate businesses in this neck of the woods. **Ellisfield Farm**, an orchard growing quinces, sweet cherries and black sour Morello cherries – a brilliant fruit for everything from jams to fortified wine – retains its tranquil pace even during the short summer cherry-picking rush. There is more tranquillity to be had on

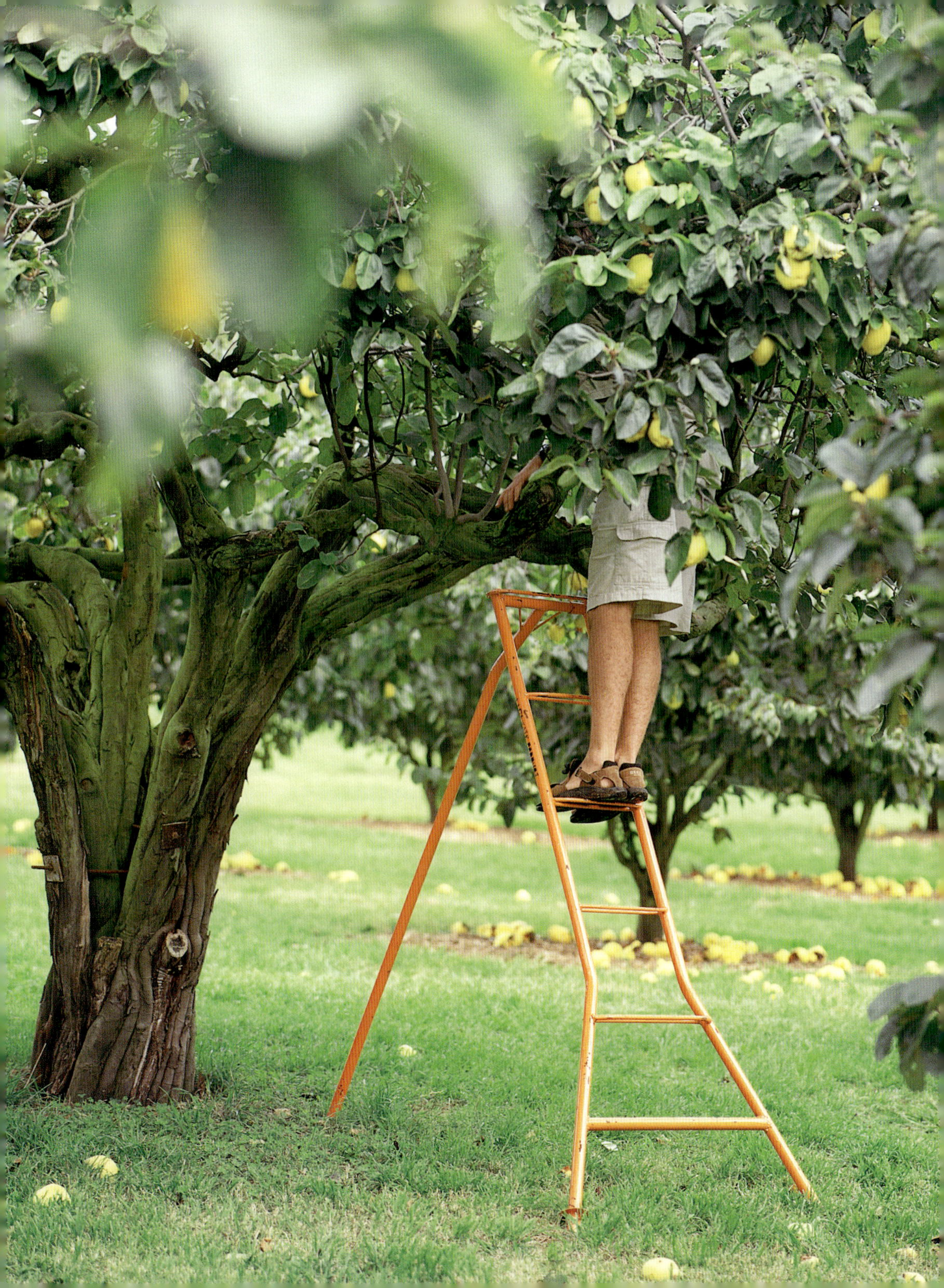

Strawberries with rose cream

Based on an old French recipe, Sunny Ridge Strawberry Farm

150 ml milk
2 eggs, separated
5 tbsp vanilla sugar
kirsch
500 g strawberries, hulled
225 ml thick cream
2–3 drops rosewater
or rose syrup

Make a small, dense custard by cooking the milk, egg yolks and 1 tablespoon of the sugar over a gentle heat. Stir in 1 tablespoon of kirsch remove from heat and chill.

Place the strawberries in a ceramic bowl and sprinkle with 3 tablespoons of sugar and the rest of the kirsch. Whip the cream to soft peaks with the rosewater or syrup. Beat egg whites with remaining sugar until stiff peaks are formed, then fold into rose cream mixture. Gently fold through custard, a little at a time. Pile strawberries in a bowl or individual dishes, top with generous dollops of rose cream and chill. Serve with sponge finger biscuits, or *langues de chat* (cat's tongues).

Serves 4

---

winding Boneo Road where you can pick up a bag of much-praised **Flinders Farm** hydroponic tomatoes from a roadside stall. The untended stall operates on an honour system – pull up, grab your bag of tomatoes, put your money in the box, drive away again. It is a wonderfully old-fashioned idea that leaves you with good tomatoes and a calming feeling of stepping back in time.

All that fruit-picking and produce-gathering can leave you feeling thirsty so it is time to head to the **Red Hill Brewery**, the Mornington Peninsula's only micro-brewery.

Red Hill Brewery is owned and operated by David and Karen Golding, who live in the small wooden house that shares the leafy property with the purpose-built brewery buildings. There is a nice sense of scale to the place – from the small hop yard where all the hops they use in their beer are grown to the café building with its pleasant sunny wooden veranda and its viewing windows into the brewery.

The pitch-roofed brewery building may look like a rustic wooden and corrugated-iron barn, but inside it is all copper-clad, stainless-steel and steam-fired action that produces three European-style ales – a pale, fruity and crisp Golden Ale, a slightly cloudy, creamy aromatic Wheat Beer and a wonderfully coppery, malt-driven Scotch Ale. You can team your ale with rustic food that uses plenty of local produce in shareable dishes inspired by 'the great beer cultures of England, Belgium and Germany'. Kicking back in the sun with an ale or two and a ploughman's platter your thoughts turn, of course, to dinner.

Criss-crossing the Mornington Peninsula foraging for food, you would have noticed fat and happy cattle grazing in fields around Flinders, Tyabb, Moorooduc and Red Hill. So where are you going to get your hands on some of that?

Somerville may not be the most picturesque town on the peninsula and, being in the peninsula's warm, flat north, isn't on the regular food and wine radar. **Somerville Village Meats** is a great excuse for a detour.

Butcher Phil Revell runs what seems like a traditional country butcher shop complete with concrete floor and plastic grass in the counter display cabinets. But look a little closer and you will notice trophies dotted around the shop for 'Best Ham off the Bone' and 'Best Strasbourg'. The award-winning smoked goods – ham, beef, cabana, chicken breast, ham hocks – are worth the trip in themselves, but Phil also stocks Peninsula Blue Ribbon Beef: free of chemicals, growth-hormones and antibiotics, sourced entirely from those pastures you noticed across the Mornington Peninsula. Come in at the right time and you might also be able to buy lamb from Phil's own peninsula farm.

Your back seat is filling up. Dinner is looking better and better. Now, all you need is a little cheese.

Red Hill Cheese

Jan and Trevor Brandon recently removed all references to French cheese from their small cheese factory's tasting room. The walls are now filled with photos of their own product and of dishes local chefs have created using Red Hill Cheese. It seems that the Brandons, after many awards and much acclaim, have finally understood that the quality they are achieving in their factory in the forest does not need the light of reflected glory to prove itself. That proof is all in the tasting.

Jan and Trevor moved to their beautiful Red Hill property about twenty-five years ago and have kept much of the block, down the end of a picturesque winding dirt road, forested with native bush. Cheese-making started as a hobby for Trevor but when he began taking cheeses to friends' places, people loved what he was doing so much that the pressure started to build for him to do it 'properly'. When he began getting requests from winery restaurants for his cheese it became apparent that they could even make a living from his hobby.

'It got to the stage where we thought that if we didn't do it we would regret it,' says Jan. 'So when the last of the kids finished uni, Trevor retired from teaching and we set this up.'

Red Hill Cheese is a very small, artisan cheese factory that processes around 50 000 litres of milk a year to make about five tonnes of cheese. Compare this with other boutique cheese makers in Australia that process 5000 litres a day or the big gorgonzola factories in Italy that go through 20 000 litres of milk an hour and you understand how small an operation Red Hill Cheese is. And that is the way the Brandons – and their customers – like it.

All of the sixteen cheeses the Brandons make are hand-made and the milk they use – organic cow's milk from Gippsland and goat's milk from nearby Main Ridge – is pasteurised at ten degrees lower than milk in the big cheese factories. Trevor Brandon says that this preserves the flavour of the milk and encourages the cheese to continue to ripen and for 'something a bit different' to happen flavour-wise.

The other major plank of the philosophy behind Red Hill Cheese is to make cheese that complements the local wines. Thus the mild, semi-hard Portsea Picnic goat cheddar has been tailored to suit the local chardonnays while their award-winning, wonderfully pongy Misty Valley soft goat cheese is brilliant with a dry sparkling wine. Trevor Brandon has even worked with local chefs to create one-off cheeses for special events or particular wine vintages, always interested in the region and in pushing the boundaries of his cheese making.

Though Red Hill Cheese is a little easier to buy away from the factory these days, making the trip down the dirt road is still the best way to obtain one of Trevor and Jan's cheeses and to get a feel for some of the unique food activity now happening on the Mornington Peninsula.

Wineries

For some people, the Mornington Peninsula begins and ends with the production of high-quality, cool-climate wines. There is much talk about the explosion of vineyards in the region in recent years (920 hectares presently under vines, a figure that has doubled since 1996), the ever-increasing cluster of cellar doors (more than fifty), the spectacle of big industry players swooping in and snapping up small wineries, and a calendar increasingly filled with wine-related events. Hearing all this you might think that the wine industry on the Mornington Peninsula is some sort of out-of-control monster that is taking on all comers and devouring everything in its path. The true picture is less dramatic but more interesting.

Of the two million visitors to the Peninsula last year, only 10 per cent visited a winery. Even though this number has doubled in the last five years, it still

The garden, vineyards, winery and wines of Moorooduc Estate.

Their award-winning, wonderfully pongy Misty Valley soft goat cheese is brilliant with a dry sparkling wine

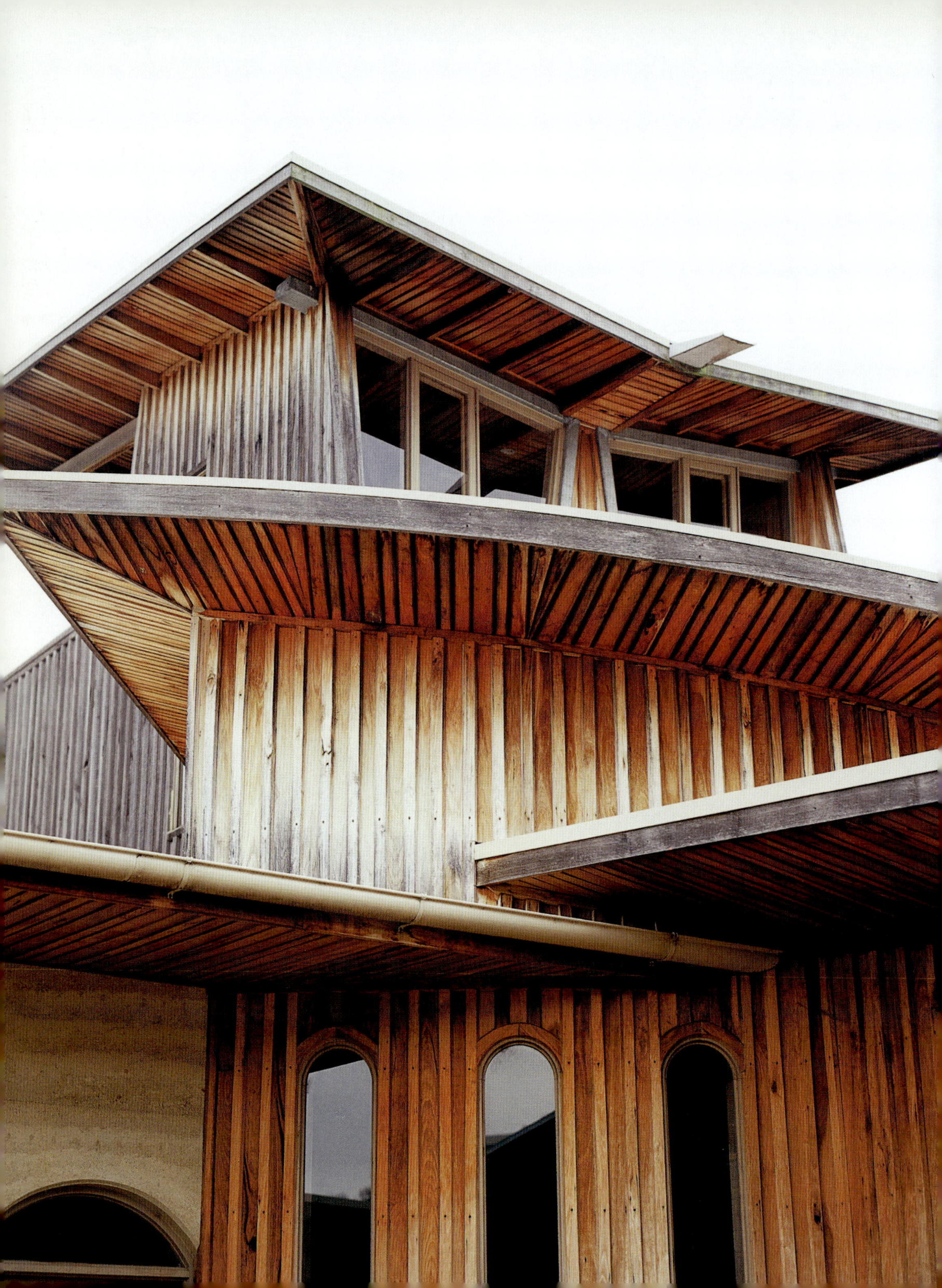

Opposite
Dramatic design and weathered timbers distinguish the Moorooduc Estate winery.

Right
Rows of vines at Mantons Creek Vineyard.

shows that most tourists come for the views rather than the vines and most can spend an entire summer on the peninsula, blissfully oblivious of all the chest beating, expansion and corporate manoeuvring happening in winemaking circles. But it also shows – given the amount of awards, accolades and column inches its wines receive – that the Mornington Peninsula wines are attracting a lot more attention than you might expect from a small, reasonably new and untouristed winemaking area. Put two and two together and you have to figure that something special is going on here.

The brief history of winemaking on the Mornington Peninsula is, like many other regions in Victoria, one of false starts, bad luck and disaffected city professionals with winemaking dreams and enough cash with which to bankroll them. Vines planted near Dromana in the nineteenth century were completely abandoned by the 1920s and others that went in during the 1950s were destroyed by bushfire a decade or so later. Nothing even remotely resembling an industry happened until the 1970s.

The 1970s were a turning point for wine in Australia generally. That decade marked the first time that sales of dry European-style table wine in Australia overtook those of fortified wine. This coincided with an increase in the numbers of Australians travelling to Europe, falling head over heals in love with the wine-growing regions of France and wanting to emulate the vigneron lifestyle when they returned home. The Mornington Peninsula's cool climate brought visions of Burgundy to more than one aspiring, Europe-bedazzled winemaker.

The Myer family started the rush at Elgee Park, followed by Nat and Rosalie White at Main Ridge. There were many others that followed but only a few – **Stonier**, **Dromana Estate**, **Moorooduc Estate** amongst them – managed to negotiate what can be a tricky, even difficult climate in which to successfully grow grapes.

Being a maritime region, the Mornington Peninsula is blessed with mild temperatures for much of the year but it can also be wet and windy with

mornington peninsula **49**

vines prone to moulds and mildews. The topography changes dramatically from one end of the peninsula to the other, resulting in a myriad microclimates and a diversity of soil types that can see one plot of land grow exceptional pinot noir grapes year after year while another just next door or over the hill might get one good year in five.

The decades since the 1970s have begun to reveal the Mornington Peninsula's strengths. While there are plots of everything from riesling to tempranillo growing, it is pinot noir, chardonnay and pinot gris vines that are most commonly planted here and have produced the most successful and regionally specific wines.

Wife-and-husband winemaking team Kathleen Quealy and Kevin McCarthy, of Main Ridge's **T'Gallant**, came to the Mornington Peninsula in the late 1980s to make pinot gris and pinot grigio. Nobody else was doing it at the time but they believed the cooler climate and red volcanic soil in the peninsula's hilly parts were perfect for creating the more complex, voluptuous pinot gris, while the warmer areas close to the coast with their lighter soil would suit the lighter more savoury pinot grigio. They were proved right and the Mornington Peninsula is now the largest producer of pinot gris in Australia.

T'Gallant, an apple orchard until Kevin and Kathleen bought it in 1994, is one of the Mornington Peninsula's most popular winery destinations. The combination of excellent, accessible wines with eye-catching unconventional labels, a lovely location and a fantastic, rustic trattoria (La Baracca) and wood-fired pizzeria (Spuntino Bar) sees the place full to capacity for much of the year. Though the Fosters Group bought the winery two years ago, Kathleen and Kevin continue to make wines as before, proving their theory that the Mornington Peninsula is an area ideally suited to producing white wine.

As some of the vineyards on the Mornington Peninsula start to reach thirty years old, the next stage of Mornington Peninsula winemaking history is getting under way. Some winemakers are deliberately narrowing their focus to pinot noir and chardonnay believing that these grapes can best achieve the heights the region is capable of. Others are experimenting with different grape varieties, matching specific types with specific pockets of land. Either way, the winemakers here are increasingly looking at single-vineyard wines, old world winemaking techniques and the whole concept of *terroir* which, on a land mass as diverse as the Mornington Peninsula, seems a mighty sensible approach.

T'Gallant Winery, one of the peninsula's most popular winery destinations, has a rustic trattoria, wood-fired pizzeria and lovely views.

Just around the corner from T'Gallant is **Mantons Creek** Vineyard. An enchanting place reached by a dirt driveway that disappears down a winding tree-lined slope, Mantons Creek feels like another world entirely. In terms of the range of restrained, elegant and Old World-influenced wines made here, it is.

Owners Michael and Judy Ablett bought the property in 2000 inheriting 19 hectares of ten-year-old vines and a remarkable number of varietals – eight in all – that they, with much-awarded contract winemaker Alex White, continue to make into a surprising and well-received range of wine.

All of the grapes at Mantons Creek – chardonnay, pinto gris, sauvignon blanc, gewürztraminer, pinot noir, pinot meunier, tempranillo and muscat – are handpicked (the slope on many of the vineyards prevents the successful use of machinery) and yield, in a good year, about three tonnes to the acre. This small, hands-on approach and the carefully crafted wines – a lean and elegant chardonnay, a lovely rosé made from three pinots, a robust tempranillo – buck the peninsula's trend towards a narrower focus and make Mantons Creek one of the most interesting wine destinations on the Mornington Peninsula.

Vines at Stonier Wines, one of the longest-established wineries on the peninsula.

There is little doubt that the winemaking industry on the Mornington Peninsula will continue to expand. Not only does it add $50 million to the Peninsula's economy every year but the depth of winemaking talent – Gary Crittenden at **Crittenden's**, Nat White at **Main Ridge Estate**, Sandro Mosele from **Port Phillip Estate** – ensures that the area's winemaking potential is a given these days – more than enough incentive for new winemakers and their dreams to give it a go.

The rate of expansion will probably be at a slower, steadier and more considered rate rather than the breakneck speed of the late 1990s. As the local winemakers become increasingly fascinated with the idea of regionality, mixing it with the big boys in terms of volume is becoming less of a goal. The Burgundian dreams of the 1970s might yet come true as the Mornington Peninsula winemakers increasingly look towards small-scale, high-quality, region-specific wines to make their mark in the world.

Stonier Wines

Established in Merricks in 1978 by Brian and Noel Stonier, **Stonier Wines** has undergone major changes since its days as a single 600-vine plot with spectacular ocean views. Big winemaking and then big brewing companies have gathered Stonier under their wings and winemakers have come and gone, but still the wines attract attention and awards.

Geraldine McFaul has been at Stonier for ten years and took over as chief winemaker from Todd Dexter (now at Yabby Lake) in 2003. She was attracted to Stonier because they only made three varieties of wine.

'I liked the idea of a region specialising,' she says. 'We have cut down to two varieties and I find that approach to have real integrity. I think it is the way that things are happening in Australia – we are moving away from that idea that everything can go everywhere. The Mornington Peninsula is a real self-selector in that respect. To me, if it is not the best you can do, why do it?'

Stonier now has 60 hectares of vines, twenty of them on the beautiful estate vineyards at Merricks, home of the Stoniers and the site of the

mornington peninsula 53

Opposite
The welcoming interior of Merrick's General Store.

winery's dramatic Daryl Jackson-designed cellar door. Other sites in five different regions have been chosen for their particular characteristics – protected from the sea winds and retaining maximum exposure to the sun.

Geraldine McFaul's philosophy – and her passion – with winemaking is based on wines that distinctly reflect the specific sites they come from. As chief winemaker at Stonier she has been making small amounts of single-vineyard wines from particular vines in the Merricks vineyard, something they have been 'mucking around with' for a few years but is now being done in a more formal, commercial way. She is loathe to generalise about a Mornington Peninsula chardonnay or a Mornington Peninsula pinot noir but when pushed, she outlines what she believes are the general regional characteristics.

'With chardonnay,' she says, 'You get incredibly powerful fruit that comes into a citrus, nut, honey character as they get older. They are quite big in terms of flavour and weight but with the Mornington Peninsula acidity bringing things together, giving it a lovely balance of richness and elegance. The pinots are quite aromatic, a lighter, more classic Burgundy style of wine – light, ethereal and with good acid.'

A tasting at the Stonier cellar door contrasting the Reserve-labelled chardonnay and pinot noir with the standard versions blended from various vineyards on the Peninsula, allows you to experience both the differences and the similarities from wines made with the same type of grape. If you are lucky, you may even get to taste one of the single-vineyard wines, sipping it in view of the specific rows of vines from which it came. It is a perfect way to understand just what this cool-climate region is capable of producing both in terms of quantity and variety.

Eating Out

One of the clearest indications that the Mornington Peninsula is being colonised by food and wine focussed Melburnians is the number of excellent restaurants now dotted around the place. The peninsula has always had good restaurants but only in small, sporadic numbers because there hasn't been the population – or the day-trippers – to support them outside of the summer months. In recent years, an influx of sea changers and people realising it is easy to pop down to the peninsula for lunch has seen dining-out become one of the Mornington Peninsula's real strengths. There are arguably more good restaurants taking advantage of the increased crowds and ever-improving local wine and food here than in any other region of Victoria.

*Specials

* Curried Parsnip Soup Served c Crispy Bacon — $11
  Wine Suggestion: Rigel '01 Chardonnay
* Ham Hock & Lentil Soup c Crusty Bread — $11
  Wine Suggestion: Rigel '02 Chardonnay
* Gnocchi alla Zucca — Potato Gnocchi c Pumpkin, Basil & a Little Chilli — $18.5
  Wine Suggestion: Rigel '02 Chardonnay
* Classic Steak Sandwich & Fries — $18
  Wine Suggestion: Rigel '00 Shiraz
* Beef Bourguignonne — Traditional French Style Beef Slow-Cooked in our Zinfandel & Served c New Potatoes — $22
  Wine Suggestion: Rigel XLV '00 Zinfandel
* Slow Simmered Spanish Chicken c Chorizo & Green Olives — $19.5
  Wine Suggestion: Rigel XLV '02 Sangiovese

The historic General Store, recently given a beautiful, award-winning makeover, highlights local produce on its shelves and its menu

Local produce, gourmet provisions, and an interesting cellar are highlights of the handsome old Merrick's General Store.

56 mornington peninsula

Don't expect to get good food everywhere you go, however. Like most beachside places in Australia, the coasts of both Western Port and Port Phillip Bay have surprisingly few good places to eat, opting for a casual even slapdash approach that often pays no attention to all the quality produce growing just kilometres away both on the land and in the sea. There are exceptions of course. Places like **Stringers Stores** and the **Green Olive Gourmet**, both in Sorrento, offer above average café fare and wave the flag for local producers and winemakers on the shelves of their produce sections. In Merricks, the historic **General Store**, recently given a beautiful, award-winning makeover, highlights some local produce on its shelves and its menu. But the biggest exception, and one of the most interesting places to eat on the Mornington Peninsula, is Dromana's **Heronswood Café**.

Made from rammed earth taken from a local quarry and with a roof thatched with local reeds, the Heronswood Café has a heart-on-its-sleeve commitment to the locally produced. Set in the beautiful grounds of the historic Heronswood house, headquarters of the environmentally aware gardening group **The Digger's Club**, the café is part of a larger effort to remind people of the diversity and deliciousness of the home-grown, the rare breed, the non mass-produced.

Many of the café's ingredients are sourced from the gardens, both the delightful 'picking' garden of herbs, beans, peas and so on that surround the café's outside tables, and the extensive fruit and vegetable plantings across the rest of the estate. Part of the joy of eating here is being introduced to things like rare-breed tomatoes and heirloom strawberries that come in an amazing

mornington peninsula 57

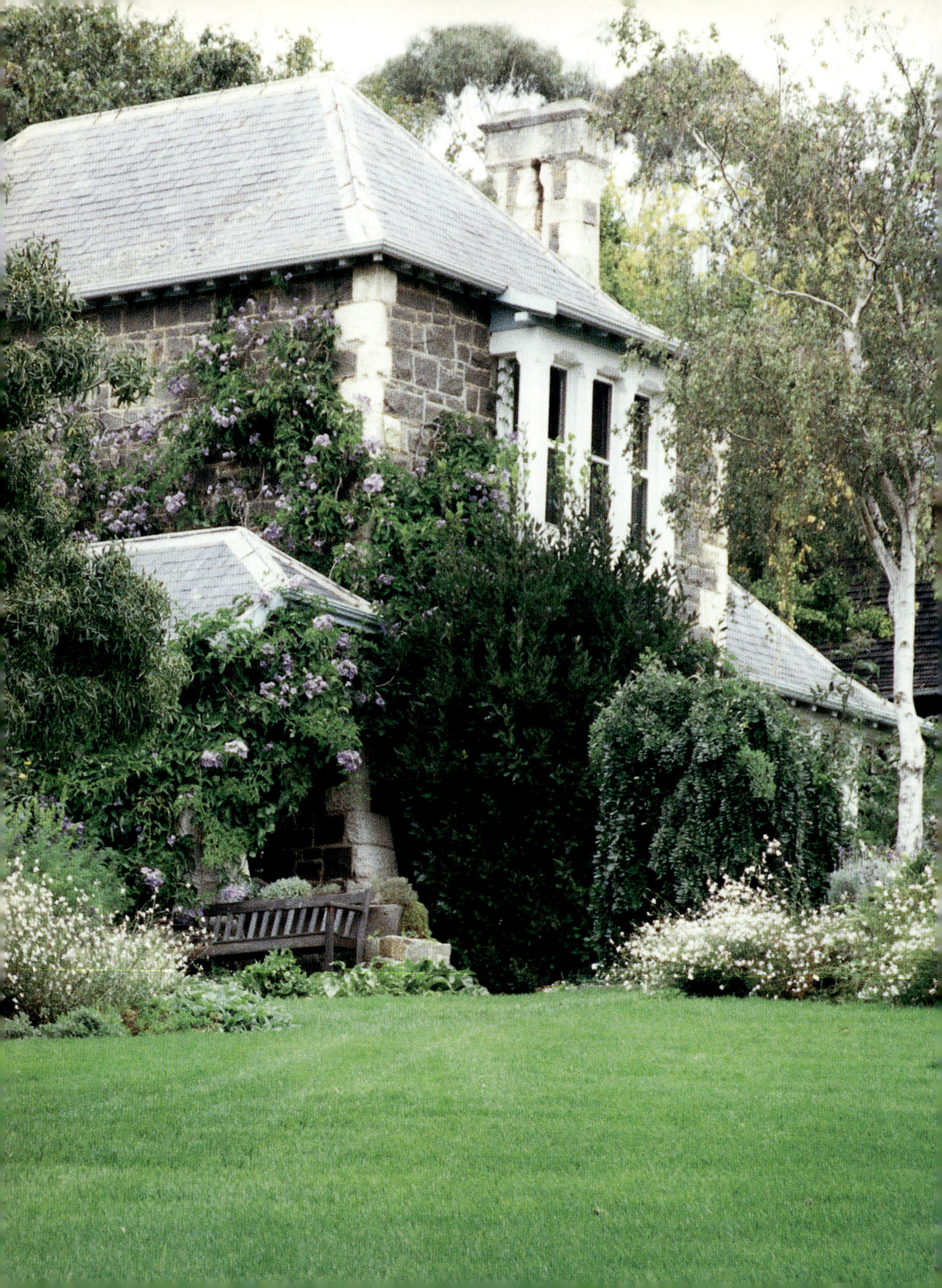

Opposite
The magnificent bluestone house at Heronswood.

variety of tastes, shades and shapes. During tomato season, for example, there can be as many as thirty different types of tomatoes growing in the gardens.

Recently refurbished by renowned chef George Biron, Heronswood Café now features an open kitchen and a menu of small tastes that you combine to make a meal. The menu changes every day depending on what comes in from the garden and will always feature something heirloom, be it a white strawberry or a sweet chocolate capsicum, an Easter egg radish or a tigerella tomato. It is not only an interesting and educative place to dine, but the food is delicious, the wine local and the gardens, with their amazing views over Port Phillip Bay, the ideal place for walking off lunch.

It is still too early to identify a particular Mornington Peninsula style but move inland a bit and there are a few things that all the best restaurants here have in common – a love of local produce, a desire to support local industry, a fanatical devotion to the seasonal and a relaxed approach that doesn't stint on attention to detail in cooking or service.

Many of the best restaurants are attached to wineries though there are some that choose to do it alone. **Bittern Cottage** has been open for twenty-five years and has become something of a Mornington Peninsula institution with its European flavours and philosophy. Owner/chefs Noel and Jenny Burrows are committed to sourcing as many of their ingredients locally as they can and the menu names local producers so you will know, for example, where the beef you are eating was grazing not so long ago.

Jill's at **Moorooduc Estate** is another place that sources many of its ingredients close to home. Housed in a striking rammed-earth building with inspiring vineyard views, Jill's is the sort of place where the eggs, vegetables and herbs on the menu come from owner/chef Jill McIntyre's coop and gardens and many of the other ingredients are sourced from local producers. Jill's bouillabaisse, for example, includes fish from local fisherman Tim Mirabella and mussels from Michael Harris' Flinders Shellfish. The approach to the food is much like Jill's husband Richard's approach to making the impressive Moorooduc Estate wines – a skilled, subtle and deceptively simple reflection of the region.

Red Hill, with its mix of artisan producers, small-scale wineries, food stores and gorgeous scenery has become one of the best places to eat on the peninsula. There is a good mix of places that will suit most moods – whether you want something casual in the sun in summer or a more hearty meal inside by the fire watching the rain fall on bare vines.

Opposite top
Chef Bernard McCarthy, his wife Rachel and their daughters at their restaurant Salix at Willow Creek.

Opposite below
Seared scallops and stuffed piquillo peppers from Salix.

The **Red Hill Brewery** not only makes and serves excellent beer but has simple excellent food, sourced from local producers, that is perfect for sharing in the sun over a pint or two.

At **Vines of Red Hill**, with its Tuscan-inspired building set amongst bush and vines, the food again leans towards the local with seriously good cooking that pays close attention to the season. **Poffs'**, the **Long Table**, and winery restaurant pioneer **Max's at Red Hill Estate**, similarly provide uniquely local experiences with food, wine, views or a lucky combination of all three.

A short drive from Red Hill, in Merricks North, you can find one of the Mornington Peninsula's best winery restaurants, **Salix at Willow Creek**. Housed in a lovely timber building with a wall of glass that overlooks the Willow Creek vineyard, Salix not only has a comfortable, stylish dining room but has recently been taken over by sea-changing Melbourne chef Bernard McCarthy.

The father of two young daughters, McCarthy decided that the hours of working in a city restaurant were robbing him of the chance to see his girls grow up. Bernard's wife Rachel, who runs the restaurant with her husband, was also happy to move to the Mornington Peninsula because it is where her mother lives and so they were spending a lot of time in the area as it was. When Salix became available, it seemed too good to turn down – a restaurant with a sound reputation, at a winery with a rapidly increasing profile, in a beautiful location just down the road from Rachel's mum.

Bernard already had a reputation as a chef fanatical about good produce and so coming to the Mornington Peninsula where he can have a 'real connection with the growers' is like a dream come true.

'The producers live just around the corner and they come to your back door with their cherries or eggs or quinces and you actually get to know them,' he says. 'I wouldn't use them if the produce wasn't good but a lot of the things you can get around here are world class.'

The menu at Salix is thick with local produce. During mushroom season, for example, you might find a twice-baked mushroom soufflé with local chestnuts and Red Hill goat's cheese, and Mornington Peninsula Prime Beef fillet will usually make the list.

Like many Mornington Peninsula sea changers, Bernard McCarthy is wondering why he didn't make the move sooner and has found the transition to shorter hours, fresh air and more time with his girls easy. What has been good for him has also been a bonus for the local restaurant scene.

Seared scallops with stuffed piquillo peppers and almond sauce

Bernard McCarthy,
Salix, Willow Creek

1 eggplant
1 tbsp chopped parsley
1 tbsp small capers, washed
salt and pepper
grated rind from ½ lemon
1 tbsp extra virgin olive oil
8 piquillo peppers

Barbecue the eggplant whole until tender and cooked. Then remove flesh and chop roughly. Add the other ingredients and fill the peppers.

Sauce
5 tbsp almond meal
1 tbsp breadcrumbs
2 tbsp sherry vinegar
1 tbsp extra virgin olive oil
1 garlic clove, crushed
1 cup water or vegetable stock
salt and pepper

Combine ingredients and blend until smooth.

To serve
24 scallops, cleaned

Warm the peppers gently in the oven. Put a splash of olive oil in a hot pan and sear scallops till three-quarters cooked.

Spoon the almond sauce into middle of a warmed plate. Stand the peppers upright on the sauce and place the seared scallops around.

Serves 4 as an entree

There may always be cheap and cheerful pizza and pasta joints on the Mornington Peninsula, but as more and more food and wine fanatics join the holiday crowds, the easier it will become to find a locally produced feed cooked with skill. The current wave of Mornington Peninsula restaurants is a good indication that the area may be finally waking up to its true potential.

Montalto Vineyard and Olive Grove

If you're looking for a place that illustrates the food and wine aspirations of the 'new' Mornington Peninsula, **Montalto Vineyard and Olive Grove** is a good place to start. The site of one of the region's most feted restaurants, Montalto combines great food and service with a host of other activities – extensive vineyards, a range of wine from estate and Peninsula-grown grapes, vegetable gardens, fruit and nut orchards, olive groves, sculpture – that show just how much good quality stuff the Mornington Peninsula is capable of producing.

Montalto is the result of a retirement project and a sea change happening simultaneously in one family. During his years as a food industry executive, John Mitchell lived in the UK and spent many holidays in the south of France

At the heart of Montalto Vineyard and Olive Grove – with its vines, vegetable, herb and fruit gardens and distinctive sculpture – is the winery restaurant.

where he and his family fell in love with the sight of vineyards growing on hills that sloped towards the sea. Seeing similarities in the landscape of the family's property at Merricks, John decided to plant a few vines after he retired. Hobby turned to passion and when the opportunity came to buy the incredibly beautiful Red Hill South site with its 4 hectares of vines, he decided to expand his horizons. Soon after, his daughter Heidi Williams, a Melbourne-based lawyer, expressed interest in joining him and the idea of Montalto as a business was born.

Montalto combines great food and service with a host of other activities – extensive vineyards, vegetable gardens, fruit and nut orchards, olive groves and sculpture

Opposite
Montalto's restaurant features vegetables, herbs, nuts and olives all grown on the property, as well as its own wines.

After eighteen months of discussion with her parents, Heidi quit her job and moved to the Mornington Peninsula with her husband Neil Williams and the business really began to take shape. Wine remained a primary focus with more vines planted across the property but a restaurant also became integral to the plan as did the idea of an olive grove and restoring the natural wetlands. The ruggedly handsome wood and glass restaurant building was constructed, sited to capture both the beauty of the property's gorgeous hinterland position and the distant sea views and, after internationally renowned chef Philippe Mouchel became involved, the new venture attracted attention both locally and in Melbourne.

Mouchel moved on after setting the restaurant's produce-driven philosophy in motion. His protégé James Redfern maintains the passion for locally grown ingredients, even overseeing, with John's wife Wendy, the planting of kitchen gardens that are supplying more and more of the restaurant's herbs and vegetables. Montalto's olives (both as table fruit and oil), nuts and wines also feature on the menu.

The 12 hectares of vineyards that follow the slopes of the property's natural amphitheatre include pinot noir, chardonnay, pinot meunier, riesling and semillon grapes. Montalto also manages another 40 hectares of vineyards across the Mornington Peninsula that include plantings of shiraz and pinot grigio. There is no winery on the site, Montalto's locally grown fruit being made into wine by winemaker Robin Brockett at Scotchman's Hill on the Bellarine Peninsula.

Not only is Montalto a hive of food and wine activity, it also hosts an annual sculpture competition with the entries carefully sited around the property from February to April. Montalto acquires the winning sculpture each year and so its permanent collection is growing alongside the grapes, nuts, olives and vegetables.

Heidi Williams has no regrets about leaving Melbourne and sees Montalto as a part of a movement on the Mornington Peninsula that is pushing the quality of both wine and food higher and higher.

'It is great to be in a business I am so passionate about, in a region I am in love with that has so much to offer,' she says. 'There is still a long way to go in many respects but that is what makes being here so exciting.'

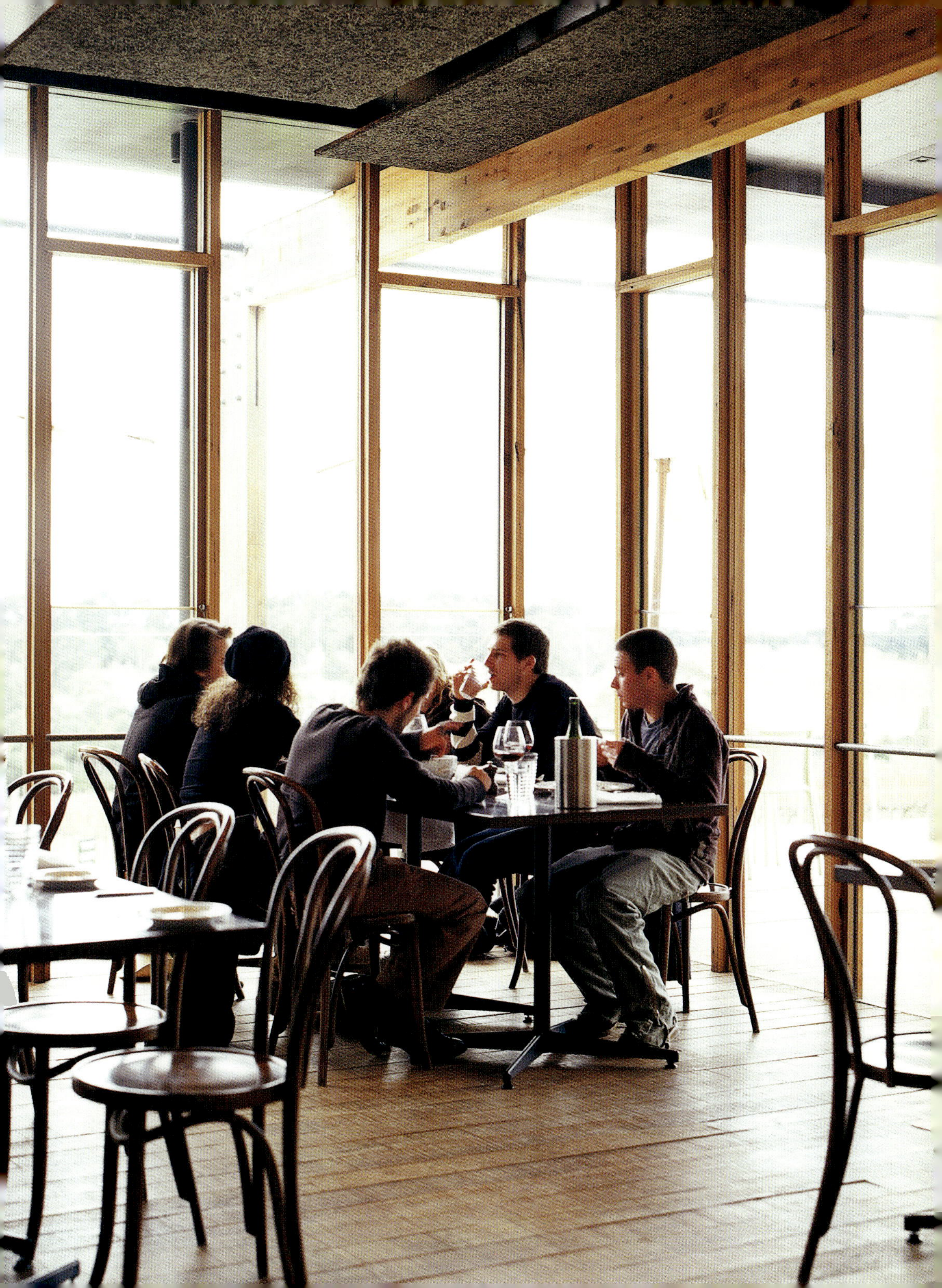

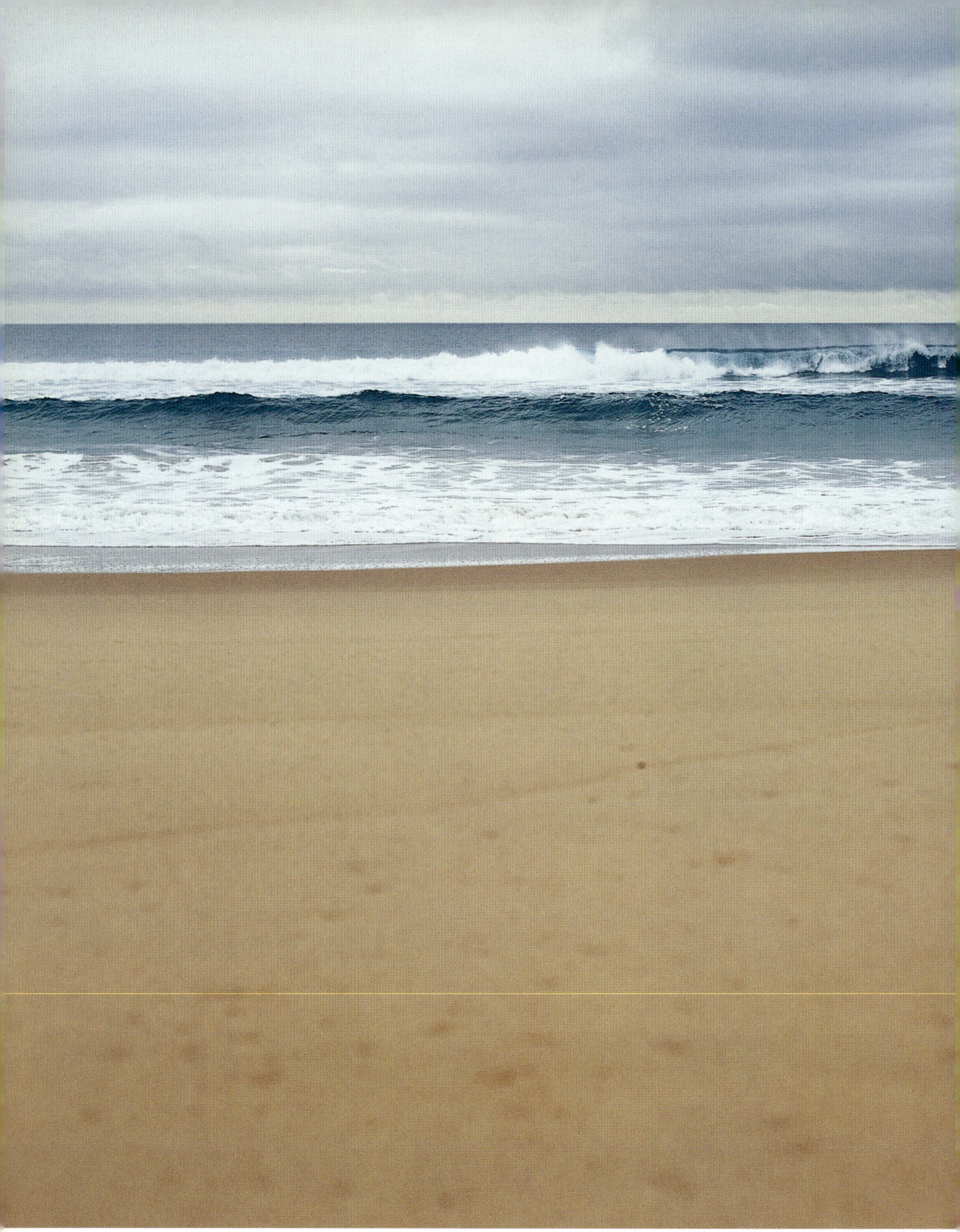

phillip island

michele curtis

phillip island

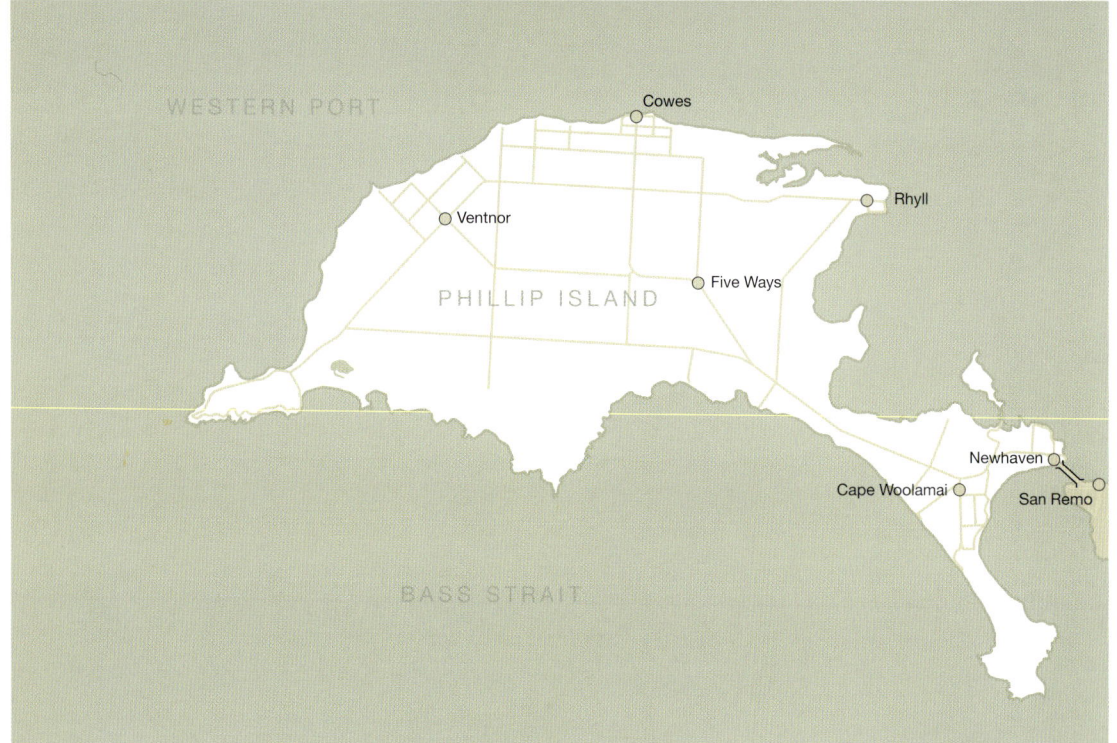

WESTERN PORT

Cowes

Rhyll

Ventnor

PHILLIP ISLAND

Five Ways

Newhaven

Cape Woolamai

San Remo

BASS STRAIT

MELBOURNE

The maritime climate contributes to the unique flavours of ingredients produced both on the island and in the surrounding waters

Above and opposite
The island's beaches and rocky coastline are a refuge for wildlife.

Phillip Island has a magical sense about it, from the moment you drive over the bridge separating this peaceful pocket of the world from the mainland. Surrounded by the waters of Western Port and Bass Strait, it has long been a traditional getaway spot for Melburnians with its stunning surf beaches, spectacular coastal scenery and easygoing ambience. The island, just 26 kilometres long and 9 kilometres wide, is less than two hours' drive from Melbourne, yet has a distinctive quality all its own. The population swells from around 5500 to 40,000 over the summer months as people make the most of its fine beaches, good fishing, family activities and visitor attractions.

One of the island's special features is its abundant wildlife – the little penguins that can be seen at Australia's number one wildlife attraction, the 'fairy penguin parade', the country's second-largest seal colony, huge numbers of shearwaters that nest on the cliffs in season, and koalas, now protected by the Koala Conservation Centre. Pelicans swoop in for their daily feed at 11.30 each morning on the beach near San Remo Fisherman's Co-op.

Fishing has always been a primary industry for Phillip Island, though for many decades wheat and chicory crops were planted in substantial numbers. Even today you can still see some of the old chicory kilns with their unusual towers and pitched roofs. The maritime climate contributes to the unique flavours of ingredients produced both on the island and in the surrounding waters. There's an abundance of fresh seafood, and a lot of it makes its way onto menus at restaurants and cafés on the island. Cowes is the culinary hub of Phillip Island with its restaurants and cafés, but there are gems at Cape Woolamai such as **White Salt Fish and Chippery**, the **San Remo Fisherman's Co-op** and **Island Primary Produce**.

Thriving seal colonies first drew sealers to the area, the traditional lands of the Bunurong people, during the 1800s. The first recorded land sale took place in 1868 and by 1872 there were 165 settlers living here. The island gained popularity in the 1920s when an access track was opened for visitors to view the penguins on the trek back to their burrows after a hard day's

Above right
The jetty at Cowes,
a popular spot for fishing.

Opposite
Fisherman John Gazan, whose family has fished off Phillip Island for generations.

Foodstores and producers

fishing. Tourism boomed with a ferry service to Cowes and the construction of grand guesthouses. The first bridge linking the island to the mainland was opened in 1940.

Just off Phillip Island is historic Churchill Island, separated by a narrow strait; it's shallow enough to wade across at low time, though a bridge allows vehicle access. The first building was built in 1866 by John Rogers and still stands today, along with the Amess Homestead built by Samuel Amess in 1872, with its many outhouses, farm machinery and period gardens. Churchill Island is now home to a monthly farmers' market, where visitors can meet the makers and growers, taste samples and load their baskets with some of the region's best and freshest produce.

The island's main industry always has been and still is fishing. At one time San Remo was the state's premium shark-fishing area. Today, due to reduced quotas and high licensing fees the number of commercial fishermen has dropped substantially.

The San Remo Fishermen's Co-op, today with more than twenty active members, has existed since the 1950s. Back then there were fifty couta boats fishing in Bass Strait, as well as a reasonable number of crayfish boats. Over time, couta have left the area and shark and crayfish have become the main catch. Today there are eight shark boats, three cray boats and one Danish seiner owned by Lucas Hill, a fisherman and chairperson of the San Remo Fishermen's Co-op. Hill has fished off Phillip Island for twenty-five years, originally as a shark fisherman, but now with his Danish seiner he trawls for flathead and whiting.

While crayfish is fished locally in waters surrounding the island the shark fishermen go out into Bass Strait for seven to ten days for both gummy and school shark. Hill says 'There was trouble with the high levels of gummy shark being caught four to five years ago. With the introduction of quotas

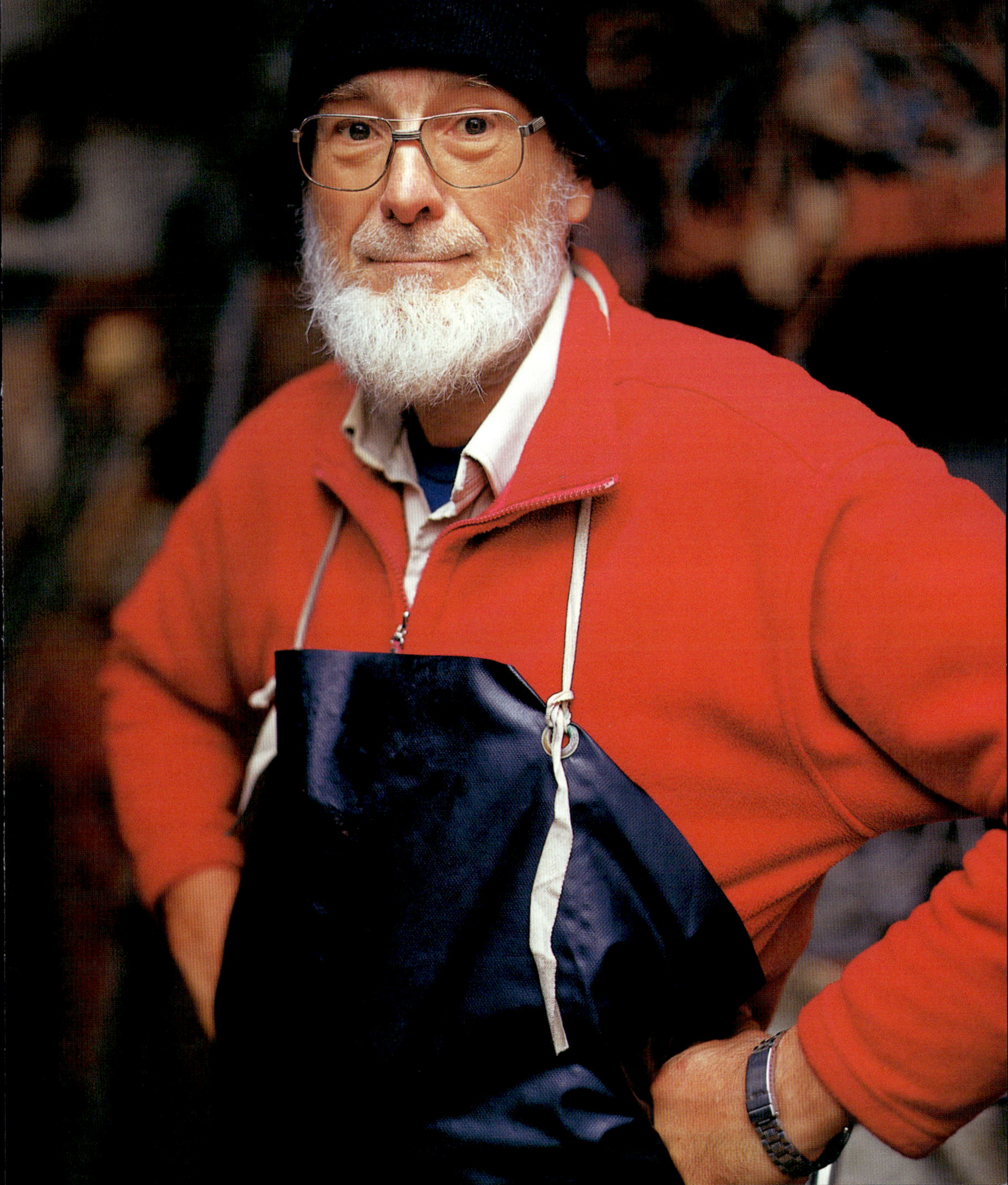

and higher licensing fees the number of commercial fisherman has dropped their catch to a sustainable level.'

Fisherman John Gazan's family has fished off Phillip Island for generations, and he attributes much of his success as a rock-flathead fisherman to the knowledge passed downover the decades. Through his twenty-five years of commercial fishing, his own experience plus tips learnt from previous generations have helped him predict certain catches in specific areas.

He has a strong environmental approach to fishing though, 'Fishermen are conservationists, we never want to do anything that will reduce our chance of catching fish next week, next year, or even next generation.' He goes so far as to say he doesn't catch his quota, preferring instead to go out each day, catch a small, fresh amount, rather than do it all in one hit.

As a member of the Victorian Bay and Inlets Fishermen's Association John Gazan is trying to get environmental accreditation for the commercial fishermen in Port Phillip and Western Port area. This involves limiting the number of commercial fishermen working in the area to help preserve it for future generations.

San Remo, just before you cross the bridge onto Phillip Island, is where you'll find the local fishing fleet, the Fishermen's Co-Op Shop (for great fish and chips) and plenty of hungry pelicans.

Fishermen's Co-op Shop

The San Remo Co-op sells most of its catch straight on to Melbourne, but it is possible to buy some of this fantastic fresh fish at the **Co-op Shop**. The shop really came about by accident. As fishermen were working close to San Remo gutting fish, they started to throw fish scraps to the pelicans. More and more pelicans came, and then people started coming to watch. 'In the end the Co-op saw that if they opened a shop they could make some

'Fishermen are conservationists, we never want to do anything that will reduce our chance of catching fish next week, next year, or even next generation'

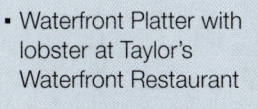

Five fishy treats

- Waterfront Platter with lobster at Taylor's Waterfront Restaurant
- Asian Octopus Salad from White Salt Gourmet Fish and Chippery, Cape Woolamai
- Island Fish Soup, Harry's on the Esplanade
- Mussels Provencale from the Island Food Store
- Flake and chips from the San Remo Fishermen's Co-op

money,' explains Hill. 'Today in the height of summer we get 300 people watching the feeding of the pelicans.'

And there are plenty more people feeding themselves. The Co-op offers good quality fish, mostly flake straight from their boats, cooked in canola oil and served with fresh chips – on a good day they sell 11,000 serves to the hungry hoards. If you prefer to cook it yourself, you might be able to choose fresh flathead, rockling, whiting, garfish, calamari and crayfish, depending on the season.

Island Primary Produce

Phillip Island may have great fish and chips, but food and wine lovers will find it offers more than that. The island's farms are responsible for some fine primary produce. Ted Walsh of **Island Primary Produce** specialises in taking beef and lamb from the paddocks of Phillip Island to the plate. Walsh explains 'We take 100 per cent Phillip Island beef and lamb and supply to a select few businesses on the island and also through our retail outlet. Although not organic we use free-range and chemical-free animals that we process in the old-fashioned manner.'

All the animals are pasture fed, which means plenty of rich green grass due to the ample rainfall, as well as an abundance of fresh air thanks to the sometimes icy southerlies. Ted likens the quality of meat produced on Phillip Island to that of King Island, which has an outstanding reputation for prime meats.

A unique feature of the island's farming is the maritime influence. Walsh truly believes there's a case difference. 'Depending on where the animals graze on the island you get a difference in flavour. If it's up near Cape Woolamai the lamb takes on a salty flavour, but the natural grass feeding gives all the animals a good flavour and texture, similar to the bygone days when meat still had flavour,' explains Ted. 'We follow the traditional methods such as milk feeding young animals… the cattle are predominantly Angus and they eat nothing bar the excellent pasture on the island.'

Island Primary Produce supplies only a handful of quality businesses on the island, such as **Harry's on the Esplanade**, the **Island Food Store** and the luxury B&B **Glen Isla House**. The RSL is lucky enough to get their schnitzel for their customers. Harry Schmidt, from Harry's, frequently makes use of the eye fillet on his menu, while the Food Store turns beef into hearty meat pies. Island residents and weekenders pick up their meat from the retail outlet, open four days a week Ventnor Road, Ventnor. Orders are welcome.

The **Churchill Produce Market**, held on the fourth Saturday of each month,

Right and below right
Herbs being cultivated and picked on the island.

Below and bottom
A staff member from Island Primary Produce and the island-grazed stock.

Weekenders flock to the market to stock-up on goodies such as jams, honey, fruit, vegetables, blueberries, asparagus from Kooweerup, wine from several Gippsland wineries and more

Left
One of the Maremma dogs that guard the free-range chickens at Freeranger.

Below and right
Phil Westwood's chickens and the free-range eggs at Freeranger.

brings a lease of life to historic Churchill Island. Manager Peter Arnold says it's a strong regional farmers' market attracting some fifty stalls at the height of the season. Weekenders flock to the market to stock-up on goodies such as jams, honey, fruit, vegetables, blueberries, asparagus from Kooweerup, wine from several Gippsland wineries. and Phil Westwood's **Freeranger** eggs from nearby Grantville.

Phil Westwood's hens lead a happy life. Guarded by Maremma dogs who protect the 800-strong flock from foxes and other natural predators, the chooks are free to roam quality pastures. 'Each flock has its own dog. They band together and the dogs will stay with the chooks to protect them,' says Westwood. This allows the hens to hunt for worms and insects as well as any natural feed they can scratch up, providing them with a healthy diet free from additives and chemicals.

The Blue Mountain Creek property is in a bushland setting off the Bass Highway on the way to Phillip Island. Each week Westwood delivers his Freeranger eggs to shops and restaurants on Phillip Island as well as many homes, and his stand can often be found at the monthly Churchill Island Farmers' Market.

Island Food Store

The island seems to attract people wanting a change of life and a more relaxed lifestyle. Two such people are Elizabeth McGrath and Jayne Menesdorffer. McGrath founded the Island Food Store in 2001 and was later joined by Menesdorffer. In 2004 the business took an extra leap and doubled its floor space, taking over a nearby shop. 'We wanted to sell more than vinegar and oil,' says Menesdorffer. For example, 'driven by customer requests we now host regular cooking classes. These might be how to cook squid,

Rack of lamb in hunan barbecue sauce

Island Food Store, Cowes

5 tbsp hoisin sauce
3 tbsp honey
2 tbsp dark soy sauce
2 tbsp dry sherry
1 tbsp oriental sesame oil
1 tbsp curry powder
1 tsp Chinese chilli sauce
4 cloves garlic, finely minced
1 tbsp grated or finely minced orange peel
1 tbsp salted black beans, rinsed and chopped
¼ cup white sesame seeds
1 rack of lamb

In a bowl, combine all barbecue sauce ingredients except sesame seeds. Place sesame seeds in a small, ungreased skillet set over high heat, and stir until light golden, about 2 minutes. Immediately pour out, let them cool momentarily, then add them to sauce ingredients. Stir well.

Place meat in a stainless steel or glass bowl and pour in sauce. Marinate for 2 hours, then drain and reserve marinade.

Prepare a charcoal fire. When coals are ash coloured, grill meat, rotating occasionally and brushing on more barbecue sauce, until medium–rare in centre. Alternatively, roast in preheated 180°C oven until meat thermometer registers 60°C.

Serves 2 as entree or 1 rack per person for main

Opposite and above
The Island Food Store specialises in regional and seasonal, home-cooked fare.

simply because it's squid season, or it may be a special Moroccan evening.'

Produce from the island features heavily. 'Our customers bring us excess from their gardens such as leeks, herbs, beetroot and pumpkins,' says Menesdorffer. 'Lizzie has her own chickens, so we use those eggs regularly as well. The Island Primary Produce beef makes its way into our pies and we use seafood caught from waters surrounding the island.'

The shop is a haven for residents and weekenders alike with a plentiful supply of top quality, locally sourced and imported fare. There are fantastic salads, ready-to-eat curries and take-home meals, quality baked goods including Phillippa's breads, imported and local cheeses, and pantry standbys such as Grinders coffee, excellent pasta, arborio rice and specialist Simon Johnson products. The Island Food Store seems to be making sure life is a little bit more relaxed for everyone.

Wineries

Phillip Island and the surrounding area, bordering on the lush Gippsland region, has a growing reputation for producing premium, cool-climate wines with full fruit flavours, and is especially renowned for its chardonnay and pinot noir. Just before you reach Phillip Island, there are a couple of small wineries with cellar doors open to the public.

The **Gurdies Winery**, off the Bass Highway on St Helier's Road, enjoys some of the region's best views across Western Port and French Island. Legend has it the name Gurdies arose from a travelling circus whose 'hurdy gurdy' or carousel rolled into the creek and became a permanent fixture.

The region surrounding the vineyard is based on sandy soil giving good drainage for the vines resulting in full fruit flavours, while the plentiful sunshine helps ripen slower-maturing grapes such as cabernet. Wine styles produced at the Gurdies include riesling, chardonnay, pinot noir, shiraz, merlot and cabernet sauvignon. The winery, established in 1982, opens every day of the year for tastings and cellar-door sales.

Catherine and David Lance always wanted a winery with a cellar door. After successfully putting their Yarra Valley winery, Diamond Valley Vineyard, on the map with its flinty pinot noir, they were ready for the challenge of producing great wine grown in a maritime climate. 'We were fascinated by Phillip Island with its cool climate and volcanic red soil, so similar to the Mornington Peninsula,' says David. 'And because we knew the grapes grown here would be so different from our Yarra Valley vineyard.' **Phillip Island Winery** is the successful result.

On the southern coast of Phillip Island, on Berrys Beach Road, an old dairy built from Mount Gambier limestone was transformed into this picturesque vineyard, complete with seventy different types of roses. You can visit the cellar door, taste the wines and enjoy a platter of food, either by the open fire on a chilly day, or in the protected courtyard with its beautiful garden and shade cloths.

In 1994 the Lances planted 2 hectares of chardonnay, sauvignon blanc, merlot and cabernet sauvignon, then added a tiny plot of pinot noir in 1998. 'Phillip Island has a lot more sunshine compared to the peninsula and we

Left to right
David Lance, who runs Phillip Island Winery with his wife Catherine; the old dairy building, the vines and the picturesque landscape.

knew that, and that the wind might be a problem.' The effect of the wind was far greater than they expected though. After planting out the vineyard they left the baby vines in their plastic tubing growing happily and went to the Yarra Valley. When they returned after a couple of weeks the vines had grown extremely well, but as soon as the vines emerged from the plastic tubing the wind burnt the heads off. Catherine says, 'We are always ready for a challenge, there was no way we were going to give up.'

The answer was to cover the entire vineyard with a unique state-of-the-art netting enclosure, the first of its kind in Australia. Under this netting the 2 hectares of close-planted vines have thrived, producing wines with true characteristics for their grape variety.

'Not only does the netting protect the vines from the wind, it also offers 15 per cent shade and protects the vines from birds and hail. As the southerlies blow in off Bass Strait the netting tricks the wind into thinking it's a hill,' says David.

The label on the estate range of wines features the distinctive net with its artful squiggle representing the roofs of the net. A second range, produced mostly from Gippsland fruit, features labels with photographs of prominent Phillip Island landmarks – watch for their Cape Woolamai Sauvignon Blanc and The Nobbies Pinot Noir.

The winery's pinot noir always sells out early. Be sure to visit just after vintage to get your hands on a bottle of a typical silky Burgundian pinot. As David states 'We're pinot people.' Certainly their track record with Diamond Valley confirms this statement and consistent reviews of the Phillip Island pinot noir support the view. The sauvignon blanc also stands out in a big way with its herbaceous fruit and minerally finish. Likewise the chardonnay 'sings its own song' according to Catherine. Matured in oak, it has a touch of lemon with a rich mellow butterscotch mouth, in an intensely fruit-driven wine.

The merlot represents more of a challenge. David explains 'It's a difficult variety to grow here … Grapes at the top of the vineyard have different characteristics to grapes from the bottom.' It's very Phillip Island though,

Opposite
The view from Taylor's Waterfront Restaurant and Gerald Taylor holding one of the restaurant's succulent lobsters.

with an intense chocolate and liquorice palate with a hint of violets. While winemaking may seem an onerous task, the Lances sum it up succinctly 'We aim to grow the best grapes possible and not bugger it up.'

A similar passion runs through **Silverwater Winery**, owned by Lionel and Lyn Hahn, in San Remo. Originally the Hahns bought the property as a weekend escape, purely because of the stunning views over Western Port, but eventually they moved to live permanently in San Remo.

They planted the vines in 1995 and struggled with the wind, eventually planting rows of melaleucas, acacias and she-oaks in between every fifteen rows of grapes to prevent damage to the grapevines. The vineyard consists of pinot gris, pinot noir, chardonnay, shiraz and cabernet sauvignon.

Lionel was advised to pull out the cabernet sauvignon, as he was told it would never ripen. Ironically, since the first vintage in 2000 the cabernet sauvignon has won three medals in its class. The true success story has been the pinot noir, recently picking up a gold medal for the 2003 vintage, plus the trophy for the best wine in the Cool Climate Wine Show. All the wines are typical cool-climate styles made in the traditional French manner; the chardonnay and pinot noir are aged for nine months in French oak, while the cabernet and shiraz take eighteen months and then undergoes a further fermentation.

Although Silverwater Winery isn't open to the public, their wines can be purchased locally from the supermarket in San Remo and from the Island Food Store in Cowes.

The property is also home to 1200 olive trees, half of them planted in a symmetrical design around the hill to produce table olives and the remainder on the lower side of the hill for oil production. The Hahns have yet to do anything with the olives, however, as they focus on the winery, and also enjoy the lifestyle that Phillip Island and its surrounds has to offer, including wonderful views, magnificent seafood and plenty of fresh air.

Eating out

While the little penguins have to swim hundreds of kilometres to get their dinner you can just walk into one of the excellent restaurants on the island and take a seat.

Without a shadow of a doubt **Harry's on the Esplanade** is the number one dining spot. Harry Schmidt's menu reflects not only the regional produce but also his German heritage. Harry has always been a chef; he gave up his highly acclaimed Mornington restaurant to move across Western Port to take advantage of the exceptional water views that Phillip Island offers from every angle.

Chilli mud crab

Taylor's Waterfront Restaurant

6 crabs
½ cup minced garlic
½ cup minced ginger
30 shallots, thinly sliced
15 small red chillies, thinly sliced
½ cup soy sauce
100 ml lime juice
4 tbsp sambal oelek
150 g palm sugar, grated
100 ml fish sauce
400 ml chicken stock
Thai basil leaves for garnish

If using fresh crabs place in freezer for 15 minutes to stun them. Bring a large pot of water to the boil and cook crabs for 4 minutes, then refresh in iced water. Remove outer shells, cut off and crack claws. Cut the bodies into quarters. Mix together garlic, ginger, shallots and red chillies. Set aside. Mix soy sauce, lime juice, sambal oelek, palm sugar, fish sauce and chicken stock together. Heat wok over a very high heat, add spice paste and fry until fragrant. Add crab pieces and fry briefly. Add soy sauce liquid and allow to simmer for 3 minutes. Add basil leaves to garnish and serve.

Serves 6–9

Harry is dedicated to his job; he has spent the last three years persuading fishermen and locals to supply him, from old Italian gardeners dropping off excess, home-grown vegetables to **Island Primary Produce** supplying high-grade meat. On top of this he travels to Melbourne once a week, twice in summer, to pick up market-fresh produce, shellfish and meats. He makes all his own ice creams, pastries, cakes and bread from scratch. 'I am from the old guard,' he says proudly. 'That's the way it should be and that's the only way I like it.'

> Harry makes the most of what is offered, from just-picked tomatoes and passionfruit to locally produced venison and goat

Working fifteen to eighteen hours a day, Harry is likely to change the menu on a whim. It may be some whiting arriving unexpectedly from a fisherman or a chance encounter with a farmer. Harry makes the most of what is offered, from just-picked tomatoes and passionfruit to locally produced venison and goat. In spring its asparagus from Kooweerup, while over summer some 20 kilos of crayfish will pass through his kitchen along with 80–100 kilos of mussels.

With wife Kirsten front-of-house they welcome the regulars, a strong band of locals who get them through the winter. Harry says 'We look after everyone, for they go away and tell their friends.' Harry's meticulous attention to detail shines through. 'Chef-owners work harder,' says Schmidt simply.

On the other side of the island **Taylor's Waterfront Restaurant** boasts three unique features: a stunning view across the surf, a prime position for watching the sunset every night, and their exceptional lobster platters. Brothers Gerald and Michael Taylor run this successful business that sees 20,000 international visitors each year, most of whom can't wait to sink their teeth into the seafood-heavy menu. While no penguins come up on the beach below, Michael says there's plenty of opportunity to spot the odd passing whale or pod of dolphins. As any fisherman will tell you, where there are dolphins, there's shark and Phillip Island is the biggest source of flake in Victoria. Some of it makes its way onto the menu here in their famous Shark Attack, a local fillet of ocean-fresh gummy shark battered and served with fries and tartare sauce.

Tourists come for the platters though. 'We use 4 to 5 tonnes of lobster

Harry Schmidt from Harry's on the Esplanade.

each season,' says Gerald. 'All of this lobster is fished for just off the coast and brought directly to us. We keep it live in special tanks in the kitchen. It's a guarantee that we serve fresh lobster.'

Tasmanian salmon and oysters, red emperor, Moreton Bay bugs, scallops and crab along with venison from nearby Bass also feature on the menu. Chef Daniel Airoldi, who worked with Jacques Reymond, joined the team recently. This classically trained French chef has brought his French influence, updating the menu and highlighting local produce.

A more casual option for dinner is the **Jetty Restaurant**, on the Esplanade in Cowes. Perched right opposite the waterfront, this modern bright dining room offers large communal tables and a classic family restaurant menu matched with local wines. Owner Vivian Viglietti says their menu is aimed at the family market and daytrippers wanting a bite to eat before heading off to the penguin parade. Diners will find a smattering of Asian dishes, such as chicken laksa or a spicy lamb rogan josh, along with distinctive – and popular – dishes such as BBQ kangaroo fillet with stir-fried vegetables and spicy plum sauce. Seafood lovers might consider a whole baby snapper with sweet chilli sauce, salad and chips. There's also a kid's menu. 'It's a busy, hectic place during summer,' says Viglietti.

Near the other side of the island, at the **White Salt Gourmet Fish and Chippery** in Cape Woolamai, Natalie Dwyer and Max Hutchinson are creating something a little more special than your standard fish and chips. Max believes in doing everything the proper way, from hand-cutting the chips and potato cakes – using potatoes sourced from Gippsland's Kooweerup – to making his own special batter using tempura flour and beer to coat the fish. Surprisingly, it's not flake and chips that is the number one seller: it's the spicy Asian octopus salad. Max tenderises the octopus, marinates it in kecap manis, coriander, ginger and chilli, then char-grills it and serves it on a bed of baby salad leaves with sweet potato chips.

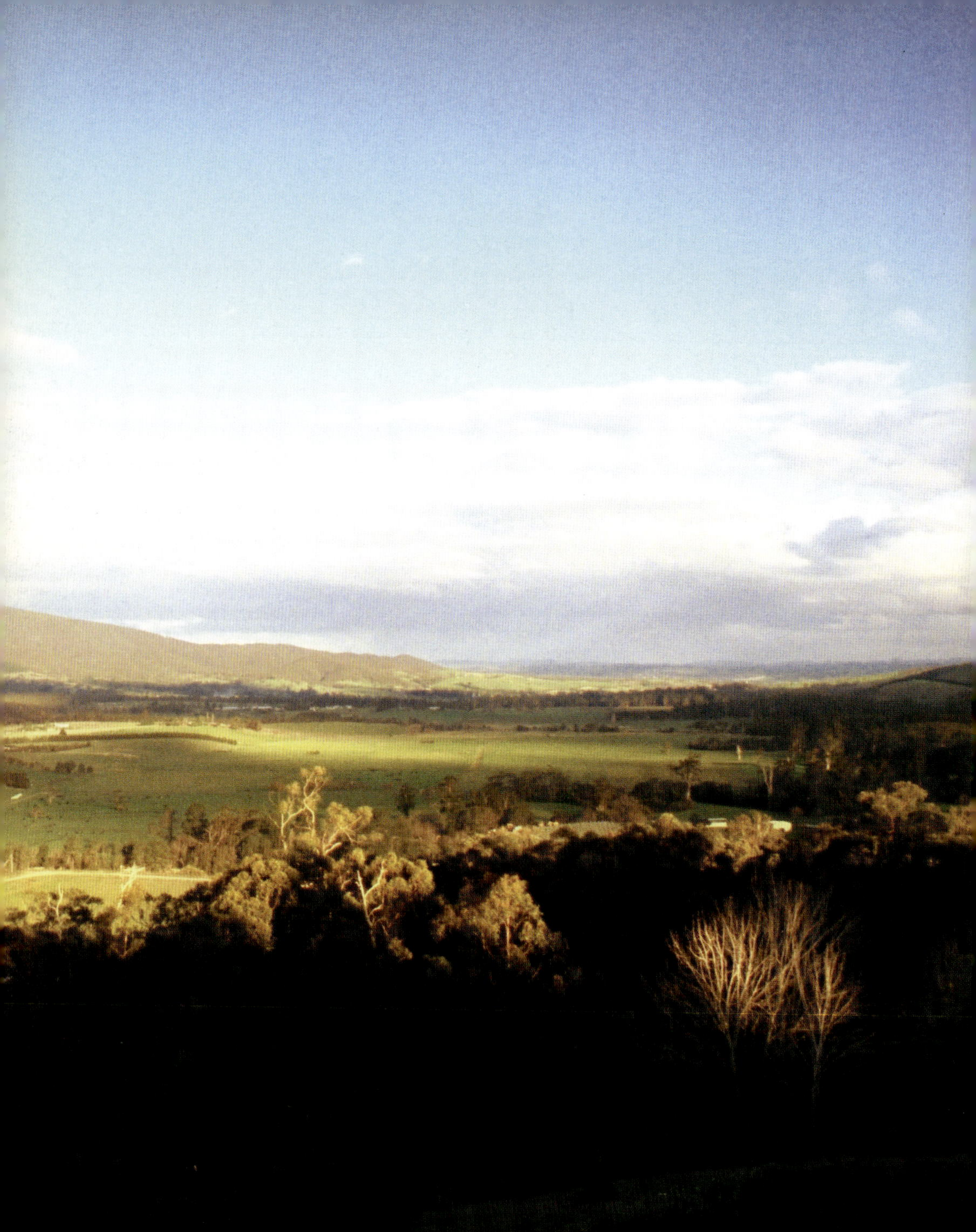

yarra valley

michael harden

yarra valley

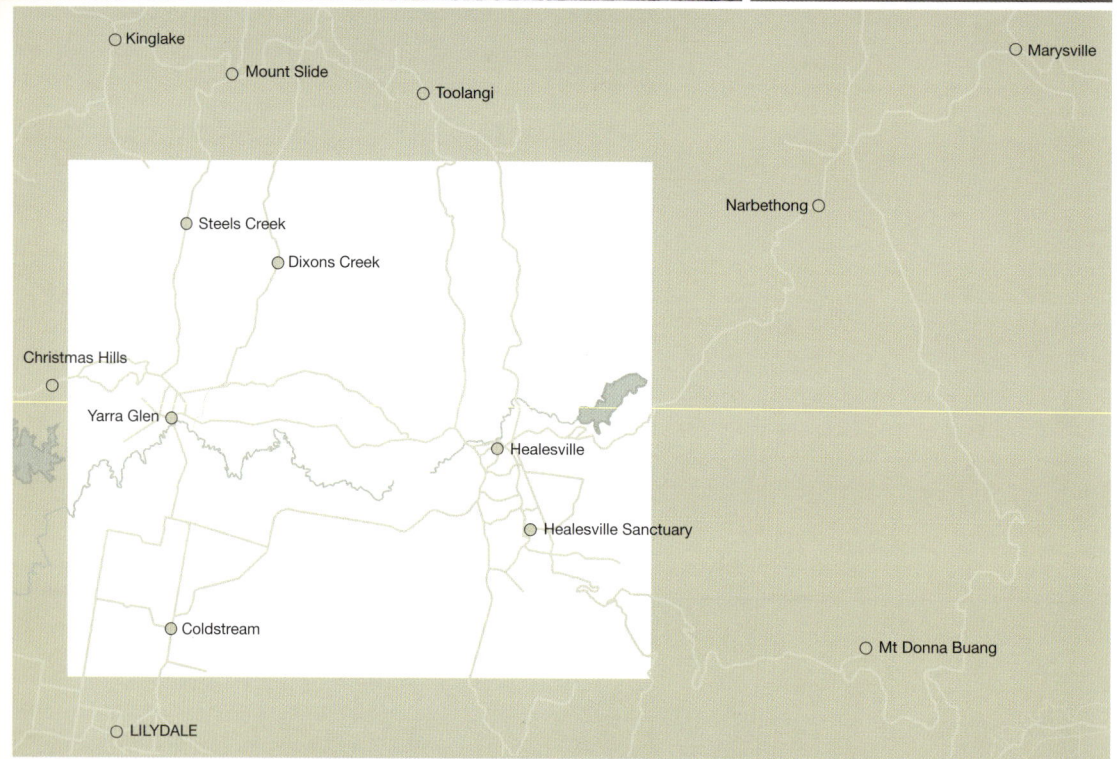

- Kinglake
- Mount Slide
- Toolangi
- Marysville
- Steels Creek
- Dixons Creek
- Narbethong
- Christmas Hills
- Yarra Glen
- Healesville
- Healesville Sanctuary
- Coldstream
- Mt Donna Buang
- LILYDALE

Blessed with a cool climate capable of producing wines of great subtlety and foods of rare variety and flavour, the region is currently in the midst of a renaissance

Above
TarraWarra Estate is notable for its distinctive architecture, magnificent landscaping and award-winning wines.

Opposite
Vineyards crisscross the Valley.

Of all the food and wine-producing regions around Melbourne, the Yarra Valley has come the furthest in understanding its true potential. Just an hour's drive from Melbourne, incredibly beautiful and abundantly fertile, the Valley is a seductive place that will have you plotting ways to reorganise your life in order to settle down there. Blessed with a cool climate capable of producing wines of great subtlety and foods of rare variety and flavour, the region is currently in the midst of a renaissance as growers, producers and business owners band together to promote and protect one of their greatest assets – the Yarra Valley name.

The beauty of the Yarra Valley has bewitched Europeans since they first stumbled upon it in the early 1800s. The soft gold afternoon light and surrounding walls of misty blue ranges, the gentle hills rippling across the valley floor, gathering mists in the shaded valleys and lush areas of bush that suddenly open to breathtaking views of pastures and vineyards, make it easy to wax lyrical.

'The whole district abounds in the picturesque, resembling closely the country between Turin and Mont Cenis in Italy,' raved an 1888 visitors' guide, and the comparisons with Italy and France continue to this day. The earliest comparisons came at a time when the Yarra Valley was enjoying its first spike of popularity, attracting record numbers of visitors from Melbourne, winning medals in international wine shows and supplying increasing volumes of milk, butter, eggs, vegetables and fruit. Looking at the Valley today with its endless vineyards and startling variety of produce – from peaches and chocolate to pigs and cheese – you could easily believe that it had been smooth sailing since the first vineyard was planted at Yering Station in 1838. But adverse economic and natural conditions meant that winemaking in the Valley was wiped out by 1937 when the last vineyards of those early vineyards were removed.

The area's farms continued to produce fruit and vegetables, nuts, eggs and milk but the vineyards fell to grazing for nearly thirty years. The 1960s saw a new generation of wineries quietly begin the business of wine again and the

Food stores and producers

whispering about the Yarra Valley and its potential to produce brilliant cool-climate wines grew louder until it turned to a roar in the late 1980s when French champagne house Moet and Chandon and some of Australia's largest wine companies moved in.

The increased wine noise finally drew appropriate attention to the excellent produce in the Valley, both from decades-old farms and new artisan producers. As more operators add to the diversity and quality of the produce here, the Yarra Valley is becoming as renowned for food as it is for wine and has become a destination not to be missed by any true food and wine lover.

Considering the mind-boggling range of food being produced in the Yarra Valley it is a miracle that it is so peaceful. The amazingly fertile area not only pumps out sizeable quantities of wine but also produces apples, pears, peaches, apricots, raspberries, blueberries, cherries, chestnuts, figs, quail, organic vegetables, honey, venison, cheese, bread, jams and pickles, ice cream, pasta, herbs, lamb, chocolate, cookies, rare-breed pork and turkeys, trout, salmon and rabbits. You might expect such a food factory to run at a frenetic pace and, sure, it picks up on the weekends and at festival times when food and wine fanatics from Melbourne descend on the Valley in droves. But no matter what else is going on in the Valley, there always seems to be a time when you are driving along a back road in search of a farm selling free-range eggs or heirloom peaches and there won't be another car in sight, and you can get that rare, peaceful feeling of being the only person for miles around.

There is so much produce in the Valley, so many farm-gates to visit, that you could spend several days and fill the back seats of several cars and still not see and taste everything. Sheer quantity is one part of the reason but also there are artisan producers scattered throughout the Yarra Valley who not only value their privacy but make, grow or breed such small quantities of their products that everything they produce is snapped up by chefs or

Above
Views across the valley from Mt Rael Winery.

Opposite
Cabernet and shiraz ageing in barrels.

05 CAB #3

Village Baker

Ciabatta $5
7 Grain $5½
COB $4½

Phillippas

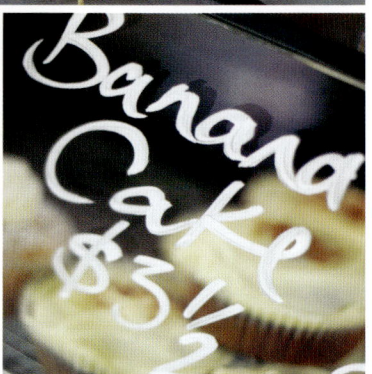

Olive $4½

Banana Cake $3½

Opposite
Healesville Harvest Produce and Wine, part of the Healesville Hotel.

those in the know long before it can hit the shops. It might be hard to get a taste of Alison Goldburn's rare-breed turkeys or to secure a loaf of **Fruition** bread, wood-fired at **Candlebark Farm**, but if you ask the right questions at the right produce store or restaurant, you might be given a tip that will allow you a rare and tasty glimpse of the Valley's true artisan side.

Mostly though, the Yarra Valley is a remarkably easy and straightforward place in which to negotiate a produce tour. This is largely due to the efforts of determined, committed locals like Suzanne Halliday (wife of wine writer and maker James Halliday) who has been instrumental in getting Yarra Valley food onto a wider stage. Halliday's championing of local food led to the formation of the Yarra Valley Regional Food Group that has brought together the area's best local producers and literally put them on the map – the Yarra Valley Regional Food Trail. This map is a vital key to much of the best stuff in the valley – informative, easy to read and a lesson to most of Victoria's other regions on how it should be done.

If you don't have time to meander along the Trail, the **Yarra Valley Farmers' Market** is held in the Barn at **Yering Station Winery** on the third Sunday of every month. The diversity of produce – jams and preserves, chocolate, walnuts, bread, wine, a brilliant range of fresh, seasonal vegetables – gives you a convenient one-stop snapshot of what the Yarra Valley has to offer.

There are also several good produce stores scattered around the Valley where time-strapped food fans can get a quick fix on what the locals are doing.

If you miss the Farmers' Market, Yering Station also has a decent produce store housed on the property in the same building as its cellar door. **Regional Fare** in nearby Yarra Glen has a good range of local products plus a selection of wines from the Yarra Valley's smaller vineyards, but the best produce store in the Valley is found in Healesville.

Healesville Harvest Produce and Wine, part of the **Healesville Hotel**, is housed in the hotel's former bottle shop, using the driveway between the buildings as an outdoor seating area. A produce store, bottle shop and café, Harvest Produce is not just about stocking local produce (though ex-Melburnian owners Michael Kennedy and Kylie Balharrie are great fans of regionally based produce) but rather about offering quality produce generally. An impressive range of locally produced stuff is stocked here – herbs from Ravensbrook Estate, cheese from the Yarra Valley Dairy, bread from Fruition, jam from Cunliffe and Waters, chocolate from Kennedy and Wilson and a small, cleverly selected group of local wines. With its

Right
Lisa, Michael and Maria Colaneri, of Yarra Valley Pasta.

counter packed full of cheeses, dips, terrines and meats, the smell of coffee in the air, locals reading newspapers around the communal table and light streaming in over shelves packed full of good local produce, Harvest Produce gives a good indication of where the Yarra Valley is right now.

Just down the road from Healesville Harvest is one of the Yarra Valley's first artisan food businesses and one of its most successful. **Yarra Valley Pasta**, run by mother and daughter team Maria and Lisa Colaneri, was started in 1997 after Maria sensed the food and wine-driven changes afoot in the Valley and decided that she wanted to play a part.

Maria, who moved to the Yarra Valley from Melbourne thirty-three years ago with husband Felix, had always made pasta at home and started her business on a similar scale with 'just a few pots of sauce and a bit of pasta'. But the handmade pasta she was producing using local free-range eggs and top quality semolina began attracting so much attention, both locally and from Melbourne, that daughter Lisa left her job to join the business and life became extremely busy. Initially Maria and Lisa ran a café, had a catering business on the side and handmade all the pasta, but after several years decided they 'needed a life' and now concentrate solely on making and selling their range of Yarra Valley Pasta that includes gnocchi, cannelloni, lasagne, and ravioli stuffed with a variety of traditional and gourmet fillings including local smoked trout and **Yarra Valley Dairy** goat's cheese.

Cheese from the ten-year-old Yarra Valley Dairy is stocked and used in many businesses across the Yarra Valley and is one of the first artisan products that drew attention to the region's possibilities. Part of a lush dairy farm called Hubertswood, owned by Mary and Leo Mooney, the Yarra Valley Dairy makes about twelve different cheeses from the 300 cows on the property that are milked twice a day, and from locally sourced goat's milk. Hubertswood has been in Mary's family for fifty years, and initially the cheese was a way for Mary to use the dairy's leftover milk. The hobby has since

Gorgonzola and dried fig ravioli

Lisa Colineri, Yarra Valley Pasta

1 x 375g pack of Yarra Valley Gorgonzola, Prosciutto & Dried Fig Ravioli
¼ cup of lemon pressed olive oil
fresh garden herbs (whatever is seasonal)
generous handful of fresh rocket
¼ fennel, shaved
1 blood orange, segmented
cold pressed extra virgin olive oil
balsamic vinegar
sea salt and pepper to taste

Place frozen ravioli directly from the freezer into a pot of boiling salted water, and cook for up to 8 minutes. Drain pasta of water and place into a pan of heated lemon pressed olive oil (being careful not to burn oil). Add fresh garden herbs and toss through.

To serve, dress the ravioli dish with a handful of fresh rocket leaves, fennel shavings and blood orange segments, lightly tossed through some cold pressed olive oil, balsamic vinegar, sea salt and cracked black pepper.

Serves 4 as an entree

turned into an award-winning line of specialist cheese that includes the renowned Persian fetta, a cow's milk fetta, marinated in herbs and oil, and a range of fromage frais.

The Yarra Valley's cheese shop and tasting room are housed in a rustic timber and corrugated-iron shed that has views over the surrounding paddocks, where cows graze in a suitably picturesque fashion. The Dairy's

From left to right
Handmade produce from Cunliffe and Waters.

Far right
Yarra Valley Dairy produces handmade farmhouse cheeses and has a restaurant in a rustic former shed.

cheese shares space with a good variety of other Yarra Valley produce – everything from honeycomb to pickles – and **The Wine Hub**, a cellar door that stocks wine from twelve of the region's smaller wineries, concentrating on places that employ young makers interested in displaying regional characteristics in small handmade wines. It is a philosophy that suits the Yarra Valley Dairy, a place that is sticking to its handmade traditions despite a groaning trophy shelf and ever-increasing demand.

A short distance across the Valley in Coldstream is another business sticking to its handmade roots. Housed in a nondescript shopfront just off the Maroondah Highway, **Cunliffe and Waters** churns out an amazing variety of brilliantly flavoured jams, pickles, preserves and sauces that are sold locally, nationally and internationally. Business owner Mandy Cunliffe, who started making jam in 'one French preserving pan on the stove at home' to get herself out of a jam of the financial kind, seems bemused by the popularity of her produce and feels 'the business is as big as it needs to be'.

'The philosophy of the business is that everything is handmade,' she says. 'The jams are made as if I was making them for myself and there are a few extra jars to give away.'

You can get Cunliffe and Waters products in many places but it is worth dropping by the shop to see the engine-room with its line of burners running down one wall, each with a bubbling concoction of the much-loved Willamette raspberry jam, tomato and capsicum relish or blood orange and ruby grapefruit marmalade, closely watched by Mandy Cunliffe or her manager Caroline Gray. Bags and boxes of ingredients, much of it locally sourced, are stacked against the walls and you get a real sense of the small-scale, dedicated approach that Cunliffe and Waters and others like it have helped draw so much attention to the Yarra Valley.

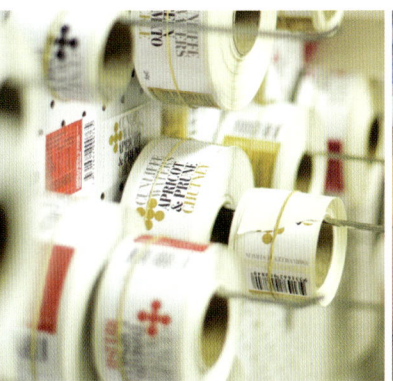

The Valley is brimming with such places – whether you are looking for salmon roe or pickles, fresh berries or chestnuts. Nose around and you never know what delicious treasures you might uncover.

Kennedy and Wilson Chocolates

It is easy to miss the small white building tucked behind a house on sleepy Briarty Road. Even if you do notice it amongst all the glorious bush and paddocks, there is nothing to indicate that behind the building's nondescript exterior some of Australia's best chocolate is being crafted. It seems both impossible and perfectly logical that such a modest building could be the heart of one of the Yarra Valley's star products. Impossible because **Kennedy and Wilson** chocolate is so revered, glamorous even, and is stocked in Australia's best food stores and hotels, is offered to Qantas first class passengers and has developed a cultish following amongst chocolate fans. Logical because it is just this sort of boutique, brilliant-quality artisan produce that sits so well with the Yarra Valley's current direction.

yarra valley 97

Kennedy and Wilson is named for its founders, Peter Wilson, winemaker and former punk band manager and his wife Juliana Kennedy. Peter was in Burgundy in his capacity as winemaker at Yarra Yering when he discovered Valrhona chocolate and developed an instant bee in his bonnet about turning his winemaker's palate and skill to making great chocolate in Australia that 'tasted of chocolate, not just sugar'. He left Yarra Yering, sourced the best equipment and ingredients – cocoa from South and Central America, milk from New Zealand, vanilla from Vanuatu – and set up the white shed at the back of his house in Briarty Road.

The small range he began producing in 1998 included bitter chocolate Cats Tongues, dreamy milk chocolate Bears and dark chocolate and cinnamon Autumn Leaves, luxury chocolate with high cocoa content, amazing richness and a voluptuously velvety texture. A couple of years ago, Peter invited Didier Cadinot to join the business to complement his existing range with a range of filled chocolates. Didier, a French chef and chocolate-maker with an impressive moustache and even more impressive CV (working for renowned chefs Paul Bocuse and Phillippe Mouchel) fitted in perfectly with Kennedy

Kennedy and Wilson's chocolates are another of the artisan-made made products coming from the Yarra Valley.

and Wilson's handmade, small-scale approach. When Peter Wilson decided to return to winemaking, Didier was there to take over the chocolate making.

While Didier maintains the fastidious quality of Peter Wilson's basic range, he continues to experiment with the filled-chocolate side of things, using many local ingredients like raspberries, pears and blackcurrants. He is even testing a range of truffles filled with locally made red wine.

Such is the prestige and the demand for Kennedy and Wilson chocolate

The fastidious quality of handmade chocolates – luxury chocolate with high cocoa content, amazing richness and a voluptuously velvety texture

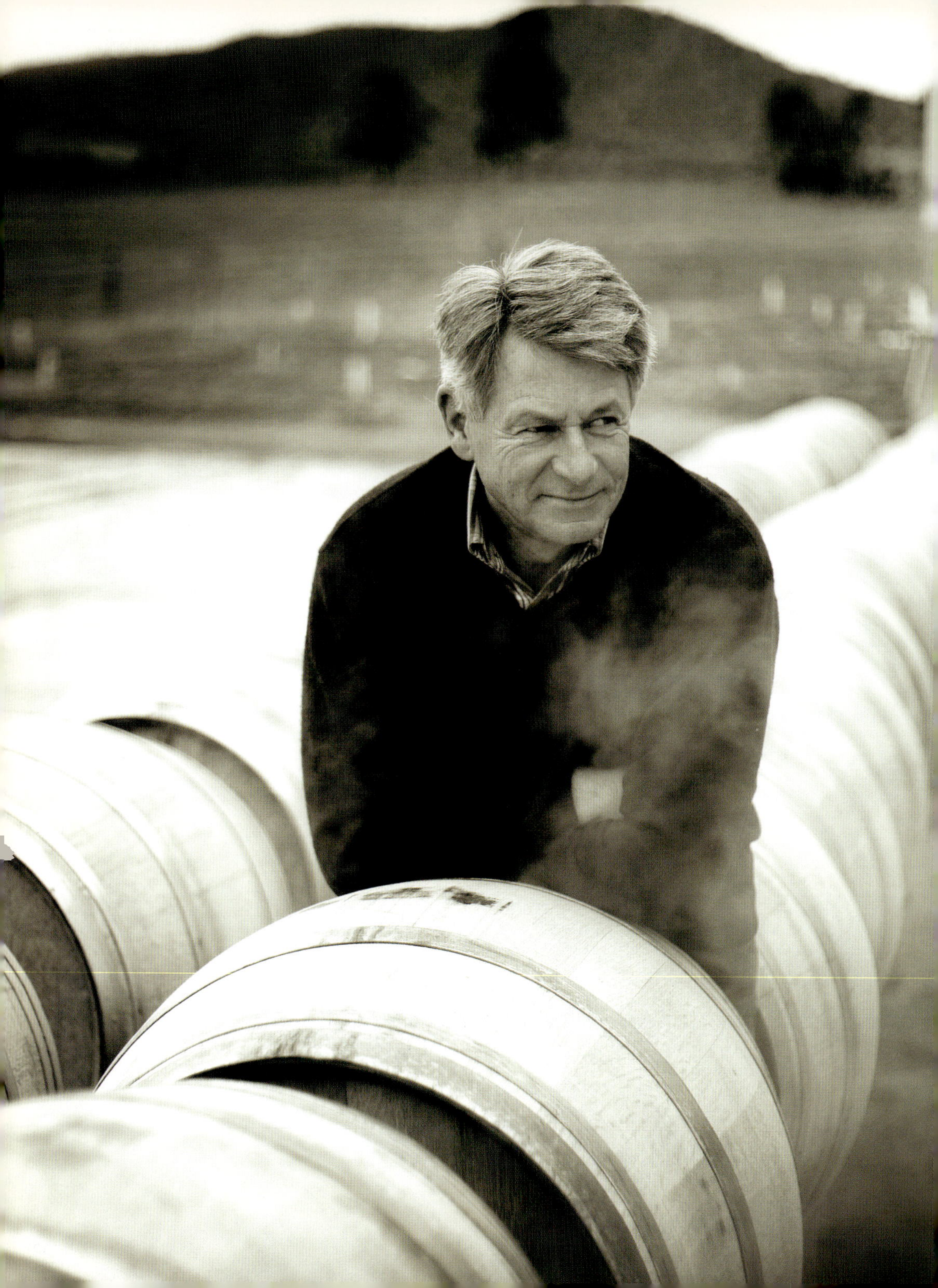

Dominique Portet produces elegant wines at his French-inspired winery.

Wineries

that there is a constant pressure to expand but, despite the lure of increased fortune through automation, there is little interest in changing the way things are done.

Christine Fryer, director and administrator of the business says, 'Kennedy and Wilson is about a craft, about making something special in a special place. There is nothing about the approach we would change because that would change what we are doing. We would rather employ three more like-minded folk who appreciate the hands-on approach than buy more machinery. You can expand but you can do it without sacrificing the quality because the quality is what makes the chocolate so unique.'

The first vines in the Yarra Valley – in fact, in Victoria – were planted in 1838 by William, Donald and James Ryrie, cattle-owning brothers who came south from drought-stricken New South Wales in search of fertile grazing land. Attracted by the lush river flats around the Yarra River they put down roots, named their property **Yering Station** and planted a kitchen garden, fruit trees and grape vines. The first wine in the area was made in 1845 but it was the arrival of Swiss settlers with aristocratic names and winemaking pretensions that really gave the Yarra Valley its first dose of success and fame.

Prestigious vineyards like **St Hubert's**, **Chateau Yering** and **Yeringberg**, became fashionable destinations for an increasing numbers of visitors from Melbourne and the wines of the area won a number of international awards including a Grand Prix at the 1889 Paris Exhibition. And then a series of man-made and natural disasters over a series of years began to sap what had been a thriving and successful industry.

The overwhelming preference in Australia for sweet fortified wine did nothing to help a cool-climate region that produced mainly dry European-style wines, and economic depression dealt the final blow. In 1900 there were 400 hectares of vines in the Yarra Valley. By 1937 there were none

Right
Cool-climate wine and winemaker Kate Goodman, from Punt Road Wines, Coldstream.

and it was nothing but cows, chickens, vegetables and fruit trees for nearly three decades.

Despite the fairytale-like slumbering of the Yarra Valley's wine industry over the next thirty years, its reputation as a potentially great wine region never went away. The combination of a wide range of soil types – from sandy loam to rich red volcanic dirt – and a climate cooler than most of Australia's wine regions ensured that the Yarra Valley stayed on the winemaking radar despite the lack of activity. The 1960s saw the establishment of **Wantirna Estate** and **Kellybrook wineries** and the subsequent arrival of current luminaries like **Mount Mary**, **Yarra Yering** and **Warramate**. The area had begun to reawaken.

Over the next couple of decades, more and more vines were planted and now-familiar names – **Diamond Valley**, **TarraWarra** – kept arriving. The whispering about the quality of chardonnay and pinot noir increased and, once again, the Yarra Valley wineries started winning awards.

The late 1980s brought the biggest changes and the greatest period of expansion. French champagne house Moet and Chandon established a vineyard at Green Point, **Coldstream Hills** was started, the De Bortoli family bought **Chateau Yarrinya** and many of Australia's largest wine companies – McWilliams, Hardy Wines, Beringer Blass – followed. Architect-designed, statement-making winery buildings appeared and the drip of visitors turned into a stream. When Yering Station was replanted with vines in 1989 on the Yarra Valley's original vineyard and a large and dramatic Robert Conti-designed building went up across from the original de Castella house a decade later, you could almost hear the Valley saying: I'm back, baby.

The rapid expansion of the 1990s has slowed but the Yarra Valley continues to experience great change. The current change has less to do with constant vineyard expansion and more to do with winemaking philosophy. The dominant wines remain chardonnay, pinot noir and

Left
TarraWarra Museum of Art, in the grounds of TarraWarra Estate, features rammed earth walls and a glass turret.

sparkling (though shiraz and cabernet are also well represented) but Yarra Valley winemakers are increasingly talking in terms of restraint, complexity and balance rather than mere fruitiness.

At **Punt Road Wines** in Coldstream, straight-talking winemaker Kate Goodman warms her back by the cellar door fire and brings a bit of lifestyle reality into the romantic notion of the winemaker's lot. The Yarra Valley is a destination coveted by many winemakers she says because 'it is only an hour from the centre of Melbourne, you can now get a decent meal and a good coffee and you can make really good wine here'. Kate, who has been at the winery since its first vintage in 2000, is responsible for making all the wine from Punt Road's 160 hectares of vineyards in five different locations around the Valley. She makes wines that reflect both their vineyard source and their grape variety and are textural 'with good mouth feel'. They are, says Kate with typical candour, the kind of wines she likes to drink because making any other types of wine 'defeats the purpose of making it really'.

'The Yarra Valley is a good place to make wines but it's challenging because it is quite a cool region,' she says. 'But that means we can make good chardonnay and pinot and some fantastic shiraz. Yarra Valley wines are quite fine compared with wines coming out of South Australia, for example, which are big and alcoholic and obvious. There is subtlety, elegance and finesse in the wines here.'

Not far from Punt Road is another Yarra Valley newcomer that is playing the elegance card – both in wine and architecture - and drawing a lot of attention. Dominique Portet, the owner of the winery **Dominique Portet**, comes from a French winemaking family from Bordeaux and was managing director of Taltarni for twenty-two years before buying his Yarra Valley patch in 2001. The Yarra Valley attracted Portet because of its 'quality and style'.

'I found fragrance and structure here – most of all structure – that reminds me of Bordeaux,' he says. Drinking his acclaimed, savoury Fontaine Rosé, or

Five great cellar doors

- Domaine Chandon at Green Point, Coldstream – some of Australia's best sparkle and great views at this impressive complex
- De Bortoli – elegant cool-climate wines served in the upstairs restaurant or downstairs at the atmospheric cellar door
- Yering Station, Yarra Glen – big bustling cellar door in the old barn
- Roundstone, Yarra Glen – ingest the beautiful setting and the hand-crafted wines
- Coldstream Hills, Coldstream – no-nonsense cellar door highlighting seriously good, cool-climate winemaking

De Bortoli Wines

the restrained and elegant Dominique Portet Sauvignon Blanc, in the French-inspired winery building surrounded by vines you may well be reminded of Bordeaux too.

Across the Valley, **TarraWarra Estate** is attracting attention for more than its award-winning chardonnay and pinot noir. Owners Marc and Eva Besen established TarraWarra on a breathtakingly lovely parcel of land near Healesville in 1982. The sunny site meant earlier ripening grapes which have given TarraWarra wines – the golden-coloured chardonnay in particular – a reputation for generosity of both flavour and alcohol. An intimate cellar door and a small, stylish glass-walled café allow visitors to savour both the wines and stunning views.

Adjacent to the winery is the **TarraWarra Museum of Art**, similarly generous though with a less obvious connection with wine. The striking new Alan Powell-designed building with its rammed-earth walls and glass turret set amongst the property's vines, houses one of the country's most important collections of Australian contemporary art. The Museum has been gifted to the Australian public by the Besen family. Art and wine have always been friendly and a building and a collection like this add weight both to the friendship and the surrounding region. The beautifully serene interior of the gallery echoes the gentle curves of the surrounding landscape and the large windows, cut dramatically into the walls of the exhibition spaces, frame some of the best views of vineyards and hills and sky that the Valley has to offer. It is as if the art of the vigneron has been given a place in the permanent collection and TarraWarra is adding more generosity and complexity to the Yarra Valley blend.

When the De Bortoli family bought the Chateau Yarrinya winery in 1987, the Yarra Valley was just beginning to flex its winemaking muscles. There was no doubt that the area had potential – Chateau Yarrinya had won the Yarra Valley's first Jimmy Watson trophy in 1978 – but it had yet to receive the whole-hearted stamp of approval that came in the 1990s. Winemakers knew that it was an excellent winemaking district and that chardonnay and pinot noir could do great things in the region but beyond that – and as far as the general wine-drinking public was concerned – it was scarcely known.

Leanne De Bortoli, who moved to the Yarra Valley with winemaking husband Steve Weber to run the new property, recalls a time when there was virtually no wine tourism in the area. In the early days, a good weekend saw a car an hour pulling into the winery, something that seems inconceivable now with the **De Bortoli** cellar door and restaurant busy every day, and on the weekend a steady stream of visitors on the Yarra Valley roads as they tour the wineries.

The popularity of the region is not the only thing that has changed at De Bortoli and Steve Weber is a good example of how the winemaking culture in the Valley is changing with the confidence brought by increased visitors and acclaim.

> More and more, embracing the notion that most of the work in a good wine comes from the vineyard rather than the winery

Spurred on by travel overseas and drinking more European wine styles, Steve has embarked on a fundamental change in philosophy about making wine in the Yarra Valley. Most importantly, he has come to believe that wine should have a sense of place and that De Bortoli should be making wines that reflect the regional characteristics of and within the Yarra Valley. More and more, he and his team are abandoning the tricks employed in many New World wineries – filtering, pumping, centrifuging – and embracing the notion that most of the work in a good wine comes from the vineyard rather than the winery.

Organic practices are being embraced, vineyards realigned to catch or lose more sun, handpicking and sorting being adopted, particularly in the vineyard's premium sites and grapes are being picked earlier at lower sugar levels. Steve is embracing the idea of minimal handling and the notion that 'the more gentle we are with the fruit and the winemaking the less we have to do – let nature look after itself'.

These practices are now being displayed in both the Gulf Station and De Bortoli Yarra Valley range of wines – elegant pinot noir, restrained chardonnay, beautifully balanced shiraz viognier – and will be even more obvious in the new limited release Reserve range Steve has been developing. Single-vineyard wines will also push the new philosophy.

There are many small wine producers in the Yarra Valley that are taking an artisan, handmade approach to wine but the fact that De Bortoli, one of the region's largest (150 hectares of vines), most recognised and consumed

Brazo de gitano – gypsy's arm with chocolate olive oil mousse

Robin Sutcliff, Executive Chef,
Healesville Hotel

Chocolate olive oil mousse
180 g Kennedy and Wilson dark couverture chocolate
¼ cup water
1 shot espresso coffee
¾ cups Grovedale extra virgin olive oil
2 tbsp Cointreau
3 Harvest Farm free-range eggs, separated
½ cup caster sugar

Melt chocolate with water and cool slightly, stir in coffee, oil and Cointreau. Whisk egg yolks with sugar over hot water until thick. Stir yolks into chocolate. Whisk egg whites to soft peaks then fold through chocolate.

Cake
200 g Kennedy and Wilson dark coverture chocolate
¼ cup water
6 Harvest Farm free-range eggs, separated
110 g caster sugar
soft butter for greasing
cocoa for dusting

Heat chocolate and water over medium heat, stirring until smooth. Cool. Whisk yolks and sugar until pale and thick, stir in chocolate mix and set aside. Whisk whites to soft peak and gently fold into chocolate mixture. Spoon into greased and paper-lined Swiss roll pan (24 cm x 30 cm) bake at 180°C for 18 to 20 minutes. Turn cake out onto a sheet of baking paper and, whilst hot, roll cake up from the long side, using the paper as a guide. Cool. When mousse is completed, gently unroll cake, spread mousse evenly over cake and re-roll.

Eating out

labels, is heading down the same path seems to show that the Yarra Valley is heading into a new, exciting era that acknowledges the region's specific characteristics. De Bortoli has hung out a sign that says 'watch this space'.

Restaurants in the Yarra Valley have been slower on the uptake than the region's food and wine producers. Until quite recently there have been relatively few restaurants in the Valley that have taken real advantage of the area's great produce and ever-increasing wine and food reputation. A tendency amongst many Yarra Valley restaurants to either pay too much attention to what was going on in Melbourne or else pile on the hokey countrified charm brought a generic blandness to much of the dining in the Valley.

Over the past couple of years, however, it seems as if a light has suddenly been switched on and the idea has dawned that using local produce not only pleases visitors looking for local colour but is also a very satisfying, interesting and exciting way to approach food, particularly in an area of such diversity and exceptional quality.

Well-recognised, established products like Yarra Valley Salmon, Yarra Valley Pasta, Kennedy and Wilson Chocolate, Yarra Valley Ice Cream, or cheese from Yarra Valley Dairy are common sights on most local menus these days – a good thing for both those products and the region's reputation. But a new batch of eating places are taking the regional produce idea beyond the famed brands and are taking advantage of backyard growers, hobbyists and small-scale producers with a passion for rare breeds and heirloom varieties.

At the **Healesville Hotel**, a beautifully restored old pub in an increasingly food-savvy town, the menu comes with a supplementary page that lists local producers whose ingredients are used by chef Robin Sutcliffe. Some of the big Yarra Valley names are on the list but there is also an entry acknowledging backyard gardeners with 'prolific green thumbs, productive gardens and old fruit trees' that supply the hotel with an array of goodies from figs, quinces and pears to lemons and limes. Harvest Farm, the home of Healesville Hotel owners Michael Kennedy and Kylie Balharrie, is also on the list thanks to the extensive kitchen gardens they are developing on their property to supply the hotel kitchen with a range of heirloom and heritage vegetables. Harvest Farm is also planted with citrus, olive and hazelnut trees that will also go straight into the kitchen and onto the menu of the Healesville Hotel.

Opposite
The handsomely restored dining room of the Healesville Hotel.

Opposite
Mt Rael Retreat, with its wonderful views of the Valley, and below, the elegant dining room.

Though he didn't move to the Yarra Valley with the express purpose of using local produce, Michael Kennedy has wholeheartedly embraced a philosophy at the hotel that is all about 'freshness and seasonality' and 'circumventing the process where things are grown here, then shipped to the markets in Melbourne and then shipped back up here'. He believes the best thing about going direct to the growers or even growing produce themselves is that it makes the journey from ground to plate as short as possible. Knowing where the food came from is reassuring and, if the beautifully cooked, clever comfort food at the **Healesville Hotel** is anything to go by, something that is deliciously well-worth pursuing.

A short distance away on the Healesville-Yarra Glen Road, you will see a turn off for **Mt Rael Retreat** and the **3777 restaurant**. A steep winding drive later and you come to the former nursery and restaurant building, transformed by Sean Lee and chef John Knoll, into a stylish modern restaurant with a series of guest rooms. Perched on the top of a hill, the restaurant with its wide veranda and walls of windows has wonderful views of the Valley. John Knoll says that people appreciate the view for its beauty but are even more impressed when he is able to point out to his customers the field where the wild mushrooms they are eating were growing that morning.

John was born locally but owned and worked in a series of eateries in Melbourne before deciding to move back to the Yarra Valley. Local produce was a big factor in his decision to return home.

'My family have orchards in the Valley and so I grew up knowing how much good produce was up here,' he says. 'I think that now there are places around the Valley that are looking for good, seasonal produce – no matter what it is.'

John mentions a place called **Waterwood Farm** where he gets fresh walnuts from a couple 'who crack them by hand in front of the TV at night' and **Yarra Valley Game Meats**, a company with a licence to shoot and sell wild rabbits that are 'organic as you can get and they taste great'. The seasonally changing menu at **3777** is as good a place as any to get a mouthful of what is happening in the Valley. And with views this good, it says something about the cooking and the produce that you notice the food at all.

At the **De Bortoli Winery Restaurant** in Dixons Creek, an enthusiastic young chef with a passion for local produce has breathed new life into one of the Yarra Valley's original restaurants. Cameron Cansdell worked with renowned Sydney chefs like Stefano Manfredi and Peter Doyle before coming to the Yarra Valley to head the De Bortoli kitchen. He is a true

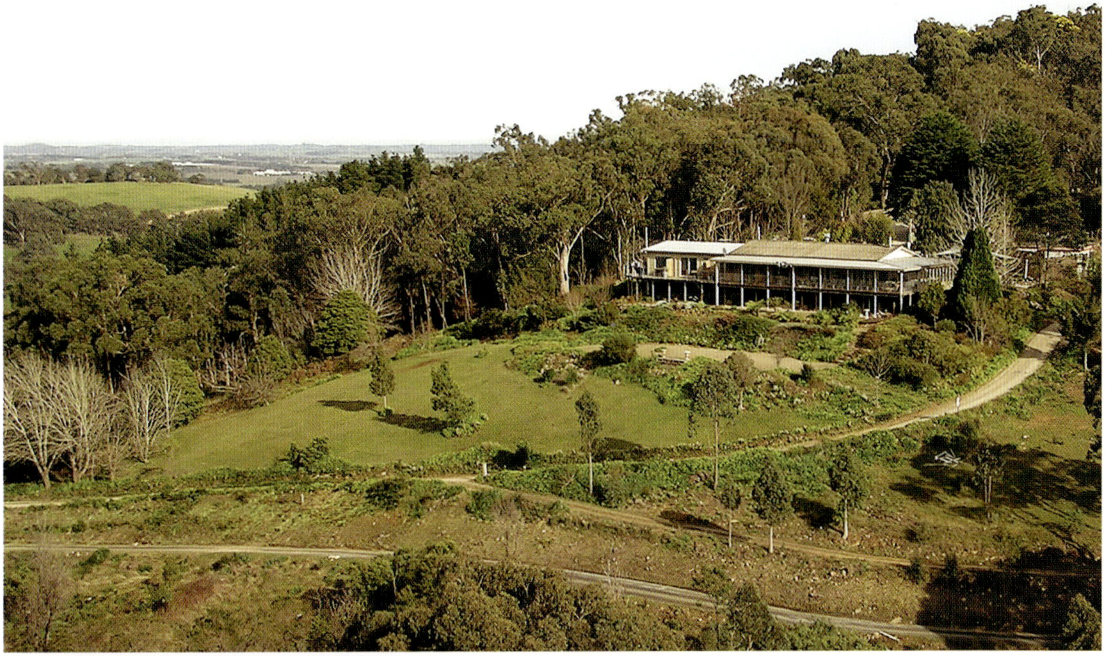

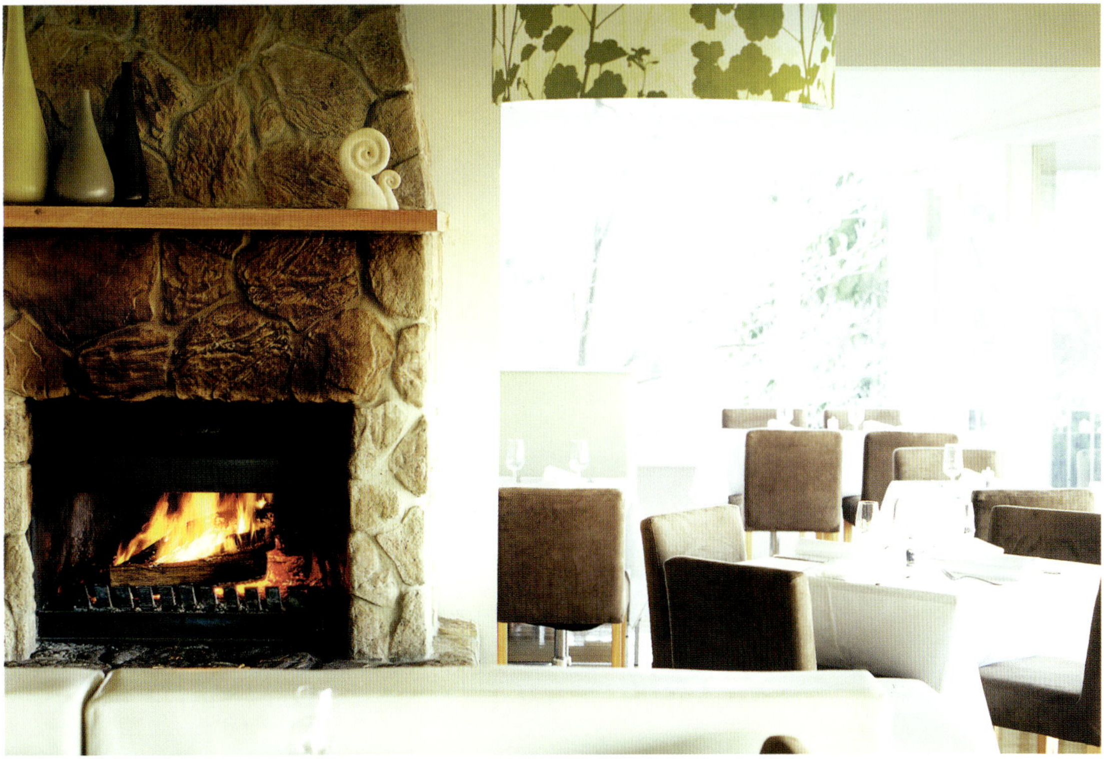

Through the door is the bakehouse, the source of both the delicious aroma and the variety of wonderfully formed loaves stacked on shelves

Left and below
Seasonal fruit and fresh-baked pie at Bella Vedere.

Opposite left
The dining room at Bella Vedere.

Opposite right
Owners Tim Sawyer and Gary Cooper, in the bakery at Bella Vedere.

forager, an artisan-produce fanatic, and spends much of his time scouring the Yarra Valley, for small-scale, high quality produce.

One of his favourite finds is the rare-breed black pigs, bred by Christine Ross in Macclesfield, that are attracting an almost cultish following among chefs both in the Yarra Valley and further afield. Cameron is also working with Leanne De Bortoli to extend the kitchen gardens for the restaurant so that they can grow more vegetables, like the heirloom tomatoes that appear in summer salads with buffalo mozzarella. There is even talk of removing some vines to make way for a larger garden – a sure sign that the passionate chef has the ear of the owners and a plan for bigger and better things.

Other winery restaurants, like those at **Yering Station** and **Rochford Estate** or newcomer **Cru** at Outlook Hill, are also increasingly pushing the local produce barrow in impressively designed dining rooms with fantastic views over the vines. An even more impressive view is the sight of all those local goodies starring on the menus, a sure sign that, finally, Yarra Valley restaurants are starting to catch on and are taking real advantage of all the good stuff growing in their own backyards.

Bella Vedere

From the outside, Bella Vedere looks like a modest two-storey house sitting amongst vineyards on the Maroondah Highway in Coldstream. The first clue that all may not be what it seems is the smell of freshly baked bread that hits you as you walk towards the big wooden front door from the gravel car park. Open the door and it is immediately obvious that there is something special going on here.

Through the door and to your left is the bakehouse, the source of both the

Nicoise torte

Gary Cooper, Belle Vedere

500 g savoury pastry

Tuna custard
1 x 375g can of good quality Italian tuna
6 eggs
400 ml cream
2 tbsp capers
salt and pepper

Topping
100 g string beans
½ cup olives
1 spanish onion
2 soft-boiled eggs
parmesan cheese
Oak leaf lettuce for serving

Preheat the oven to 180ºC. Roll out the pastry, and line a lightly greased 30 cm flan dish. Bake blind in the preheated oven for 10 minutes. Cool.

Puree the tuna in half of its oil. Add the lightly beaten eggs and cream, capers, and salt and pepper to taste. Mix well. Pour the tuna custard into the baked pastry shell and cook at 180ºC until the custard is just set (about 15 to 20 minutes), then let cool.

Blanch beans. De-pip the olives. Slice the onion very finely. Peel the soft-boiled eggs. Scatter the beans, olives and onion over the tuna custard tart. Break the soft-boiled egg and scatter over the tart, then shave some parmesan on top. Serve with dressed oak leaf lettuce.

Opposite above
The open kitchen at Bella Vedere. David (left) with owner/chef Gary Cooper.

Opposite bottom
Gary Cooper's Nicoise torte, served at Bella Vedere.

delicious aroma and of the variety of wonderfully formed loaves stacked on shelves further up the wide hallway. The hallway leads you past the bread and the open kitchen (complete with a tempting array of cakes sitting on the counter) and into the green-walled dining room with its open fireplace and windows that bring the surrounding vineyard into the room. The kitchen has been designed so that there is a clear view into it from the restaurant and the cooking process – whether it is a rare-breed pig being broken down, a fish being filleted, croutons being fried in a pan or an enormous pot of stock simmering on the stove – is all part of the experience here. It is a wonderfully warm and welcoming environment, obviously a restaurant, but with the relaxed atmosphere of somebody's home.

Bella Vedere is owned by Tim Sawyer and chef Gary Cooper and is partly inspired by the philosophy and approach of Alice Waters at her famed Californian restaurant Chez Panisse. Gary has been working in the Yarra Valley for about fifteen years and has built up a strong relationship with many local breeders and growers and is a staunch advocate of regional produce. He seems equally passionate about all aspects of Bella Vedere: his lovely airy kitchen, the dégustation dinners they hold twice a week, the garden that increasingly supplies produce for the restaurant, the smokehouse and cooking school that are being developed and the box of globe artichokes that were dropped in by a local gardener the day before.

'I love the fact that we can dig in the dirt and grow things and that we can pull things out of the ground and they will be on the menu a short time later,' says Gary. 'I love that I can have relationships with tiny growers where I can help them out with a bit of cash and a tarte tartin and they can help me out by bringing me fantastic zucchini flowers. I never have to wait for a truck to arrive with my produce – I can go out and get it myself or the grower will come to the door.'

Though Bella Vedere is obviously a business venture, it also has a strong philosophical edge where the owners can demonstrate practically their approach to food and life. A place like this where you can taste the silver beet you saw the kitchen staff pulling from the garden half an hour ago is the ideal way to demonstrate how much more flavour really fresh food has. An open, accessible kitchen means that you can communicate directly with the chefs about the cakes sitting on the counter and become a little more involved with your food and where it has come from. But the fact that you can get skilfully cooked, simply handled and very delicious food is probably the best way for Gary and Tim to get their point across, and the biggest reason why Bella Vedere is attracting so much attention both in and outside of the Yarra Valley.

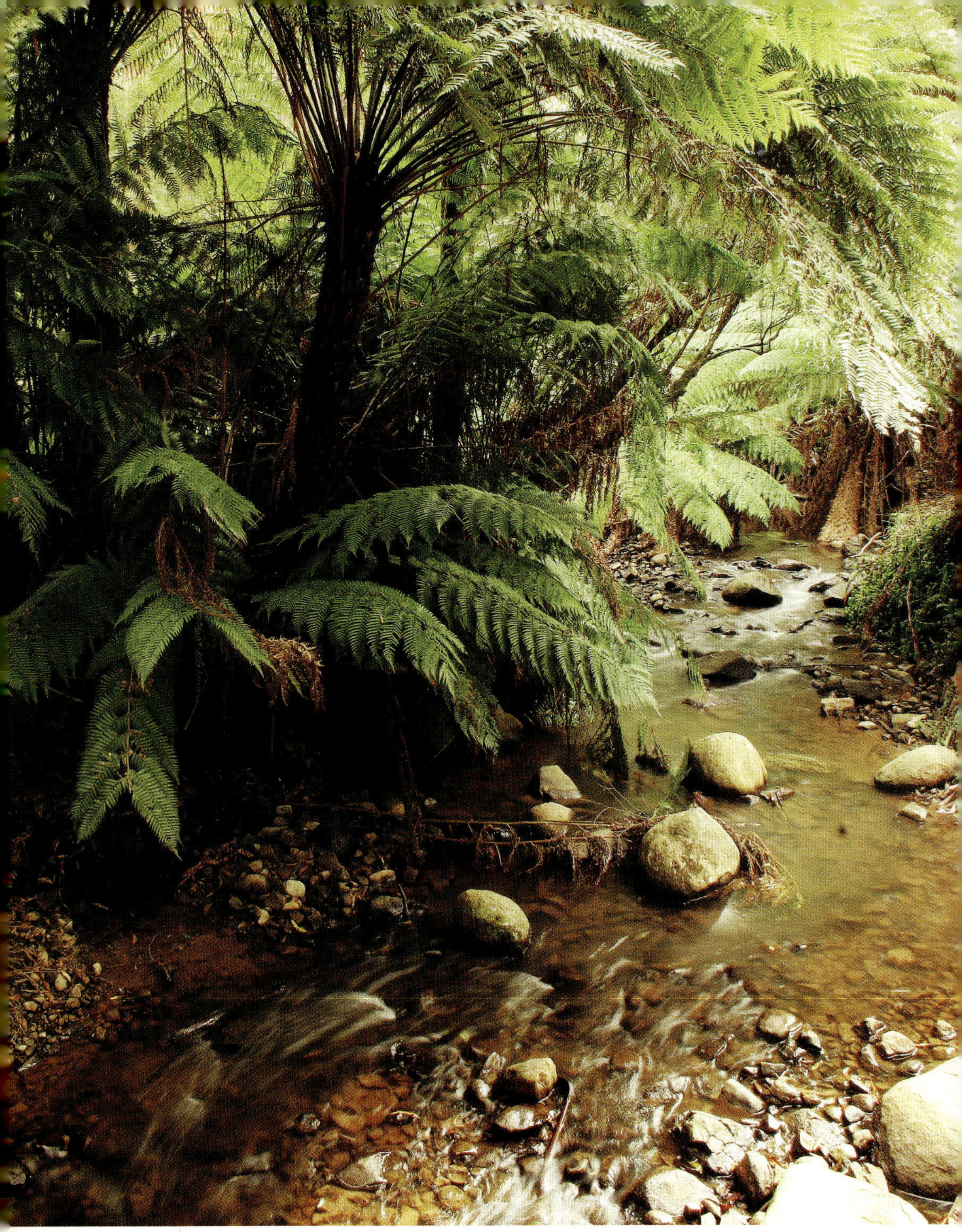

dandenong ranges

michael harden

dandenong ranges

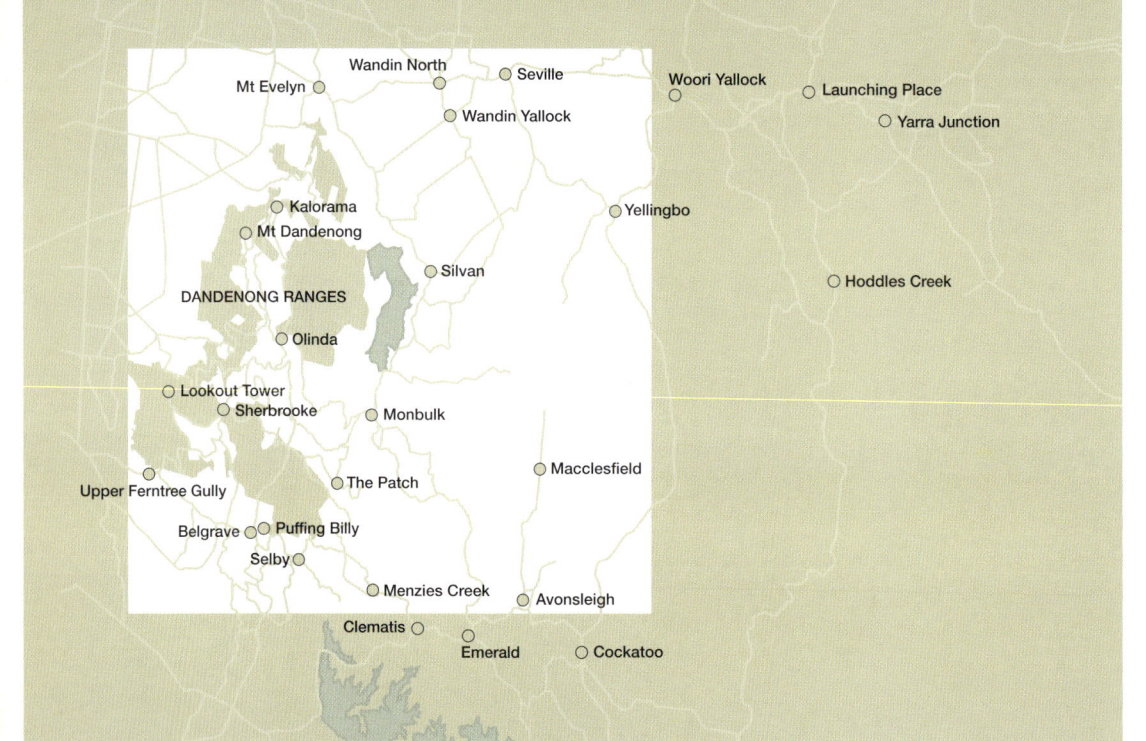

DANDENONG RANGES

- Mt Evelyn
- Wandin North
- Seville
- Wandin Yallock
- Woori Yallock
- Launching Place
- Yarra Junction
- Kalorama
- Mt Dandenong
- Silvan
- Yellingbo
- Hoddles Creek
- Olinda
- Lookout Tower
- Sherbrooke
- Monbulk
- Macclesfield
- Upper Ferntree Gully
- The Patch
- Belgrave
- Puffing Billy
- Selby
- Menzies Creek
- Avonsleigh
- Clematis
- Emerald
- Cockatoo

MELBOURNE / dandenongs

You can find farms producing fabulous fruit – berries in particular – and roadside stalls selling everything from chestnuts and vegetables to eggs and homemade preserves

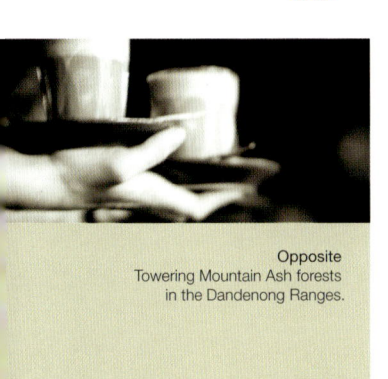

Opposite
Towering Mountain Ash forests in the Dandenong Ranges.

The clichéd view of the Dandenong Ranges is of beautiful scenery, Devonshire teas, craft shops and lace-choked B&B's. As with many clichés, there is a core of truth to this view, but these magnificently forested mountains on the outer edge of Melbourne also harbour a unique and interesting food culture that exists amongst the doilies, comfortable handknits and homemade scones.

Driving towards the Dandenong Ranges from Melbourne, it seems as if the suburbs will never end. But as you approach the foothills, the unbroken mass of shopping strips, traffic lights and houses abruptly runs out of steam. Suddenly you're negotiating narrow, winding roads surrounded by forests of towering eucalypts and enormous tree ferns – broken only by the occasional picturesque village that emerges briefly from the forest – before the trees and silence take over again. It is this magical feeling of being spirited away from the city, combined with a distinctly English feel to the architecture and gardens that has kept the Dandenongs on the tourist radar since the late 1800s.

Only a couple of decades after the first Europeans ventured into the area called Corhanwarrabul ('high' or 'lofty') by the indigenous inhabitants, the ranges became a place for Melburnians to escape the city heat in summer and revel in the cloud-shrouded frosty chill in winter. Almost destroyed by Melbourne's insatiable need for timber (Dandenong forests were reduced from more than 10,500 hectares in 1867 to a little under 1620 hectares by the 1970s), the Dandenong Ranges were saved in many ways by tourists wanting to keep a little nature in their lives. Much of the felled native bush has been replanted with imported trees and plants, though the Dandenong Ranges National Park that dominates the region now includes more than 3000 hectares of protected Mountain Ash-dominated bush.

For food and wine lovers, the Dandenongs present an interesting challenge. Unlike many of Victoria's other regions, the ranges don't have a large food-producing base (though there are commercial farms in the area) and many of the dining places tow the traditional Dandenong Ranges tourist line,

Right
Signs of fresh and fresh-baked produce in the hills.

Opposite
Roads weave past the district's lush ferns and Mountain Ash.

Foodstores and producers

pretending to be in England with menus to match. But there are treasures to be found if you persevere and ask the locals. In backyards and small farms there is an interesting variety of goods being produced, albeit on a fairly small scale. Get off the track a little and you can find farms producing fabulous fruit – berries in particular – and roadside stalls selling everything from chestnuts and vegetables to eggs and home-made preserves.

There are also restaurants, cafés and produce stores in the area that are taking advantage of the good local stuff, serving it up in ways that may have you struggling to remember the Dandenong Ranges you thought you knew. As a food region, it may not have the size and diversity of its close neighbour the Yarra Valley, but for true food and wine foragers, that makes discovering the gems here even more special.

In some tourist brochures, the Dandenong Ranges are grouped together with the Yarra Valley as if the area is a mountainous outpost of the glamorous winemaking area rather than a region in its own right. With this in mind, to find specific information about the region it is worth checking out the literature on the Yarra Valley alongside anything you might find on the ranges. The excellent and extensive Yarra Valley Food Trail map, for example, includes a number of Dandenong Ranges producers and produce stores in its extensive coverage of the food being grown and produced in the region.

Not surprisingly, most of the producing action in the region happens on the Yarra Valley side of the ranges around Silvan, Monbulk and Seville, where the soil is rich, red and volcanic, the climate mostly mild and the rainfall almost dependable. Those who like the farm-gate experience will find the pickings best around Silvan where there are a number of pick-your-own fruit and berry farms. One of the most outstanding (and oldest) of these is **R L Chapman and Sons** on Parker Road where, during the summer berry season, you can pick your own – or simply pick up – strawberries, cherries, raspberries, blackberries, young-berries and boysenberries. Just next door is **Blue Hills Cherries and Berries**

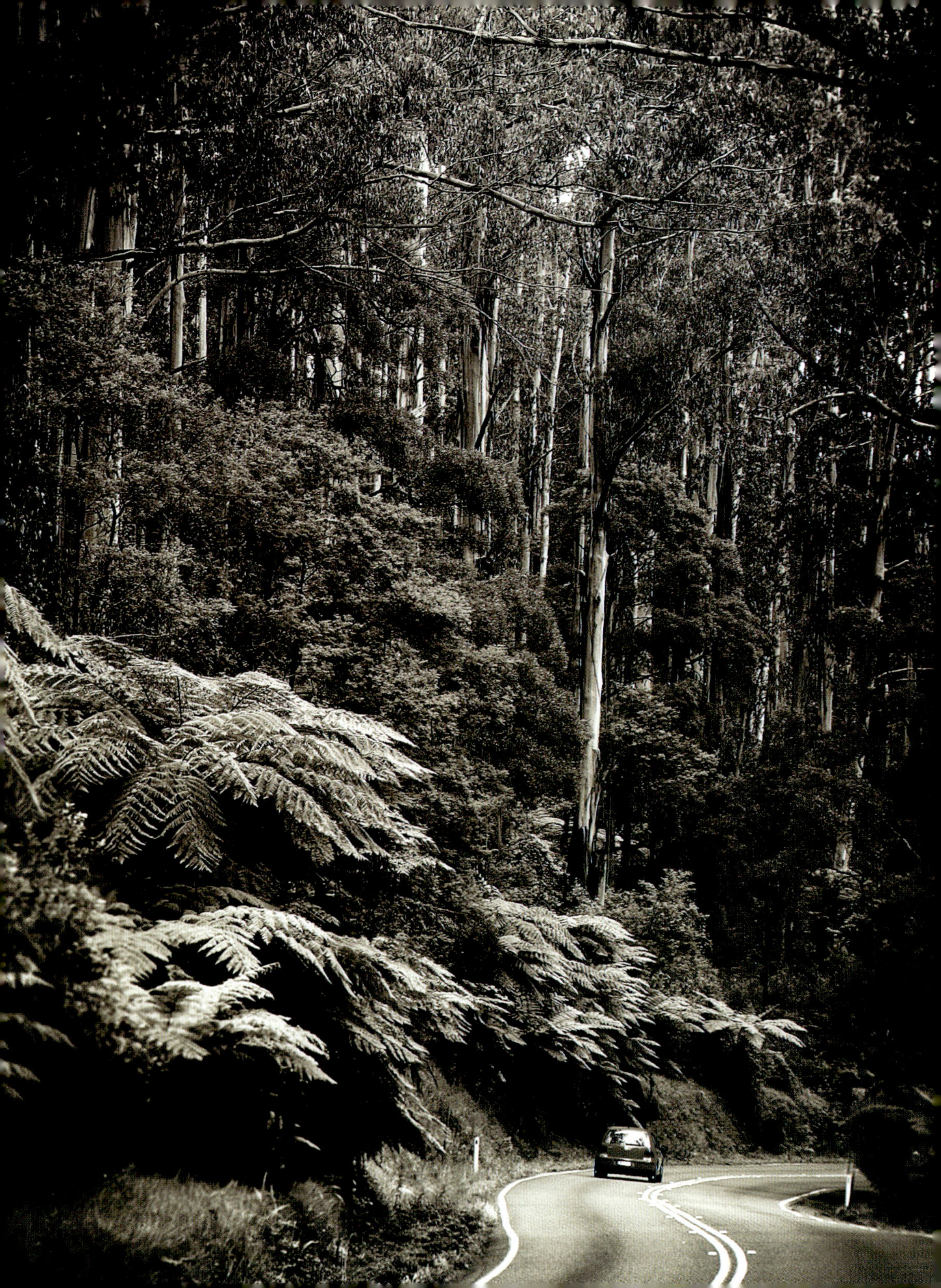

Five hands-on food experiences

- Gather chestnuts at Ruefleur Chestnuts, Olinda
- Catch your own trout at the Australian Rainbow Trout Farm, Macclesfield
- Pick raspberries and blackberries at the Big Berry U-Pick, Hoddles Creek
- Taste wine at the cellar door of Paternoster Wines, Emerald
- Pick red currants at Emily Hill Farm, Emerald

where you can also pick your own berries in season or, in the off-season, buy frozen fruit, jams and sauces.

Further up into the forests at the top of the hills there may be little evidence of farms but there is still good, fresh produce to be had.

At Olinda – the highest of the Dandenong Ranges villages and one of the prettiest – the fledgling **Olinda Village Produce Market** is held every Saturday in a quaint square called Parsons Walk. Local honey and bread, organic and biodynamic food and free-range eggs are featured every week amongst a seasonally changing array of goods. Much of the produce is sourced in the Dandenongs and the Yarra Valley, but the market is set up as much for locals as it is for tourists so the emphasis is on the quality of the produce rather then where it came from.

Just above the Produce Market you'll find the shop belonging to one of the market's movers and shakers, Tricia Jonescu of **Herbicious Delicious**. It is a store devoted to the glory of food and eating in all its many forms and stocks an eclectic and interesting array of food-related goods, homewares and an extensive range of herbs and spices. Tricia, who owns the shop with three friends, says that the eccentric nature of the business comes from the four partners each stocking what they like. 'It's always changing as we all go through our fads,' says Tricia. 'The only rules are to keep it interesting and to celebrate the fun of eating and entertaining.'

Also in Olinda, on the Mount Dandenong Tourist Road, is the Dandenong Ranges best wine store, **Olinda Cellars**. Run by Ross Wilson, a former wine broker and a man obsessed by boutique and hard-to-get cult wines, the attractive shop with its wooden floors and cathedral ceilings, carries mainly Australian wines and boutique beer from microbreweries across the state and country. There is a strong Yarra Valley focus in the store's wine mix with an impressive showing from some of that region's prestigious smaller wineries like **Yarra Yering**, **Mount Mary** and **Yeringberg**. Ross's other specialty and source of pride is to be able to source 'almost any wine' through his knowledge and contacts from six years as a wine broker. Ross is a local boy who dreamed about opening a shop like this in the area and has not only fulfilled his dream but has met with great approval in the Dandenongs too. Talk to any local wine buff about the arrival of Olinda Cellars and the happiness and relief in their voice is palpable.

Folly Farm, also in Olinda, is an ideal place to soak up a bit of traditional Dandenongs atmosphere while also getting your hands on some garden-fresh blueberries (in summer) and locally grown chestnuts (in autumn). The B&B **Blueberry Farm** also boasts superb gardens designed in 1936 by Edna Walling and the blueberries are amongst the sweetest and juiciest around.

Tea lovers should make the journey over to Sassafras, a quaint little village at the junction of the Mountain Highway and the Mount Dandenong Tourist Road. **Tea Leaves** is a treasure trove of a store that boasts 'the largest range of teas and teapots in Melbourne'. Amongst the teapots great and small is a range of more than 300 different teas, infusions and tisanes both from well-known tea-producing countries like China and India and from less obvious places like Papua New Guinea, Kenya and Vietnam. There are nearly eighty varieties of flavoured tea – from coconut to whiskey – organic and decaffeinated teas and a decent range of coffee for the java addicts. You can also discover some handy tips on how to brew the perfect cuppa.

The best idea when trawling for food in the Dandenong Ranges is to keep your eyes peeled and get chatting with the owners of the shops you like. That way, you won't miss the little roadside stall selling brilliant, warm roasted chestnuts or jars of excellent raspberry jam and you'll see that there is a whole lot more to the Dandenongs than Devonshire tea.

Silvan Estate Raspberries

There are some well-travelled chefs in some of Melbourne's finest restaurants who reckon the raspberries from **Silvan Estate** are amongst the sweetest and tastiest in the world. So around 4.30 every morning of the summer raspberry season, the Silvan Estate truck pulls onto Hollis Road in Silvan on a delivery run to city restaurants like Circa, ezard and Fenix, whose quality-mad chefs wouldn't have any other raspberries on their menus.

When you taste a Silvan Estate raspberry the acclaim is easy to understand. What is surprising, however, is that Silvan Estate's owners Pam Vroland and Jeremy Tisdall have been growing raspberries for less than seven years and started their farm 'knowing nothing about raspberries except that we liked them'.

Jeremy's corporate background and Pam's career in the arts and the rag trade were perhaps not the ideal backgrounds for raspberry growers but the couple did their homework and decided that the red soil and mild climate of Silvan, an area with an established fruit and flower growing history, would be a good place to pursue the perfect berry.

It has been something of a trial and error journey for them. Jeremy says that there is not much hard knowledge on how to grow a great-tasting raspberry

Right
Silvan Estate raspberries.

Far right and opposite
Luscious cup cakes from the kitchen of the Crabapple Bakery.

and 'why one farm can produce flavoursome fruit and another can't is still something of a mystery'. Some of the things they have learnt in seven years – that the chillier the winter, the better the flavour and that 'a good splash of rain seems to be the final step in the ripening process' – still seem to be more like theories than hard and fast rules.

Part of the success of **Silvan Estate** must come from the fact that their fruit is completely mollycoddled. Even before they go into the ground, some of the

There is a whole lot more to the Dandenongs than just Devonshire tea

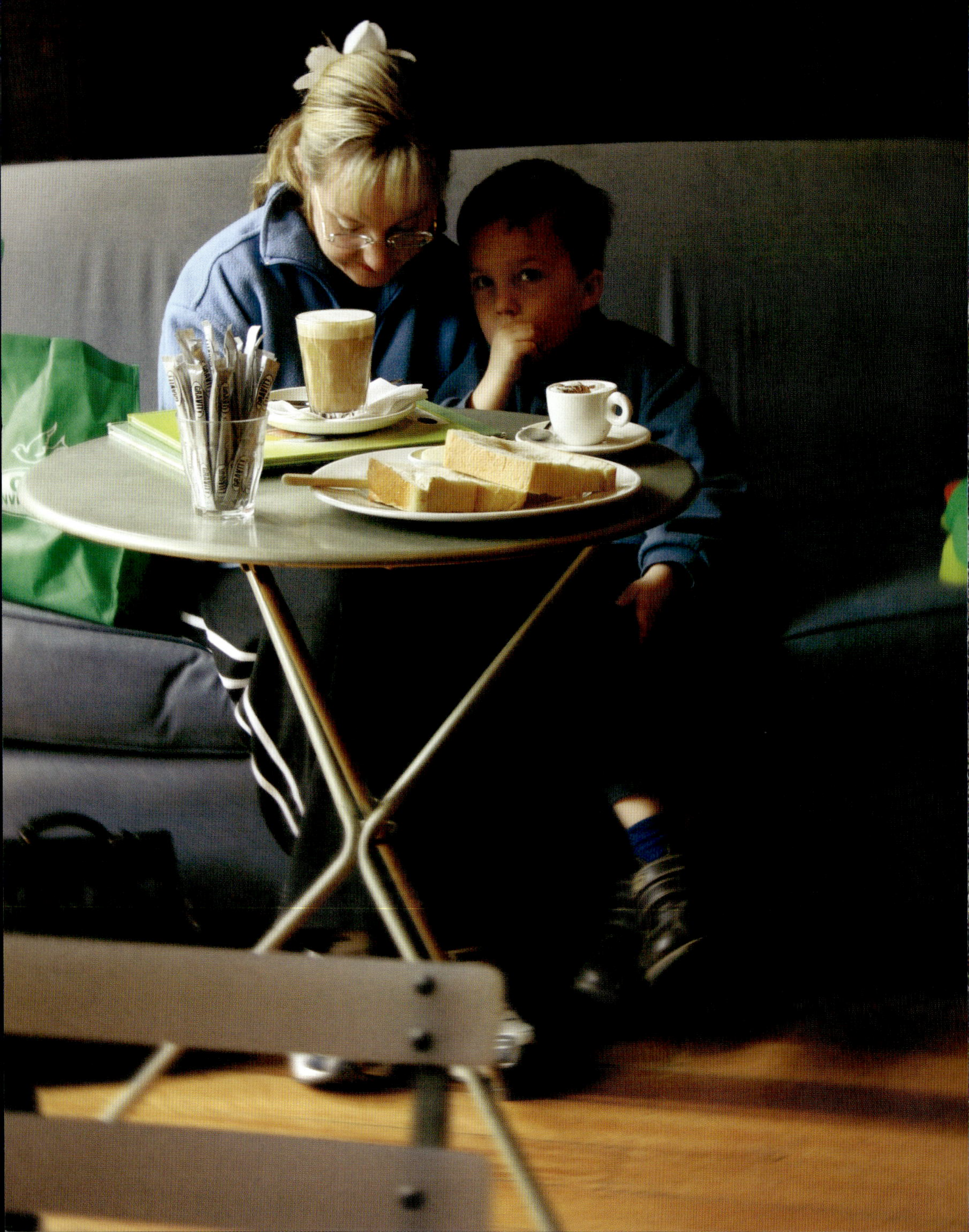

Right
Enjoying a quiet coffee at café and food store, Ripe, Sassafrass.

canes are refrigerated to emulate a good winter chill. Once planted, the canes are well pruned, watered with care (too much water and the flavour is diluted), the fruit is picked by hand when it is perfectly ripe (to ensure just the right sugar levels) and then immediately packed, lidded and refrigerated so that it remains in top condition when it is delivered by Jeremy the next day. Fruit that is damaged by rain or bruised during the picking process is frozen and sold when the raspberries are out of season, or to businesses for use in things like jam and ice cream. It is a point of pride for Pam and Jeremy that the fresh berries they sell are always in perfect condition whether they are delivered to the city or sold at their farm-gate.

In addition to the 3 hectares of raspberries – Chilliwack, Tulameen, Serpells Willamette varieties among them – Silvan Estate also grows redcurrants, blackberries, blueberries, boysenberries, tayberries and youngberries. International students and backpackers do much of the picking and Pam notes that pickers from some countries seem to have a natural affinity with certain berries. French girls, she says, 'are the best at picking red currants'; an untapped marketing angle if ever there was one.

Silvan Estate doesn't offer a pick-your-own experience but purchase a punnet from the packing shed, pop a sweet juicy morsel in your mouth and see how quickly a truly mollycoddled raspberry can put a smile back on your face and make you glad the work has already been done.

Carolyn Deutsher and Ripe

In the Dandenong Ranges it seems all roads lead to **Ripe**. Ask any food-savvy local about what is happening with food and wine in the area and you will be inevitably pointed in the direction of this brilliant little produce store and café in the pretty village of Sassafras.

Owner Carolyn Deutsher opened Ripe almost six years ago though in a smaller shop up the street from the former house it now calls home. Originally the business was all about produce – from small-scale, artisan businesses, preferably from nearby – but it also had a couple of tables in the shop where people could have a quick coffee or a baguette filled with something from one of the shelves in the store. As popular as the produce side of Ripe was, the café became ever more packed and so when the opportunity to move into the newer, larger premises came, Carolyn packed up her stock of Jam Lady Jam, Kennedy and Wilson Chocolate, Yarra Valley Ice Cream and her excellent range of Yarra Valley wine made by small producers, and moved down the street.

Zeppole, a traditional Italian pastry

Drew Colpman, Ripe

1 large or two small potatoes
125 g plain flour
12.5 g unsalted butter
(12.5 not 125)
60 g caster sugar
10 g active yeast
2 eggs, beaten but kept separate
80 g jam or custard
peanut or vegetable oil for cooking

Peel and boil potatoes until soft. In the meantime measure out all ingredients and put oil on to heat slowly.

Once potatoes are cooked mash until smooth. Take 125 grams of mash, then add the flour, butter sugar and yeast. Mix in an electric or hand mixer until firm and work for at least 5 minutes. Once desired texture has been reached, add the well-combined eggs one at a time and work in well.

Put dough onto floured surface and cut into circles. Prove for 10 to 20 minutes, then fry in 160º–170ºC oil. Place in oven for 5 minutes then roll in sugar and fill with jam or custard.

Serves 4

Above and opposite
Shelves stacked with gourmet fare, fresh cakes, pastries and fudge, plus good coffee entice regulars at Ripe, in Sassafras.

The current incarnation of **Ripe** is a charming, warm and comfortable place that feels both familiar and unique. There is no sign outside but the packed shelves full of pears in brandy or handmade soap or olive oil that greet you the moment you walk through the front door immediately tell you that this is the right place. Around the corner is the counter with its open kitchen, over-worked coffee machine and case full of fantastic meats and cheeses, dips and terrines. There is a fireplace in the main dining area, a veranda out the back and, everywhere you look, evidence of how much good food and wine there is to be consumed. It is one of those places that, even with the queue for tables that happens most lunch times, the pace remains relaxed, the staff affable and the mood peaceful.

The menu at **Ripe** changes every day, uses as much local product as possible, and is fiercely seasonal. In fact, it seems Carolyn is happiest when she can use local products, particularly from the people she has come to know since opening her store. She mentions Anne Creber and her range of pickles, sauces and vinegars called **Whispers from Provence**. 'Anne makes us this beautiful elderflower cordial that comes from the same tree on her property every year,' says Carolyn. 'I've started to refer to it as our tree.'

Though obviously pleased with the success of her business, Carolyn seems more pleased that the heartfelt philosophy on which Ripe is based has been accepted and embraced by so many people.

'I put my spirit and my soul into Ripe,' she says. 'It is important for me to have a place that is humble, a place that feeds people well, a place that is connected to the community in terms of the people who come here to eat and the products I put on the shelves. Making more money is not important to me but providing good food to everybody is.'

Eating Out

As with most aspects of food and wine in the Dandenong Ranges, the area's restaurant scene is inextricably – and not particularly accurately – linked to Devonshire tea. There is no doubt that there are plenty of tearooms in the ranges,

At Miss Marple's Tea Rooms jumbo scones are served with homemade raspberry jam, a generous amount of cream and large pots of tea

alongside pie shops and places like the Bavarian-style **Cuckoo Restaurant** (which has been offering a smorgasbord since the 1950s), but there is a wider selection of dining experiences nestled in the hills if you are willing to look.

If you're here to experience the tried-and-true, however, not just any old tearoom will do. For the full Dandenong Ranges Devonshire Tea Experience, you need to set the compass for Sassafras the home of **Miss Marple's Tea Rooms** for the last twenty years. This quaint Agatha Christie-themed, mock-English shop with its floral tablecloths and curtains not only has the Dandenong Ranges Devonshire atmosphere down pat but it does the scone, jam and cream business very well, particularly if you're into quantity as well as quality.

Owner Jennifer Cook says that the large, square, 'shearer's' scones are baked in big batches and crowded together in the oven so they tend to rise higher than a conventional scone. The jumbo scones are served with homemade raspberry jam (made from local berries) a generous amount of cream and large pots of tea. Size is a point of pride at Miss Marple's so if you choose not to have the big scones, you can have a big sundae, big toasted sandwich or an enormous Ploughman's Lunch.

Left and opposite
Miss Marple's Tea Rooms, Sassafras.

Pie shops are also integral to the traditional Dandenong food outing, so if you are continuing that theme, head for Olinda and the award-winning **Pie in the Sky**. Owner/chef Dennis Sideras originally opened Pie in the Sky as a traditional tearoom, but decided to include homemade pies to give his place a point of difference amongst all the other sandwich and quiche places. The pies took off – particularly after he began winning gold medals in the nationwide Great Aussie Pie competition – and they now account for 95 per cent of Dennis' trade.

There are about fifteen pies on the **Pie in the Sky** menu but Dennis says his traditional Aussie meat pie with good quality beef (coarsely ground 'so you can't cheat with what is in the pie like you can with finely ground mince') and served with tomato sauce is probably his best seller. His gourmet range – pork pies, chicken korma pies, spinach fetta and rice pies – all walk out the door in good numbers as well, and Dennis has recently begun ordering special boxes for the increasing number of tourists from Malaysia and Singapore who have heard of his pie-making prowess and are ordering up big and taking the pies back home on the plane as edible Aussie souvenirs.

To complete the Dandenong tourist food experience you probably need to include a visit to **SkyHigh** at Mount Dandenong. Worth the trip for the absolutely spectacular views over Melbourne alone, the facilities at SkyHigh have had a recent refurbishment and now include a reasonable bistro and café with lots of windows taking advantage of the gob-smacking vista. Go up there at night, order a beer or a glass of wine and watch Melbourne shimmer like a jewel.

If you want to see what Dandenong Ranges restaurants are capable of beyond the traditional, **LadyHawke** in Mount Dandenong is an excellent place to start.

Right
Fresh from the oven at Pie in the Sky, Olinda.

Opposite
Troy Payne and Fleur O'Hare at the quirky and colourful LadyHawke in Mount Dandenong.

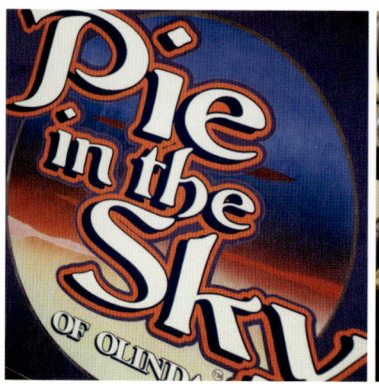

This wonderful little restaurant, housed in a homey 1920s building surrounded by lush trees, is a scone-free zone, the menu being more about Middle Eastern flavours and excellent local produce.

Owners Troy Payne and Fleur O'Hare are young and enthusiastic refugees from Melbourne who spent a couple of years getting their restaurant together, painting and renovating it themselves while they held down jobs in the city. The result is a quirky and colourful place with a welcoming atmosphere that is a cross between nanna's lounge room and a groovy inner-city café. There is no

Troy bakes his own bread, gets tomatoes from his garden and sources as much local produce as he can

Young and enthusiastic chef Ben Higgs sources much of Wild Oak's produce from the ranges and the Yarra Valley

lace to be seen anywhere. Fleur says that their aim was to create a completely relaxed feel to the place so that people would be as comfortable coming on their own as they would in a group. Watching people curled up with a coffee and the newspaper in the reading room, or joining friends for a meal near the fireplace, you can see that LadyHawke is working pretty much as they hoped it would.

The secret of LadyHawke's success (apart from Fleur's smile) is Troy's terrific food. He may have worked with and been influenced by chefs like Jacques Reymond, Andrew Blake and, most recently, Greg Malouf but having his own kitchen, his own kitchen garden and his own ideas have allowed him to give the food a unique spin. He says he is as much influenced by his grandmother as he is by anybody else and has Fleur's eighty-two-year-old grandmother working with him in LadyHawke's small kitchen.

Troy bakes his own bread, gets tomatoes and herbs from his garden and sources as much local produce as he can. There's not a lot of produce grown in the Dandenongs, he says, 'but when you do find things you leap at them'. The result is a restaurant that is unique in the area and one that should be included on the itinerary of any food lover to the ranges.

Left and opposite
Seasonal food, a stylish dining space and chef Ben Higgs, all at Wild Oak, Olinda.

There are other places in the Dandenongs that are also pushing a modern, produce-driven barrow. **Wild Oak** in Olinda, owned by another young and enthusiastic chef, Ben Higgs, sources much of its produce from the ranges and the Yarra Valley and has a big Yarra Valley focus on its wine list. Also in Olinda is **Credo**, a bright and modern Italian joint that is all about clean lines and modern Italian flavours.

Lemon myrtle tea sorbet

Paperbark Café,
Kuranga Native Nursery,
Mount Evelyn

½ cup tea leaves
4 cups water
30 g lemon myrtle leaves
2½ cups sugar
¼ cup glucose syrup
juice of 1 lemon

Add tea leaves to 1 cup boiling water, strain when the leaves begin to sink, and set aside to cool.

Place lemon myrtle leaves into 1 cup boiling water and leave there until cold and then strain. Put sugar, glucose, lemon juice and 2 cups water into a pot and bring to the boil. Chill well and then mix with the tea and lemon myrtle waters. Partly freeze the mixture, then beat and refreeze. (May also be churned in an ice-cream machine).

Serves 4

Paperbark Café at Kuranga Native Nursery

It may not have the biggest restaurant scene in the state, but the Dandenong Ranges has a broader dining culture than the Devonshire tradition might have you believe. Dig beyond the surface and the gems soon make themselves apparent.

There are scones on the menu at the **Paperbark Café** but they're unlike any other you'll find in the Dandenong Ranges. Flavoured with the cinnamon/coffee taste of wattleseed, the scones come served with jam made from native bush fruit, cream and a wonderfully sweet butter flecked with slices of macadamia nut. It's a Devonshire tea, Jim, but not as we know it.

Paperbark Café is part of the **Kuranga Native Nursery** in Mount Evelyn, a nursery that not only stocks 3500 varieties of exclusively Australian native plants but has a fantastic produce store that includes jams, honey, pasta, olive oils and mustards with Australian bush flavours.

Kuranga recently moved to this larger site from its original home established in Ringwood in 1983 by owners Evan Lucas and Leanne Weston. A fanatical following among local, national and international gardeners prompted the move to the Dandenong Ranges and Kuranga seems well situated in its new location – away from the European tree areas that are higher up in the ranges and amongst gum trees alive with the cackle of kookaburras.

The new site gives the nursery increased space for an even greater variety of plants and also allows the business to push another passion – the flavours of bush food. The nursery has a small section of bush-food plants for sale at the moment – lemon myrtle, macadamia, mountain pepper, riberry (lilli pilli) – a range that will soon be expanded with more plants being grown here and at another site in nearby Wandin. The plants are not just grown for sale, however. They are there to supply the Paperbark Café, to help spread the word on how good these flavours really are.

Faith Samuel heads the kitchen at Paperbark and uses the ingredients grown at the nursery in a skilled, interesting and subtle way. An open sandwich might include a bush chutney, or chicken marinated with wild lime, while for breakfast you can get local fruit poached with lemon myrtle or porridge flavoured with wattleseed. There is nothing gimmicky about the cooking and you could easily indulge in many of the dishes in this light and airy place without being aware that you are eating in a bush-food café.

Paperbark Café takes a refreshingly relaxed approach to the often-misunderstood flavours of the Australian bush, an attitude that should put it on the map of any food foragers seeking something a little different.

Opposite
Flavours of the Australian bush from the Kuranga Native Nursery and Paperbark Café.

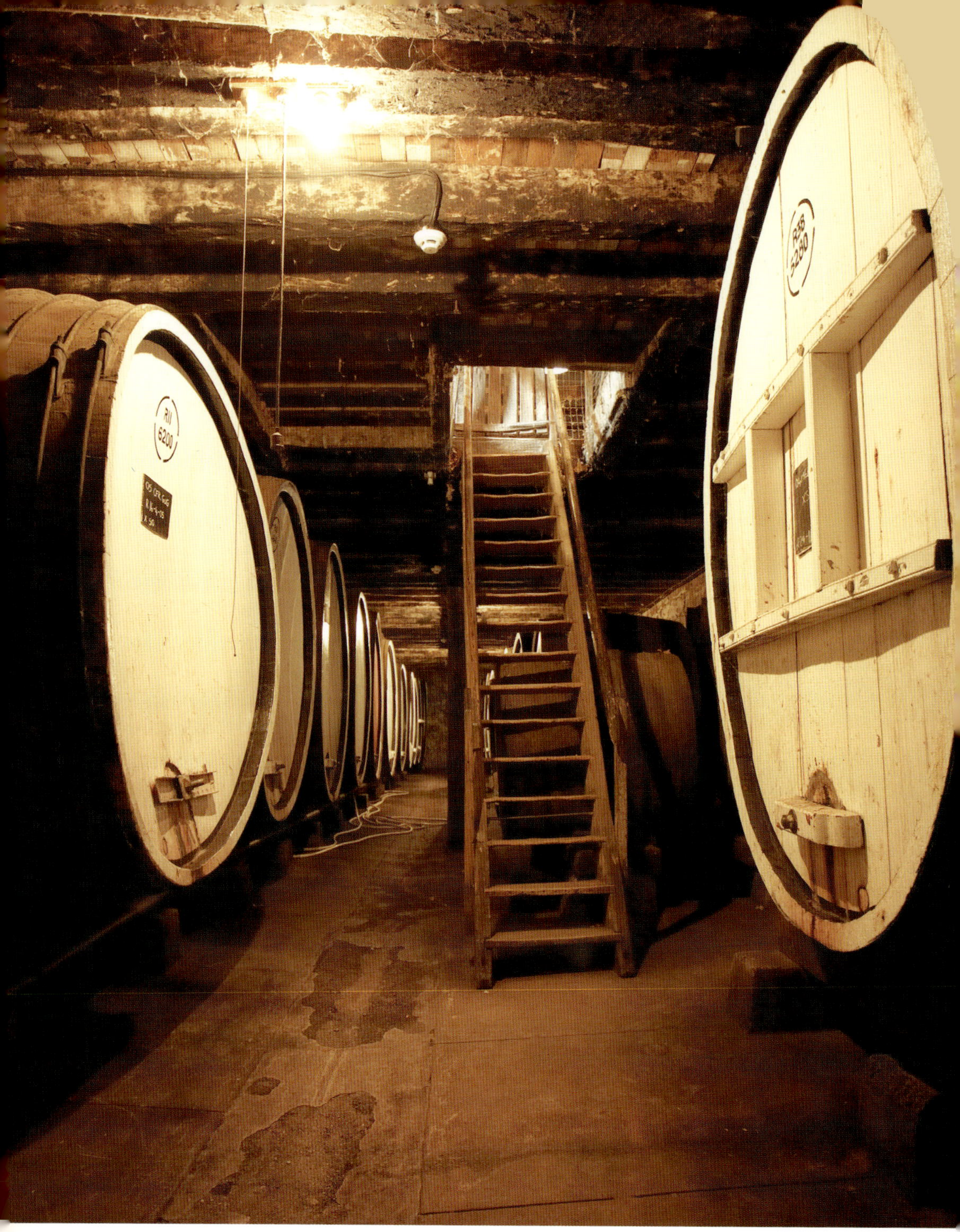
R11
6200
R38
5280

nagambie and strathbogie ranges

michael harden

nagambie and strathbogie ranges

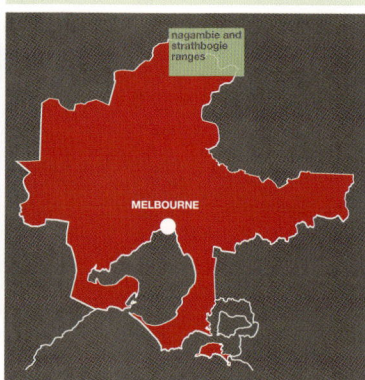

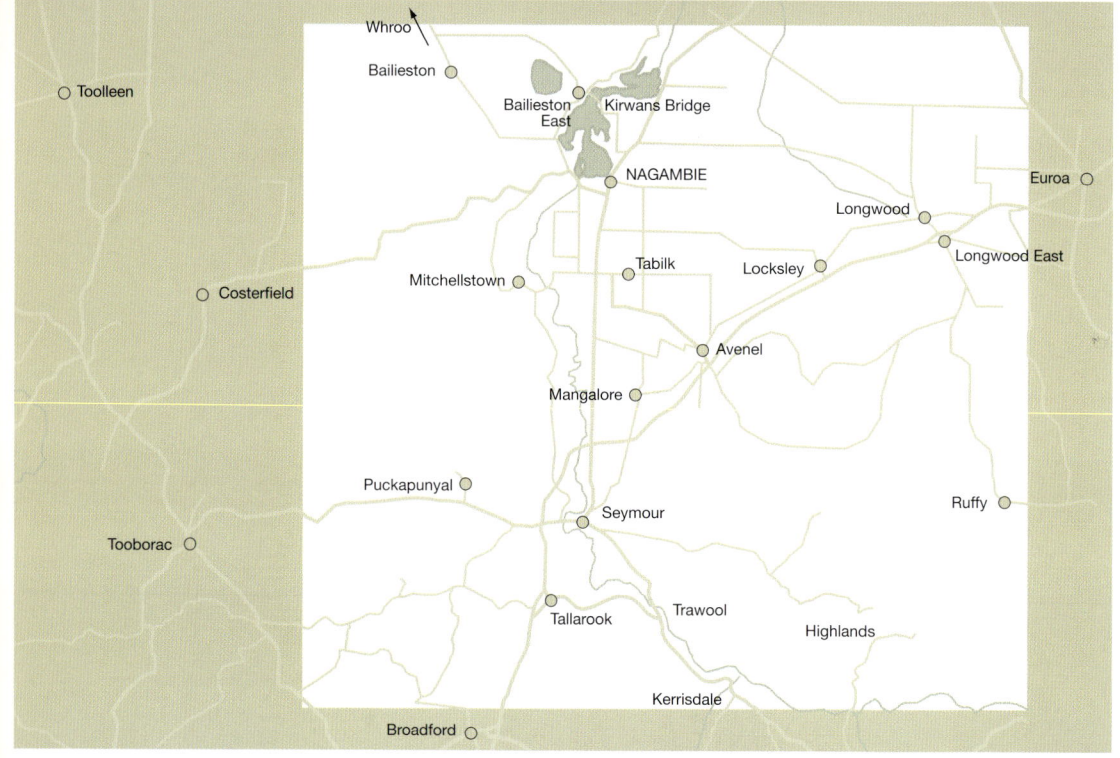

Toolleen

Whroo
Bailieston
Bailieston East
Kirwans Bridge
NAGAMBIE
Longwood
Euroa
Costerfield
Mitchellstown
Tabilk
Locksley
Longwood East
Avenel
Mangalore
Puckapunyal
Ruffy
Tooborac
Seymour
Trawool
Highlands
Tallarook
Kerrisdale
Broadford

This ruggedly handsome region features one of Australia's oldest wineries and some of Victoria's best beef, lamb, fruit and vegetables

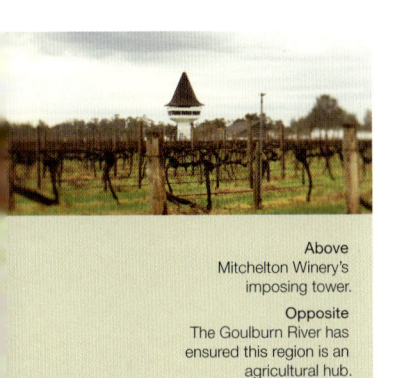

Above
Mitchelton Winery's imposing tower.

Opposite
The Goulburn River has ensured this region is an agricultural hub.

If you're interested in observing a great food and wine area in the making, set your compass for the region surrounding the town of Nagambie. Less than an hour and a half from Melbourne, this ruggedly handsome region of mountains and rivers, fields and lakes has, until recently, been virtually invisible to all but the keenest food and wine foragers despite the presence of one of Australia's oldest wineries and some of Victoria's best beef, lamb, fruit and vegetables. But things are changing. Local businesses – cellar doors, produce stores, butchers, restaurants – are waking up to the untapped potential in the often remarkable local produce, while an increasing number of growers are branching out and planting a wider variety of fruit and vegetables, buoyed by the dawning realisation that this region can truly deliver the food and wine goods.

An abundance of water, courtesy of the Goulburn River, and a warm mild climate has meant that the area around Nagambie has been on the farming map since the early 1800s. The discovery of gold in the region in the early nineteenth century brought an influx of people, many of whom stayed to try their luck at farming when the gold ran out. While much of the initial farming involved sheep and cattle, grapevines were being planted by the 1850s on the river flats around the Goulburn River. Amongst the first major growers were a group of Melbourne businessmen who established the **Tahbilk Estate** in 1860, a gorgeously positioned winery, still in operation, that has not only secured the Nagambie Lakes area's ongoing reputation for winemaking but has been instrumental in highlighting the region's affinity with Rhone varietals like shiraz and marsanne.

The 1891 completion of the Goulburn Weir – a remarkable engineering feat that uses the Goulburn River to irrigate half a million hectares of farmland – ensured the region's longevity as an agricultural hub, but its distance from Melbourne meant fewer tourists and less recognition than other food-producing regions like the Yarra Valley. Over the last few years, however, dramatic improvements to the roads have slashed the travelling time to Melbourne,

Five great local products

- Strathbogie Beef Sausages
- Alpi 'Ruffy Blend' Organic Tea
- Purbrick and Crawford Raspberry Jam
- Adrian and Valda Martin's cherries
- Vazzoler Cheese Two-Year-Old Cheddar

Opposite
The picturesque Goulburn River flows through the region.

which has seen the numbers of tourists increasing as well as more city folk looking for a 'tree change' moving into the area to plant vines, grow olive trees, make cheese or simply wave the flag for the local producers.

Part of the beauty of visiting the area around Nagambie now is that it is still in the early stages of becoming a food and wine destination. You may have to look a little harder, ask a few more questions of the locals and travel a few more dusty, pitted dirt roads before you find what you are looking for. But what makes this kind of hunt doubly satisfying is that there is an increasing number of real treasures to be found at the end of the trail.

Foodstores and producers

While there is plenty of great fruit, vegetables, nuts, olives, eggs, honey, herbs, beef and lamb produced around Nagambie and the nearby Strathbogie Ranges, the farm-gate experience in this neck of the woods is still fairly undiscovered. Finding the places that sell produce from their sheds is a matter of keeping your eyes peeled and talking to the locals. You may not be able to buy much direct from local producers, though there are ways around that.

Local woman Di Mc Donald grows some of the sweetest, reddest, juiciest rhubarb you will ever taste, on a plot of land at the **Tahbilk Estate winery**.

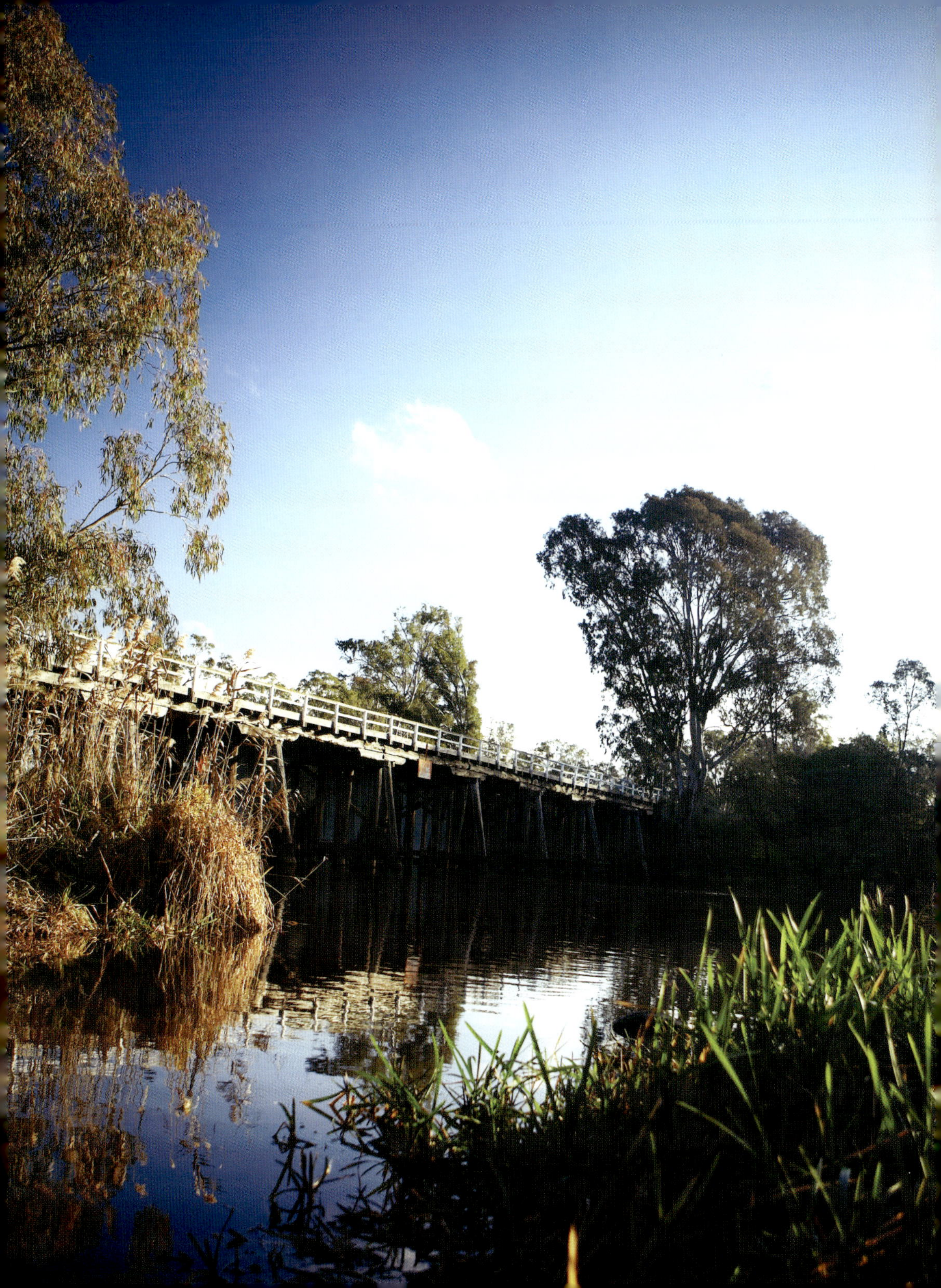

Right, this page
Harvest Home B&B provides fresh produce and old-fashioned charm.

Opposite
Biodynamic fruit, and growers Adrian and Valda Martin.

Di also grows a few raspberries but mainly concentrates on cultivating her heirloom rhubarb using organic farming methods. The rhubarb seems to love her for it and it deservedly receives rave reviews from everybody who has tasted it. Some Nagambie locals even go so far as to claim that Di 'has put rhubarb back on the map'. Despite the raves, it is often easier to buy a bunch of Di's rhubarb at one of the farmers' markets in Melbourne than it is to source it locally. Luckily there are a couple of fairly new produce stores – **the Goulburn Terrace Cellar Door** in Nagambie and the **Ruffy Produce Store** in Ruffy – that stock small amounts of local produce and often include Di's rhubarb. Arrive at the right time and you might get lucky.

Another product finding its way into an increasing number of the region's shops is **Strathbogie Beef**. David and Libby Hamilton run the **Bellagreen Cattle Farm and Stud** in the Strathbogie Ranges and have recently begun producing a small range of products from their grass-fed stock. The range includes prime cuts of steak, beautifully flavoured beef sausages, kabana, mince and finely sliced smoked eye fillet, all of which are meticulously labelled and numbered so that the meat can be traced back to the very paddock where the stock once grazed.

Avenel is a good place to head for a taste of the local stuff. While the town's small butcher is a decent source of local beef and lamb, the real food event here is Suzi McKay's sprawling and eccentric **Harvest Home**. The dining-room menu at this unique pub/guesthouse teems with local products but if you want to get your hands on some of Suzi's ingredients, there is a small produce market held in the sheltered, ramshackle garden on the second Sunday of every month. Seek out Brian Bowring and Jessica Bateman, who grow a fantastic range of vegetables for the Harvest Home kitchen and always have a small stall under a tree at the produce market. During summer there could be up to seven varieties of tomato available while at other times there is a brilliant range of garlic, pumpkins, leeks, broccoli, carrots and broad beans.

Cheese lovers should take the very pretty back road out of Nagambie and wind their way north to the **Longleat** cellar door in Murchison. The thirty-year-old Longleat vineyard is now home to **Murchison Wines**, made by Guido Vazzoler, and Vazzoler Cheese, handmade by Sandra Vazzoler. Inspired by the small cheesemakers in Italy's north, Sandra makes a small range of cheese from local cow's milk that includes a white mould, marinated fetta, subtly tangy blue vein and two-year-old cheddar. A vine-covered pergola at the cellar door is just the place to sit back and enjoy the quiet over a tasting plate of these delicious handmade cheeses and a glass or two of Guido's nicely restrained shiraz.

The Nagambie area's warm climate has attracted a number of olive growers who are beginning to produce some very promising olive oil. Keep an eye out for **Nagambie Gold**, produced by Susie Moscovitch and her husband Leon. Though now a city dweller Susie grew up in Nagambie and has planted 1200 olive trees on land that has been in her family for three generations. The impressive peppery, hazelnut flavours of their unfiltered oil seems to point to the region's great olive oil potential.

There is great produce in the Nagambie region. Its food and wine frontier status simply means you have to try a little harder to find it.

Adrian and Valda Martin's Biodynamic Fruit

Adrian Martin reckons that his orchard sits on 'the best bit of land in Ruffy'. That may well be, but even the most untrained and citified eye can see that this bio-dynamic orchard on McLeans Lane is certainly one of the prettiest and well-kept farms you could hope to come across. Looking at its elegant rows of carefully tended fruit trees, it seems logical that this lovely place should produce such delicious, intensely flavoured fruit.

Adrian and his wife Valda grew flowers for the commercial market in Melbourne for many years but had always grown a small number of peaches and, with orchardists on both sides of their family, an orchard was something that Adrian always had in the back of his mind. The Strathbogie Ranges

TAHBILK ESTATE

Opposite
Tahbilk Estate, home of one of the oldest wineries in Australia.

property they bought was a sheep and oats farm initially but when that business 'fell over', Adrian decided to take a gamble and grow fruit in a place where there were virtually no other orchards.

Having become increasingly concerned over the use of agricultural chemicals while they were growing flowers, Adrian and Valda decided to move in the opposite direction from conventional commercial practices and farm by biodynamic principles. They began planting the orchard on the sunny north-facing slope in 1992 and gained biodynamic certification in 1996.

There are 10 hectares of fruit trees on the Martins' orchard with cherries, peaches, plums and apples the main crops. Adrian planned the orchard so that he and Valda can handle most of the picking and packing work themselves. The orchard contains several varieties of peaches that ripen from late December until March but the trees have been planted so that only one variety of peach ripens per week, ensuring the picking remains manageable for two people. The only time Adrian and Valda need to hire workers is during the shorter and more intense cherry season.

Adrian is very proud of the response he gets to the beauty and flavour of his fruit and is a true believer when it comes to the biodynamic principles under which his farm operates, but there is nothing of the zealot about him. Instead he talks modestly about picking the fruit 'as ripe as we can' and then sorting and packing it with minimal handling before he puts it on the ute and drives it to the market in Melbourne.

During the season you can drive through the stone gates at the entrance to the orchard, make your way up the olive-lined driveway (the Martins are planning to make olive oil) to the packing shed and buy just-picked fruit. Be warned though: the way these cherries taste, you may finish them before you reach the gate. If you spot any jars of cherries or plums in syrup or bottles of cherry juice (a sideline to use up any excess or slightly damaged fruit) snap them up. That way, long after the fresh fruit is a distant, sweet memory you'll have something to keep you going until the cherries ripen again.

Wineries

Unlike many of Victoria's wine regions, the area around Nagambie has had an unbroken winemaking history dating back to the 1850s. Despite this longevity, the area's unique geographical and climatic conditions were only officially acknowledged in 1993. Subsequently, the Nagambie Lakes Wine Region is one of the newest in Victoria, even though it contains some of the oldest vines in the world. It might seem confusing at first but stick with it because,

The Nagambie Lakes Wine Region is the only winemaking region in Australia where the climate is dramatically influenced by an inland water mass combined with the increasing number of cool-climate, high-altitude wineries in the neighbouring Strathbogie Ranges, this part of the world contains some seriously good fun for wine lovers.

At present, the Nagambie Lakes Wine Region is the only winemaking region in Australia – and one of only six in the world – where the climate is dramatically influenced by an inland water mass. So despite the inland setting, the presence of the Goulburn River and various lakes and lagoons make the region milder and more humid than you might expect. Such is the effect of these waterways on the grapes (slower to ripen, delicate but full flavours) that to be included in the region, a winery has to be no further than three kilometres from water.

Tahbilk Estate, established in 1860 and run by the Purbrick family since 1925, is the region's best-known winery and one of Australia's oldest. The 1214-hectare property has 11 kilometres of river frontage and a beautiful wetlands area that has been restored and developed to include a series of walks for winery visitors and a stylish café. Visiting the original riverfront Tahbilk 'village' with its iconic tower and original, atmospheric cellars is like

Left and opposite
An idyllic setting, classic wines and the new Wetlands Café at Chateau Tahbilk.

strolling through a movie set. There are old blacksmith shops, tiny workers' cottages and a fantastic cellar door in the same building as the original oak fermenters that are still used for Tahbilk's red wines.

It is all very pretty and historic, but Tahbilk also mixes substance with the style. The 168-hectare vineyard (including the plot of shiraz planted in 1866) includes many of the Rhone varietals for which the region is becoming increasingly recognised – shiraz, marsanne, rousanne, viognier – and its

Right and opposite
Mitchelton Winery, on a bend of the Goulburn River, is known for its Spanish-influenced winery buildings.

marsanne planting is the largest of any single vineyard in the world. Tahbilk has won a swag of awards over the years and is highly regarded for the longevity and structure of its red wines, particularly the Reserve shiraz made with grapes from the winery's 1933 vineyard. Its success with marsanne has been such that it virtually 'owns' the variety in Australia.

Not far from Tahbilk (a 45 minute boat ride up the river for those with some time to spare) is another of the area's well-known wineries with another landmark tower. **Mitchelton** was established in 1973 and the impressive Spanish-influenced winery buildings – including the tower with its observation deck offering brilliant views over the estate – show that tourism was very much on the agenda in the early days. Now Mitchelton, with its wonderful river-snuggled position, is concentrating more on the business of wine and is producing some excellent riesling under its **Blackwood Park** label and some good versions of the Rhone varietals – shiraz, marsanne, viognier, mouvedre and rousanne.

Tourists haven't been forgotten at Mitchelton though and it remains a lovely place to stroll or picnic by the Goulburn River, eat lunch in the consistently good restaurant and visit the well-run cellar door with its small range of local produce. One of the advantages of visiting Mitchelton's cellar door is that you get to taste and buy wines that are not available anywhere else. The winery makes small runs of wines from particularly good parcels of estate-grown grapes – perhaps a straight rousanne – that will only be sold at the cellar door. Similarly there will be small releases of aged riesling and marsanne on sale from time to time.

Also in the area is **David Traeger Wines**. Established in 1984, the winery has several vineyards, one of which has been producing grapes continuously for more than a hundred years. The long established, non-irrigated vines are low yielding and produce intensely flavoured grapes. David Traeger Wines operates a cellar door in the main street of Nagambie – next to the tourist information centre – where you can try his small but finessed range of wines that includes a viognier and an excellent shiraz that is partly made from grapes from the old vines at the vineyard in Graytown.

The Nagambie Lakes Wine Region is a good blend of new and old wineries and because of the specific geographical requirements will always remain a fairly small club. It is interesting to see some newer wineries in the area are expanding their repertoire and experimenting with the dominant styles, ensuring the region – steeped in all that wine-making history – does not lapse into being a wine museum.

Goulburn Terrace

If you want a taste of the new food and wine energy that is beginning to bubble in the Nagambie region, the **Goulburn Terrace** cellar door is the perfect place to start. Winemakers Greta Moon and Mike Boudry bought the romantically rickety general store at the north end of Nagambie's main drag without knowing what they would do with it; Greta simply liked the look of the empty 1920s building with its wooden floors and old Bushell's commercials painted on the windows. It was only after they had bought the old shop that they realised it was the ideal cellar-door location for their **Goulburn Terrace Winery**, 8 kilometres away on the banks of the Goulburn River.

Initially the shopfront was a fairly straightforward operation where they sold their wine alongside a bit of local produce – organic vegetables and fruit, handmade pickles and preserves, local olive oil – and other gourmet ingredients brought up from Melbourne. But the style of wine they were making – the restrained, savoury Midnight Shiraz; an elegant, richly textured chardonnay; a steely, complex cabernet sauvignon – was strongly influenced by their admiration for European wine styles and really shone when it was teamed with food. There was enough room in the shop for a small kitchen, and Greta (who, Mike explains, 'has an immense food knowledge') was interested in cooking local ingredients to go with their wine, so they decided to add more food to their cellar-door selection.

Goulburn Terrace is not a restaurant but more a shopfront expression of Greta and Mike's philosophy towards food, wine, hospitality and conviviality. It only opens on weekends, and if Greta and Mike have to be away, it stays closed. There are a couple of wooden tables with mismatched wooden chairs, an old deli fridge full of fresh produce, excellent coffee and tea, homemade sourdough bread and a fridge full of juices and cheese, buckets of stock and olives. It is a good place to go not just because of the convivial atmosphere, great music and delicious cooking, but because Greta and Mike are an incredibly rich source of information about everything that is happening in the area to do with food and wine.

In some ways, Greta and Mike represent the classic Nagambie district's 'tree changers', both representing and driving the evolution of the local food and wine culture.

Greta owned Au Go Go records in Melbourne for many years but had always liked wine and the idea of growing grapes. After looking around the state for a site, she bought her riverside property, attracted by the 'forgiving' climate and the plentiful water, and planted it with chardonnay and cabernet. Sensing the

Right and opposite
Greta Moon and Mike Boudry run their Goulburn Terrace Winery and, in Nagambie's main street, the shopfront Goulburn Terrace cellar door-cum-weekend-restaurant.

The region's best dining experiences take advantage of the rural atmosphere and excellent local produce (both food and wine)

Sammy's potato galette thing

Helen McDougall,
Ruffy Produce Store

Shortcrust pastry
240 g plain flour
180 g cold unsalted butter, cubed
pinch salt
3 tbps cold water

Topping
3 onions, caramelised
500 g kipfler potatoes, finely sliced
120 g Donnybrook or Milawa Blue cheese
sea salt and black pepper

For the pastry, whiz all the ingredients except water in food processor. Add water and whiz again until pastry comes together. Knead lightly, wrap in plastic and refrigerate for 30 minutes. Roll out to approximately 1 cm thick, to cover rectangular baking sheet. Prick pastry with fork.

Cover pastry with caramelised onions then kiplfer potatoes arranged in layers on top. Sprinkle with sea salt and black pepper then crumble cheese over the top. Bake at 175°C degrees for about 30 minutes, or until edges of potato start to lightly brown.

Serve warm with greens and perhaps some sliced fennel.

Serves 4

Above and opposite
Mitchelton Winery combines an enviable, river position, an interesting cellar door and a well-established restaurant.

winds of change in the record-buying business, she decided to study wine science and met Mike who was over from London to complete the same course and stay on in Australia to plant grapes and make wine. They teamed up, produced their first vintage in 1999, moved into the area fulltime in 2000 and fully committed to their winemaking when Greta closed Au Go Go in 2003. Their range of wine continues to expand and reflects their desire to keep things interesting. A sparkling marsanne is on its way and they have just released a viognier and a rousanne alongside their range of shiraz, chardonnay and cabernet. Try Goulburn Terrace wine with some of Greta's food in the old general store and get a glimpse of how the Nagambie region is progressing.

Eating Out

You won't find much in the way of slick city eateries in the Nagambie area's tiny restaurant scene and here's hoping that it remains that way. The region's best dining experiences avoid both faux city style and hokey country charm clichés and instead take advantage of the rural atmosphere and excellent local produce (both food and wine), dishing up simply cooked food with a refreshing lack of pretension.

Not many of the wineries in the region have restaurants attached but the one at the **Mitchelton Winery** is a valuable lesson on how to do it right. The purpose-built restaurant building takes advantage of its superb location with a wall of glass framing a tranquil bush-strewn stretch of the Goulburn River and the large whitewashed dining room with its classic 1970s look – cathedral ceilings, large open fireplace – is an ideal setting for making merry over lunch with a couple of glasses of wine. Each dish on the menu of simply cooked, often locally sourced food is matched with a Mitchelton wine so you can get an idea of the winery's range, and the nicely maintained grounds around the restaurant are a picturesque location to walk off your lunch.

The **Traawool Shed Café**, south of Nagambie, is a relaxed and comfortable kind of place with friendly service and a menu of well-cooked, rustic food that

Right
Harvest B&B, in Avenel.

Far right
Geoff and Chris Callan, who run the Wetlands Café at Chateau Tahbilk.

takes advantage of some of the region's produce. The wine list favours local wines from Nagambie, Traawool and the Strathbogie Ranges, many of which are available by the glass so you can do a virtual winery crawl over the course of a very enjoyable meal.

The dining room at **Harvest Home** in Avenel offers one of the region's best opportunities to taste local produce being used to delicious effect. The room's eccentric mix of old-world Victoriana and thrift-store chic is a perfect setting for Suzi McKay's take on regional cooking (a la Alice Waters at California's Chez Panisse) and it is a guarantee that most of the ingredients she uses were plucked from a field nearby. An enticing wine list makes the dinner-and-bed packages at Harvest Home a sensible and often memorable option.

With other places like the **Goulburn Terrace** and **Longleat Vineyard** cellar doors and the **Wetlands Café** at **Tahbilk Estate** also in the neighbourhood, eating out in this neck of the woods increasingly offers its own relaxed and unpretentious dining style.

Ruffy Produce Store

Driving into the tiny town of Ruffy through the ruggedly beautiful Strathbogie Ranges, it seems inconceivable that a place this small and isolated could harbour a food business that has been turning heads far and wide. But pull up a seat at one of the tables inside the **Ruffy Produce Store** or, if the weather is fine, one of the outside tables scattered across a well-tended lawn and you begin to understand why all those cars are parked out the front every weekend.

Helen McDougall originally bought the former general store to use as a kitchen for making her rapidly growing McDougall and MacLean range of jams and preserves, but the idea of using the space as a produce store and café proved 'irresistible'. An energetic and passionate woman, Helen found herself

Above
The landscape around Nagambie and the Strathbogie Ranges district.

driven by the concept of stocking only local produce and cooking with local ingredients and, three years later, that drive has turned the **Ruffy Produce Store** into a showcase of everything local that is good to eat and drink.

In the centre of the simple, homey shop there is a range of organic and biodynamic fruit and vegetables, free-range eggs and bags of locally grown walnuts. On the various shelves you can find Alpi organic peppermint, echinacea and lemongrass tea (the only place the brand is stocked other than Donovan's restaurant in Melbourne), homemade cordials flavoured with lemon verbena, bergamot and elderflower, bottled plums in syrup from **Adrian Martin's** nearby biodynamic orchard, as well as Helen's own brilliant Ruffy Produce range of jams and preserves that includes a rhubarb chutney, fennel and cucumber pickles and fig conserve. One shelf is dedicated to wines from the small wineries scattered throughout the district, many of which have no cellar door of their own. In the fridge there are sausages, steaks and kabana from Strathbogie Beef and a range of smoked meats from the butcher in nearby Euroa. **Split Rock Mineral Water** – a well-known brand in Melbourne – comes from a spring in the Strathbogie Ranges and so also finds a place in the fridge. One of the nicest things about the store is that it also stocks more mundane but essential items like milk and newspapers, adding to the down-to-earth atmosphere.

The menu at the Ruffy Produce Store changes regularly and with the seasons. The food is beautifully cooked, keeping things simple and letting the wonderful ingredients speak for themselves. Those wanting to get a decent dose of the local foodstuffs should order a produce platter 'with everything that we sell that is from around here'. Team it with a glass or two of the local wines and you begin to understand why this area is finally starting to attract the attention it deserves.

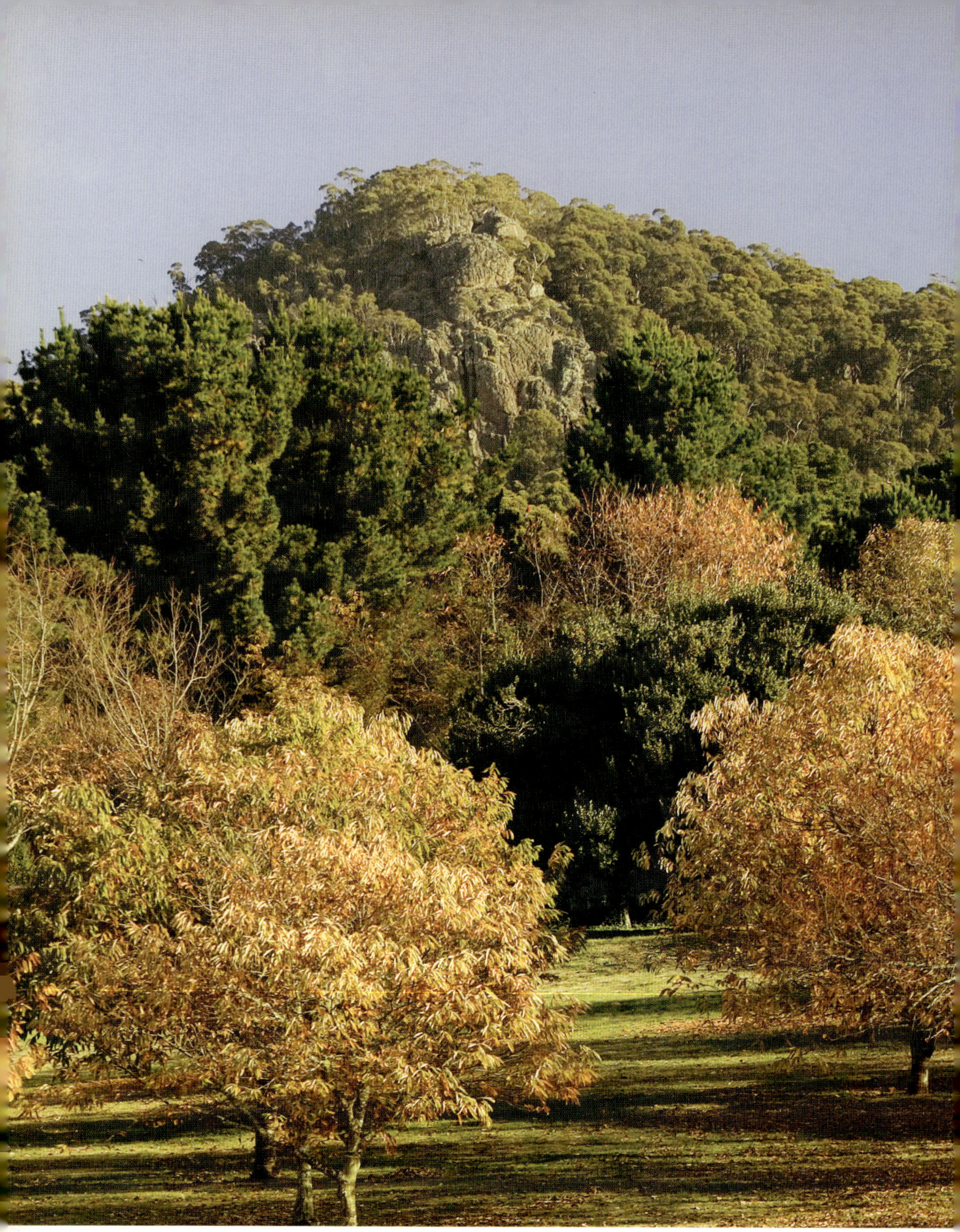

macedon ranges

claude forell

macedon ranges

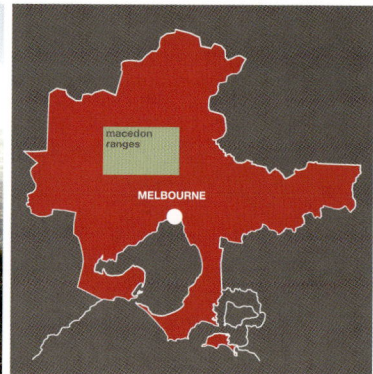

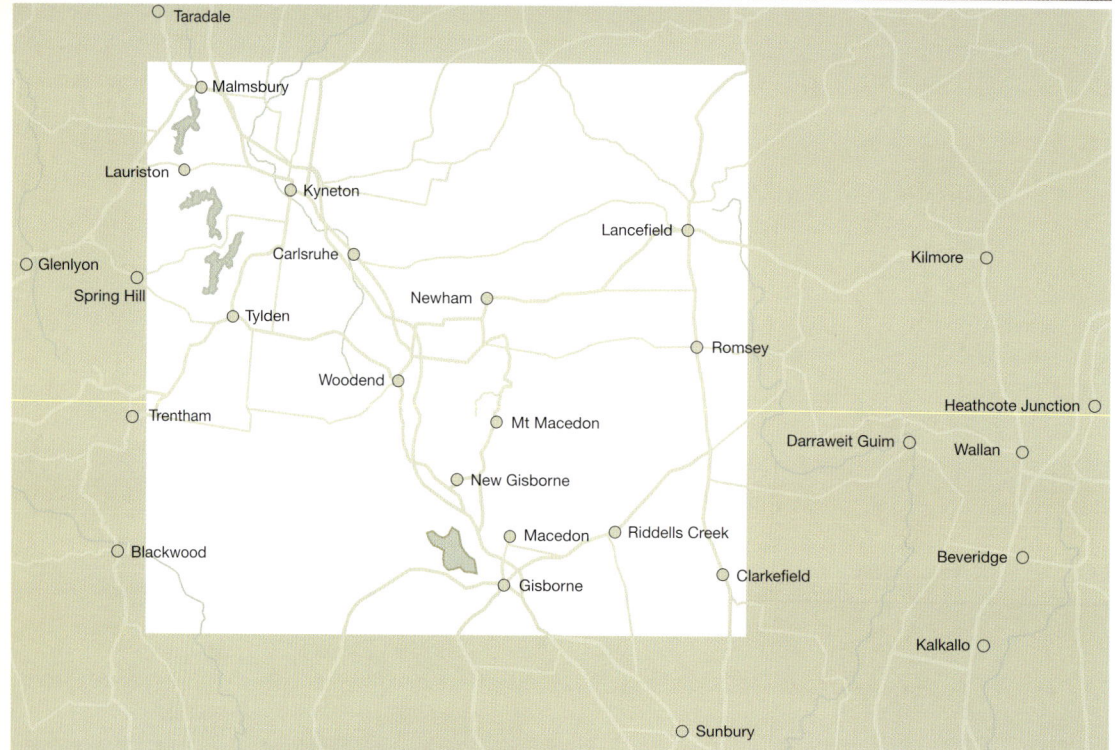

Taradale
Malmsbury
Lauriston
Kyneton
Glenlyon
Spring Hill
Carlsruhe
Lancefield
Kilmore
Tylden
Newham
Trentham
Woodend
Romsey
Heathcote Junction
Mt Macedon
Darraweit Guim
Wallan
New Gisborne
Blackwood
Macedon
Riddells Creek
Beveridge
Gisborne
Clarkefield
Kalkallo
Sunbury

The area is producing some exceptional wines.... there are flourishing olive groves, berry farms, and producers of specialty foodstuffs, as well as enticing restaurants, cafés, gourmet food shops and even a boutique brewery

Above
Roadside mail delivery near Malmsbury.

Opposite
Hanging Rock, an impressive outcrop on the northern side of Mount Macedon.

Foodstores and producers

The Macedon Ranges and its surrounds are cool, in more ways than one. They offer a crisp climate that is producing some exceptional wines, and they are increasingly fashionable as a destination for those seeking fine quality regional and seasonal produce.

As early as the 1860s, wealthy Melburnians built cottages, then mansions, on the mountain slopes to escape the city's summer heat. A decade earlier, inns and shops at its foot served local timber cutters and prospectors on the way to the Bendigo goldfields. Now the Macedon region is Victoria's youngest and coolest (you could say coldest) wine-growing district, grapes replacing potatoes as the principal crop. The flamboyant Hungarian restaurateur, Tom Lazar, was the first to recognise the potential, establishing Virgin Hills in 1968. The higher slopes have proved ideal for pinot noir and chardonnay, hence some fine sparkling wines; the northern, more granitic areas produce excellent cool-climate shiraz and riesling. Much of the area is marginal for wine growing. Stuart Anderson, local elder statesman of winemaking, says the best wines come from vineyards with the best sites: that is, with the most favourable aspect of soil, slope and aspect to the sun. By contrast, the warmer, lower and drier Sunbury region proved successful for viticulture as far back as the 1860s. None of its original vineyards survived as such until wine growing resumed in the 1970s and, as further north, has gathered pace.

Although not as bountiful as the closely associated Daylesford region, the area from Sunbury to Kyneton now also boasts flourishing olive groves, berry farms and producers of specialty added-value foodstuffs, such as jams, sauces and biscuits. There are also a growing number of enticing restaurants, cafés and gourmet food shops, and even a boutique brewery. Diana Marsland has regular classes, often using regional produce, in her cooking school in Woodend.

After just three years, the **Lancefield and District Farmers' Market** has been named the best farmers' market in the state. For visitors, it's a convenient way of discovering what the region has to offer in food and wine. Every fourth

macedon ranges **159**

Right
The road leading
up to the 'Mount'.

Opposite
Ian Gutner at
Knight Granite Hills.

Saturday of the month (the third in December), from 9 am to 1 pm, you may browse, taste and buy among some forty stalls in the central plantation of the town's main street. You will find a variety of fresh and value-added produce, including wines from boutique vineyards, alongside live poultry, herbs and other farm-based products. The market's success owes much to its dynamic organisers, Megan ('Meggs') Hannes-Paterson and Vivien Philpotts, who hope to expand it to sixty-five stalls.

Depending on seasonal harvest times, Daylesford Organics will be there with their crisp, freshly picked apples, and **Fernleigh Farm** with their straight-from-the-ground organic potato varieties and carrots. Kyneton Olive Oil and Macedon Grove Olives (of which more below) will have their products on display. Under the intriguing **Lovers Chase** label, Michael Wuttke offers a robust, peppery olive oil from his 80-hectare olive grove on the ridge that divides Lancefield and Kilmore. The colder than usual climate here means a lower yield of more intense flavour and higher quality.

Honey anyone? Chris Dawson, and his wife June are usually there from Kyneton. They take bees to the Murray, Riverina and Mount Buller in the appropriate season for their distinctive red gum, orange blossom and mountain honeys. They sell most of their four to six varieties of honey at local markets, including Woodend and Kyneton, as well as here. How does the cookie crumble? Most delectably, if you choose them from the **Cookie Crumbs** stall. An enterprising young couple, Luke Stevens and Amy Bodilly, of Tylden, make wonderful chocolate fig-and-hazelnut, cherry-and-orange and ginger biscuits, among other varieties, including their popular birdseed Anzacs (with dates, sunflower and pumpkin seeds). Cookie Crumbs are also available at Cliffy's in Daylesford, Bites in Woodend, and MC's in Gisborne.

Do you remember Wildings café in Hawthorn or more recently their popular restaurant in Trentham's old Cosmopolitan Hotel? Well, Chris and Anna Wilding have moved to Woodend and now are making an unusual range of specialty

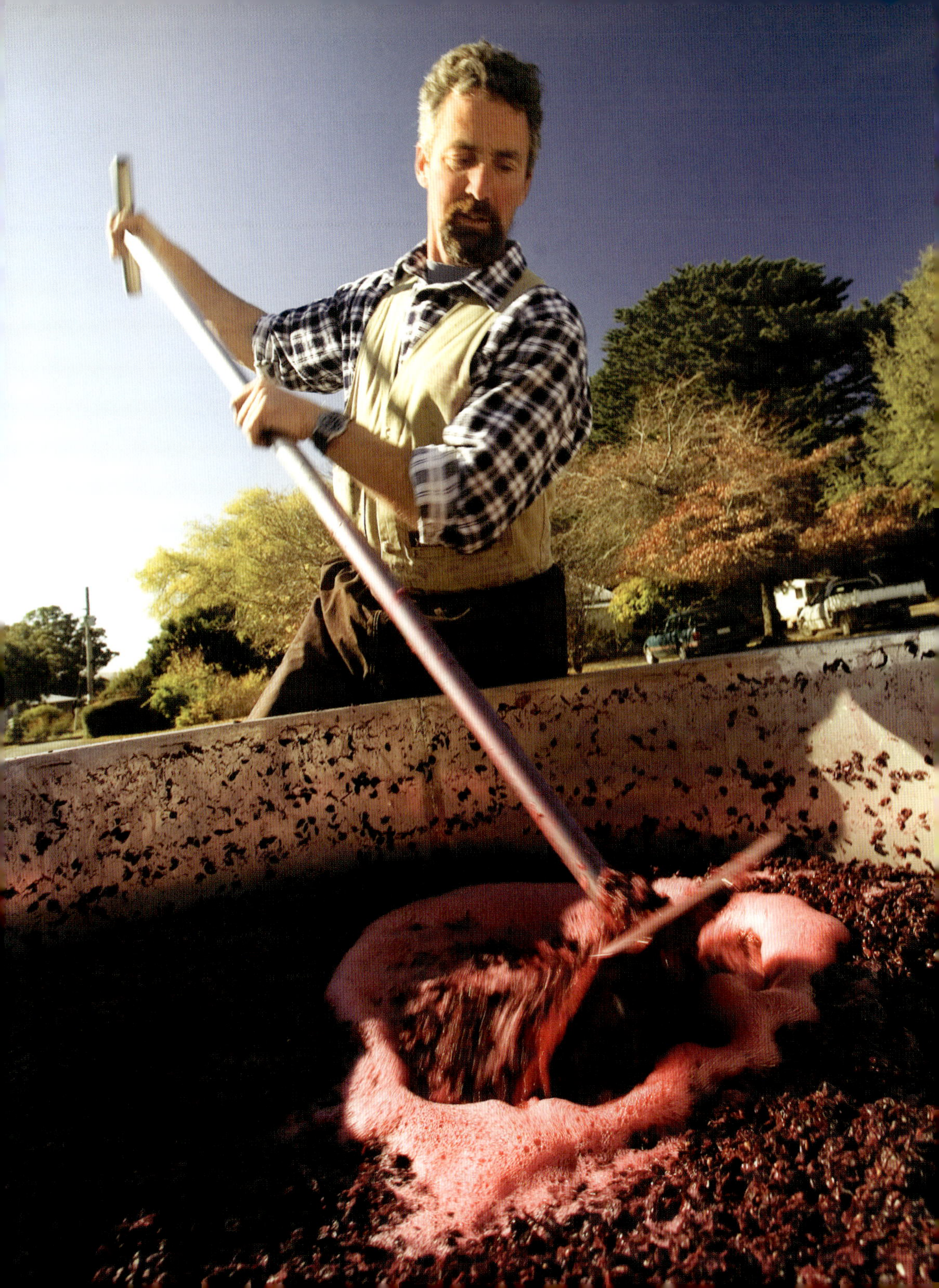

This page and opposite Lancefield and District Farmers' Market offers locally grown produce, handmade and homemade goods, pure local honey and more.

food products, such as bourbon vanilla meringues (delicious with macerated strawberries and cream), fig and balsamic paste (great with creamy blue cheese or brie), nougat and chocolate-drizzled honeycomb. Then they have such exotic spices as za'atar, chermoula and Cajun spice. Regulars at the Lancefield market, the Wildings also do catering and their products are available at about twenty-four metropolitan and country shops.

Pud for all Seasons live up to their name. At Elphinstone, Karen Kelly and Cassandra Gunter make traditional puddings for Christmas ('great-grandma's recipe') and a splendid double-chocolate, orange and Cointreau creation for Easter, as well as special puds for Mother's Day and Father's Day, with a sauce to go with each. And their little chocolate-coated 'pud balls' always score a goal. Also often represented at the market, from north of the Macedon region, are **Michel's Fine Biscuits** of Castlemaine. Michel Mussett has won remarkable acclaim (and export orders) since she expanded her boutique range from fruit mince pies and hazelnut shortbread to twenty-five varieties of superb sweet and savoury biscuits.

When it comes to jams, chutneys and sauces, there's plenty to choose from at the market. Former oil-rig worker Don Turner from Heathcote will be showing off his It's Treats range, all made without preservatives or colourings. Olive Branch Preserves of Taradale catch the eye with their quirky labels like Trampy Tomato Relish (it goes with everything), Shimmering Shiraz Jelly (sweetly made from local fruit) and Devilish Date and Lime Chutney (the devil is in the chilli detail).

Say cheese. Although located just north of the region, Carla Meurs or Ann-Marie Monda are usually at the market with their Holy Goat organic chèvre range, which they handmake with milk from their well cared for goat herd using traditional French soft curd processes. The different styles range from fresh to aged, and from creamy fromage frais to ash-coated, natural rind cheeses, each with its distinct flavour and texture.

The **Kyneton Olive Oil** story begins in 1954 when Felice Trovatello arrived in Australia with one suitcase and few words of English. A visit to central Victoria reminded him of Calabria and inspired him to plant an olive grove 20 kilometres east of Kyneton towards Heathcote. The family business has grown, collecting numerous awards for its Gourmet Blend, Family Selection and infused virgin olive oils, Nonna's olives and tapanade. They have regular 'open weekends'. **Macedon Grove Olives** is a much younger and more specialised concern. Chris and Julie Green have a small grove near Gisborne of 700 trees, all cultivated organically, and concentrate on bottling handpicked table olives.

Cherries are my favourite fruit and if we didn't grow our own at Glenlyon chances are that we'd be heading off to **Mount Gisborne Cherries** during the season. Their cherry orchard is planted with twenty-two varieties that ripen progressively on these cool mountain slopes over six to eight weeks from mid-December to the end of January. They are open daily for farm-gate sales during this period, except on extremely hot days. Take the Sunbury/South Gisborne exit from the Calder Freeway and head west about 4.5 kilometres.

As well as organically grown blueberries, the farm boasts hazelnuts, heritage apples, lavender and roses and a glorious labyrinth of trees

The **Woodend Berry Farm** on the road to Trentham invites visitors to pick blueberries during the summer season. American Jahne Hope-Williams, a yoga teacher and ordained minister, took it over seven years ago. As well as organically grown blueberries, the farm boasts hazelnuts, heritage apples, lavender and roses, and a glorious one-acre labyrinth of 2500 trees. Raspberries won't be ready for some years. After the picking season, the farm shop is open on Sundays (look for the roadside sign) to sell frozen berries, jams and lavender products. In late 2005, the farm's first vintage of blueberry wine, made at The Swillery near Redesdale, went on sale.

Maloa Gourmet Delights in Woodend's shopping strip is both a congenial daytime café and gourmet provedore, offering such regional produce as Macedon olives, Beatties Shortbread and cheese biscuits, goodies from

Wildings and Puds for All Seasons, and Annie Smithers Jams. Owner Denise Grantham has also recently acquired Marian's Kitchen and is now making and selling its range of tangy pickles, relishes and chutneys.

Kyneton is the shopfront home of **Emelia's Piquant Sauces**, which now enjoy distribution from Tasmania to North Queensland, and have won many prizes, especially for their pickled onions. Undaunted by bankruptcy resulting from the collapse of their quarry business, feisty Emelia Prendergast and her husband regained pride and prosperity with something totally different. All her sauces, made on the premises and distinguished by a red chilli in every jar, are perfect for stir-fries and barbecues. Her favourite Sweet Serendipity Sauce contains local honey, raspberries, garlic and onion among other ingredients.

Wineries

When the esteemed wine writer, consultant and show judge James Halliday published his comprehensive Australian Wine Compendium in 1985, he could list only six wineries in the Macedon region, including Sunbury. They were Cope-Williams, Craiglee, Flynn and Williams, Goona Warra, Knight's Granite Hills and Virgin Hills. Four of these are still open to visitors. Now there are about sixty vignerons in the Macedon-Daylesford region, with about ten of those near Daylesford (see page 00) and about twenty in the Sunbury area.

Sunbury District

Craiglee, renowned for its great cool-climate shiraz and admirable chardonnay, can trace its history to 1864, when James Johnston, member of Parliament and a founder of the *Argus* newspaper, planted a variety of vines on 16 acres (around 6.5 hectares) and won awards in Europe with his wines. The last vintage of the Johnston era was made in 1927 and all the vines were pulled out in the 1940s. The Carmody farming family bought the land in 1961 and were persuaded to diversify into growing grapes in 1976. The Carmodys, who planted shiraz, chardonnay, cabernet and sauvignon blanc, pioneered the sustained revival of viticulture in the Sunbury area. Patrick Carmody is now concentrating on his carefully tended, slow-ripening shiraz, his aim being to 'grow clean fruit and make wine that will give people pleasure up to twelve years later'. On most Sundays or by appointment, he will welcome visitors to the original bluestone winery built to last in 1868.

Across the road is another historic property, **Goona Warra**, founded in 1858 by James Goodall Francis, who later became premier of Victoria. The vineyard produced wines until the early 1900s and fell into neglect until Melbourne

Right
Well-established vines at Craiglee winery in the Sunbury district.

Far right
Cope-Williams Winery, near Romsey.

Opposite
The Great Hall at Goona Warra, Sunbury.

lawyer John Barnier and his architect wife Elizabeth bought the property in 1982. John has replanted a wide variety of vines, both here and on nearby land leased from the local water authority. His wines, most notably pinot noir, cabernet franc, chardonnay and semillon/sauvignon blanc are made now on the Victoria University of Technology's Sunbury campus.

A lingering Sunday lunch in the **Great Hall of Goona Warra** – the restored original bluestone winery built into a hillside of this historic vineyard first planted in 1863 – has long been an institution, but changes were afoot as we went to press. John and Elizabeth Barnier were planning to build a larger café, opening out to a garden terrace, and tasting room out from the Great Hall's upper level, to cater for more guests more days of the week.

Wildwood is more than a hobby for plastic surgeon Wayne Stott, who grew up on a neighbouring hill property. He returned here in 1983 and progressively planted almost 13 hectares of chardonnay, pinot noir, cabernet sauvignon, cabernet franc, shiraz and petit verdot. Having taken a wine science degree, he has increasingly taken charge of the winemaking on the estate.

For a pleasant lunch away from the crowds, and with a marvellous panoramic view of the distant city skyline and Port Phillip Bay on clear days, Wildwood is perfect. This small vineyard has a charming little café and sheltered terrace with a wood-fired oven, and from late 2005 will open five days a week to serve simple meals like gourmet pizzas from the oven, house-made gnocchi with veal shank ragu, and bullboar sausages to enjoy with a glass or two of the estate's own wines.

Another winery restaurant with a glorious view, but on a larger scale, is **Estelle's** at the Andraos brothers' **Olde Winilba vineyard**. On the foundations of an abandoned 1860s hillside winery high above Sunbury, the Lebanese brothers have built an impressive new bluestone winery, cellars and tasting room with a restaurant above. Here we found another familiar face from the past, that of Joseph, the white-haired former maître d' at the Hilton's Cliveden Room. At Estelle's (named for Sam Andraos' teenage daughter) the big seller is

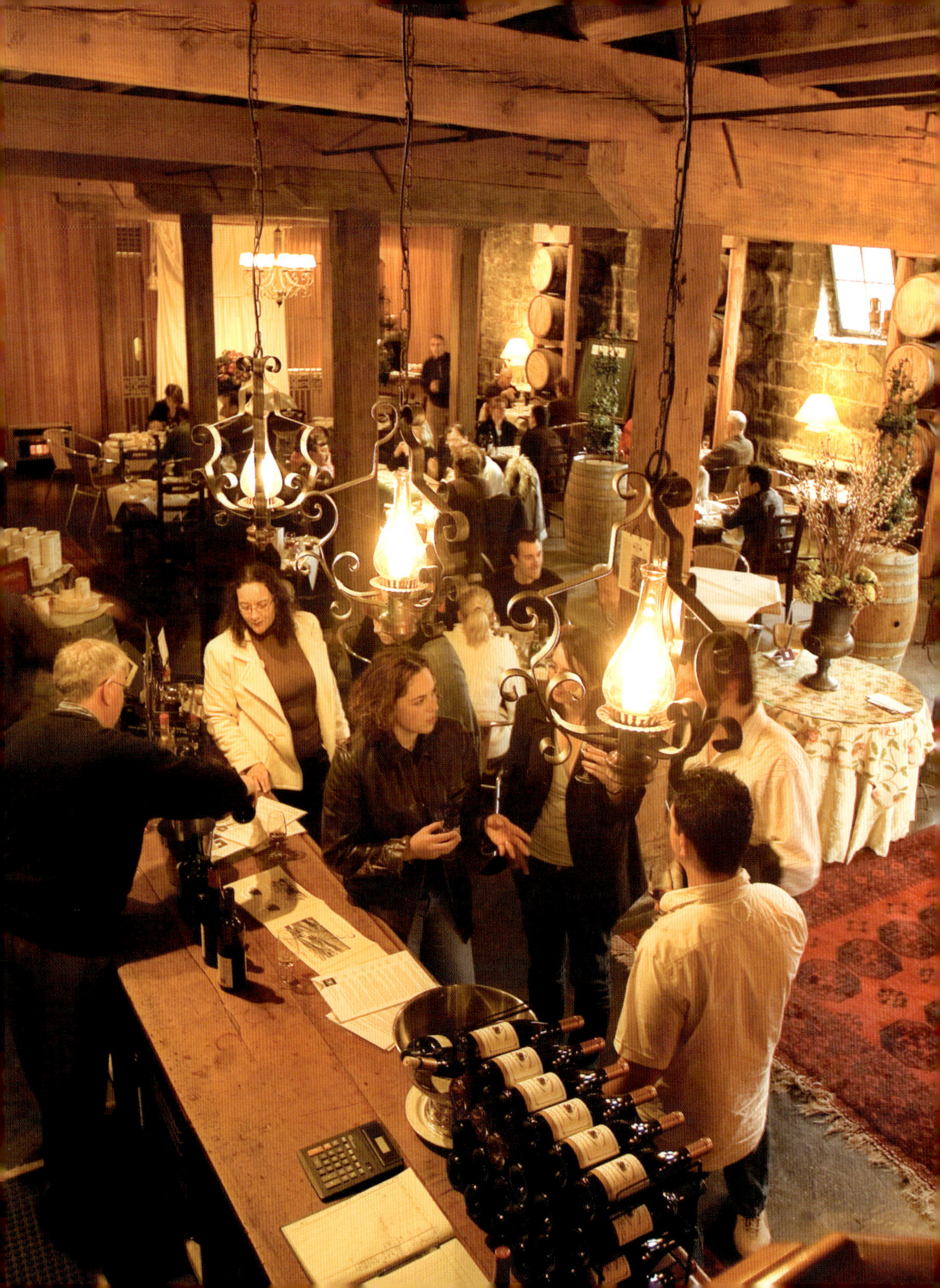

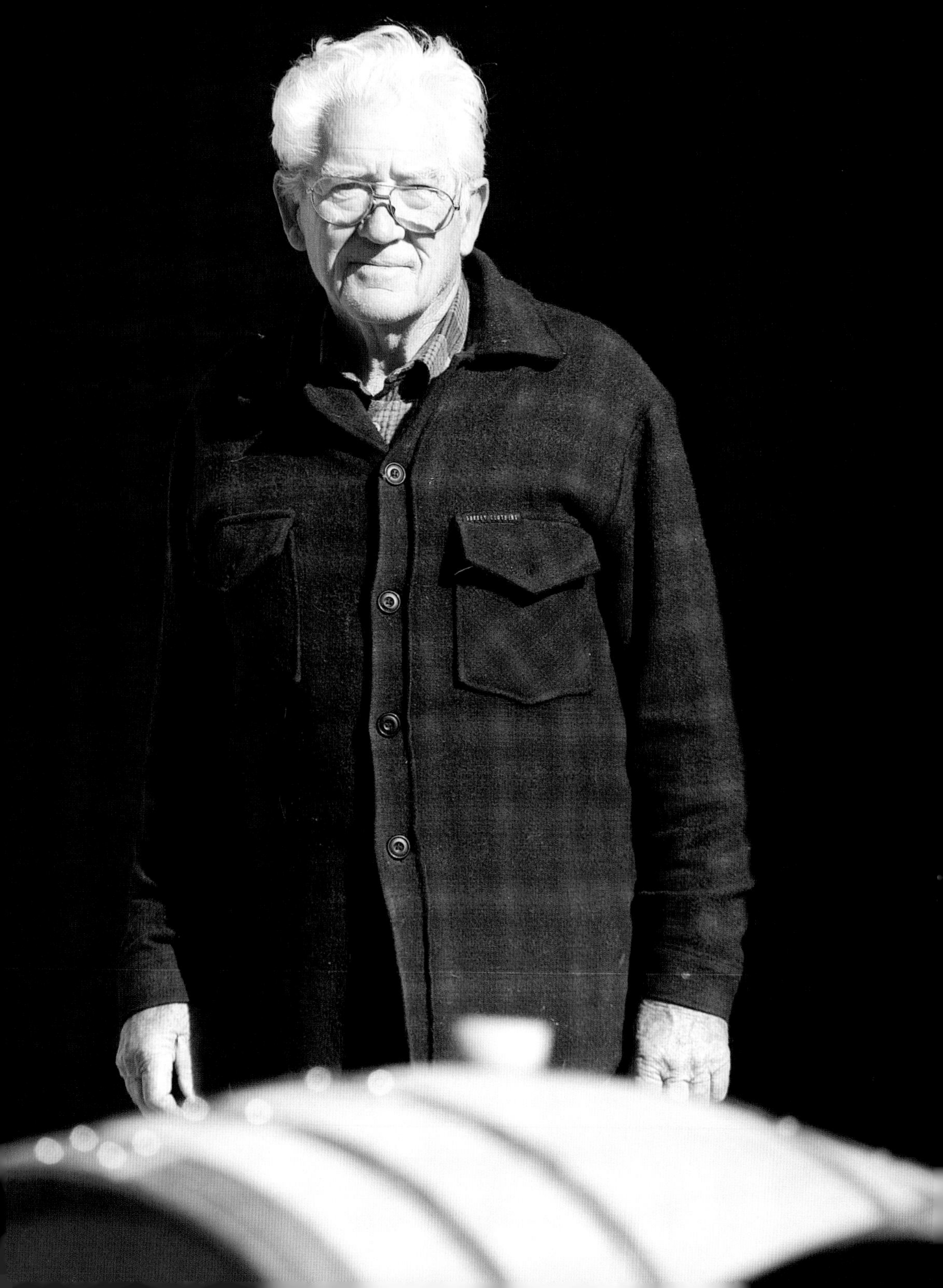

Opposite
Gordon Knight, of the family winery Knight Granite Hills.

the Andraos steak, which goes perfectly with their trophy-winning '98 shiraz and the spectacular view.

The Sunbury region's two biggest winery restaurants are to be found on and just off the Melton Highway at Rockbank. Both are owned by Italian families with a construction and property background who have invested heavily in establishing local vineyards. Melburnians who remember Avanti restaurant in Carlton will find its former owner, Joseph Brancaleone, as the genial host of the new **Avanti** at **Witchmount**, the restaurant in the towered bluestone building that forms part of the Ramunno family's winery complex. At weekends, the place is buzzing with large parties, family groups and couples tucking into such favourites as Waygu ragu gnocchi and saltimbocca alla Romana finished with chardonnay and sage sauce. Round the corner, directly on the highway, is the expansive **Galli Estate** with its huge vaulted-roof restaurant, complete with massive fireplace between the tasting counter and large dining area. Here the menu is traditional Italian with a liberal use of the estate wines.

Halfway between Sunbury and Riddells Creek is **Longview Creek**, a seventeen-year-old vineyard of white and red varietals that Bill and Karen Ashbury took over in 2003. At weekends Karen offers 'tasting platters', using produce from their own property and the region, or coffee with her homemade cakes.

Gisborne

Only one vineyard is always open to the public in the Gisborne region. For easier recognition Bob and Barbara Nixon changed the name of their Mawarra Estate to **Gisborne Peak Wines**. Bob's first planting in 1978 of sylvaner riesling proved unsatisfactory, but against the odds his trial with a batch of semillon cuttings has resulted in a fine wine that's refreshing to drink now but worth cellaring for up to ten years. The Nixons also grow chardonnay, pinot noir and a little shiraz; John Ellis makes their range of wines, which now also includes a slighter sweeter Allegro Semillon, a Duet 80/20 chardonnay/semillon blend, and a rosé to come. Barbara offers visitors to this picturesque property cheese platters on weekdays and pizzas from the wood-fired oven at weekends.

Veteran vigneron Stuart Anderson, now semi-retired near Gisborne, has three top-class properties under his wing as winemaker or mentor. James Halliday has declared **Bindi** of Gisborne one of Victoria's icons of small-production, high-priced chardonnay and pinot noir vintages. Under Anderson's tutelage, owner Michael Dhillon is increasingly taking over responsibility for the winemaking. At **Mount Gisborne Wines**, retired Canadian academic David Ell

Opposite top
Cobaw Ridge owner Alan Cooper.

Opposite below
The cellar door at Cobaw Ridge.

grows and makes, under Anderson's guidance, chardonnay and pinot noir. **Epis** and **Epis & Williams** are separate brands from different vineyards, both owned by Essendon football hero Alec Epis for whom Anderson makes the wines. Their chardonnay and pinot noir are grown in two favourably sited vineyards on the western slopes of Mt Macedon; their cabernet sauvignon (soon to be augmented by some merlot) comes from vines planted thirty years ago near Kyneton by Macedon-region pioneer Laurie Williams (of **Flynn & Williams**).

Macedon and Kyneton District

Four generations of the Knight family had been grazing cattle and sheep near Baynton before Gordon Knight switched to viticulture in 1970, at first selling grapes to Virgin Hills. His son Llew is now in charge of all aspects of one of Victoria's most successful small family wineries, **Knight Granite Hills**, winning numerous Australian and international awards. Granite Hills is, unusually for this region, an outstanding exponent of cool-climate riesling, the cooler nights in these hills facilitating good acid retention and slower ripening. Shiraz of great balance and structure is the estate's other icon. 'Our aim is always to make the best wine we can possibly make,' says Knight, and that includes a highly esteemed chardonnay. He also grows and makes cabernet sauvignon, pinot noir and merlot, plus a sparkling wine (60/40 chardonnay/pinot) that is sent to Petaluma for tirage and disgorging. Some of his premium wines are exported to Britain and the US; cellar-door (open daily) accounts for about 10 per cent of sales.

In the same spectacular granite highlands as Knight, but more secluded, self-proclaimed purists Alan and Nelly Cooper lovingly tend their vines and craft their wines of individual character and style with minimal interference at **Cobaw Ridge**. They bought their property in 1982, built a mud-brick house and planted their first vines in 1985. In 1994 they were inspired to cut down their cabernet sauvignon vines and graft lagrein, a variety from the Alto Adige region of alpine north-east Italy (formerly Austrian South Tyrol). Cobaw Ridge Lagrein, an impressive full-bodied wine, is highly sought after in its distinctive tall bottles. The Coopers also have a Rhone-style blend with a difference: a spicy shiraz with a touch of viognier for fragrance and lift, as well as chardonnay and pinot noir. They're open daily for cellar-door sales. Alan Cooper also makes the highly esteemed pinot noir for the owners of the small Patrick's Vineyard on the southern slopes of the Cobaw Ranges, where an 1862 cottage stands as a reminder of early settlement.

Also near Kyneton are some smaller players. **Candlebark Hill**, near Kyneton, established by David Forster in 1987, produces small quantities of pinot noir,

Five great regional wines

- Macedon NV Brut Cuvee (Hanging Rock): a richer, fuller, more mature sparkling wine than most of its Australian competitors

- Knight Granite Hills Riesling: an elegant but full-flavoured wine

- Bindi Chardonnay: an iconic chardonnay of immense power and lingering complexity

- Curly Flat Pinot Noir: an outstanding, complex, well-rounded wine

- Craiglee Shiraz: acclaimed as one of the finest examples of an Australian cool-climate shiraz

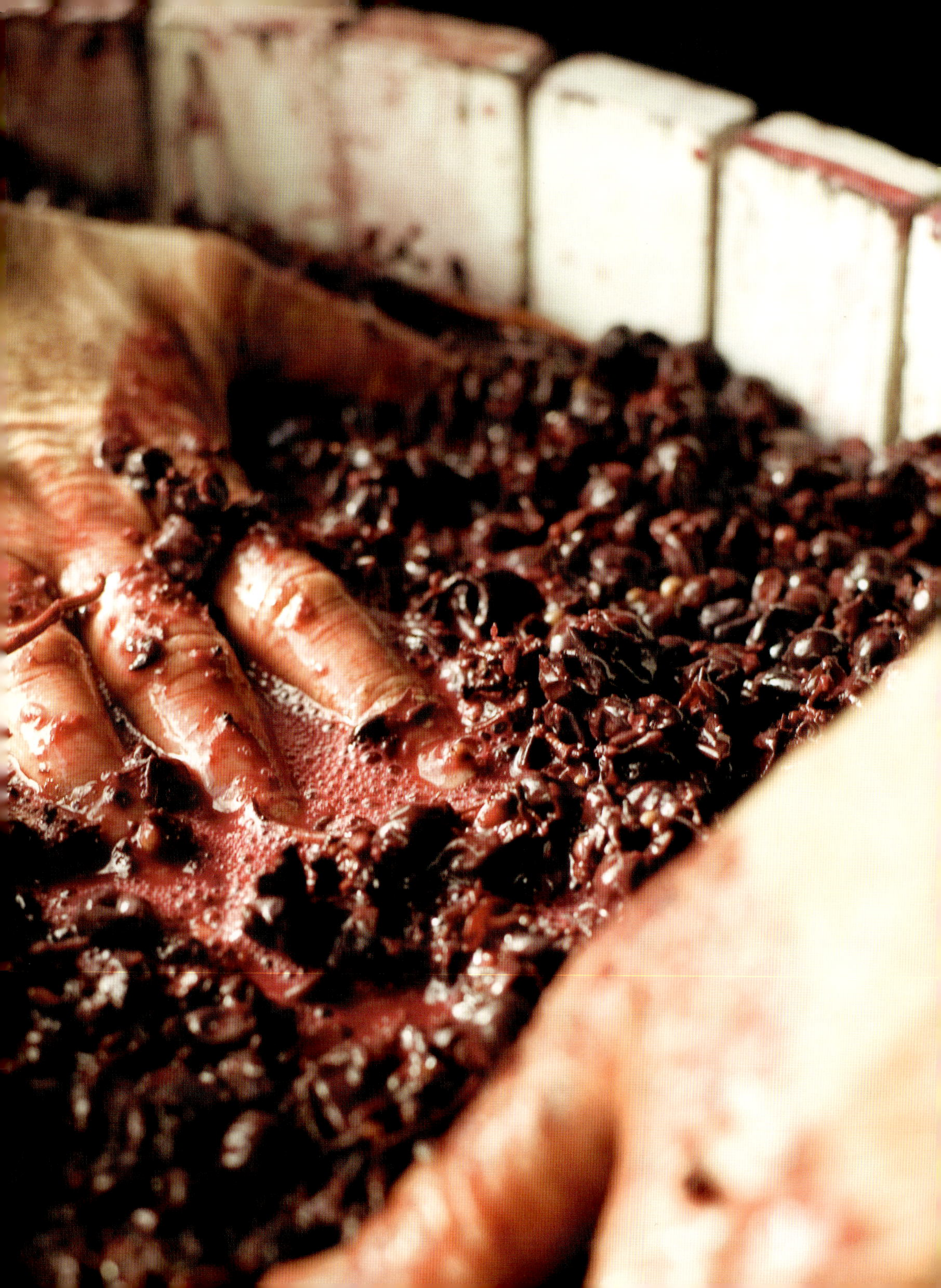

the Bordeaux reds and chardonnay. Llew Knight is consultant winemaker. (Open Sundays). **Kyneton Ridge Estate**, grows mostly top-quality pinot noir on its glorious 40-hectare site, which includes B&B accommodation and a function room. The vineyard is owned by John Boucher, a descendant of three generations of winemakers, and his wife Pauline Russell. (Open weekends).

North of Mt Macedon, and within a marvellous view of its legendary namesake, is **Hanging Rock Winery**, the region's biggest producer and winemaker for a number of smaller growers. (See the profile on John Elllis p. 183.)

High on the side of the mountain is **Mt Macedon Winery**, a small family concern that has estate-grown chardonnay, pinot noir, cabernet merlot, shiraz and sparkling wine. (Open daily). West of Woodend are two small wineries. John Ellis makes the small quantities of pinot noir grown by Barry Elliott, an orthopaedic surgeon, at **Chanters Ridge**. His wine is available at the Tylden general store. Chris Cormack is another small pinot noir specialist at **Pegeric** (the name honours his parents, Peg and Eric) with the help of Llew Knight.

Since he planted his first grapes near Romsey in 1977, former English architect Gordon Cope-Williams has developed his **Coniston** estate into a winery complex that embraces an indoor royal tennis court (the game played by Henry VIII at Hampton Court when he wasn't swapping wives), a cricket oval that's the Victorian home to the Lord's Taverners, villa accommodation and banquet rooms. David Cowburn has taken over the winery, which has the region's only facilities for making sparkling wines. The Cope-Williams range includes the esteemed ROMSEY vintage and non-vintage bruts, a new sparkling rosé, chardonnay and pinot noir.

Lancefield area

Further north on either side of Lancefield, are the **Glen Erin** and **Cleveland** estates, both now run predominantly as conference and leisure centres in a vineyard setting. Although perhaps more noteworthy for their accommodation and dining facilities than for their wines, David Cowburn makes a good sparkling wine (Macedon Brut), pinot noir and pinot gris for Cleveland.

The Grange Restaurant at Glen Erin is in an extension of the 1860s homestead, looking out on a sunny terrace and rows of vine beyond. Chef Nigel Stainwell has a flair for Mediterranean, Asian and Australian fusion cuisine, supported by a regionally focussed wine list. Cleveland has been taken over by the Grange Group of Conference Centres, but the restaurant in the former stables of the picturesque 1889 homestead is still open for weekend lunch. The splendid dining room of the homestead is only for houseguests and receptions.

Rochford winery has undergone a change of ownership, and is not open to visitors; at time of writing its high-quality pinot noir grapes were being sent to be made at the associated Eyton winery in the Yarra Valley. On the northern slopes of Rochford Hill, **Braewattie** is a small vineyard owned by Des Ryan and his wife Maggi. They grow chardonnay and pinot noir; these, and a fine sparkling wine, are made by contract. **MorganField Vineyard** is a newcomer near Lancefield with 4 hectares of premium chardonnay, pinot noir and cabernet sauvignon. Mark and Gina Morgan welcome visitors to their cellar door for tastings and gourmet platters at weekends.

North-east of Lancefield, **Portree** is open at weekends; in warmer weather visitors may relax in the sheltered courtyard to try Ken Murchison's highly rated chardonnay, pinot noir and blanc de blanc sparkling wine. He also offers his Damask (a crisp rosé) and Quarry Red (a Loire-style blend of cabernet franc and merlot). Nearby is **Mt William**, where the Cousins family grow pinot noir, chardonnay, cabernet franc and merlot. Their 1999 blanc de blanc sparkling wine, made by John Ellis, won a trophy at the Macedon wine show. Light snacks are available at weekends in the lovely gardens or in the intimate tasting room.

Right and opposite
Cleveland Estate provides luxury accommodation and dining in a vineyard setting.

The restaurant in the former stables of the picturesque 1889 homestead is open for weekend lunches

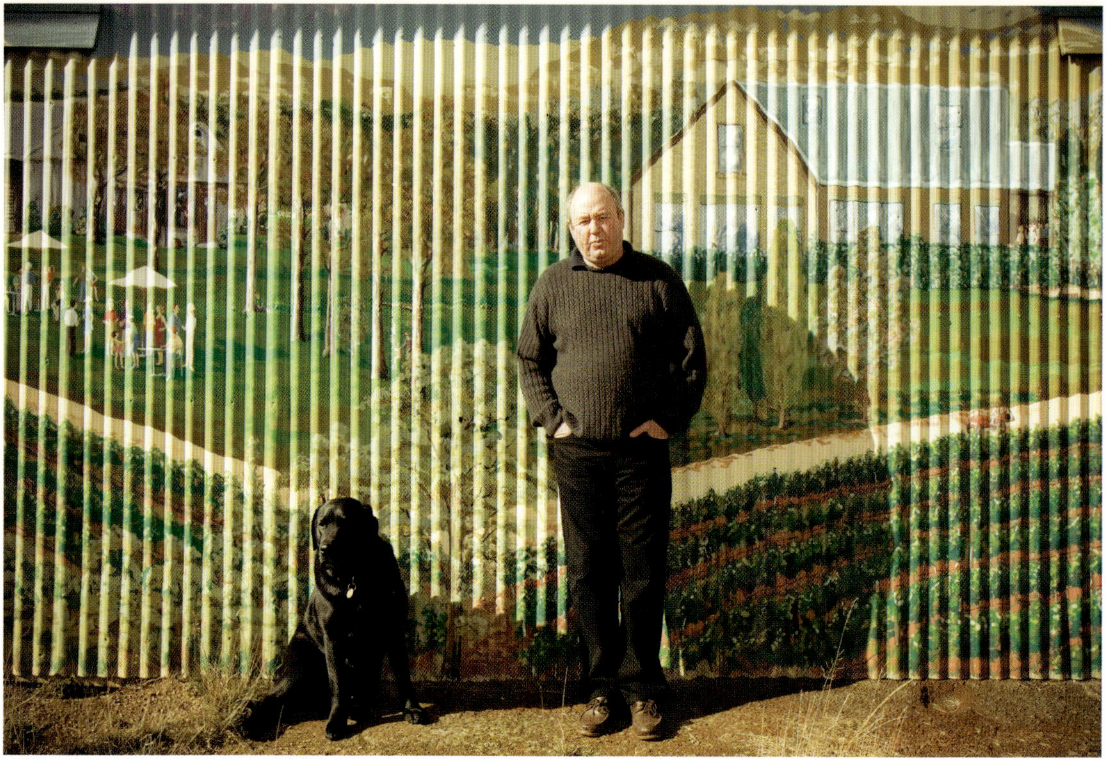

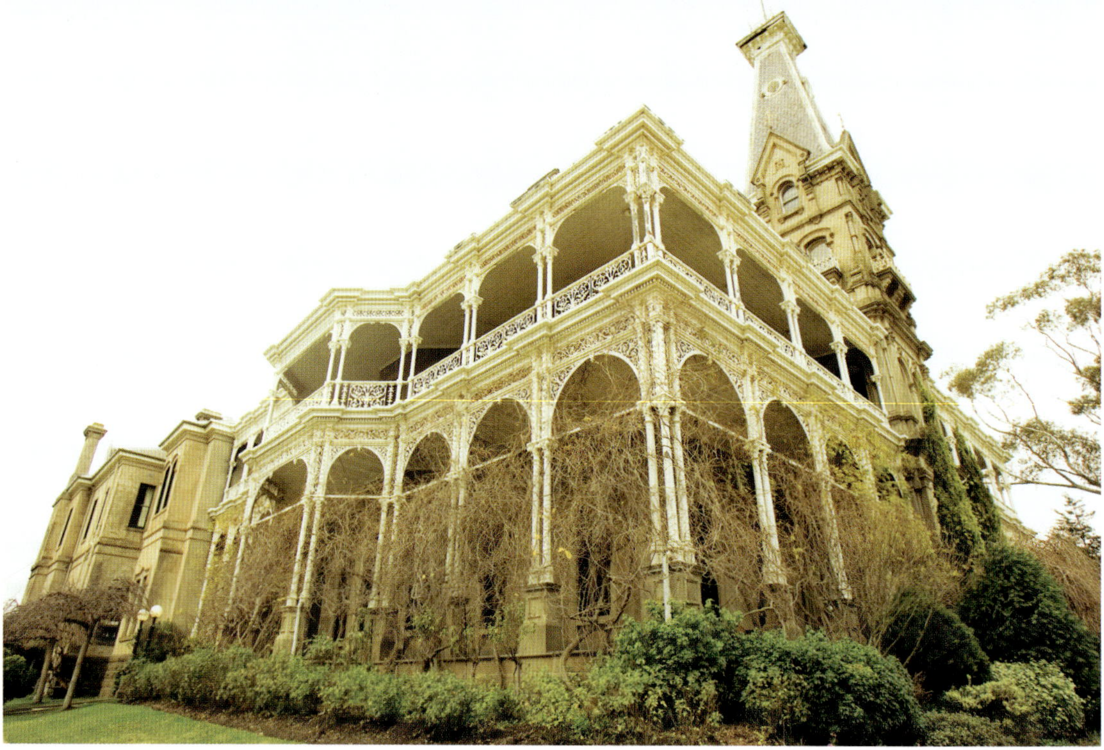

Eating out

Sunbury to Macedon

At Sunbury, **Rupertswood** – former family seat of Australia's first family of baronets, the Clarkes – was one of Australia's grandest private mansions and is known as 'the birthplace of the Ashes'. Restored to its 1874 glory, it is now open for private banquets in high Victorian style. Its imposing bluestone gatehouse of 1875 has also opened as the **Gatehouse Café**, serving inexpensive lunches Wednesday to Sunday, and scones with jam from the estate's own strawberries, in an old-world setting with period artworks. The manager of both properties, Domenic Romeo, is a keen supporter of regional produce and wines.

Nearby is **Café Adagio**, once a doctor's surgery in a 1930s house, which has been transformed by Judith Watson into a bright, inviting café and art gallery. It's an attractive spot for coffee and cake or good-value lunches Monday to Friday, and may open for dinner on Friday and Saturday nights.

It's worth the diversion to Gisborne to visit **The Deli**, which dares to be different by bringing in regional and imported gourmet foodstuffs that you would not normally find in a small country town. Craig Carnell and Tim Buzza are passionate foodies, and justifiably proud of the Illy caffe lattes and French hot chocolates they serve in new double-wall Bodum glasses (they don't burn your fingers!). Locals love the communal table in the café section where they can drop in to meet friends.

Just as exciting for Macedon village is the designer-chic new **Sitka Foodstore and Café**, where Clare Jeffries draws on her experience at Peter Rowland Catering and The Essential Ingredient to offer weekend breakfasts and lunch, plus coffee and cake Wednesday to Sunday, on tables handcrafted from local timber. She also stocks an impressive range of produce and wines from the Daylesford and Macedon regions among other deli items.

Woodend

Formerly Richard and Jeanne Pratt's corporate country retreat, **Campaspe House** in Woodend is a gracious, English-style 1920s mansion in secluded gardens designed by Edna Walling, against a bushland background. It's now a weekday executive conference centre and weekend leisure retreat and an elegant weekend restaurant that opens to a garden terrace. Owner Milton Collins and chef Brad Lobb (ex-Warrenmang and also Frangos and Frangos), are staunch promoters of regional produce and wines, and present them in such fine style. Expect such individually crafted dishes as pancetta-wrapped Tuki trout with Trentham potato puffs or seared Kyneton beef with an organic Nicola potato and rosemary cake.

Opposite top
Ken Murchison from Portree Wines.

Opposite below
The magnificent mansion Rupertswood at Sunbury.

Slow braise of capretto

Brad Lobb, Campaspe House, Woodend

1 baby goat (about 5 kg before boning), cut into 2 cm cubes (ask your butcher)
2 brown onions
3 large ripe tomatoes
½ cup continental parsley
250 g risoni pasta
100 g chopped Istra pancetta
2 tbsp thyme
1 tbsp finely chopped rosemary
salt and pepper
8 cloves garlic, crushed
1 cup Kyneton extra virgin olive oil
1 bottle Hanging Rock white wine
200 ml chicken stock
100 g parmesan
200 g ciabatta breadcrumbs, roughly chopped
extra parsley to serve

Place the goat pieces into a shallow baking dish.

Rough chop onions, tomatoes and parsley.

Scatter the onion, tomato, risoni, pancetta, thyme, rosemary and parsley on top of the meat and season with salt and pepper.

Add the garlic, then drizzle the meat with olive oil and almost cover the meat with the wine and chicken stock.

Sprinkle with coarsely grated parmesan and breadcrumbs. Bake, uncovered, in a moderate (180ºC) oven for 1½ hours or until tender, occasionally basting the meat with its own juices.

Serve with all the juices and extra chopped parsley on top.

Serves 6

Above
Holgate Bar and Restaurant in Woodend serves its own handcrafted beers.

Opposite above
Sequoia in Woodend serves modern Italian fare.

Opposite bottom
Brad Lobb, Chef at Woodend's Campaspe House.

Smart casual **Sequoia** is a stylish newcomer that looks as if it would be more at home in fashionable South Yarra. Much-travelled chef Damian Sandercock uses as much regional produce as possible for his flavour-driven modern Italian fare that includes an ever-changing $55 five-course dégustation menu.
The lunch specials of two courses and a glass of wine for $22 are a bargain; even the a-la-carte lunch list offers excellent value. Check the shelves for such hard-to-find regional wines as Bindi and Patrick's Vineyard pinot noir, and Cobaw Ridge Lagrein.

If classic beer is your preferred beverage, then drop in to Woodend's **Holgate Bar and Restaurant** in the historic **Keatings Hotel**, where Paul and Natasha Holgate serve, along with superior pub grub, full malt ales and lagers handcrafted by traditional natural methods in their own brewhouse. Some are available only on tap here; others are widely available in the region and in Melbourne in liquor stores, bars and restaurants. For casual, café-style breakfast and lunch, or good coffee and cake, **Café Colenso** in the town's old bakehouse has a loyal local following. It's cosy inside and sunny on the deck beside the old wood-fired oven. **Schatzi's** ('sweetheart's') is a cosy little shopfront café with a heart-shaped logo and nostalgic Austrian dishes. Maureen Wilson's **Not Just Fudge Café** is a popular spot for morning and afternoon tea, plus a choice of thirty-five tantalising varieties of handmade fudge.

Malmsbury

A popular pitstop on the Calder Highway, the quaint old **Malmsbury Bakery**, in Malmsbury, is renowned for its pies, cakes and bread. At time of writing, its enterprising owner, Jan Grant, was planning to open the Malmsbury Provedore in a restored 1860s bakery as a showcase for produce grown and produced along the 'Calder corridor' as far as Mildura. She had already signed up about forty producers.

Annie Smithers

Kyneton should be so lucky. So should Annie Smithers. Kyneton again has a restaurant of note, not too uppity but a lovely little bistrot with a provincial French accent. And Smithers again has a place of her own in the country, cooking what she most loves to cook, and making preserves from local fruit. She has been cooking professionally, mostly for others, for twenty-one years. Versatile celebrity chef Iain Hewitson taught her to be innovative. 'Hewie's recipes were always ahead of their time. Something of his creativity has always stayed with me,' she says. From trendsetting Stephanie Alexander she learnt regard for good, seasonal ingredients and the integrity with which she prepared them. As head chef at Lake House under the exacting direction of Alla Wolf-Tasker, Smithers realised the importance of kitchen management and discipline.

There have been other gigs in the city and country, from cheffing at Kaye's on King, preparing rustic Italian-style dishes at the glorious Lavandula lavender farm, to helping out at Ballarat's top café, L'Espresso, and turning out pizzas at the Malmsbury bakery. She even slaved as a labourer for a landscape gardener for money to realise an ambitious dream of offering classic, fixed-price dinners in a romantic, old-world setting for just a few guests at a time. Her Linton House in Daylesford won critical acclaim but it wasn't viable. A subsequent stint with ultra-perfectionist Geoff Lindsay at restaurant-of-the-year Pearl left her 'shattered'.

Now she has found her niche. Making jams and jellies from fresh, seasonal fruit of the region with partner Mim Beaumont, a trained horticulturalist and Angus cattle grazier, was to be her principal business. (Try the naughtily named Bordello jelly, made with rosehips, hawthorn berries and French crab apples.) But she missed cooking and seized an opportunity to open her new **Annie Smithers Bistrot** in an 1850s building on Kyneton's historic Piper Street. French-inspired cooking may not be the latest gastronomic fad among city sophisticates, but it suits her preferred style and, she believes, the community and region of which has chosen to be part.

Not haute cuisine, not expensive, but food 'recognisable by people who are not foodies, yet requiring a degree of technical skill that distinguishes it from home cooking'. It might be a perfect béarnaise and Nicola pommes frites with the grilled porterhouse or a fine beurre blanc with the fish. Rather than use pre-cut and packaged portions, she prefers to buy 'the whole beast', be it a duck or an Angus carcases from her partner's property. This could mean duck-breast crepe with cherry jelly, confit of duck leg, and duck-neck sausages. Her beef stews are proving as popular as her steaks.

Opposite
Anne Smithers' Bistrot in Kyneton's historic Piper Street.

Double baked 'holy goat' cheese souffle

Annie Smithers,
Annie Smithers Bistrot, Kyneton

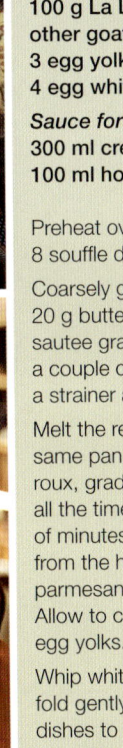

3 zucchini
80 g butter
60 g flour
350 ml milk
1 tbsp cream
1 tbsp parmesan
100 g La Luna or other goat's cheese
3 egg yolks
4 egg whites

Sauce for re-heating
300 ml cream, mixed with
100 ml homemade tomato sauce

Preheat oven to 190°C. Butter 8 souffle dishes.

Coarsely grate zucchini, melt 20 g butter in a frying pan and sautee grated zucchini for a couple of minutes. Place into a strainer and set aside to drain.

Melt the remaining butter in the same pan, mix in flour to form a roux, gradually add milk, stirring all the time. Cook for a couple of minutes to thicken. Remove from the heat and stir in cream, parmesan and goat's cheese. Allow to cool slightly, then add egg yolks.

Whip whites to stiff peaks and fold gently into mix. Fill souffle dishes to about 1 cm below rim and bake for approximately 20 minutes. Remove from dishes.

When ready to serve, place soufflés in individual gratin dishes, pour over warmed cream and tomato mix and bake in a hot oven for ten minutes until puffy and lightly coloured. Serve immediately.

Serves 8

Right
Early morning landscape around Lancefield.

Opposite
The vines of Curly Flat vineyard, and winegrower Phillip Moraghan.

Increasingly, Annie Smithers is becoming involved in the Slow Food movement and passionate about organic farming and environmental sustainability. 'Small growers of specialised foodstuffs are doing great things, and we must encourage them to maintain quality and supply," she says. 'Respect for what comes from the land has become part of my philosophy.'

The Moraghans of Curly Flat

Great wines are grown, not made. That's a maxim that Phillip Moraghan firmly believes and that is why he prefers to be known as a grower of grapes rather than a winemaker, although he supervises – passionately, even obsessively – both aspects of the business at his and wife Jeni's **Curly Flat** vineyard. Both are dedicated to producing wines of exceptional quality – there is no room for small players in the competitive middle market – and even their second label, Williams Crossing, is a premium wine. The Moraghans were both corporate high-flyers with international connections before they were bitten by the 'burgundy bug' and searched for a cool-climate property within a 100-kilometre radius of Melbourne with the aim of producing a great pinot noir. Completing an MBA degree in Switzerland, cycling in the French countryside and tasting such wines as La Tache in the mid-1980s were turning points in Phil's choice of career change.

Moraghan found the place of his dream near Lancefield in 1989 and set about learning all he could, first about viticulture and then about winemaking, with the help of such eminent mentors as Llew Knight, Laurie Williams (both pioneer vignerons of the Macedon region) and Gary Farr, whose iconic Bannockburn pinot noir he greatly admires. He also studied viticulture in Wagga and worked in vineyards and wineries here and in the United States to gain experience. His first planting of chardonnay in 1991 was disaster: the root stocks were past their use-by date and a year later he had to rip them out. Now he and Jeni have 14 hectares planted with immaculate rows of pinot noir (65 per cent), chardonnay (30 per cent) and pinot gris (5 per cent). The first vintages were contracted out; since 2002 Phil has taken charge of winemaking in their state-of-the-art and still expanding winery.

Growing the grapes is Phil's priority; he is a firm believer in the French concept of *terroir* as the primary determinant of great wine. Here the cool climate, red soil, drainage, rainfall and aspect to the sun on the slopes are all components of that, and Phil helps those along by expensive lyre trellising, lucerne mulching, and irrigating as little as possible. Even different plots within his small vineyard produce wines with discernible differences, the best, from a rocky ridge, he has termed his 'grand cruiser'. But he is equally meticulous about the winemaking, compromising as little possible.

The Moraghans' serious investment and painstaking approach have paid off with critical acclaim, exports to the United States and Britain, and sales to mail-order clients and top restaurants. Although not listed on the tourist wine trails, they will welcome visitors and have future plans for proper cellar-door facilities and wine dinners with guest chefs such as Luke Mangan.

Why 'Curly Flat'? It's a tribute to the whimsical cartoonist Michael Leunig (to whom curly-haired Phil bears an uncanny physical resemblance) and his mythical Curly Flat with a vineyard whose workers wax eloquent about how they feel after drinking its wines.

John Ellis of Hanging Rock

Taking a break from a busy vintage within sight of the legendary Hanging Rock, trailblazing vigneron John Ellis admits that his winemaking style has been contentious, but knows that his persistence has been vindicated. The ultra-cool Macedon Ranges region is sparkling wine country and that is what drew him there after an eye-opening, career-changing visit to Champagne in France in 1981. Ten years earlier he had graduated dux of Roseworthy Agricultural College, then learnt to make white wine with John Vickery at Leo Buring, became foundation winemaker at Rosemount, and with his wife Ann – daughter of renowned Hunter Valley winemaker Murray Tyrrell – moved to Echuca to establish Tisdall Wines.

The ultra-cool Macedon Ranges region is sparkling wine country and that is what drew John Ellis of Hanging Rock Winery to the district

Opposite top
The mysterious Hanging Rock near Woodend.

Opposite below
John Ellis of Hanging Rock Vineyard.

In 1982 the couple bought a rundown grazing property, Jim Jim, on the northern slopes of Mt Macedon, planted vines and built a modern winery with the aim of producing, among other wines, a great sparkling wine. Most Australian bubblies were, and are, what Ellis calls aperitif or celebratory wines: fresh, light, fruit-driven and delicate. He wanted to make a richer, fuller, more mature wine to go with food, similar to a Krug or Bollinger. His yeasty Macedon cuvées polarised critics and customers, some regarding them as 'too big, bold and brassy'. Leading wine judge and writer James Halliday was dismissive until he tried the Macedon VIII at Hanging Rock in 2003. 'You win, Ellis' he said, admitting he never liked the style before. 'I have never tasted a better Australian sparkling wine.'

What makes the Macedon distinctive is that the base wines, pinot noir and chardonnay, are matured in old oak barrels for two years before the cuvée is put together, giving it an evolved yeastiness and nuttiness. Ellis also uses what sherry makers in Spain call the solera method. He keeps a little of each vintage, blended in a tank, adding to it each year as some is taken out. This blending of young and aged adds to each cuvée's subtle complexity and character.

Of course, there is more to Ellis and **Hanging Rock Winery** than the Macedon. His acclaimed Heathcote shiraz, some of it from a vineyard he established there with Athol Guy of The Seekers fame, is another flagship wine. Then there is super-premium Jim Jim sauvignon blanc, gewürztraminer and pinot gris, other super-premium, premium wines and lower-priced Rock range varietals and blends made with grapes from other regions. Hanging Rock now is the dominant winery of the region, also making wines for a number of smaller growers. Hanging Rock wines have won numerous trophies and gold medals.

Ellis has proved his point with his Macedon sparkling wines but he is not stubbornly single-minded. In late 2005, he is releasing a more light-hearted pink bubbly in the young celebratory style, labelled Hanging Rock Rose Brut. Then, for the sparkling wine connoisseur, there will be a re-release of the Macedon VI, which will have spent nine years on yeast lees. It will be called Macedon LD (for late disgorged). Ellis confidently believes that this seriously aged wine will set a new standard in the panoply of Australian wines.

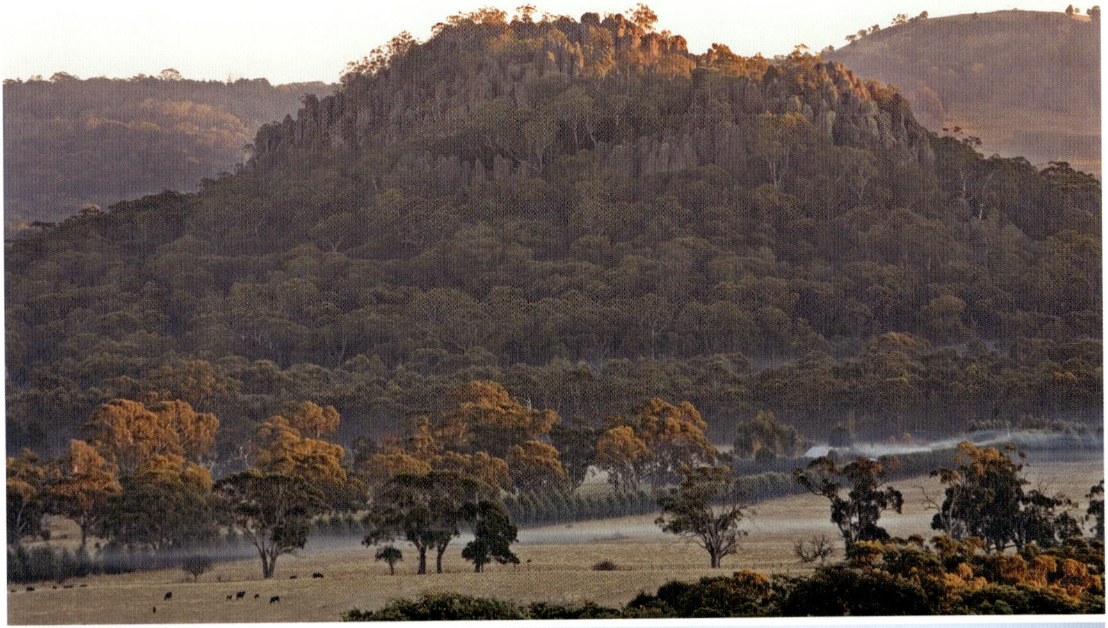

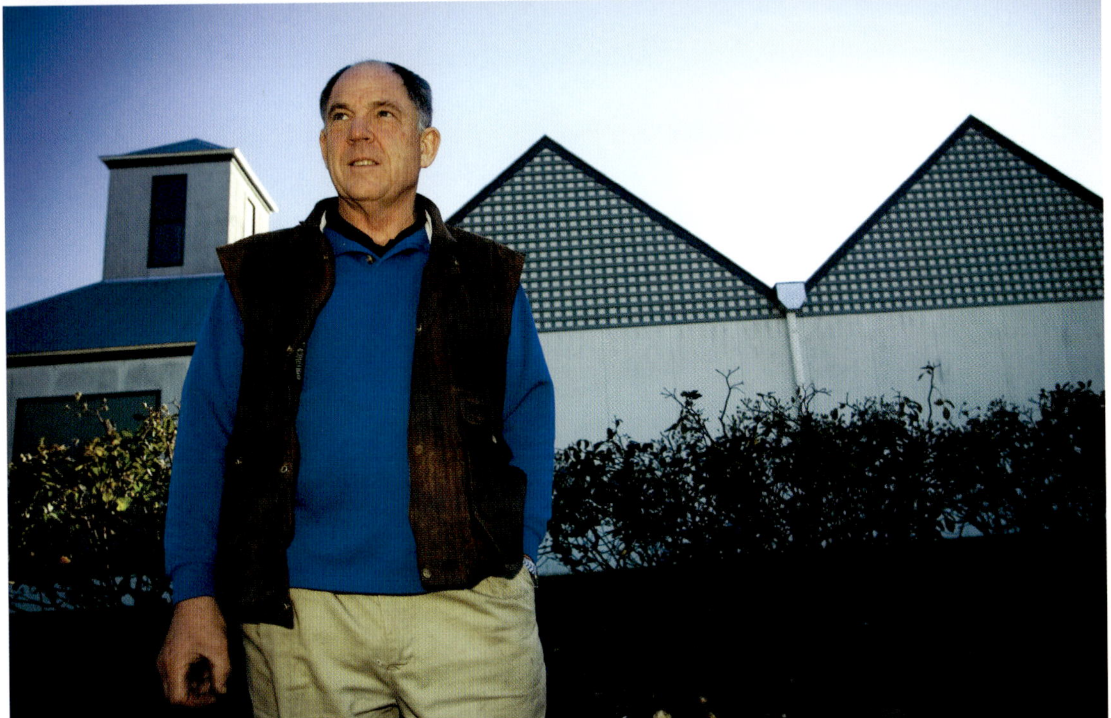

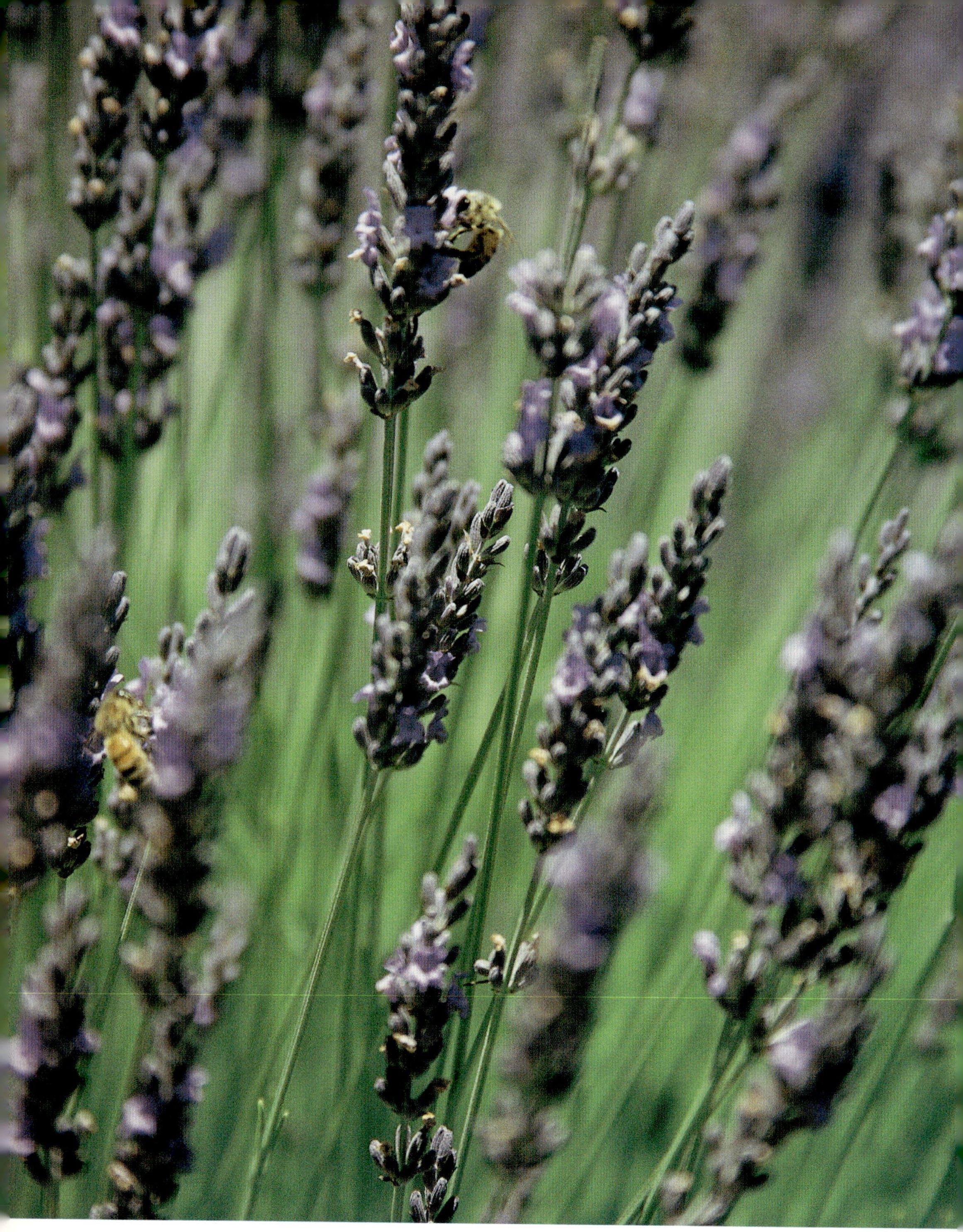

daylesford
claude forell

daylesford

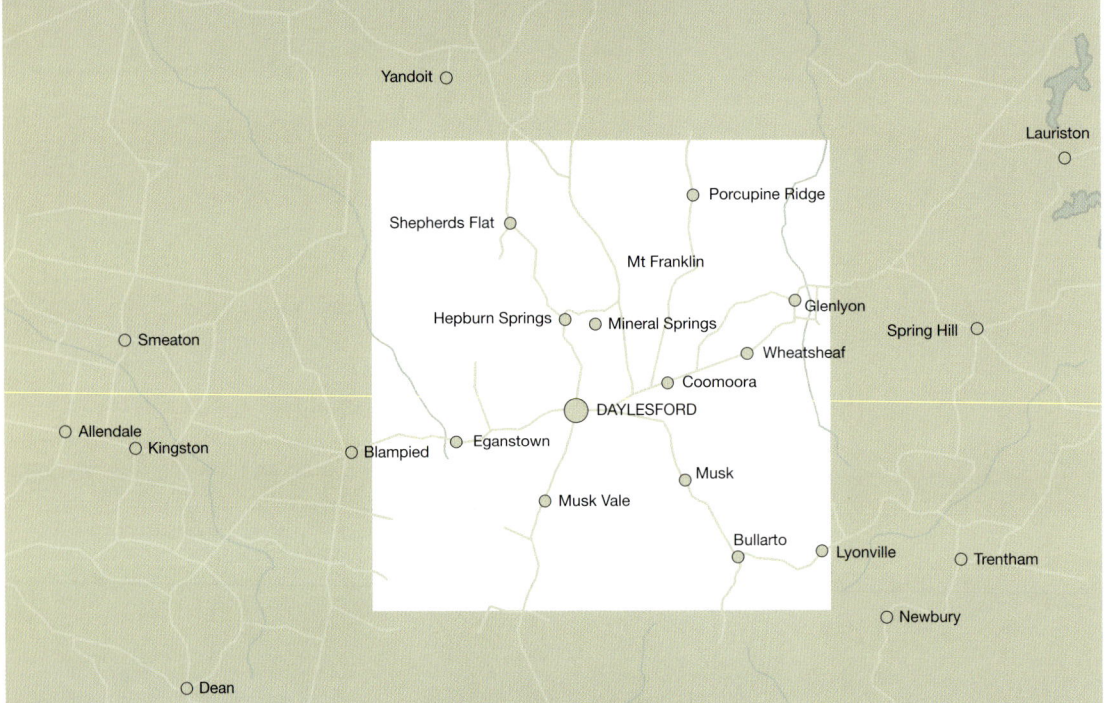

Yandoit
Lauriston
Porcupine Ridge
Shepherds Flat
Mt Franklin
Hepburn Springs   Mineral Springs
Glenlyon
Wheatsheaf   Spring Hill
Smeaton
Coomoora
DAYLESFORD
Allendale
Kingston   Blampied   Eganstown
Musk
Musk Vale
Bullarto
Lyonville   Trentham
Newbury
Dean

MELBOURNE

Critically acclaimed restaurants, cafés, good-food pubs and produce stores draw on fresh, seasonal produce from a host of specialist growers as well as offering cool-climate wines

Above
One of the stained-glass windows at The Convent in Daylesford.

Opposite
Sault restaurant, near Daylesford, is housed in a French-style building of local sandstone.

The funkiest town on Earth? Yes, a British travel writer in 2005 put Daylesford at the top of his list of the world's 'best funky towns', praising its rich cultural heritage, its bounty of good food and wine, its vibrant café and arts scenes, its mineral springs, spas and holistic therapists. In short, a place for relaxation and indulgence, with a touch of cosmopolitan style, all in a picturesque highlands setting only ninety minutes north-west of Melbourne. It wasn't always thus. Daylesford and its twin Hepburn Springs have in turn been frenzied, fashionable and forlorn until their relatively recent revival as an enchanting place in which to live or linger.

First came the squatters and timber cutters who, in the 1830s and 40s, displaced the Djadja Wurrung people of the Loddon Valley. Then in the 1850s, hordes of prospectors were lured by finds of gold in the bushland creeks and gullies. Many were from northern Italy and the troubled Swiss Italian-speaking canton of Ticino. As the gold petered out, those who stayed settled into small farms and businesses, and had the foresight in 1868 to reserve for the public Australia's biggest cluster of mineral springs. With the coming of the railway in 1881, the district developed as a fashionable place to stay in grand guesthouses and 'take the waters'. Then Daylesford and Hepburn Springs sank into sad decline with the onset of the 1930s depression and World War II.

The opening of **Lake House** in 1984 – an isolated rustic restaurant that has evolved into an internationally recognised luxury retreat – was a turning point. Alla Wolf-Tasker's Russian parents had bought a cottage on Wombat Hill in the 1960s, drawn, along with other East Europeans, by the mineral springs and scenic similarities to their homelands. They, like the earlier Swiss and Italian settlers, also brought a love of food and wine, and growing their own fruit and vegetables. Further impetus came in the 1990s when Tina Banitska converted an abandoned convent into an outstanding art gallery–café and Jim Frangos transformed a boisterous old pub into a civilised café-restaurant.

The rejuvenation gathered pace over the past ten years. The Hepburn Spa Centre and some of the heritage guesthouses have been restored and

Right
Lavandula, with its rustic buildings and fields of lavender, at Shepherds Flat.

Opposite
The view across Daylesford from Wombat Hill.

Foodstores and producers

renovated. A myriad self-contained cottages, boutique B&Bs and luxury retreats have sprung up, many offering massage and health therapies. Some have glorious views over water or distant hills; others nestle in tranquil gardens of native flora. Daylesford and its immediate surrounds now can boast of what I would judge to be regional Victoria's greatest concentration of critically acclaimed restaurants, cafés, good-food pubs and produce stores. What's more, they now are able to draw on fresh, seasonal produce from a host of small specialist – including organic – growers with whom they have developed a symbiotic relationship, as well as offer cool-climate wines from the region's burgeoning small vineyards and neighbouring Macedon Ranges. Visitors can also buy local produce at Sunday markets, roadside stalls and cellar doors. There is so much to see and savour.

You are never far from good food and wine in the spa country. Wherever you drive, look out for farm-gate and cellar-door signs, or indulge yourself in such wonderful provedores as **Cliffy's** in Daylesford. Seasonal produce includes freshly picked berries, cherries, chestnuts, crisp apples and stone fruits, new potatoes, culinary and medicinal herbs, and an array of organic vegetables. All year round, you can buy free-range eggs, honey, locally made smallgoods such as prosciutto and salami, fresh and smoked trout, award-winning chocolates, fresh pasta, organic cake mixes, and chutneys, jams and jellies. Bullboar sausages and Tukidale lamb are distinctive specialities of the region.

Some larger-scale producers have been long established: the market gardens and apple, pear, peach and apricot orchards of Bacchus Marsh, for instance (it's worth the diversion from the Western Freeway to check the road-side stalls east of the town), and the potato growers north and west of Daylesford. Many of the newer, smaller producers have banded together as Daylesford Macedon Produce (DMP), promoting their farm-gate logo as a sign of quality and commitment. They are supported by such restaurants as **Lake House**, which

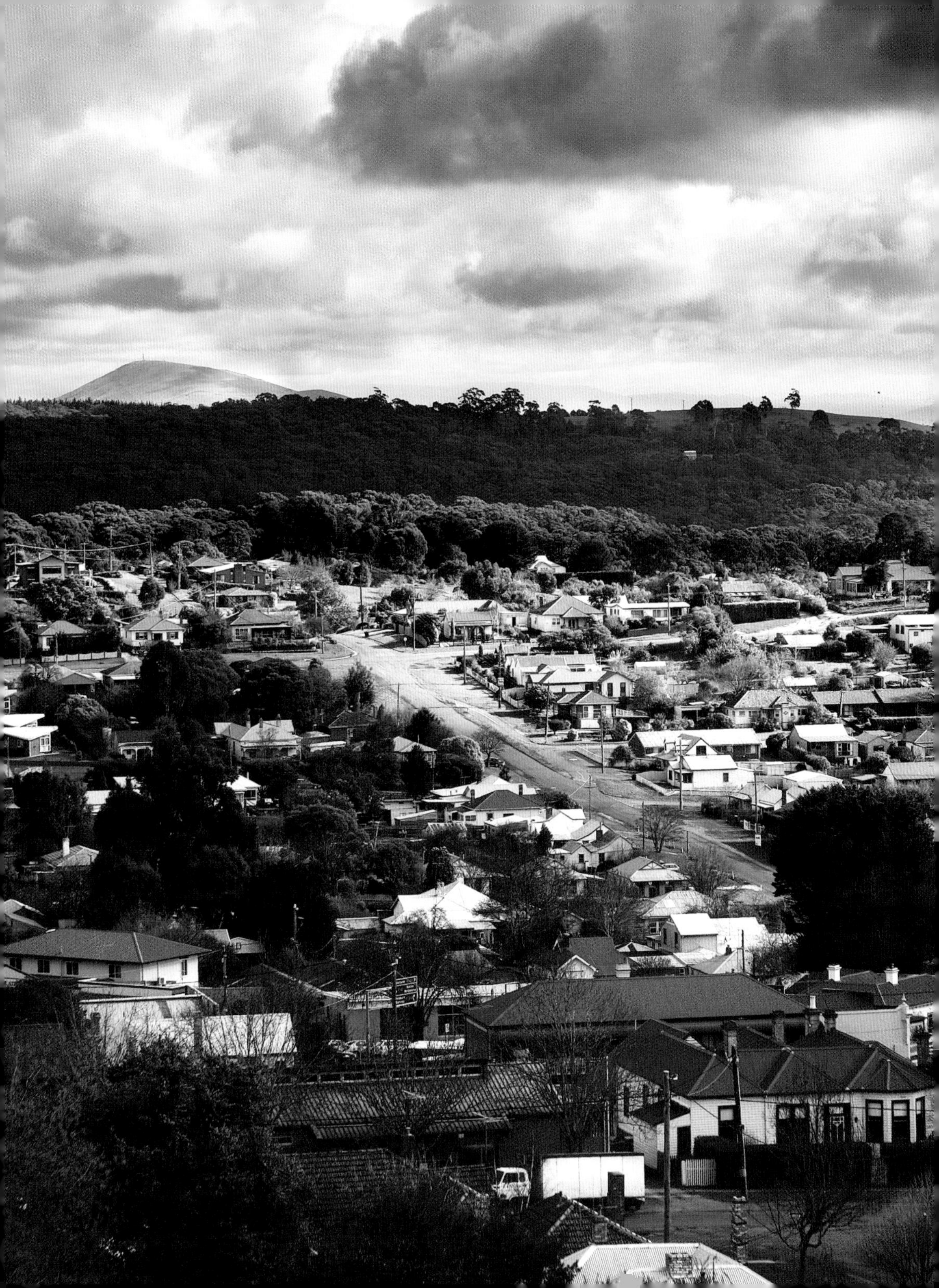

Just-picked organic vegetables and organic beer from the Fernleigh Farm Shop in Bullarto.

lists its regional suppliers in its menus. DMP reaches beyond the tourist-designated spa district to embrace such farmhouse specialists as **Meredith Dairy**, renowned for its goat's and sheep's milk cheeses, and **Sutton Grange Organic Farm**, noted for its Holy Goat chèvre.

Bite into a freshly picked, tree-ripened apple at **Organic Wholefoods and Harvest Café** and be astonished by the difference from the typical supermarket fruit that's been prematurely picked and kept in a cool store. And, thanks to careful farming practices, it will be free of the blemishes many people associate with organic fruit. Brendan Eisner and Kate Ullman will soon have forty varieties of apples from 1000 trees on their 22-hectare orchard tucked away in picturesque bush-land at Muskvale. Their season begins with gorgeous red-skinned, pink-fleshed Jersey Macs as early as December and finish with Pink Lady and Fuji apples in late May. They'll also have salad greens, greenhouse tomatoes and garlic over summer. Signs on the Daylesford–Ballarat Road will indicate when they're open.

Their apples may be more easily accessible from the **Fernleigh Farm shop** at Bullarto. The little shop sells not only Fernleigh's own produce, including organic old-style pork, Nicola and kipfler potatoes, carrots and truss tomatoes in summer, but also a range of other organic and biodynamic products. These include Warialda Belted Galloway beef, Stoney Creek flaxseed meal and cold-pressed olive oil, Glenbar organic beer brewed by Holgates in Woodend, and Hanging Rock springwater from Tylden. 'Every product has a story and comes from people we know,' says Fiona Chambers.

For the best prosciutto, I always drop in to **Istra**, off the Daylesford–Woodend Road at Musk. The Jurcan family use traditional Croatian methods of salting, spicing and smoking pork on this former potato farm to make bacon, hams, ribs, kassler, hocks, kaiserfleisch, hot and mild salami and other smallgoods and fresh sausages to fry or barbecue. Sebastian Jurcan or his mother Lidia are happy to let visitors sample their wares.

As Istra and Fernleigh are pork specialists, they don't stock the region's famous bullboar sausages, spicy reminders of its Swiss-Italian heritage. Around Yandoit just about every family of Swiss-Italian origin has its own recipe, handed down through the generations and jealously guarded, but it's no secret that bullboars are made of lean beef and pork (hence the name), coarsely minced and mixed with red wine, garlic, seasoning and such spices as cinnamon, cloves, nutmeg and allspice. The best commercial bullboars are made by butchers Ross Barker at Newstead and Neil Watts of the **Sausage Corner** in Kyneton; you'll also find good bullboars at the butcher shops in Daylesford.)

Opposite
Beekeeper Des O'Toole and his cold-extracted pure honey.

What about a taste of honey? When in Daylesford, drive down the Lake Jubilee Road to **Des O'Toole's Honey**, the second of the two honey roadside stalls along here. A former sawmiller turned beekeeper, Des runs the business with his wife Debi. Des is quite a character and makes top-quality, cold-extracted honey and honeycomb (which Lake House offers at breakfast). You can taste the difference from the highly processed commercial brands. The O'Tooles take their bees near and far to capture the flavours of desert flowers, orange blossom, manna gum and others for their six varieties of honey. You can also find their honey at the Daylesford market on Sundays and at Tonna's and Nicho's supermarkets in Daylesford. The other beekeeper, Barry McCahon, also has honey for sale on this road but sends most of his production in bulk to Melbourne for repackaging.

Organic Sunrise Foods, of Korweinguboora, is another small, enterprising agribusiness with a niche market. Richard and Lia Dobson produce a range of high-quality, certified organic pre-mixes for the home kitchen to make falafel, sunflower almond muffins and biscuits, buckwheat pancakes, burnt-butter biscuits and Dutch butter cake. They are also one of Lake House's trusted suppliers of their organic herbs, elderflowers and elderberries. A strong supporter of the Slow Food movement, Richard spent some months in Italy in mid-2005 on a fellowship to study sustainable organic food production and to train chefs to understand its nutritional benefits.

At **Stellas Naturally Fine Foods** in Daylesford, Pamela Storm and Ross Mongan make traditional sourdough breads, fresh pasta and wheat-free muesli, all well known and eagerly sought after locally and in Castlemaine. Sourdough starters and pasta-making can trace their local history back to the goldfields and the Swiss-Italian settlers. Crusty white, wholemeal, pumpkin and polenta, fig and aniseed, and mixed fruit loaves, warm from the oven, sell quickly at **Health Foods Naturally** in Daylesford and at the **Hepburn General Store**. So do the durum semolina and whole egg pasta varieties, all sold fresh.

Visiting foodies with limited time will find a beguiling cornucopia of good things to eat and drink from this and neighbouring regions at **Cliffy's** jocularly named 'emporium' and café. The weatherboard (and seemingly weather-beaten) building, uprooted from the gold diggings and plonked down in Daylesford more than a century ago, looks like an old-world rustic general store, which it was for decades. It was run by local character Cliffy Hauser, until Mary Ellis and Geoffrey Gray took it on four years ago. Like Alla Wolf-Tasker, Ellis had been frustrated by the difficulties of procuring local

Pure
HONEY
For Sale
O'TOOLE
DAYLESFORD
DES O'TOOLE'S
PURE HONEY
YELLOW BOX
Natural Blend

produce for their Hepburn Springs' guesthouse, **Liberty House**. 'We bought the old building and the barn behind, put in a kitchen and started the shop and café,' she explains. 'The idea was to stock it with what we could source from local farms and small producers, bring in really delicious cheese and other deli items, and cook some honest-to-goodness country food. Unlike supermarkets, who demand volume and continuity of supply, we offer what is regional and freshly seasonal, and provide an assured market for small local producers whose products are good.'

Country Cuisine has its own shop just out of Daylesford on the Midland Highway towards Ballarat. Philippa Wooller began making raspberry vinegar and jam from local berries in her home kitchen at Bullarto nine years ago. Now she runs a large-scale business making some sixty varieties of jams, preserved fruits, chutneys, sauces, marinades and flavoured vinegars, even winning export orders from the upper-crust London store, Harvey Nichols (which also stocks some Lake House preserves).

In Daylesford, **Tonna's greengrocery** stocks organic produce from the region; so does Organic Wholefoods and Harvest Café, which Anita Hoare and

> For those who appreciate the finest handmade chocolates, the 8-kilometre trip from Daylesford to the Chocolate Mill at Mt Franklin is a must

Scott Kinnear took over in early 2005. Here you'll find Captains Creek organic and preservative-free wines, Clancy's biodynamic eggs, and Fernleigh meats. Lola Orr supplies them with her unique 'Bullarto pink' potatoes and 'fantastic Swedes and turnips" from her Bullarto farm. It's also worth popping into the **Gourmet Larder**, Daylesford's best deli, which also stocks good things from the Daylesford and Macedon regions as well as famous-name gourmet foodstuffs from elsewhere.

For those who appreciate the finest handmade chocolates, the 8-kilometre trip from Daylesford to the **Chocolate Mill** at Mt Franklin is both a must and a delight. Here, in their unique owner-built, environmentally friendly strawbale and earth-render house, Canadian-born Chris Weippert and partner Jennifer Gregory make seventy varieties of chocolates, using Callebaut couverture chocolate from Belgium and no artificial ingredients or preservatives. They make their own caramel and ganache, and even dry their own chillies for their popular chilli chocolates. What also makes their chocolates so special, apart from their commitment to the highest quality, is that all are freshly made – many to their own creative composition – and sold only on their own premises.

Summer is berry time around Daylesford. Renamed **Trewhella Farm**, the former Musk Berry Farm has been taken over by biodynamic herb growers Liz Burns and Peter Liddelow across the road. They will continue to open it at weekends for luscious raspberries, brambleberries, red and black currants, and then from late January, blueberries and thornless blackberries, as well as their herbs. And like the previous owners, they intend to make jams, vinegars and wonderful ice creams with their fruit.

You will find many of the region's food and wine producers displaying their wares at the annual **Glenlyon Fair** on the last Sunday of July. It's held in the hamlet's community hall, about 10 kilometres from Daylesford on the Malmsbury Road.

Wineries

The Daylesford and Spa Country wineries are few in number and small in size, classified as the western frontier of the Macedon Ranges wine region. The easiest way to find the six main ones – all on or off the Daylesford–Malmsbury Road – is to pick up their combined brochure and map at the Daylesford Information Centre.

Ellender Estate is perhaps the prettiest of these properties, secluded in picturesque countryside still abounding with kangaroos. Dentist Graham Ellender and his wife Jenny lost their first vintage to frost after having planted 3.6 hectares with pinot noir, chardonnay, sauvignon blanc and pinot gris in 1996. The Burgundian-style pinot noir and a new sparkling wine, both made with meticulous care, are their top drops, but Graham, who studied brewing in England before coming to Australia, also makes some other wines with fruit from other regions. Their tasting room and terrace overlook a river-pebble lined stream flowing into an ornamental lake of paddling ducks. On Sundays Jenny offers 'budburst platters' with bread from the wood-fired oven, and plans to expand her range of dishes to include pizzas and casseroles from the oven.

Big Shed Wines is the change-of-life passion of former Edinburgh University geneticist and molecular biologist Ken Jones, whose winery takes it name from the erstwhile horse-farm stables on the hillside. With the advice of neighbouring vignerons, he established a small acreage of pinot noir and applied his scientific background to winemaking. He welcomes visitors to his intimate little tasting

Five great experiences in the spa country

- Drinks on the terrace and a dégustation dinner at Lake House
- Lunch or afternoon tea at Lavandula among the lavender
- Checking out the superb chocs at the Chocolate Mill
- Browsing through Cliffy's produce 'emporium'
- Catching your own trout for lunch at Tuki

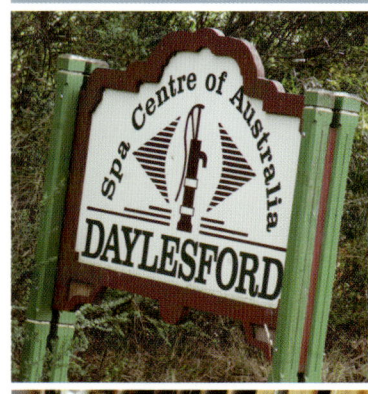

Opposite, clockwise from top left
Stone building at Lavandula; garden-fresh produce at Cliffy's in Daylesford; line up of rods for trout-fishing at Tuki Retreat, near Smeaton; Daylesford, the spa centre.

room and, as well as his estate-grown pinot, offers several other red and white wines made from bought-in grapes.

Nearby **Sandy Farm** is a small family-owned vineyard specialising in classic-style cabernet sauvignon, cabernet franc, merlot and pinot noir. Most of the wine is sold to a loyal group of regular customers, leaving little for cellar-door sales. Look for their roadside signs when they are open. Further along is the beautifully sited **Kangaroo Hill Vineyard and Winery**. Strong believers in organic principles, Jan Ward and Andre Deutsch chose this spot on a volcanic plug with underground springs and a sunny northern aspect to grow 1.80 unirrigated hectares of pinot noir, making their first vintage from their own fruit in 2003. They also make small quantities of cabernet and sauvignon blanc from Yarra Valley grapes. Not listed in the wineries brochure, **Wombat Forest Vineyard**, secluded by bushland near Denver, has progressed from growing to making full-bodied cabernet and light, fruity pinot noir.

Nearer Malmsbury, **Zig Zag** has undergone several changes of ownership since the first vines of this region were planted in 1972 by journalist-turned-restaurateur Roger Aldridge, who had rebuilt The Mill at Malmsbury. Eric and Anne Bellchambers now have 4 hectares of pinot noir, cabernet sauvignon, merlot, shiraz and riesling on the unirrigated vineyard that produces wines of low yields but intense colours and distinct flavours. Previous owner Alan Stevens helps to make the wines. At neighbouring **Basalt Ridge**, ex-army engineer Bernie O'Day grows 6 hectares of sauvignon blanc, cabernet sauvignon, merlot and pinot noir, and buys in shiraz and cabernet franc. He concentrates on growing but enjoys the winemaking, applying his knowledge of chemistry but preferring 'not to fiddle too much' with the process. He sells mainly from the cellar door, which also offers simple snacks prepared by his wife Adele at weekends other than peak vintage time.

Four other wineries are not listed on the wineries trail. At **Captains Creek Organic Wines**, at Blampied off the Daylesford–Ballarat Road, Doug and Carolyn May grow pinot noir and chardonnay and make full-bodied, well-balanced wines with subtle oak characters. They plan soon to begin cellar-door sales. The former potato farm now also grows organic cool-climate vegetables, apples, nashi pears, chestnuts, walnuts and hazelnuts. **Sailors Falls Estate**, near Sault restaurant about 7 kilometres south of Daylesford, specialises in fragrant, spicy pinot gris. Robert and Margaret McDonald have also planted some pinot noir, gewürztraminer and gamay grapes, and were hoping to open cellar door facilities in late 2005. At Creswick, consultant and contract winemaker Roland Koval (formerly at St Leonards and Warrenmang) produces small quantities of premium wines sourced from a Spring Hill vineyard under his **Cavalier** label, mainly for restaurants in the Daylesford region.

Eating Out

Seasons are distinctive in Daylesford. You can feel it in the air: balmy in summer, crisp in winter. You can see it in the trees around the lake, burgeoning in spring, golden in autumn. **Lake House** celebrates the seasons with its menus. Early autumn is my favourite time here, when highland hare cannelloni may come with spiced carrot puree, duck breast is lacquered with pomegranate, and luscious baked figs are filled with chocolate. But this is an outstanding restaurant in any season, whether to enjoy a superb tasting platter with drinks on the terraces or a dégustation banquet by the fireside.

Alla Wolf-Tasker spends less time in the kitchen these days, but remains the inspiration and driving force of her dedicated team, and the focus of her network of regional suppliers. Lake House is a resplendent reminder that fine dining can flourish without pomposity or pretension in country Victoria,

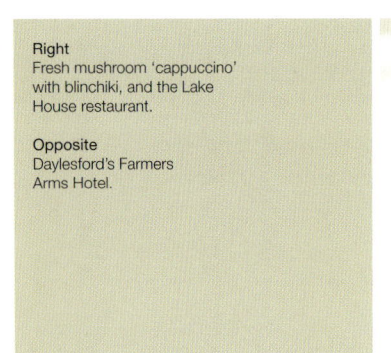

Right
Fresh mushroom 'cappuccino' with blinchiki, and the Lake House restaurant.

Opposite
Daylesford's Farmers Arms Hotel.

drawing on the seasonal harvests of its regional environment, bolstered by an exceptional wine list and waiters who know their job and do it deftly with a smile. The Lake House experience is not to be missed, and if you can stay over in one of the luxurious lakeside suites, so much the better.

If the **Farmers Arms Hotel** is not the best good-food pub in the state, it's certainly a contender. You wouldn't think so if judging by its squat, mellowed red-brick exterior or even by its idiosyncratic dining room with its disparate

Lamb's fry with horseradish yoghurt, potatoes and kaiserfleisch

Andrew Dennis, Farmers Arms Hotel, Daylesford

12 very thin slices kaiserfleisch
500 g small waxy potatoes
500 g lamb's fry
1 small horseradish root*
½ cup thick natural yoghurt
45 ml extra virgin olive oil
1 cup fresh dill fronds
juice of ½ lemon
salt and freshly
ground white pepper
*Use fresh horseradish root or 'minced fresh horseradish' in a jar.

Place the kaiserfleisch in a heavy-based frying pan over a medium heat and fry until crisp. Drain on absorbent paper.

Bring the potatoes to the boil in salted water and simmer until tender.

Trim lamb's fry of any membrane and gristle and then slice into 1 cm-thick pieces. Set aside.

Peel the horseradish root and chop roughly. Add to a food processor and mince finely. Add the yoghurt and pulse until incorporated.

Drain the potatoes and dice them to about 3 cm-thick cubes while still warm. Dress the potatoes liberally with the horseradish yoghurt, olive oil, dill and lemon juice. Season to taste.

In a large heavy-based frying pan over a high heat, with a little oil, fry the liver until crisp on both sides (about 1 minute on each side; be careful not to overcook). Season in the pan. Drain on absorbent paper.

Place some of the potato salad on the bottom of each serving plate and then layer the pieces of crisp kaiserfleisch and lamb's fry on top of this. Garnish with extra fronds of dill and a drizzle of extra virgin olive oil.

Serves 4 as an entrée

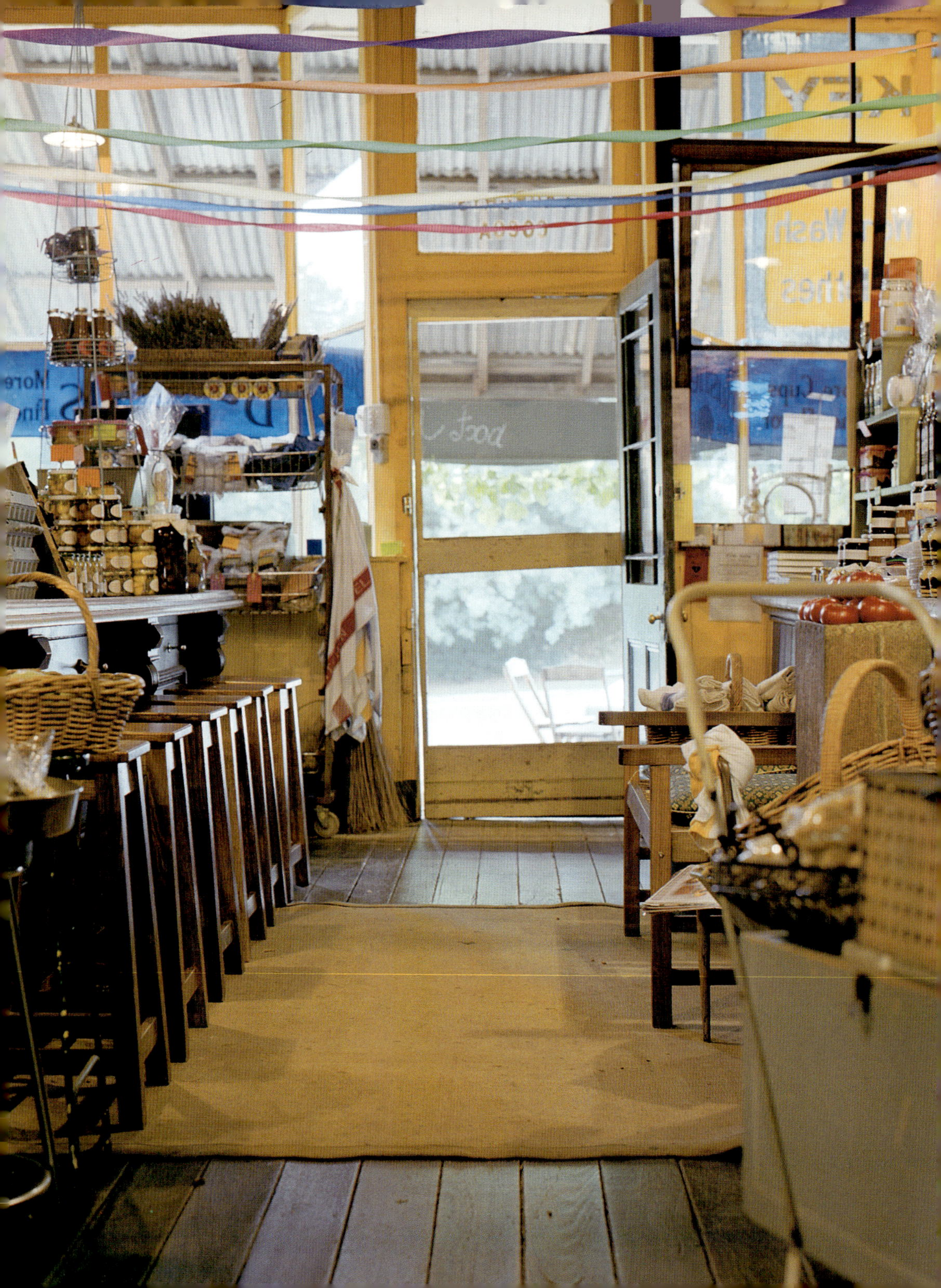

Above
Sault restaurant, outside Daylesford, has a Mediterranean-inspired menu and lovely views.

Opposite
The relaxed country interior of Cliffy's in Daylesford.

assortment of chairs and light fittings. Local farmers whose forebears used to bend the elbow in the bar on market days still prop at the bar for a beer (maybe one brewed by Holgate in Woodend) but the real action is at the tables. Genial host Frank Moylan knows his wines, and chef Andrew Dennis's food has a tantalising, flavour-driven Mediterranean-Levantine inspiration, ranging from merguez sausages with rosewater yoghurt to chicken with preserved lemon, olive tagine and labne.

Mercato is a new restaurant, but a good one. Beautifully renovated in an inviting contemporary style, the street-front building almost next to Cliffy's bears no resemblance to its 1864 origin as a hotel or former lives as a grocery store, maternity hospital and 1920s tearooms. Owner-chef Richard Mee has come here with experience in international hotels and country resorts, and draws on regional produce to present elegantly composed dishes that are rich in flavour. Expect the likes of seared loin of Tuki lamb on potato crushed with Kyneton olive oil, or Western Plains pork on creamy parsnip mash with French beans.

When Jim Frangos bought the old Belvedere Hotel in the centre of Daylesford in 1973, its nickname of the 'Swinging Arms' bore witness to its roughhouse reputation. It took him some years to transform it progressively into a civilised, old-world European-style coffee palace and restaurant renamed **Frangos and Frangos**, with yet unrealised plans for upstairs accommodation, garden courtyard and wine cellar rooms. Now the original café is for more serious dining; for more casual snacking, Koukla's offers pizzas from the wood-fired oven, pastas and lighter dishes. One or the other, sometimes both, open daily.

Built of local sandstone to resemble a French provencale villa, **Sault** fronts fields of lavender rippling down to a man-made lake against a backdrop of the Wombat Forest. Seven kilometres short of Daylesford on the road from the Western Freeway, it's under capable new management. Chef Benjamin O'Brien's menu zips around the Mediterranean, skipping from French onion

Opposite
Lunch beneath the trees at La Trattoria, Lavandula, at Shepherds Flat.

soup and cassoulet bubbling with Istra sausage and kassler, to Tunisian goat stew and Moroccan seven-vegetable couscous. Followed by, naturally, a lavender brûlée with rosemary biscotti. There's a great view by day, and romantic atmosphere at night.

With its historic buildings, lovely gardens and fields of lavender, olives and grapes, **Lavandula** – about ten minutes drive north of Daylesford at Shepherds Flat – is a delightful place to visit, imbued with the heritage of its Swiss-Italian founders of more than a hundred and fifty years ago. Its rustic **La Trattoria** daytime café has moved to a grey barn with French shutter windows, opening out to a grove of young ash trees for al fresco teas with lavender scones, jam and cream. Chef Jess Scarce also cooks more substantial lunch dishes, such as provencal chicken aromatic with saffron, and Western Plains pork with crab apple. Check the rows of preserves and relishes made with fruit from the farm and other local growers.

Lucini's at the Old Macaroni Factory is another place steeped in history and throbbing with character. Maria Viola, fourth-generation member of Australia's first pasta manufacturers, has lovingly restored this 146-year-old stone building in Hepburn Springs as a museum – a tribute to her family and other Swiss-Italian pioneers. It's listed by the National Trust and noted for its evocative murals and frescoes. At weekends, Maria serves hearty dishes of pasta, made to family recipes, on old timber tables lit by colonial-era oil lamps, and leads a feisty rendition of 'That's Amore'. It's great fun and the guided tours are well worthwhile.

For more serious dining in Hepburn Springs, **Misto** has won solid local support since Nicolas and Bridgette Dowling, formerly at Sault, took it over nearly three years ago. Tuki lamb is usually on the menu, among other dishes of Mediterranean inspiration. **The Springs Retreat** is an old pub morphed into an expensively transformed country-house retreat, now managed by the Peppers Group. Its formal **Deco Restaurant**, open every night, is a strong supporter of regional produce and wines, and its casual **Retreat Café** can be recommended for inexpensive lunches. New to town is the **Red Star Café**, opened by Ed and Lynette Banks, formerly of the Pavilion Café. All red, white and black, complete with sofas and bookshelves – it was furnished to resemble their sitting room – it is particularly popular for its breakfasts and inexpensive lunches.

Daylesford has a lively café scene all year, and seems to have more places doing breakfast than anywhere else in country Victoria. The **Convent Gallery** is one of the town's major tourist attractions. Once the palatial 1860s residence

Jess's fresh fig salad

Jess Scarce, Lavandula, Shepherds Flat

fresh green figs, sliced in rounds
rocket, de-stemmed
pecorino cheese, shaved
Marsala walnuts
extra virgin olive oil
sea salt

Arrange the rocket and figs in two layers to give height.

Add walnuts and shaved cheese.

Drizzle over extra virgin olive oil from Rose Creek Estate, Colmo's Paddock or Orchard of St Francis.

Add a sprinkle of sea salt.

Marsala walnuts
100 g butter
100 g soft brown sugar
½ cup walnuts
100 ml marsala

Melt together the butter and sugar. Add the walnuts and Marsala and warm together for 5 minutes, tossing. Cool.

of the gold commissioner, it was expanded in the 1880s to become the Holy Cross Convent and girls' boarding school. Artist Tina Banitska has transformed it into an outstanding temple of art and crafts galleries, from paintings and sculptures to jewellery and textiles. Its wittily named **Bad Habits Café** serves substantial breakfasts, light lunches and morning and afternoon teas. Another drawcard for visitors is the **Boathouse Café** with its terrace on the edge of Lake Daylesford. The ducks and geese on the grassy banks outside the converted boatshed look as contented as the customers enjoying the idyllic view and simple meals. Alternatively, enjoy a traditional afternoon tea and a fabulous view of the lake on Sundays or Mondays at the **Ambleside guesthouse**. In the warmer months, take a stroll through the botanical gardens high up on Wombat Hill and drop in at the café for refreshments.

Breakfast and Beer, with its quirky décor and spiral iron staircase, is something different. Dutch-born Stefan Overzier offers 200 varieties of British, European, Asian and Australian beers, lagers, ales and pilsners, yummy breakfasts (with eggs and fruit from Daylesford Organics), light lunches and snacky platters to go with the beer. At weekends, you may be served by

Right and opposite
The Convent in Daylesford features cafés, art and craft galleries and shop, lovely gardens and a splendid tower with a lookout.

fourteen-year-old Liam, who won the barista competition at Hepburn's Swiss-Italian fiesta. Newer still is the tiny **Della's on Vincent**, with a distinctive French provincial look and menu. **Sweet Decadence** is the place for hot chocolate (try the one with a touch of chilli) and good coffee with delicious cakes or a selection of their own chocolates, freshly made upstairs. **Cliffy's** and the **Harvest Café** do simple, unpretentious country food, **Koukla's** is the place for wood-fired pizzas, **Not Just Muffins** is just that, offering a range of budget-price snacks,

The Convent Gallery, one of the town's major tourist attractions, was once the palatial 1860s residence of the gold commissioner, and later a boarding school

Soup of daylesford chestnuts

Alla Wolf-Tasker,
Lake House, Daylesford

1 kg fresh chestnuts
75 g butter
2 shallots, finely chopped
⅓ cup porcini powder (available from specialty stores, otherwise grind powder in a processor)
1 tbsp balsamic vnegar
2 tbsp dry sherry
4 cups water
500 ml cream
1 tbsp black truffle olive oil
salt and pepper to taste

Preheat the oven to 175°C. Cut a cross in the rounded side of the nuts. Place them on a baking tray and roast until browned and the skins begin to burst, 7 to 8 minutes. Alternatively they can be boiled to soften the skin. Whichever method, ensure outer skin is pierced before cooking.

When coolish, peel the nuts and also discard the inner skins. Melt butter in a large soup pot. Add shallots and cook until soft. Add chestnuts, raise heat and cook, stirring, until chestnuts are golden. Stir in the porcini powder, vinegar, sherry and 4 cups of water. Add cream and stir, scraping any residue from the bottom.

Lower the heat and simmer for 20 minutes. Puree soup in a blender and stir in the truffle oil. Reheat the soup. (It should be warm, not piping hot.) Season with salt and pepper if necessary. Blitz with a hand-held blender to create a frothy texture.

At Lake House, the soup is served in little demitasse cups alongside 'blinchiki' – Russian crepes, filled with wild rice, chestnuts and local forest mushrooms.

Serves 6

Opposite
Alla Wolf-Tasker, at her award-winning Lake House restaurant.

Alla Wolf-Tasker, Lake House

and as for the rest, just cruise Vincent Street and take your pick.

Eating out in the quaint old bushland town of Trentham has seen a few changes. **The Chimney** takes its name from its freestanding, double-sided fireplace, and offers such German-Austrian dishes as Istra kassler with sauerkraut and dumpling, bratwurst with red cabbage and fried potatoes, followed by a delicious apfelstrudel or sachertorte with cream, plus local wines. Movie night (classic oldies) and theme dinners are a feature. Since its acclaimed founding partner-chef left in 2005, **Issan Thai** is not what it was. The fare now is both Thai and Chinese, with two sittings of yum cha on Sundays. Trentham's historic **Cosmopolitan Hotel**, popular for its better-than-average-pub-grub bistro, was gutted by fire in June 2005, but its owners plan to restore it.

The lovely old **Garden of St Erth** near Blackwood, established by the much-loved schoolmaster and gardening writer Tom Garnett and run by the Digger's Club, has a little rustic weekend café where chef Alistair White creates simple but delicious dishes from home-grown and other local produce. It's closed during the cold winter months.

Alla Wolf-Tasker can talk about food till the cows come home – or rather, the fromage frais comes in – with understanding, love and enthusiasm. She is rapturous about the virtues of organic carrots straight from the ground, vine-ripened tomatoes that have never been in a fridge, wild mushrooms picked by her daughter Larissa after the first autumn rains and offered to her **Lake House** guests that evening in Russian blinchiki with a mushroom cappuccino. Regionality, seasonality and freshness are guiding principles. Culinary integrity, creativity and caring are her hallmarks.

The success of Lake House did not come easily or immediately. When she and her husband Allan bought the property in 1979 it was a scruffy hillside paddock of gorse bushes and wrecked cars sloping down to a swampy inlet of Lake Daylesford. Neighbours were bemused when they planted trees on land someone had once paid to clear; local authorities couldn't understand why anyone would want to open a new restaurant in the town. They worked hard at weekends to build their dream, working in Melbourne during the week as teachers (she had a cooking school). They opened the restaurant in 1984, bringing fresh produce from the Queen Victoria market because so little was to be had locally.

Wolf-Tasker had always wanted to be a cook. Her Russian immigrant parents, who had instilled in her a European appreciation of good food, were

Opposite
Fiona Chambers of
Fernleigh Farm at Bullarto.

dismayed at such a career choice. But she persisted, working in restaurants and cafés during her student years, saving up to travel to France, being 'knocked out' by the charcuteries, patisseries and street markets of Paris, doing a Cordon Bleu course, and noting that many of the best French restaurants were in the country, close to their sources of food and wine. She was determined to open a restaurant of her own.

Why Daylesford, and at a time when half the shops in the town were closed and day-trippers came mainly to fill flagons with mineral water from the springs? Wolf-Tasker had spent happy holidays with her parents at the little 'dacha' they had bought in Daylesford in the 1960s. She and Allan saw an opportunity there and seized it. It took a while for visitors, accustomed to a Sunday drive to the country for Devonshire tea, to realise that you could also eat at a real restaurant out of town. As Lake House's reputation for fine food and wine grew, the need for on-site accommodation became apparent. And so, slowly, Lake House has evolved as an outstanding luxury resort, set in glorious landscaped gardens sweeping down to the lake. It has won numerous awards for its food, wine list, accommodation and professionalism. Alla is active in promoting the region's tourist attractions and food producers. Allan's evocative paintings and prints hang in the restaurant and guestrooms, and he supervises the selection of wines. In my judgment, having eaten there often over twenty years, Lake House is Victoria's best all-round regional restaurant, comparable with Melbourne's very finest.

Fernleigh Farm

The little prepubescent pig, snuffling happily with its siblings in a paddock untainted by chemicals, didn't know it was going off to market in the morning. That's life, blissful while it lasts, for these rare Wessex saddlebacks, all pretty in black with white markings and pink snouts. Fiona Chambers is passionate about her pigs, but unsentimental. If these clean, free-range pigs weren't raised to become old-style organic pork, she believes, the endangered breed would die out, leaving the field to large-scale 'factory farming' of commercial breeds. There are now fewer than seventy-five registered breeders of Wessex saddlebacks left in the world, none in England where they originated, and Chambers has collected all the remaining bloodlines over the past ten years.

In spite of her special interest in her pigs, they represent only 5 per cent of **Fernleigh Farm**'s $1 million-a-year turnover of all-organic produce. Carrots account for 70 per cent; potatoes (notably Nicola, kipfler and pink fir, plus the more common sebago) for 15 per cent; and glasshouse tomato and capsicums,

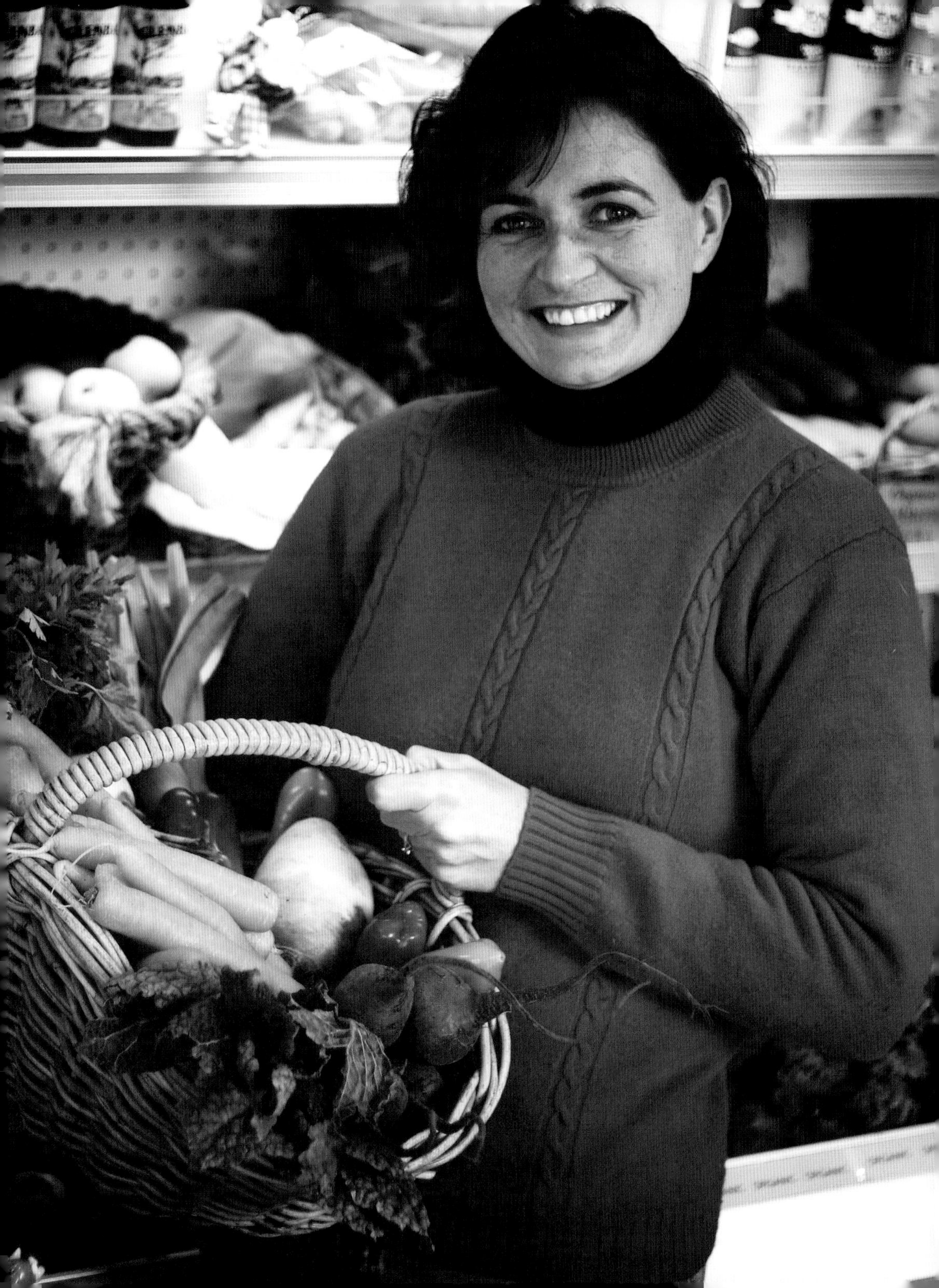

and mixed vegetable for sale locally, for the remaining 10 per cent. Chambers had always wanted to be farmer. She and her husband Nicholas – they met at Dookie Agricultural College – bought the 40-hectare property at Bullarto near Daylesford in 1988, converted to organics in 1990, and realised that only intensive farming of high-value, cool-climate crops would be sustainable on the rich, fertile soil. Within two years they were exporting fresh carrot juice, then fresh carrots, to Japan. Now they supply Coles supermarkets nationally with their organic carrots, as well as specialist organic produce shops.

Successful exporting and national distribution to choosy companies accounts for most of Fernleigh Farm's income, but it is not where Fiona Chambers' heart lies. She fervently believes that as much as possible of their produce should stay in the region or be accessible to visitors. 'In the old days, many city dwellers had relatives on the land and were familiar with farm life and fresh produce,' she says. 'Now with the drift of young people to the cities and the trend toward large-scale farming, people have lost that connection. They tend to buy food in supermarkets where it has become a faceless commodity that demands uniformity and consistency.'

On visits to Europe and the United States she noted the growing popularity of farm shops, street stalls and farmers' markets offering fresh produce. Another tour on a Churchill Fellowship led her to study how to persuade conventional farmers to adapt to organic production. Hence the opening last summer of a farm shop at Fernleigh, open most days of the week, with a range of produce from their own land and other organic and biodynamic growers. 'We want to encourage people to come in, see the farm, ask questions about the food and organic farming, and enjoy the variety and seasonality of fresh food. It is also so important for this region.' The Chambers plan to enhance the farm experience by developing farm and bushland trails, so that people 'can enjoy the fresh air and get their shoes dirty'.

The Joneses of Tuki Retreat

In farming as in investment, diversity can be the antidote to adversity. At **Tuki Retreat** near Smeaton, north of Ballarat and west of Daylesford, Robert and Jan Jones have proved the point with more imagination, enterprise and success than most. Visitors should not be deterred by the approach of seemingly desolate stoney rises. Over a ridge they will behold a magnificent vista and a veritable oasis. It's a retreat of snug colonial-style, bluestone guest cottages, rustic daytime restaurant in the old stables, and working sheep and trout farm on a 550-hectare property where sheep have grazed since the 1850s.

Tuki Retreat, near Smeaton, is a working sheep and trout farm but also offers bluestone guest cottages and a rustic restaurant.

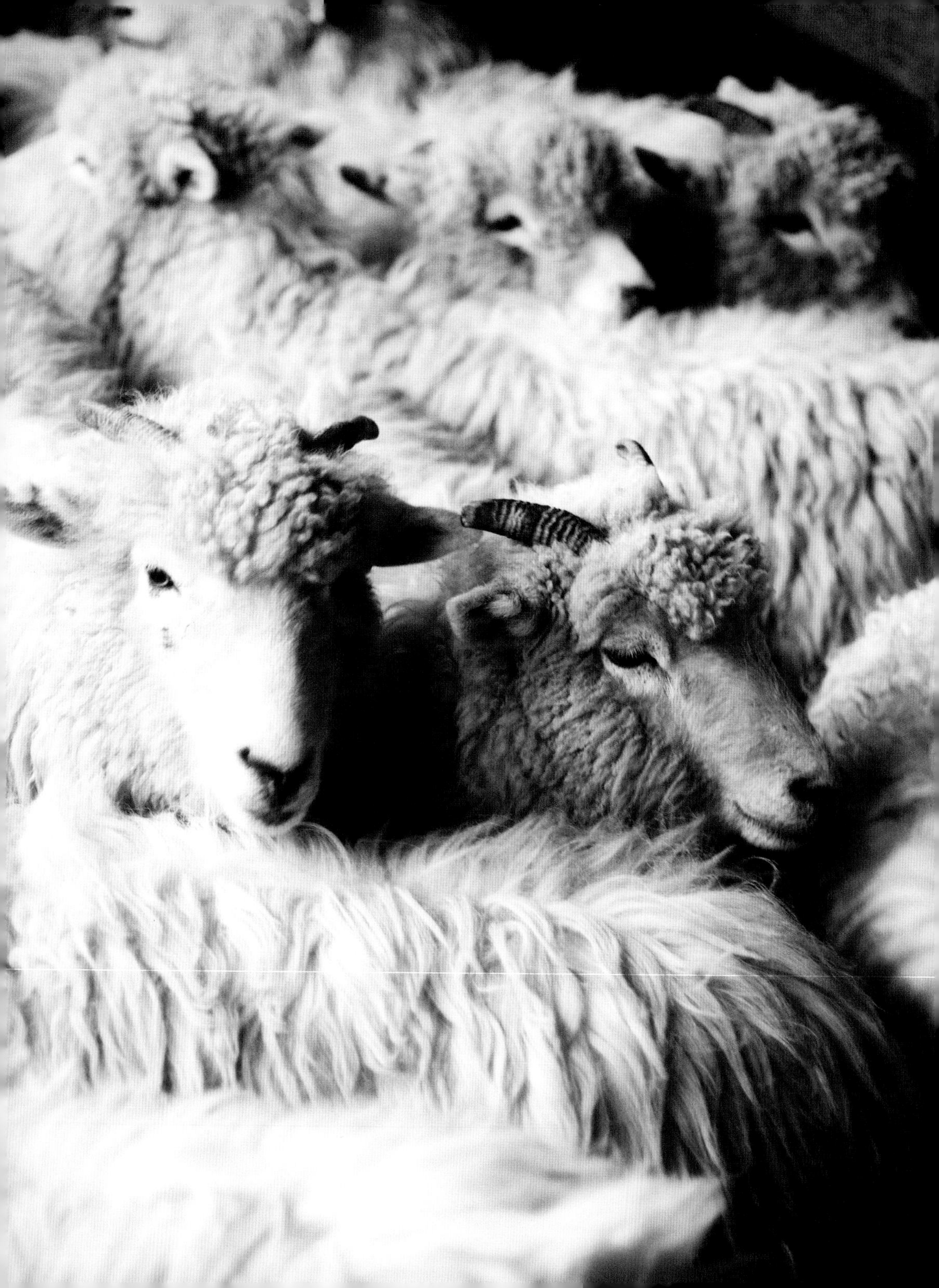

Opposite
Tukidale sheep at Tuki Retreat.

Rob's father Don came here in the 1940s and later introduced a rare flock of Tukidale sheep, a New Zealand-bred variation of Romsey Marsh, prized mainly for their quality carpet wool and excellent meat of distinctively sweet flavour and tender texture. Then the family developed terraced ponds of rainbow trout, both as a source of fresh and smoked fish and trout pâté for sale and as an added tourist attraction. The pools are graded for a progression of angling skills. Learners can easily catch hand-fed fish so tame that they almost jump into a net; experienced anglers need to cast a deft line to lure elusive fish already accustomed to stalking their insect prey. Rob, who took over management of the farm in 1985, or sons David, twenty-one, and Alistair, nineteen, are happy to help novices clean and even cook their catch, to enjoy expertly filleted at the table for lunch or packaged to take home.

Tuki lamb and smallgoods, smoked trout and trout pâté, now appear on the menus of many of the best known restaurants of the goldfields and spa regions, including **Lake House**, **Warrenmang**, **Mercato**, **Convent Gallery** and **Peppers Springs Retreat**. In Tuki Retreat's own restaurant, guests can tuck into Tuki roast lamb, Tuki lamb sausages and Tuki burgers for lunch. If you fancy an offally good lamb's fry, Rob may be happy to oblige on request.

The integrated business has steadily expanded and improved. The family now slaughters and butchers its own meat on the property, and smokes its lamb and trout products on the premises over smouldering messmate. An extended open-air terrace is a perfect spot for lunch with a view that can only be described as idyllic. The best way to enjoy all that Tuki has to offer is to stay in one of the cosily furnished cottages, with dinner brought to your table by the fireside. With the third generation as adept in all aspects of the farm work, from wrangling sheep to trout angling, it will be hard to keep up with the multi-skilled, ever-so-hospitable Joneses.

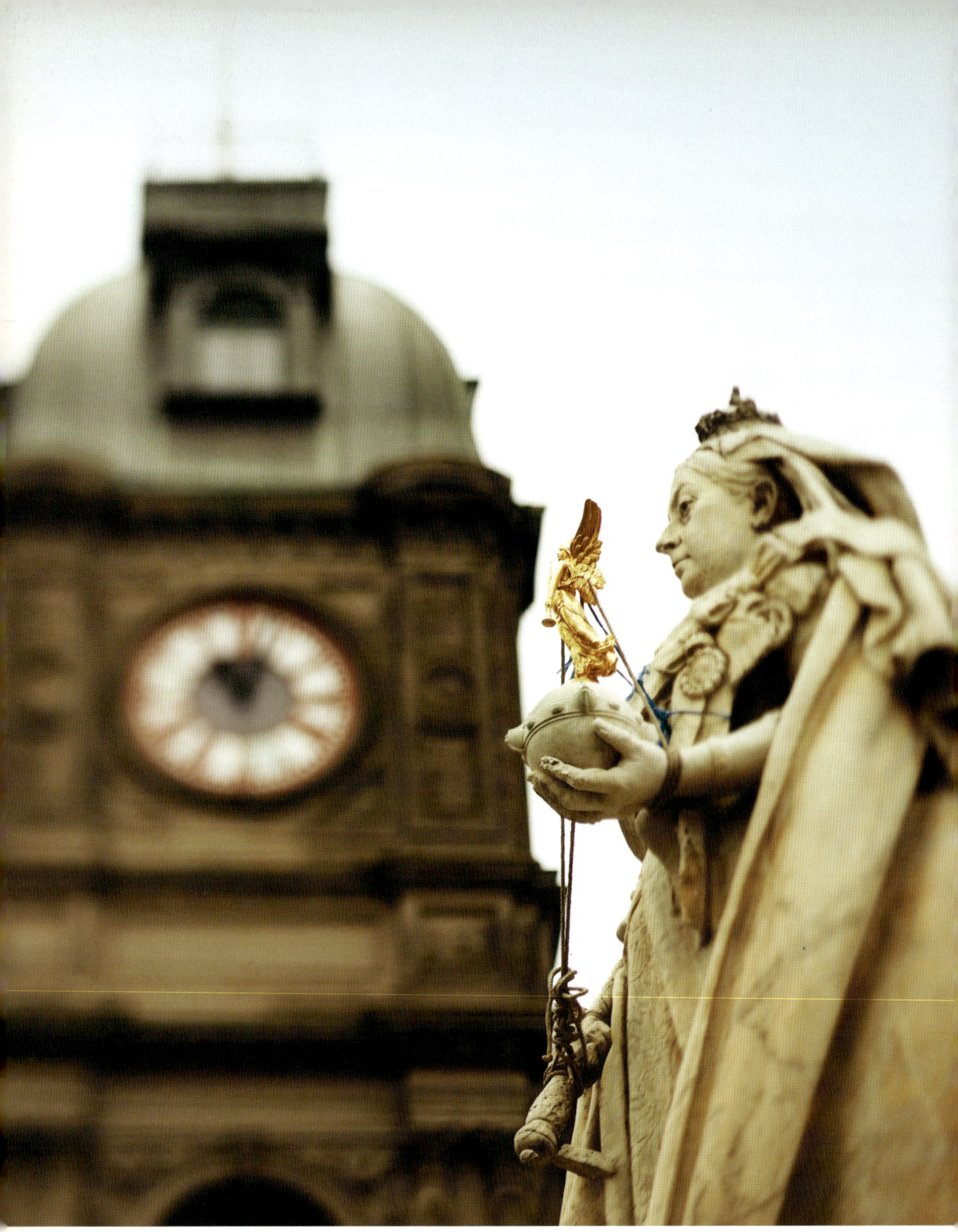

ballarat

michele curtis

ballarat

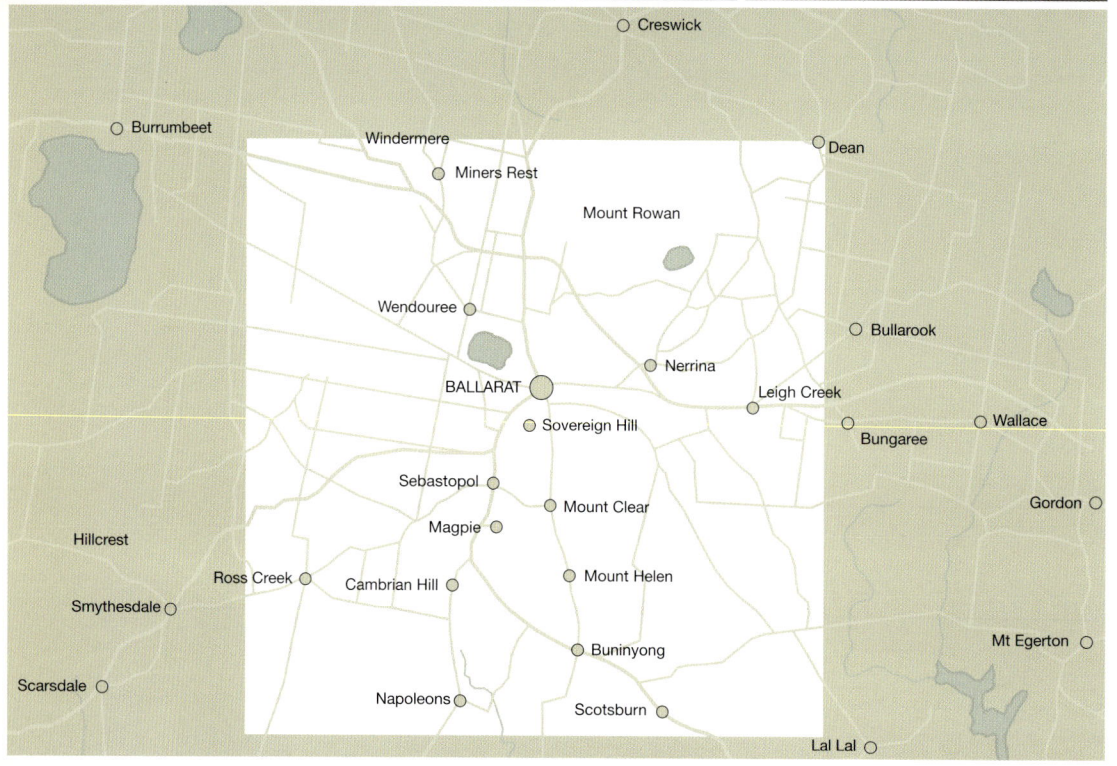

Creswick
Burrumbeet
Windermere
Dean
Miners Rest
Mount Rowan
Wendouree
Bullarook
Nerrina
BALLARAT
Leigh Creek
Sovereign Hill
Wallace
Bungaree
Sebastopol
Mount Clear
Gordon
Magpie
Hillcrest
Ross Creek
Mount Helen
Cambrian Hill
Smythesdale
Mt Egerton
Buninyong
Scarsdale
Napoleons
Scotsburn
Lal Lal

Vignerons, chefs, restaurateurs, bakers, produce growers and others are transforming the food and wine scene… there are many reasons for food and wine lovers to stay and explore

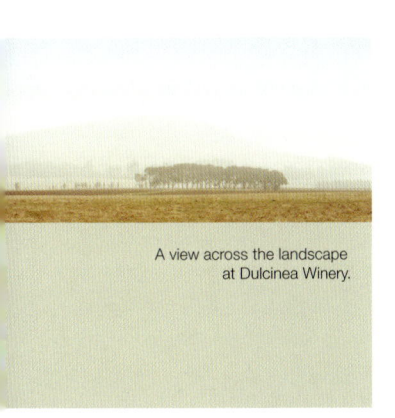

A view across the landscape at Dulcinea Winery.

Ballarat, with its wide tree-lined streets full of splendid Victorian and Edwardian architecture, is Victoria's largest inland city. Famous for its gold discoveries, it was the site of the famed Eureka uprising in 1854, when gold diggers staged a short but bloody battle to defend their 'rights and liberties'. The starry blue and white Southern Cross flag that the miners raised then still flies from many a local vantage point as a reminder of the town's historic times.

The town's ornate wedding-cake architecture reflects its Victorian and Edwardian heritage, but behind these elaborate facades and along the wide, tree-lined boulevards there is a quiet revolution going on as vignerons, chefs, restaurateurs, bakers, produce growers and others are quietly transforming the food and wine scene. Where once visitors flocked to Sovereign Hill and the Ballarat Wildlife Park for the day then drove back to Melbourne, there are now many reasons for food and wine lovers to stay and explore. This town boasts some excellent restaurants and cafés in all price ranges, as well as historic hotels and B&Bs if you'd like to stay longer.

Visitors to Ballarat can experience the gold rush days at Sovereign Hill, explore the Eureka Stockade at the Eureka Centre, enjoy one of Ballarat's many festivals and explore the local botanical gardens and Lake Wendouree, while art lovers will take delight in the exceptional Ballarat Fine Art Gallery, Victoria's largest and oldest provincial gallery. The surrounding districts are home to the Great Grape Touring wine route. This self-drive road will take you through wine districts such as the Pyrenees, Grampians and Ballarat. The region's big-bodied, cool-climate wines are a perfect match for the local produce of Western District lamb, beef, pork, venison, rabbit, pheasant and trout.

Gold was discovered in the district in August 1851. By October of that year there were over 2000 diggers searching the area for gold and by the end of that year Ballarat had been surveyed and plans drawn up to establish a township. By 1853 the number of gold miners had increased to 20,000 and some 9926 kilos of gold had been discovered, including the Welcome Nugget which, at almost 69 kilos, is the second-largest gold nugget ever found in the world.

Right
A glimpse of Ballarat's imposing Victorian-era architecture.

Opposite
Sovereign Hill, a reminder of the district's goldmining heritage.

Foodstores and producers

Initially a 5-kilometre stretch of canvas tents, the township of Ballarat developed as more substantial buildings, such as a proper hotel, a post office and Christ Church Anglican Cathedral in 1854, were built. As the gold diggings turned to shaft mining, often with the backing of large companies to finance the drilling and excavation, residents arrived from all over the world to search for gold. The population of Ballarat rose to 64,000 in 1868 with some 300 mining companies working in the fields surrounding the community. Foundries followed, along with woollen and flour mills and breweries. Farming emerged after the Land Act of 1861 opened up land for settlement. Agricultural businesses helped Ballarat to survive the 1870 depression and today still provide a strong work base for the town's people. Local industry is strong and with rich pastures in the surrounding areas there's no shortage of good produce grown and produced close by making Ballarat a remarkable district.

When a group of Scottish squatters left drought-stricken Geelong in 1837 in search of better grazing pastures, and laid eyes on the land that would eventually become Ballarat, they discovered more than gold in nearby Buninyong. Ballarat and the surrounding Western District proved to be outstanding grazing country, ideal for farming beef and lamb. Local butcher **John Harbour** not only sells the best of the Western District meat in his shop, his family farms lamb on what he believes are the finest pastures in the world.

'We breed only traditional British breeds such as Shropshire, Suffolk and Dorset lambs,' says John. 'The region is famous for its quality lamb and beef, especially Hereford and Angus cattle. I'm regionally focussed on sourcing products that reflect the uniqueness of the Ballarat region. My family has a reputation of producing the best livestock in the region.'

From free-range **Western Plains** pork, free-range eggs from **Greeneggs** in the nearby Grampians and **Bendigo Cheese** to the supreme class of his homemade smallgoods such as hams, sausages, bacon and black and white

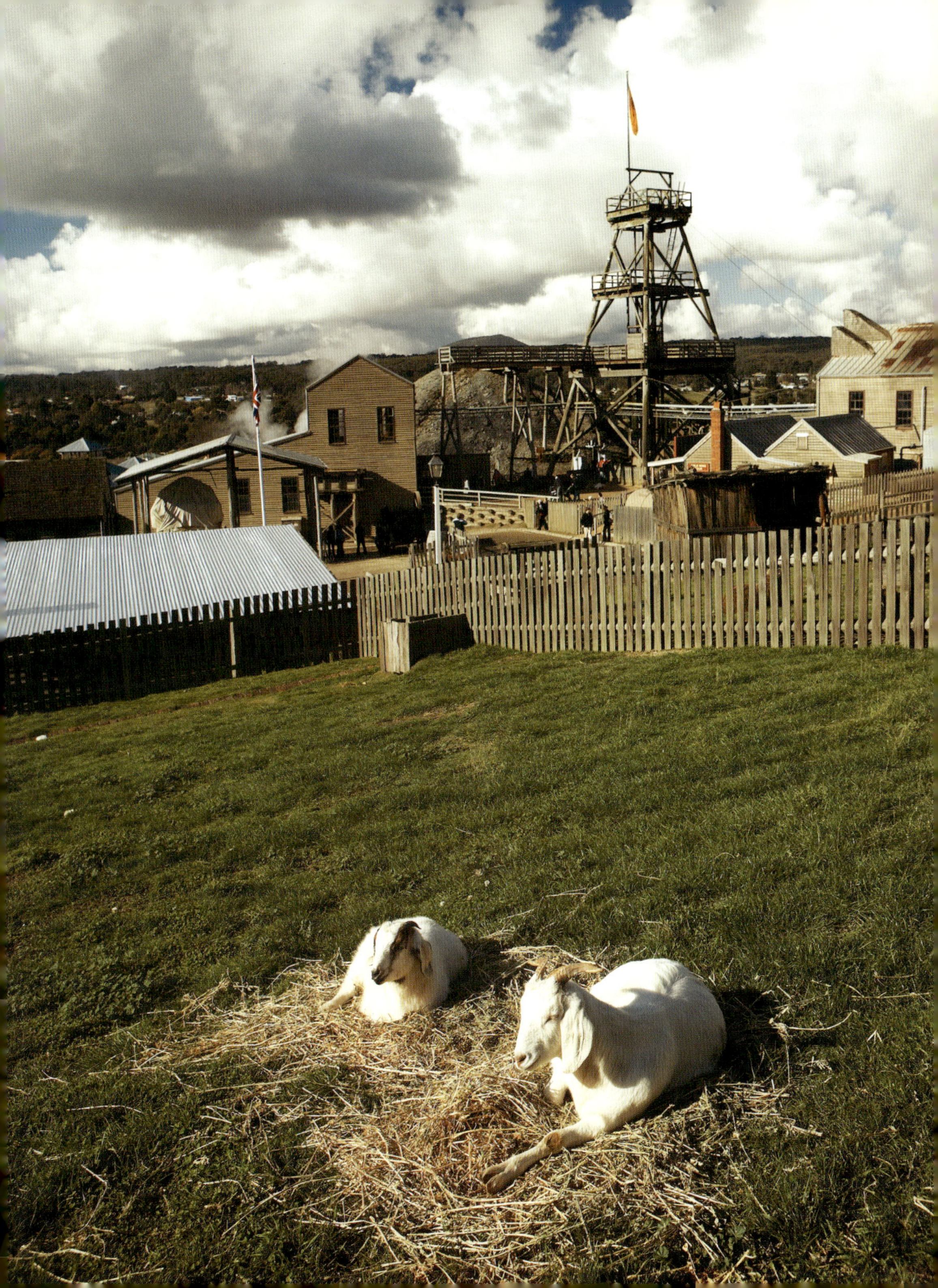

puddings his shop is a food lover's delight. Servicing many of the local businesses, who proudly state 'John Harbour meats' on the menu, John believes these restaurants represent Ballarat well and make the most of local produce and wines.

The Western District may be home to the best pastures and meats, but you need someone such as John Harbour who is passionate and righteous on following through on traditional butchering methods. 'All our beef is aged for three weeks on the whole carcass, giving it a richer flavour without too much moisture loss,' he says. With thirty years under his butcher's belt, eleven of those in his own shop he believes in doing things the proper way, taking no shortcuts whilst buying only whole animals and not just the prime cuts.

His customers appreciate the extra effort he takes. John considers his customers part of one big happy family, with the third generation of customers now shopping for his outstanding quality meat. Game is also important in this region and John sells squab, partridge, venison and wild rabbits as well as young goat in season. The attention to detail follows through to his smoking methods as well. 'We use only traditional recipes and utilise local hardwoods for smoking our meats,' says John.

Right and opposite
Ballarat butcher John Harbour sells the best of Western District meat, including handmade smallgoods.

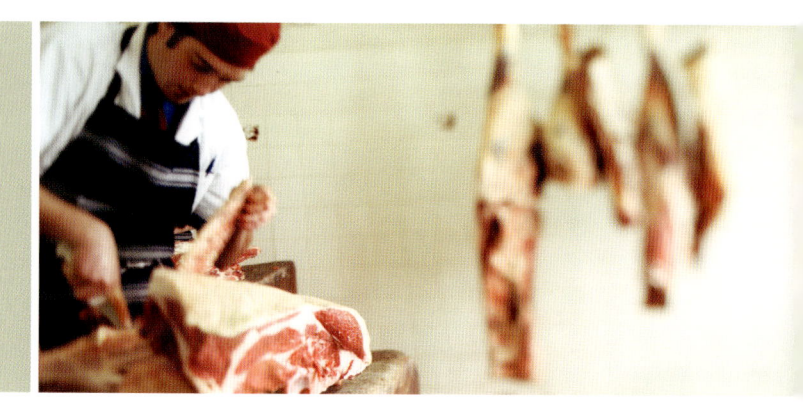

Grant Campbell of **Goldfields Organics** is equally passionate about his meat. His point of difference is his biodynamic meat, also grown locally from Stawell to Maldon. 'The region's growing diversity is excellent,' says Grant. 'Because we use no chemicals, fertilisers or additives it makes a big difference to the taste of the meat.' The growth in biodynamic meats has been phenomenal in the last five years. 'People are aware of what they are eating, being better educated at school about the environment and what we put into our bellies,' says Grant.

John Harbour is passionate and righteous on following through on traditional butchering methods. He doesn't believe in taking shortcuts

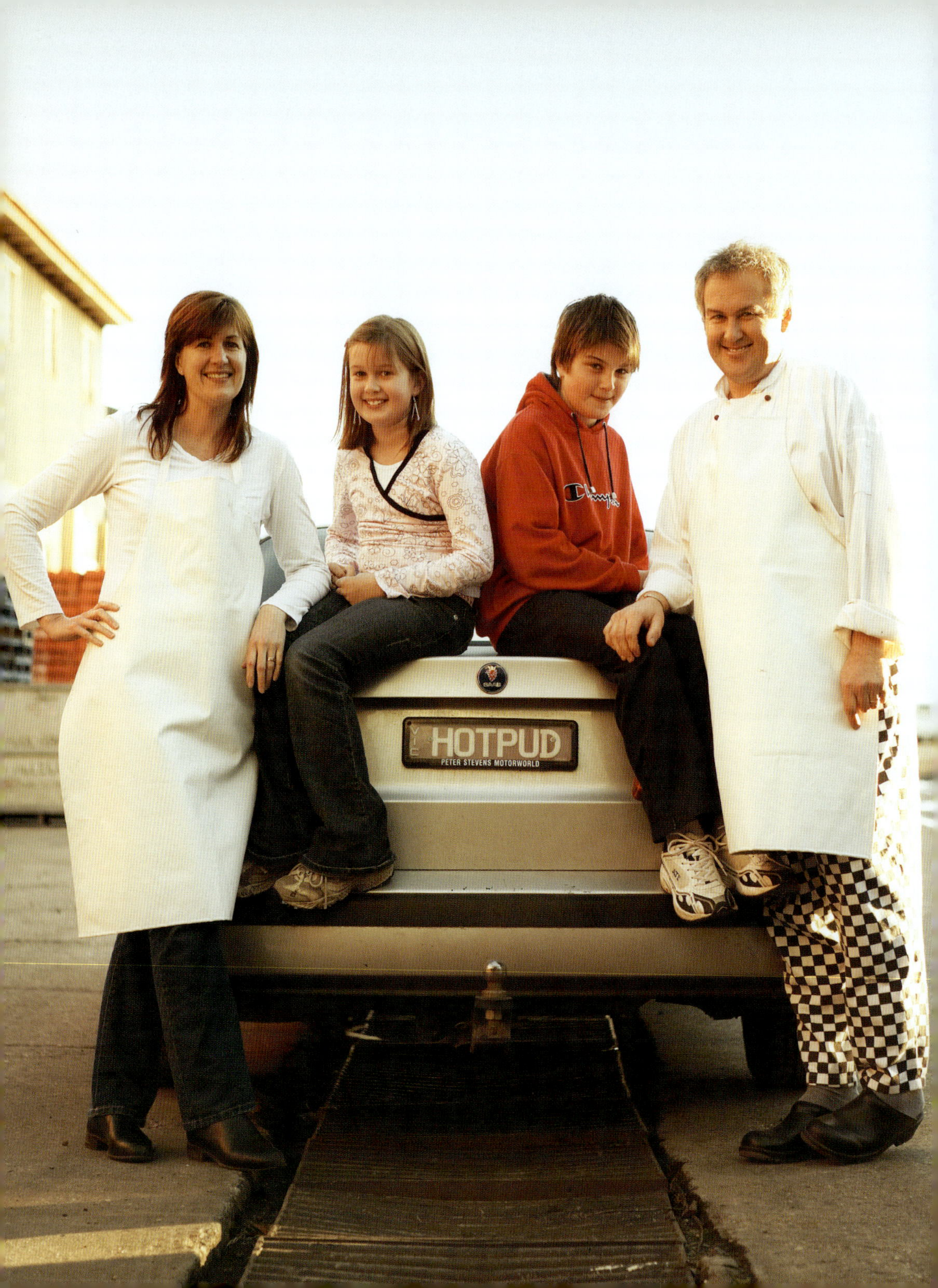
HOTPUD
PETER STEVENS MOTORWORLD

Above
Gourmet fare from Tiggies Puddings.

Opposite
Chefs Amanda Hayes and her husband John, who set up Tiggies Puddings, with their children, Mimi and Oliver.

Aside from meat Grant sells vegetables from local growers. 'Ballarat is renowned for its growing pastures, in particular the potatoes grown in the area,' notes Grant, who also farms lamb, cattle and chicken. 'Our farm has 300 chickens which provide us with enough eggs for the shops, as well as lamb and beef.'

Wallace, just east of Ballarat, is one of the coldest parts of Victoria and ideal for growing walnuts, which require a crisp, cold climate. **Wellwood Wallace Walnuts** has established a farm there and made a name for themselves with their first class walnuts and cold-pressed walnut oil. The trees are grown in the old fashioned manner, with plenty of space between each tree and following organic principles. According to owner Erich Mayer the exceptional taste of the walnuts is because the trees are not sprayed with artificial fertilisers and are air-dried in silos to preserve their fine flavour. Erich also says 'Our walnut oil is different – because it's cold pressed to retain its delicate nutty flavour and preserve the vitamins found in the nuts.'

City restaurants known for fine dining, such as Grossi Florentino and Pearl, use Wellwood's refined oils, but you can also pick up their produce at specialist local foodstores.

Springhill Farm has been producing quality handmade sweet slices for twelve years, after humble beginnings at Springhill Farm in Bacchus Marsh. Jo Barber believes that small producers have to be passionate about what they do to drive their business and is eagerly awaiting council approval for a new state-of-the-art facility for Springhill to call home.

Originally school children visited Springhill to spend a day on the farm, and were given a fresh muesli bar to eat on the bus on the way home. Twenty years ago fresh muesli bars were almost unheard of – now, as well as the original muesli slice, the range includes a Belgian chocolate-coated oat finger biscuit, wild berry and nougat, and specialist biscuits such as gluten-free and d'light slice. 'The gluten-free bar has achieved exactly what we wanted,' says Barber. 'A great tasting bar that appeals to wheat-intolerant people as well as ordinary customers who buy it just for the taste.' Stop in to local shops such as the Olive Grove and Wilson's Fruit and Vegetables to sample Springhill's wholesome slices.

Chef Amanda Hayes and her husband John moved to Buninyong for a quieter life, making puddings and running a country restaurant. After being recognised by *The Age Good Food Guide*, however, life became a bit too busy and they decided to just focus on puddings. **Tiggies Puddings**, a range of rich, luscious puddings made to an old family recipe, is the result. Hayes explains 'We have grown a lot in a small amount of time... This business gives us a good quality of life and allows us to support the local community as we source products such as flour, eggs and cream.'

The puddings come in three varieties; traditional, date and orange and fig and ginger, as well as bite-sized, chocolate-coated plum puddings. Although popular year round, Amanda says at Christmas time Ballarat 'comes alive with puddings'. International airlines are even ordering these delectable morsels for their business-class passengers. Tiggies has recently started baking individual cheesecakes, which are available in foodstores, both in Ballarat and Melbourne, along with the rest of the range.

Darriwill Farm – a small chain of gourmet shops stocking the best of country produce – has found a home for one of its stores in Ballarat's main street. The store, beautifully styled with pale blue walls and wooden shelves, boasts local products such as Tiggies' chocolate-coated puddings, Darriwill wines and products made and sourced on the Darriwill farm property at Bannockburn.

Trevor Wilson, of **Wilson's Fruit and Vegetables**, has taken the family business his father Arthur started in the 1940s and broadened its horizons. What began as a market garden and orchard has grown into a large greengrocers stocking some terrific local foodstuffs. The quality selection

Opposite
Fresh and packaged gourmet provisions are available at Darriwill Farm in Ballarat's main street.

Right
Dulcinea Winery, at Sulky near Ballarat, overlooks Mount Beckworth.

of apples, oranges, potatoes, carrots and lettuces is supplemented by farm-fresh produce, such as pumpkins in winter and berries in summer, from the Wilson family's own market garden. This is also the place to source specialist goodies such as Tiggies Puddings, Springhill Farm slices, Meredith cheeses, local Des O'Toole's honey and Decadent Alternatives, a Buninyong company producing gluten-free biscuits. Fresh fruit and vegetables are still at the heart of the business, though, and the quality ensures that business has never been better.

Wineries

As one of Australia's best-preserved gold-rush towns, Ballarat charms visitors with its sights and stories – and now it charms the senses as well. As the coolest of the three regions on the Great Grape Touring Road (the Pyrenees, Grampians and Ballarat), Ballarat is developing a reputation for its cool-climate chardonnay, pinot noir and – courtesy of **Yellowglen Vineyards** and **Whitehorse Wines** – its sparkling wines.

Ballarat district wineries are a showcase for cool-climate wines. Long, cool ripening periods and low fruit yields produce earthy, fruit flavours, typical of the wines from the area's mostly boutique wineries. Vignerons and winemakers producing the notoriously fickle pinot noir grape in particular have learnt to take advantage of the low temperatures and yields. The results are subtly fragrant, complex wines of many layers. Climate, plus passion and commitment, are resulting in nationally acclaimed, premium quality wines.

If you visit the cellar doors you might sample wine in a sophisticated tasting room, an underground tunnel or in a rustic environment of old-world, farm-gate charm. Winemakers are keen to share their experiences and their produce. Plenty of cellar-door discussion and information are the trademarks of a visit, and the unique characteristics of the wines form a lasting impression when sampled in the spectacular surrounds.

Rod Stott from **Dulcinea Winery** runs an old-fashioned cellar door

Opposite
Rod Stott of Dulcinea Winery, and a view across the property.

following two rules: visitors should make themselves at home and should help themselves to the wines lined up on the bar. The varieties range from sparkling chardonnay, sauvignon blanc, pinot noir, and cabernet sauvignon to sweeter wines such as frontignac and a tawny port, many of which are award-winning.

Back in 1977 Rod decided to become a winemaker and moved to Sulky, near Ballarat, as he believed he needed to be close to a provincial city. They set up their small winery on the Ballarat–Daylesford Road, on the side of a hill, overlooking Mount Beckworth.

The winery faces north, getting full sun which is good for ripening grapes. But the winery is on some of the oldest and most depleted soil in Australia which calls for some compensation. 'We knew we would have to supplement the poor soil to cope with the full sun, so we've built the soil up with hummus and straw, so it's a big sponge holding on to all the rainfall,' explains Stott. 'It's been a big challenge. Over the years the 2.4 hectares of vines have struggled. Originally we got 16 tonnes of grapes from the vines, now its down to 8 tonnes, largely due to lack of rainfall.'

The vineyard started off as a 'fruit salad', Stott says. 'We planted a bit of everything, as we didn't know what grapes were going to work. Even now we still experiment, planting some unusual German varieties of grapes just to see what's going to happen.'

Paul and Jane Lesock, from **Mount Beckworth Wines**, came especially to the Ballarat region for its cool climate conditions. According to Jane these conditions produce typical characteristics in their wines, such as the fresh, crisp stone-fruit flavours in their chardonnay and the plummy cherry flavours of the pinot noir, also with a hint of spice coming from a micro-climate over that planting.

Recent drought conditions have concentrated the flavours of the wines, and the dry has kept disease down. Jane says '2003 was our hardest vintage with very little rain. 2005 is looking excellent, we're very happy with the fruit and the juice we got. It was a late harvest, with a great finish to our season.'

They also produce a shiraz, which is very soft with substantially more spice, and a cabernet–merlot blend. The Lesock's have focussed on selling their wines regionally, with great support from restaurants in Ballarat, nearby Clunes and Daylesford.

One of the original winemakers of the area is Noel Myers from **Whitehorse Wines**, the second winery in the area after Yellowglen. Like Yellowglen,

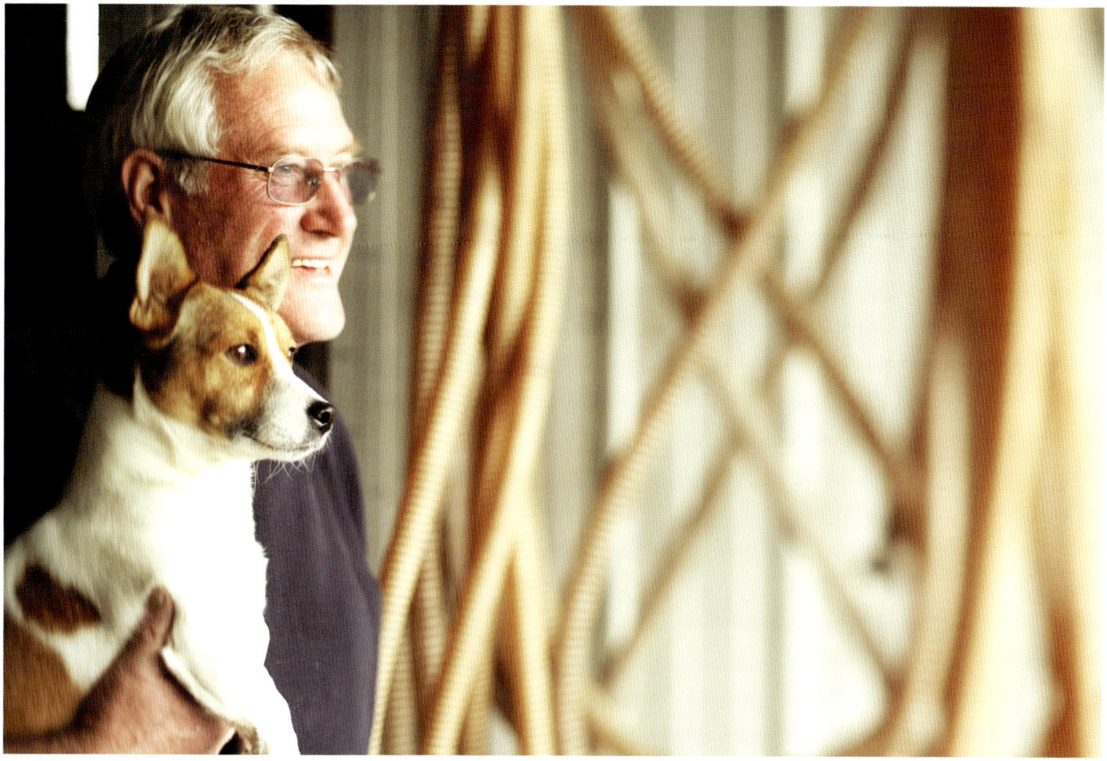

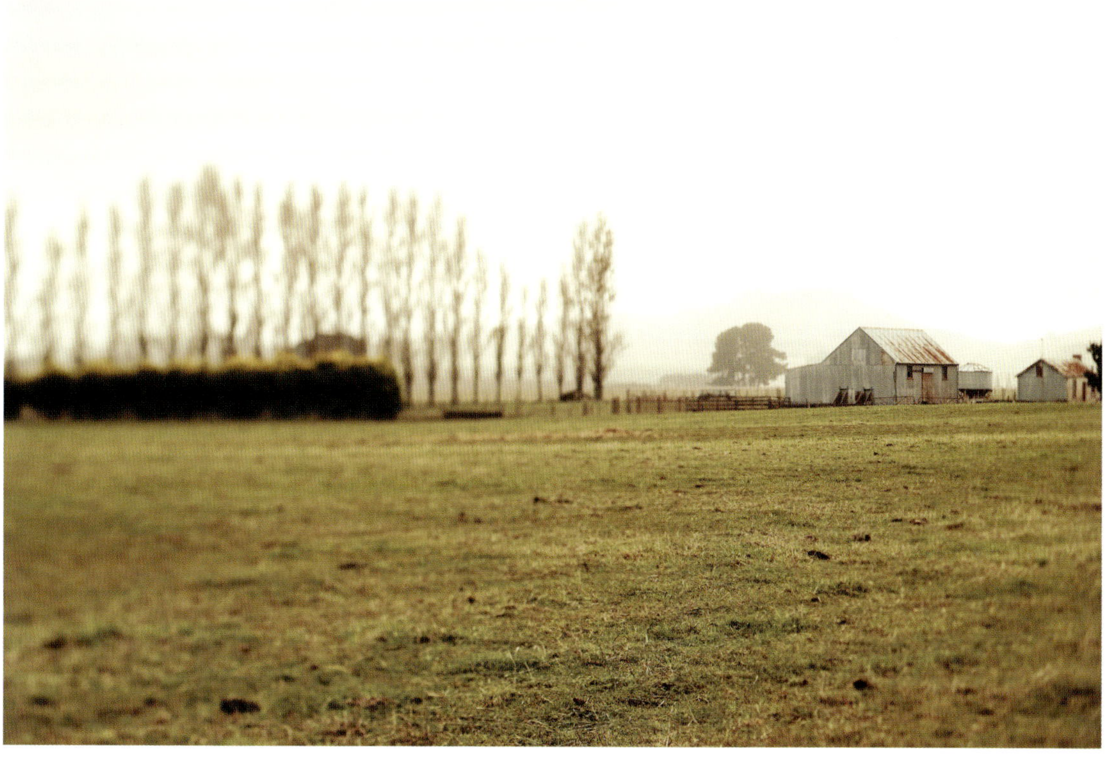

White chocolate and mascarpone tart

Peter Ford, Café Companis, Ballarat Art Gallery

Basic sweet pastry
300 g plain flour
200 g unsalted butter
100 g caster sugar
1 tbsp vanilla essence
1 egg yolk

Rub ingredients together, form pastry into a ball and leave to rest for at least 30 minutes. Roll out the pastry and line a greased 26-cm deep flan tin. Blind bake the pastry shell in a 170°C oven for approximately 20 minutes. Remove paper, and leave for 3 to 5 minutes to colour slightly.

Chocolate/mascarpone filling
75 g white chocolate
65 ml pure cream
3 eggs
110 g caster sugar
140 g mascarpone

Melt white chocolate with pure cream in a double saucepan or bowl over hot water. Whisk eggs and sugar together. Combine both mixes and fold in mascarpone. Fill the pastry shell and bake in a slow oven (120°C) for 30 to 40 minutes until set. Allow to cool and serve at room temperature.

Serves 12–14

Opposite
Chef Peter Ford, caterer and owner of Café Companis, at the Ballarat Fine Art Gallery, and a sample of his fine food.

Myers makes sparkling wines, citing the cool climate as the best to grow pinot and chardonnay, the two main varieties of grapes used in champagne, or sparkling wine. 'Like Champagne in France, Ballarat is a cool climate,' says Myers. 'To make good sparkling wines you need a long, slow ripening period to get good fruit flavours.' Whitehorse Wines makes a Ballarat cuvee with pinot noir, pinot meunier and chardonnay, a sparkling pinot noir, and a brut sparkling with pinot and chardonnay. Unlike warm wine-growing areas of Australia, Ballarat's climate can have an adverse effect on small winemakers of the area.

Norman Latta from **Eastern Peake** agrees on the complexity of cool-climate wine areas 'It's a pretty tough place, not every vintage works well, but when it's right, it's sensational,' he says. Ballarat is good to Latta, whose vineyard lies just north-west of Ballarat. 'I started off growing grapes for Mount Langhi (in western Victoria) as a part-time interest,' says Latta, 'then an opportunity arose where I could do it fulltime and Trevor Mast, winemaker at Langhi, suggested I do it myself – he's been quite a mentor.' Latta's first vintage was 1995 and his vines are currently twenty years old. As his whole vineyard is non-irrigated, the drought has been hard for Latta.

'The soil is a minor factor,' believes Latta. Throughout his vineyard he can distinguish three different types of soil, all volcanic and varying in colour, but none of this soil is of goldmining extrusion. The biggest issue is the climate, influencing the vintage enormously. Not enough sun and the grapes will not ripen. The cool climate produces complex wines with high acid levels, making them ideal for drinking with food. According to Latta, the chardonnay shows the most regional consistency, being lime, citrus with a honeysuckle nose, while the pinots of the area are more influenced by the individual winemaker, depending on how much the wines are oaked and post-fermented.

Eating out

A strong regional food and wine culture is evolving in Ballarat, with locally produced wines and local ingredients featuring on menus at many of the town's restaurants, cafés, pubs and clubs. Some of the grand nineteenth-century hotels, with their inspiring architecture, have recently undergone renovations, creating a wonderful environment to enjoy the region's produce and bringing a fresh lease of life to Ballarat's accommodation offerings.

An exceptional example is **Craig's Royal Hotel**, on Lydiard Street, an ornate Italianate structure – the oldest section dating back to 1862 – reflecting the grandeur and affluence of the era. Complete with colonnaded

Right and opposite
Café life at Ballarat's L'Espresso.

verandas, iron and lacework portico and the historic cedar bar it has had its share of famous visitors over the years including American author Mark Twain and legions of dukes, duchesses and princes. Today it offers casual bistro meals and superb accommodation.

Nearby is the **Ansonia**, an elegant boutique hotel offering intimate accommodation in a handsomely renovated Victorian building. The Restaurant, overseen by Heidi Jensen, offers breakfast, lunch and dinner in luxurious surroundings. The fine country dining puts an accent on regional produce such as Mount Doran venison and pigeon and trout and lamb from Tuki, near Smeaton. Roger Permezel loves the cellar he inherited when he took over managing the hotel. 'It has some real gems stashed away,' he says. 'The local Tom Boy Hills wines are almost exclusive to us; we have many vintages of their pinot noir which we feature on our menu.'

Chef Peter Ford claims the network of clients he built up while chef at the Ansonia has ensured the success of his catering business. Since 2004 he has run **Café Companis** at the Ballarat Fine Art Gallery, as well as servicing his catering clients. The gallery, Australia's largest and oldest regional gallery, is a prestigious venue. Customers can experience Ford's fine food in the bright modern café, hung with modern art. It provides delightful surroundings in which to enjoy a quick bite to eat, a more substantial lunch or just a coffee and one of his wonderful cakes, such as the seasonal quince tarte tatin or the rich walnut rose cakes.

'In Ballarat I have access to plenty of boutique producers,' explains Ford. 'These guys may not be good at self promotion, but they'll come to the kitchen door quietly with their fantastic produce.' With a steady of stream of suppliers bringing luxuries such as Fallow venison, partridge and squab, he makes the most of his ingredients on both the menu at the café and when catering.

L'Espresso owner Greg Wood grew up in Ballarat and after living for a while in Melbourne returned to Ballarat to open a specialist record shop in

Risotto with porcini mushrooms, red wine and thyme

Greg Wood, L'Espresso

100 g dried porcini mushrooms
1.5 litres warm water
1 bottle of medium-bodied red wine
400 g field mushrooms
1 bunch thyme
extra virgin olive oil
sea salt and pepper
1 onion, finely diced
4 tbsp butter
500 g Ferron carnaroli rice
parmigiano or grana padano

Soak dried porcini in 1.5 litres warm water for at least 1 hour. Reserve the water to be used as stock and roughly chop the porcini.

Reduce the volume of red wine by half over medium heat, reserve. Bake field mushrooms in moderate oven, sprinkled with thyme, little oil, salt and pepper. Bring reduced wine and porcini water to simmering.

Gently fry diced onion in 2 tablespoons butter and 2 tablespoons olive oil until translucent. Add rice, half teaspoon sea salt and stir constantly for 2 to 3 minutes. Follow classic rule of risotto making from now on, adding a ladle at a time of red wine, then porcini water. After 10 minutes, add chopped porcini and field mushrooms and continue ladling process until risotto is perfect consistency. Total cooking time should be about 20 minutes.

Turn off heat, add 2 tablespoons butter, plenty of grated parmigiano, pepper and salt to taste, stir gently for 2 minutes, then serve.

Serves 6.

'We use local produce whenever we can. At the moment we're serving local berries with French toast for breakfast.'

Below and opposite
The colourful and eclectic world of Bibo Bistro, in Sturt Street, Ballarat.

1976. 'After 10 years we knew we had to do something else,' says Wood. 'In 1986 we started the café, starting simply making gelati, serving coffees, and offering simple things for lunch... over the years we began to get more sophisticated and the food became more complex.'

Wood uses local produce whenever possible. 'We have used Meredith cheeses more or less since they started,' he says. 'John Harbour supplies us with local meat, then there's Tuki trout farm and Skipton eels – we use what we can when we get the opportunity.'

Situated in Sturt Street, **L'Espresso** is the perfect first stop after the drive from Melbourne, offering something for everyone, from hearty breakfasts and heart-starting coffees through to their Italian-influenced menu. There's also the chance to pick up a loaf of Irrewarra bread or the fabulous gelati that is made on the premises. A small selection of Italian pasta and arborio rice is for sale, though most customers take the easy option, sit back enjoy the intimate atmosphere and let the chefs do the hard work.

The music side of business still survives – the walls are stacked with specialist jazz and rhythm and blues CDs – and Greg believes most CDs are sold to people travelling to and from Melbourne who stop-off for the best coffee in Ballarat.

Bibo Bistro in Sturt Street serves fantastic Grinders coffee in this cosy retro café. This intimate space is quirky and eclectic, decorated with 1950's *Women's Weekly* wallpaper to add to the retro ambience. One elderly customer even features as a model in one of the scenes. Owner Charlie Graham sources food from the region whenever he can: 'We use local produce when possible. At the moment we're serving local berries with French toast for

Above and opposite
Mason's Café and Foodstore makes the most of regional and seasonal foods.

breakfast.' Breakfast is huge for Bibo with a big menu. It's just as hard to choose at lunch, with the selection ranging from braised lamb shanks and nasi goreng to risotto, pasta and vegetable stacks.

A more formal dining experience can be had at the award-winning **Tozer's Restaurant**, set in historic Bakery Hill. Kim Tozer had professional and sentimental reasons for moving to Ballarat two years ago. As he explains, 'It's on the doorstep of fantastic regions such as the Pyrenees, Bellarine and the Grampians. This gives us access to regional produce that's top quality, most of it sourced from within a thirty-minute drive.'

The restaurant is modern regional with a simple, yet stylish dining room, set with crystal glasses, silver cutlery and white tablecloths. Kim says that in Ballarat he can trade directly with his suppliers. 'I deal with the winemakers directly, our goat breeder brings in the meat himself, I don't have to deal with reps and it adds a personal touch to the dining experience. All the dishes on the menu have a regional influence, whether it's John Harbour's meats, local fish from Tuki trout farm, Meredith cheeses or locally grown fruit and vegetables.'

Slightly off the beaten track in Ballarat, in Drummond Street, is **Mason's Café and Foodstore**. Viv Mason believes customers trust them and come back for the hearty and healthy food produced each day from the kitchen. 'We make a lot of our own stuff,' she says, 'such as cakes, preserves and good wholesome food. We make the most of regional and seasonal products.' The café is a delight to sit in with its polished floorboards, whitewashed walls and shelves lined with goodies such as Meredith cheeses, Irrewarra's handmade sourdough breads, and Mason's own dips, cakes and tarts.

There are dining options beyond Ballarat's main street of course. Lake Wendouree, partly surrounded by Ballarat's Botanical Gardens, is a favourite venue for boating, fishing, walking and running and, of course, eating and drinking. **Pipers on Parade**, in a heritage-listed building, caters for weddings and conferences, but is also open for breakfast, coffee or lunch. The **Boatshed Restaurant**, with its deck overlooking the lake, is a popular choice amongst families.

Hope Bakery, Sovereign Hill

At Sovereign Hill, one of Victoria's leading tourist attractions, John Cirac, baker at the **Hope Bakery** in the main street of Sovereign Hill, pays great attention to detail.

Hope Bakery is based on a business that existed in Ballarat in the 1850s. At that time bakeries would have provided fresh bread for local families as well as lines of sweet pastries and fancy biscuits, a tradition that still continues. The Hope Bakery produces pies, pastries, cakes, buns and sweet tarts from a wood-fired oven that has been modelled on an original 1850s oven from Buninyong. The door of the oven is an original from Trahar's Foundry, one of the first in Ballarat and thought to have been made in the 1850s.

John Cirac has a long tradition with wood-fired ovens, starting work as a baker in Croatia before immigrating to Australia in the 1980s. At the Hope Bakery recipes are sourced from books of the time, such as Mrs Beeton's cookbook, and newspapers, though many have been adapted to modern needs, following traditional methods as closely as possible while adhering to today's food safety requirements.

Cirac loves the interaction of talking to the visitors and showing off his wares. Visit at around 11 am in the morning to see trays of pies emerging from the oven; over 1000 pass through the oven every day. Cirac starts the morning at around 6 am by lighting the fire in the firebox on the side of the oven. After about an hour and a half, when the smoke has died down, the baking begins with traditional loaves of bread, followed by pies, pastries and scrolls, then biscuits and sweets. Every little detail reflects how baking was in

Top five golden treats

- Hearty meat pies from Sovereign Hill
- Tiggies' delectable chocolate-coated pudding slices
- Walnut rose cakes at Café Companis in the Ballarat Art Gallery
- Old-fashioned spiced apple cake at Mason's Café and Foodstore
- Homemade baked beans with polenta, parmigiano and spiced sausage at L'Espresso

Damper recipe

John Cirac, Sovereign Hill

Taking a washing tin dish, and clearing off the dirt a little, six or eight pannicans of flour are thrown in; a half tablespoonful of carbonate of salt, the like quantity of tartaric acid, and a spoonful of salt are them mixed together in a pannican, and then well mingled with dry flour. Water is then poured in, the whole thoroughly knuckled, rolled into a good shaped loaf, and tumbled at once into warmed camp oven. Fire is applied beneath and a couple of hours or less will turn out a loaf fit to set before a queen.

Taken from *Nothing but Gold, The Diggers of 1852* by Robyn Annear

Hope Bakery at Sovereign Hill bakes classic pies and Cornish pasties, cakes, tarts and more in its historic wood-fired oven.

the gold-rush era, even to the squares of hessian sack used as oven mitts. And the wholesome flavour and lack of premixes and additives make these golden delights some of the best pies in the area.

Original Cornish pasties are a time-honoured classic, cleverly conceived as a two-course meal – one end being traditional meat and vegetable filling, while the other end provides dessert in the form of stewed apple. Other perennial favourites include Eccles cakes, Banbury tarts, Chelsea buns, miners biscuits, vanilla slices and rock cakes. Cirac revels in the challenge of dealing with the wood-fired oven and the influx of visitors.

There are other edible delights at Sovereign Hill. In 1974, traditional sweet-making equipment was moved to Sovereign Hill and a daily spectacle takes place as confectioners mould and shape hot sugar into traditional lollies such as bull's eyes, lollipops and sugared almonds, some of which are available at the local shops.

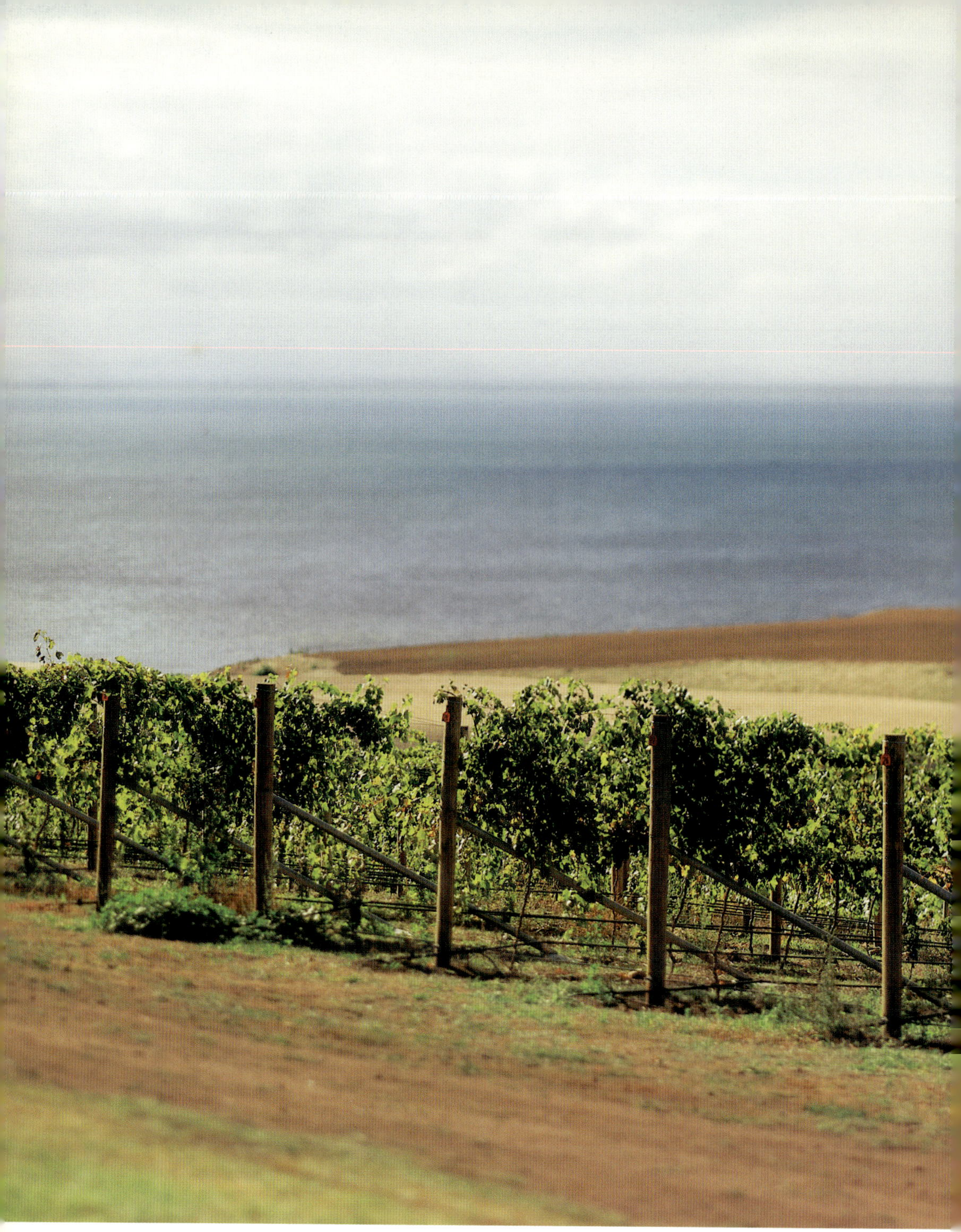

bellarine

allan campion

bellarine

MELBOURNE

bellarine

Lara
Corio
Batesford
PORT PHILLIP
Portarlington
CORIO BAY
Fyansford
Bellarine
Indented Head
GEELONG
Clifton Springs
Ceres
Drysdale
St Leonards
Waurn Ponds
Leopold
Wallington
Marcus Hill
Ocean Grove
Queenscliff
Breamlea
Barwon Heads
Point Lonsdale
Bellbrae
Portsea
Torquay
Sorrento
BASS STRAIT

There are a multitude of options and opportunities for those wanting to eat out, and take advantage of the area's seasonal and regional produce

Above
The pier at Queenscliff is a popular spot for fishing.

Opposite
The Black Lighthouse at Queenscliff.

The Bellarine Peninsula is a treasure trove for food and wine lovers.
Tiny bay-hugging towns and coastal villages offer a warm welcome for visitors, parking is a breeze and there's a relaxed bayside ambience. The region is surrounded by water on three sides with the usually calm waters of Corio Bay along its northern shore, the more variable conditions of Port Phillip Bay to the east and finally the ocean beaches along the southern coast overlooking Bass Strait. Hilltop vistas offer stunning water views across the bay to Melbourne and the Mornington Peninsula. The Surfcoast Highway, which skirts the western edge of the Bellarine Peninsula and passes through Torquay, is also the major link between Geelong and the Great Ocean Road.

Most visitors head down the Bellarine Highway with historic Queenscliff as their main destination. Here wide boulevards, renovated old hotels and views across The Rip to Portsea and Sorrento have been attracting weekend visitors for generations. To leave the peninsula after visiting only Queenscliff, though, is like visiting Paris and leaving after seeing the Eiffel Tower. There is a lot more to see and do, to discover and experience in this still somewhat sleepy corner of Victoria.

Everywhere the wide, open landscape allows expansive skies to make their presence felt. Explore peaceful Portarlington and enjoy a relaxing wander along the waterfront and fishing pier. Drive across the bridge into Barwon Heads and enjoy your very own sea change in this delightful town.

Make the journey to Clifton Springs and you'll experience a whole other side to the Bellarine Peninsula. The northern part of the peninsula near Clifton Springs and Bellarine overlooks Corio Bay and enjoys water views to Geelong and the Melbourne skyline. This is also home to the majority of the local vineyards and wineries, many of which welcome visitors for tastings and wine sales. The combination of maritime climate with bay breezes, excellent soil and a hands-on approach to winemaking has produced a boutique wine region that is recognised as one of the country's best.

Most of the local estates are family owned with well-known names such as **Scotchmans Hill**, **Bellarine Estate** and **Kilgour Estate**. Varieties like pinot

Right
Vines at Scotchmans Hill Estate.

Opposite
The historic Ozone Hotel in Queenscliff

Foodstores and producers

noir, shiraz and chardonnay do well here and renowned wine writer James Halliday remarked in his *Wine Atlas of Australia and New Zealand Wines* that Geelong wines are renowned for their 'depth of colour, bouquet and flavour'. Unlike those from warmer Australian winemaking regions, Bellarine wines are usually more European in style, subtle and delicate rather than big and bold, and wonderful to enjoy with food.

The Bellarine Peninsula has a multitude of options and opportunities for those wanting to eat out, and take advantage of the area's seasonal and regional produce. There's fine dining in splendid, renovated Victorian-era hotels and stylish vineyard restaurants, casual cafés and even fish and chips to be savoured on the foreshore.

The Peninsula also has many produce growers who regularly open their farm gates to food lovers. This creates a unique opportunity to meet the growers and taste farm-fresh ingredients. Tomatoes, olives, fresh herbs, lemons, blueberries and strawberries are readily available along country lanes and from rustic bush properties. Here, coast meets country, bush meets beach. It's not hard to see why this beautiful region has become a favourite destination for food and wine lovers or those simply seeking a sea change.

The farming life of the peninsula began with English navigator Matthew Flinders who reported on 'good grass and well-wooded slopes' after his journey through Port Phillip and Corio Bay in 1802. It was Melbourne's founder, John Batman, however, who was impressed with the Bellarine Peninsula and purchased 100,000 acres (40 000 hectares) of land there from Aboriginal people. Batman reported on the excellent black volcanic soil around Bellarine Hills, an area where much of the wine industry is now concentrated. 'I found the hills of a most superior description,' Batman wrote at the time.

His positive reports back to Van Diemen's Land led to settlers first grazing sheep on the peninsula, followed by agricultural plantings of wheat and

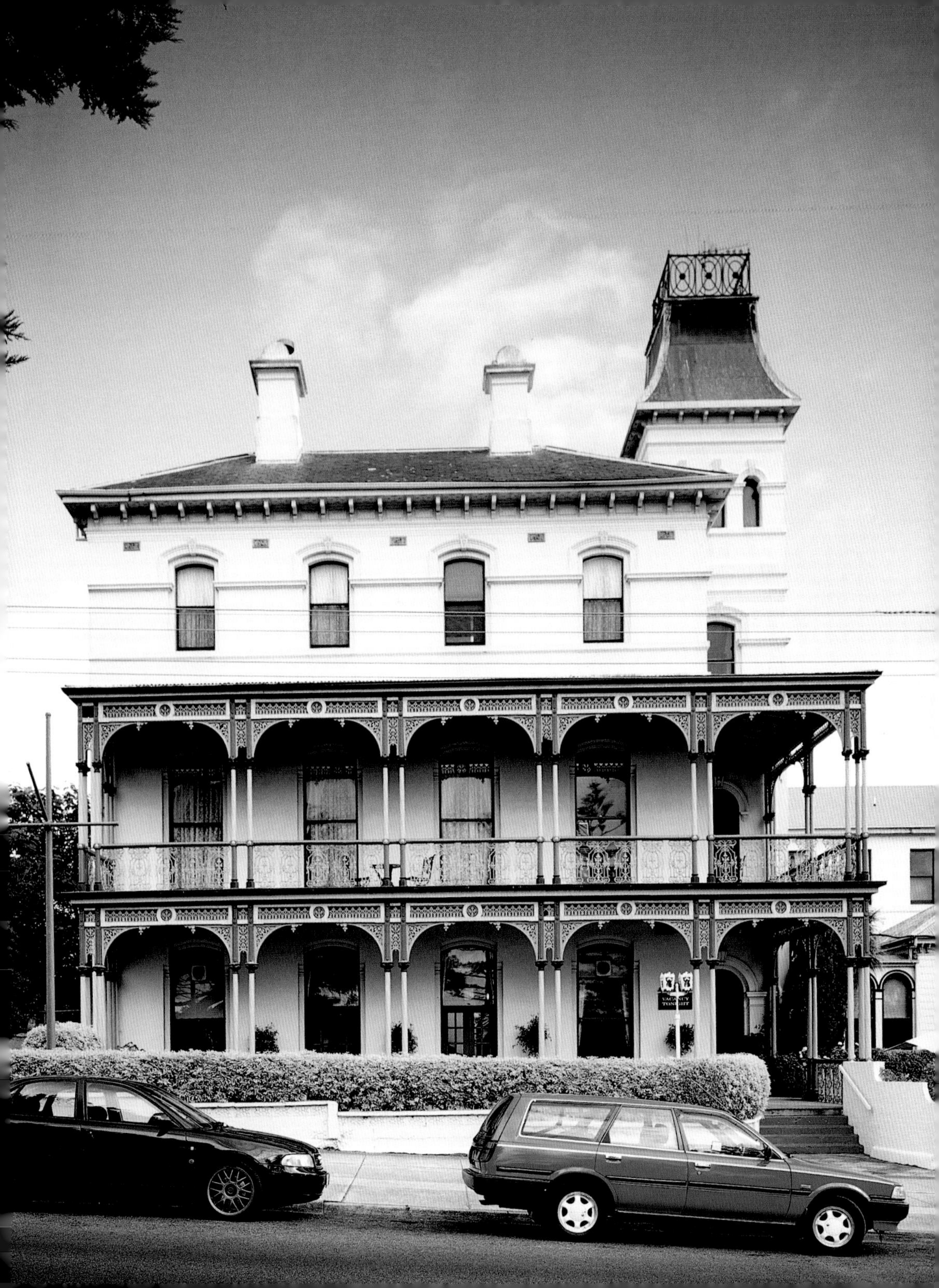

Olive bread

Renate Kint, Manzanillo Grove, Drysdale

600 g bread flour
100 g chopped black olives
1 tbsp salt
1 sachet dried yeast
4 tbsp Manzanillo Grove olive oil
300 ml warm water
sea salt for tray

Preheat oven to 220°C.

Mix flour, olives, salt, and yeast in a bowl.

Add oil to water. Make well in flour, add oil and water and mix to a dough. Then knead for 15 minutes or process with dough hook until dough springs back.

Place dough in oiled bowl and cover with clean towel for 45 minutes.

Knock back and work into log shape. Wrap completely in floured towel and stand for 30 minutes in a warm place.

Scatter sea salt on a baking tray. Place dough on the tray and bake in preheated oven for 20 minutes.

Herbs or green olives could also be used as flavouring.

Makes 1 loaf

Opposite
Olive grove and olives at Manzanillo Grove, Drysdale.

barley. Within fifteen years the area was described as the granary of the colony, such was the agricultural output. The Western District of Victoria later became the main area for growing grain, leading Bellarine farmers to switch to crops such as potatoes, peas and onions.

Today the Bellarine Peninsula is still occupied by many small farms and properties, although much of the well-wooded slopes as described by Flinders have made way for grass-filled paddocks. Now there are berries, olives, tomatoes, lettuces and grapes galore. **Tuckerberry Hill Blueberries**, in Becks Road, Drysdale, is an ideal spot for visitors looking for farm-fresh fruit. During the season, from December through to March, the opportunity to pick your own fruit is very appealing for food lovers. At **Wallington Strawberry Farm**, in Wallington Road, Wallington you can pick your own sun-ripened berries, full of flavour and sweetness, from a wide selection of varieties through the season between September and May.

Andrew Pearson's hydroponic tomatoes, herbs and lettuce are a godsend for local chefs. Instead of having to rely on produce from Melbourne they can now source beautiful, fresh ingredients grown on their doorstep along Yarram Creek Lane, at Point Lonsdale. Keen foodies can even visit the property to pick up their own supplies.

The property was established when Pearson decided to live permanently in Point Lonsdale, after spending all of his summer holidays there since 1955. 'As we only had 20 acres we needed to put in a crop that was intensive, without depleting the resource and also one where we could get an immediate return, and hydroponics provided that perfectly.' They now grow many different tomato varieties including cherry tomatoes on the vine. Lettuces such as red and green oak leaf, baby cos and coral have been joined recently by Asian greens such as tat soi. Herb varieties embrace everything from flat leaf parsley to basil, chives and coriander.

According to Pearson one of the benefits of hydroponic produce is that they never pick green tomatoes. 'We only pick when the tomatoes are ripe and really ready to eat. It definitely helps with the quality and the taste. Our herbs and lettuces too can be kept in water at home and will stay much fresher than conventionally grown ingredients.'

Supplies are delivered fresh to local restaurants such as **Athelstane House**, the **Vue Grand** and the restaurant at **Oakdene Winery**. However Pearson loves it best when food lovers come to buy direct from the property. 'I really enjoy letting consumers see what we grow and how we do it so they

Queenscliff – a little history

There's little doubt that Queenscliff is the premier destination on the Bellarine Peninsula when it comes to weekend stays and B&B getaways. The town has a distinctive legacy of hotels built in the 1880s, when money it seems was no object. What endows Queenscliff with much of its character is the combination of these grand establishments with the more modest buildings of the same era – worker's cottages, fishermen's shacks, small shops and civic buildings. Many have been restored or converted into guesthouses, cafes and restaurants, art galleries and boutiques.

Queenscliff's position at the entrance to Port Phillip Bay brought the first white settlers here. The town is believed to have been first settled in the 1830s by pilot boat operators who steered ships through The Rip, a notoriously hazardous stretch of water less than 3 kilometres wide between Point Lonsdale and Point Nepean.

As in neighboring Geelong, the discovery of gold in the 1850s brought growth and newfound wealth. Shipping increased dramatically, land sales were introduced and the town was officially named in honour of Queen Victoria. Incidentally, it was Charles La Trobe, governor of the day, and his wife, Sophie de Montmollin, who encouraged vignerons from her home region of Neuchâtel in Switzerland to settle in the colony and establish vineyards in the Geelong region.

Great Britain's involvement in the Crimea War in the mid 1850s led to the instillation of three large cannons as defence against any possible Russian attack, and fear of Russian invasion was taken seriously enough for Fort Queenscliff to be built in the 1880s.

Following the arrival of the railway in 1879 Queenscliff flourished, with grand hotels, guesthouses and restaurants built. Wealthy families and members of Melbourne society spent summers here, arriving by train or paddle steamer and staying at the many elegant establishments that lined the wide streets. Families relaxed under the pine trees along the foreshore, others took trips on ferries complete with bands and dancing. Doctors advised their patients to recuperate from illness by 'taking the air' here. Over time, however, new destinations were discovered and Queenscliff lost its position as a fashionable holiday resort, especially in the period after World War 1. But Queenscliff was still home to fishermen, ferry operators, soldiers, merchants and boat builders, who contributed to the town's survival over the lean years.

Luckily, the hotels were kept busy enough to survive the years, faded but intact, until renewed interest in the town as a holiday destination in the 1980s. It's as if time has stood still in Queenscliff leaving a beautiful 19th century town preserved for us to enjoy today.

Above left
The fishing marina at Queenscliff.

Above right
Cold-pressed olive oil from the olives at Manzanillo Grove.

can trust the ingredients completely. There's nothing better than seeing children and adults enjoy farm-fresh produce.'

Olives are another of the peninsula's growing food industries with neat rows of striking green trees appearing on hillsides and paddocks right across the region. **Bellarine Golden Olive** near Drysdale produce a selection of oils, some enhanced with lemon or basil. **Lighthouse Olive Oil** is a favourite with local chefs and visitors who are interested in trying a true regional product.

Renate and Len Kint established their **Manzanillo Grove** in Drysdale in 1997 planting over 4500 olive trees covering six varieties. They grow a lot of Manzanillo olives, which are usually considered ideal for pickling, but they are finding the oils to be of a terrific quality. 'We felt that if grapes grow well here, olives will too,' says Renate Kint. 'And so far we've been right in that assumption. The size of our property means we can still stay quite hands-on, which allows us to pick and crush our olives within twenty-four hours. This keeps all of the flavours and health benefits in the oil, and you can't ask for better than that.'

The Kints have set up a farm shop right in the olive grove so visitors can come and taste the oils where they have been grown. Renate is also working on a range of cosmetics using the property's olive oil. 'We're taking a totally natural and chemical-free approach and producing moisturiser, bath wash and face scrubs.'

Another important food producer in this region is apiarist Mark Cornell who has many beehives around the peninsula. He finds the profusion of native trees and their seasonal flowers provide him with wonderful flavours in his honey. Depending on the season his **Leopold Honey** varies from a pale gold through to a dark, rich colour, with varying flavours to match.

If you're looking for somewhere to source top quality local food and wine make a beeline for **Farm Foods** in Queenscliff. This one-stop shop combines butcher, food and wine store in one. All manner of local ingredients are on

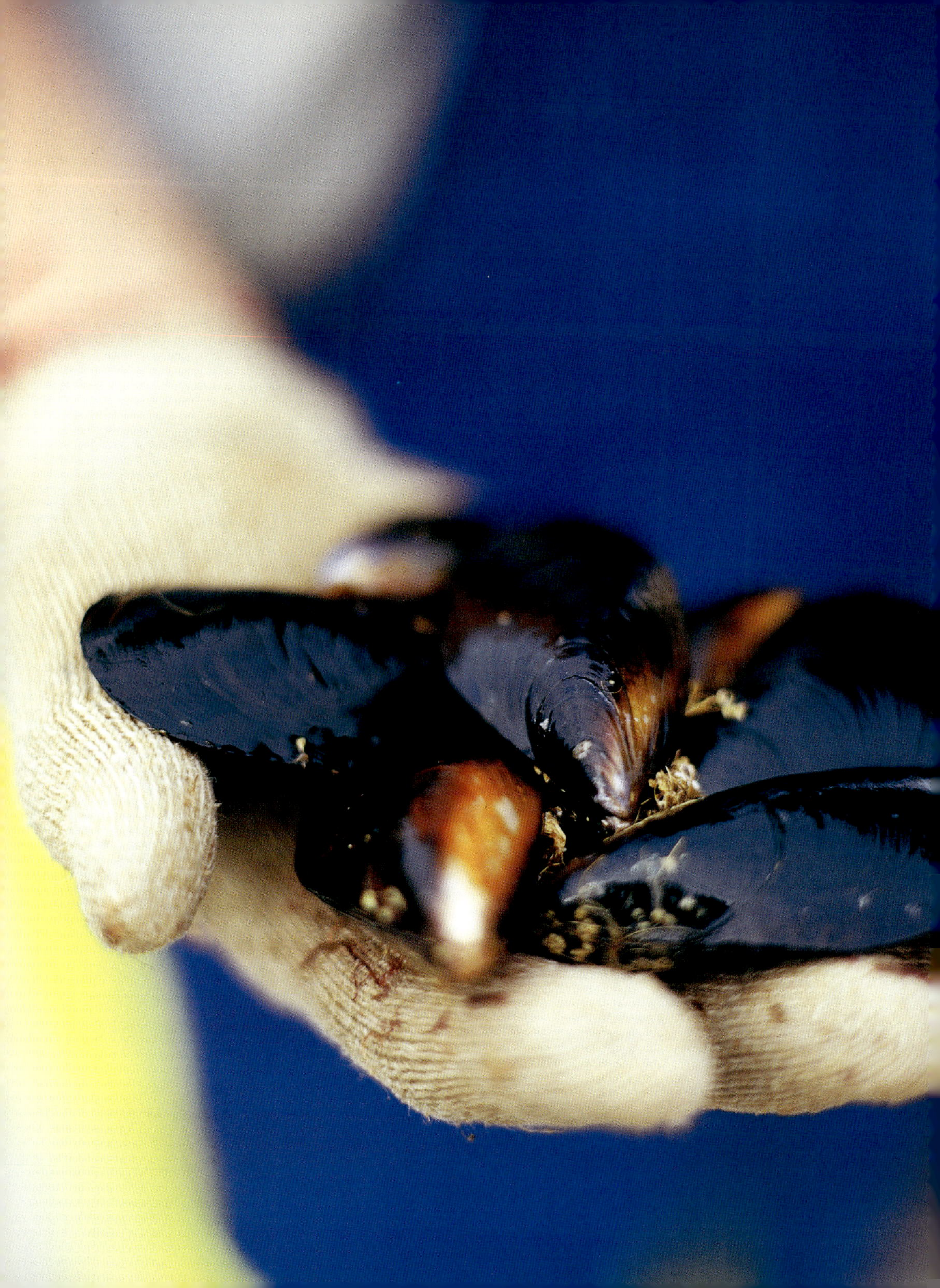

offer from Zen and La Madre breads to Meredith cheese and Manzanillo and Lighthouse olive oils. As well, you'll find gourmet produce from well-known foodie names such as Maggie Beer, Peter Watson and Stefano de Pieri stacked on the shelves.

The deli stocks only the best local lamb, pork and beef. The beef is particularly good, having been aged on the bone before going in-store. And if you are thinking barbecue, check out the top range of sausages. All of them are made with natural casings with the Guinness, herb and garlic variety in strong demand. A floor-to-ceiling wall of wine at the rear of the store is a boon for those trying to source local releases. Brands such as Bellarine Estate, Scotchmans Hill, Pettavel and Mt Moriac are all represented.

Fisheries

The history of Bellarine Peninsula is tied in with the history of the local fishing industry. Many of those currently plying the local waters are from second- and third-generation fishing families. The waters off Portarlington have been at the centre of mussel production for around twenty years and the local pier is a favourite spot for mussel lovers to pick up supplies straight off the boat.

Aussie Blue Mussels is the industry's major player, growing blue lip mussels on ropes suspended in the cool, clear local waters. The mussels are harvested and brought back to Portarlington for packing and distribution across the east coast of Australia. Seafood lovers looking for a kilo or two of tender, fresh mussels regularly stop-off at Aussie Blue's outlet on the main road into Portarlington.

Manager Rob Hede explains that they have recently achieved organic certification due to the pristine waters where the mussels are grown and the attention to detail during production. 'We get many people through here who love mussels and all are keen to talk about their favourite way of preparing them. The best was a Maltese lady who stuffs the mussels with breadcrumbs, herbs and garlic, ties up the shells and bakes them in the oven. They sounded amazing.'

Above and opposite
Blue lip mussels from Aussie Blue Mussels in Portarlington.

Right
Portarlington Bakery
in Portarlington's
main street.

Opposite
Baker Paul Fox, who
established Starfish
Bakery in Barwon Heads.

The **Coovara Fresh Fish Trawler** in Queenscliff Harbour is well known to visitors, with the daily catch displayed. Everything is straight from the sea, glistening with freshness, and guaranteeing an exceptional seafood meal.

If you prefer your fish ready-cooked and served with a paper-wrapped portion of golden chips, then the Bellarine Peninsula has plenty to offer. **Boatman's** in Portarlington has been a favourite with families for years now. **Flippin' Fresh Seafoods** at Torquay serves great flake and chips, whiting packs or a fish-bites pack for children. At Queenscliff, the **Trident Fish Bar** on Gellibrand Street does a busy trade with visitors looking for a quick, fresh meal of fish and chips (and delicious battered scallops) to carry across to the park and enjoy beneath the pines.

Bakeries

A number of bakeries on the Bellarine Peninsula provide locals and visitors with great breads, pastries, and sweet treats. **Portarlington Bakehouse**, which first opened in 1882 to serve the needs of the then growing region, is once again in business. The beautiful weatherboard building stands on the main street overlooking Point Richards, the pier and Port Phillip Bay.

Former chef Terry Christofi looked over the bakery when a friend bought it in 2001. 'It was an amazing, raw building with a terrific history, although the bakery oven hadn't been fired up for fifty years.' The oven in question – an enormous wood-fired oven constructed from 20,000 bricks – is now producing many hundreds of loaves of bread daily.

The oven is fired-up each night at midnight and the team of three bakers, headed up by Christofi, get to work. 'I find the heat produced by the oven produces a terrific crust on the breads, particularly the crunchy, pasta dura loaves.' Besides bread, the oven also churns out an impressive selection of cakes, pastries, muffins and tarts, eagerly snapped up during the bakery's enormous breakfast and lunch trade.

'Most of the tradesmen thought we were mad keeping the original timbers,

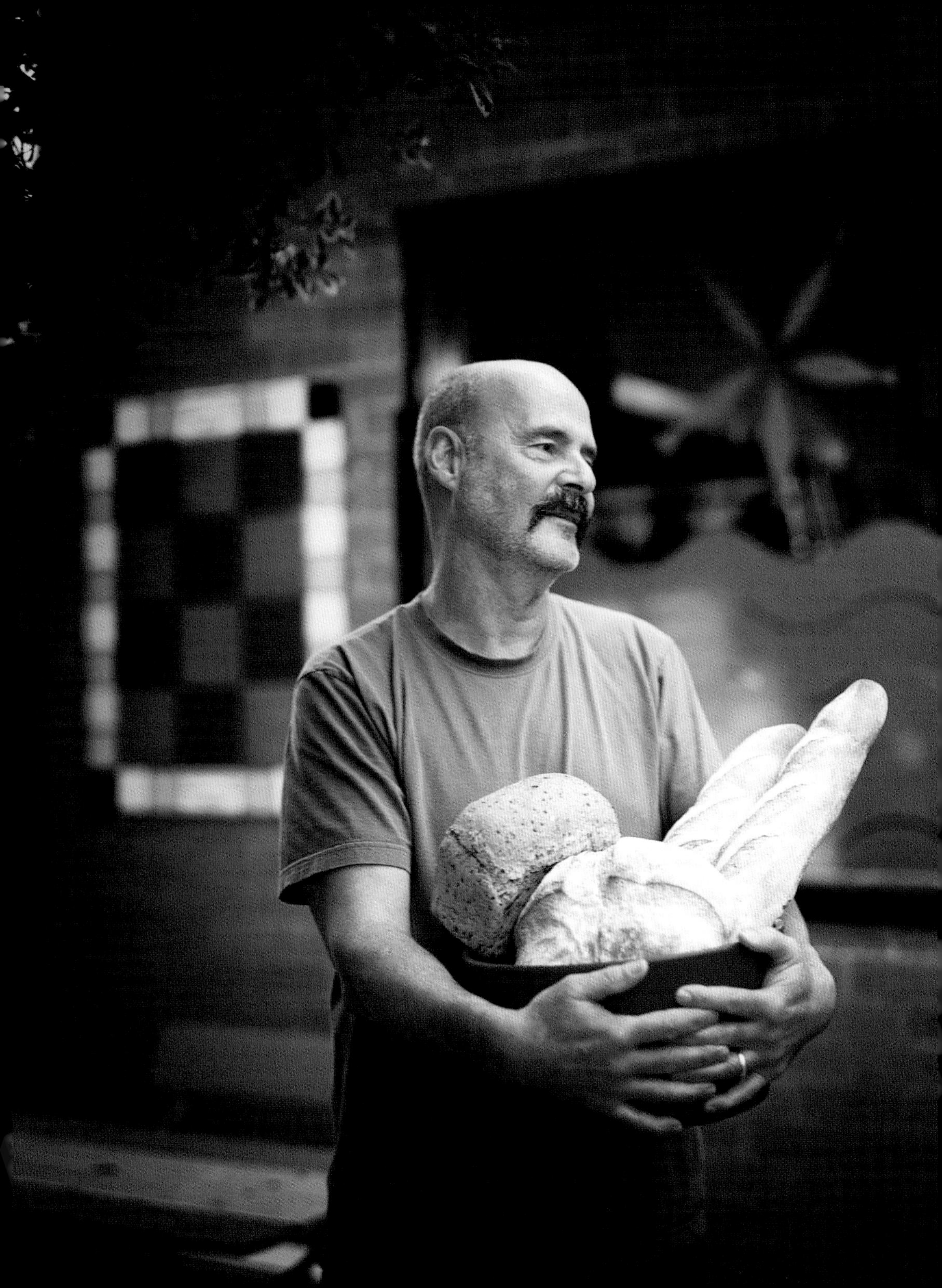

Right
Sweet treats and a window view from Starfish Bakery.

Opposite
Old wine barrels at Bellarine Estate winery.

windows and floors,' says Christofi. 'We still use the original bakery's counter today as our bread table. We knew this could become a real destination for people if we kept the building's history and feel intact.' So would he go back to being a chef? 'No way, baking bread is really satisfying, it brings a lot of pleasure to people. Also, everyone can afford it, not just those with plenty of money.'

Paul Fox at **Starfish Bakery** in Barwon Heads is another peninsula baker who has been creating excellent sourdough breads, cakes, biscuits and muffins for many years. Starfish Bakery has created a terrific niche for itself in the Barwon Heads community.

Over time, Fox has discovered what customers really love and he consistently provides it. The 'Squishy' (fried egg, bacon and herb mayonnaise in a soft roll) is legendary. Starfish's green eggs and ham breakfast (parsley, spinach and celery give the eggs their name) is also renowned and has been on the menu since the bakery opened. The made-on-the-premises breads range from crusty casalinga and baguettes, to unusual flavoured loafs like wakame and kelp or pumpkin, almond and polenta.

Muffins, brownies, biscuits and cakes cater for those with a sweet tooth, with almond Toscana cake and rich brownies baked in muffin tins two firm favourites. The bakery has recently extended its repertoire adding a changing menu of ready-to-go meals, which take inspiration from across the world. You might find a hearty Latvian goulash, gorgeous meatballs in a herb and tomato sauce, or a vegetarian dish of spiced rice with almonds, lentils and cashews.

Wineries

Bellarine Estate

The Bellarine Peninsula has a growing number of wineries offering the full cellar-door and restaurant experience, with **Bellarine Estate** one of the latest to catering for visitors. The vineyard was established on a hillside between Drysdale and Portarlington almost a decade ago by Peter and Lizette Kenny. They planted a varied selection of grape varieties, starting with chardonnay and

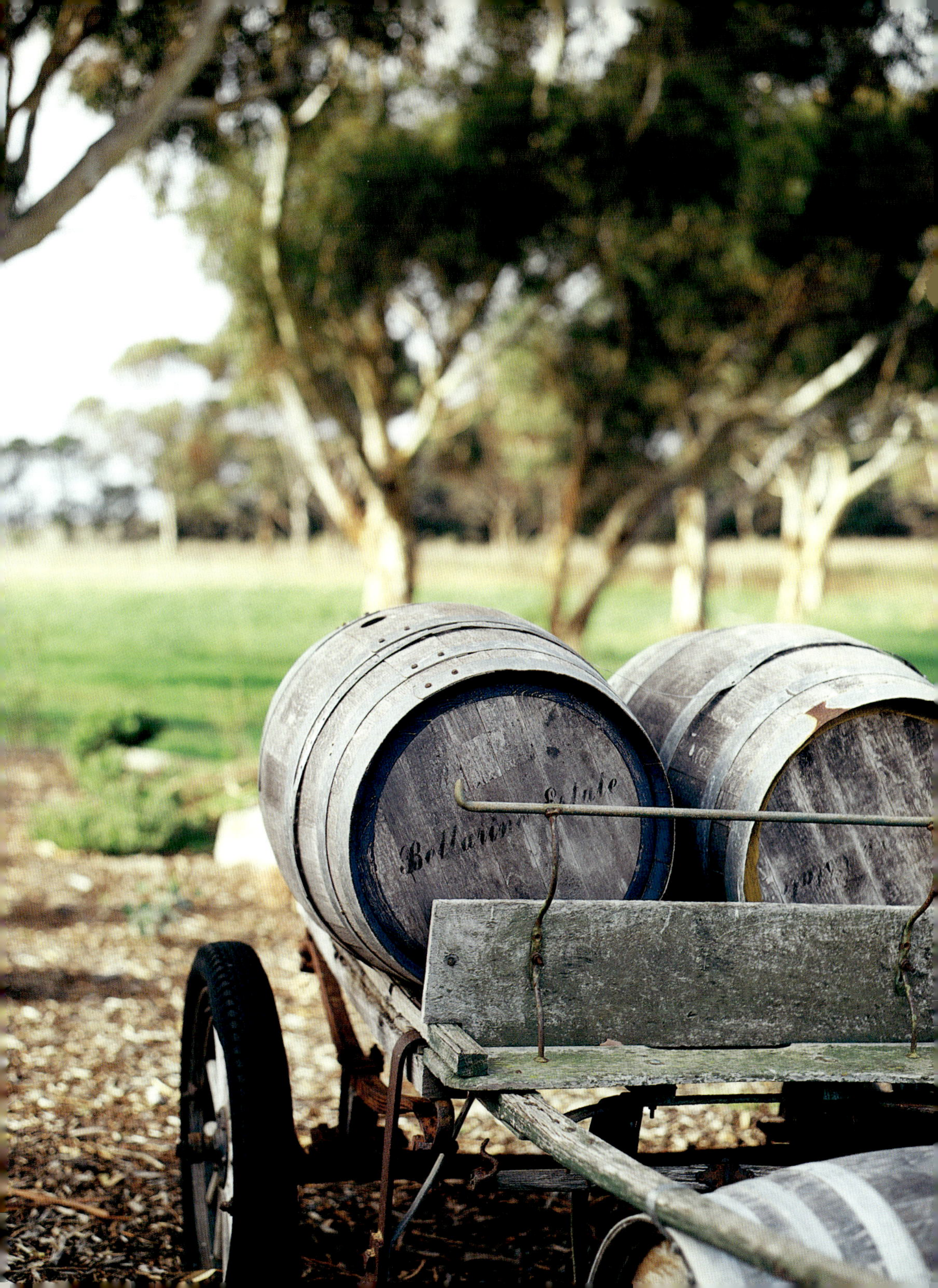
Estate

Salad of bellarine figs with prosciutto and dill

Julian Melican, Bellarine Estate

1 red capsicum
6 large figs
8 slices of prosciutto
200 g rocket salad leaves
half a bunch of dill
100 ml extra virgin olive oil

Roast the capsicum in a hot oven, 200°C, till the skin has browned and starts to bubble. Remove from the oven, cover with foil and allow to cool. When cool, peel the skin off, cut capsicum from top to bottom and open out flat, remove the seeds, then cut capsicum into 4 large squares.

To make the dressing, break off 4 sprigs of dill and place to the side (this is a garnish to complete the dish). Place the remaining dill in a pan and cover with the oil. Place the pan on the lowest heat and slowly heat the oil for 15 minutes. Remove and allow to cool.

Stand the 4 figs upright and make 2 diagonal cuts into the top of each fig about one-third of the way down the fig. Place your thumb and forefingers at the bottom of the fig and gently squeeze in so that the flesh is revealed.

Cut the last 2 figs in half. Place a half a fig as the base and the full fig on top, lay out a slice of prosciutto and place the stacked figs at one end on their side and wrap the prosciutto around the figs.

To serve, place a slice of capsicum on the plate, then some rocket leaves, then the prosciutto-wrapped fig on the rocket, drizzle some of the dill-infused oil around the dish and serve with a sprig of dill.

Serves 4

Opposite
The award-winning Bellarine Estate winery has both a cellar door and restaurant.

shiraz, then followed by sauvignon blanc, viognier, pinot noir, shiraz and merlot.

'The search for a perfect site took us five years, but we knew the combination of good soil, nearby hills to provide a wind break, plenty of sunshine and cool nights were just what we were looking for,' explains Peter Kenny. Recent tests have shown their gut instinct was spot-on as the area's volcanic soils are set above a limestone base, which is about as good as it gets for growing wine grapes.

The first wines were made in 1999, then the Kennys took the next step. 'We knew we had a great location on the main road and great views so a tasting facility was essential. We'd have lots of visitors in the morning and afternoon, but no one at lunchtime, so the next step was to offer food.' A 30-seater café with an outdoor eating area has now grown to a 120-seater indoor/outdoor dining room. The contemporary space features a glass wall, providing loads of natural light and views of the winery's vine-covered hills.

Julian Melican now runs this part of the estate's operation after many years as manager at the Vue Grand Hotel in Queenscliff. 'We source fantastic local seafood such as King George whiting, calamari, snapper, mussels, plus beef and lamb from the Western District. There are also a few market gardeners who come by with seasonal ingredients like figs, fuji apples, tomatoes, herbs and pumpkins. We even have sausages made to our own recipe by our local Drysdale butcher.'

Julian has also taken wine and food matching to a new level by including a tasting of an estate wine with each dish. 'It's proved really popular. We have customers who say they don't usually like pinot, but that was fantastic. Then they buy a bottle of it from the cellar door on their way out.'

'Having a professional running the restaurant means we can get on with running the wine business,' according to Peter Kenny. And getting on with it they are. Accolades and awards have come from far and wide for Bellarine Estate. Their 2000 Two Wives Shiraz took the silver medal at the 2003 San Francisco International Wine Competition while the 2001 release took the Chairman's Trophy at the 2003 Le Concours des Vins du Victoria. Julian's Merlot has picked up medals at numerous wine shows, from Ballarat to as far afield as San Fransisco. Their chardonnay received a 5-star rating in *Winestate* magazine.

The Kennys have also developed a strategy of naming their wines after family members. Hence Julian's Merlot, Phil's Fetish Pinot Noir and James' Paddock Chardonnay. 'We want customers to remember these wines, so they can order Phil's Pinot not just a Bellarine Estate pinot.'

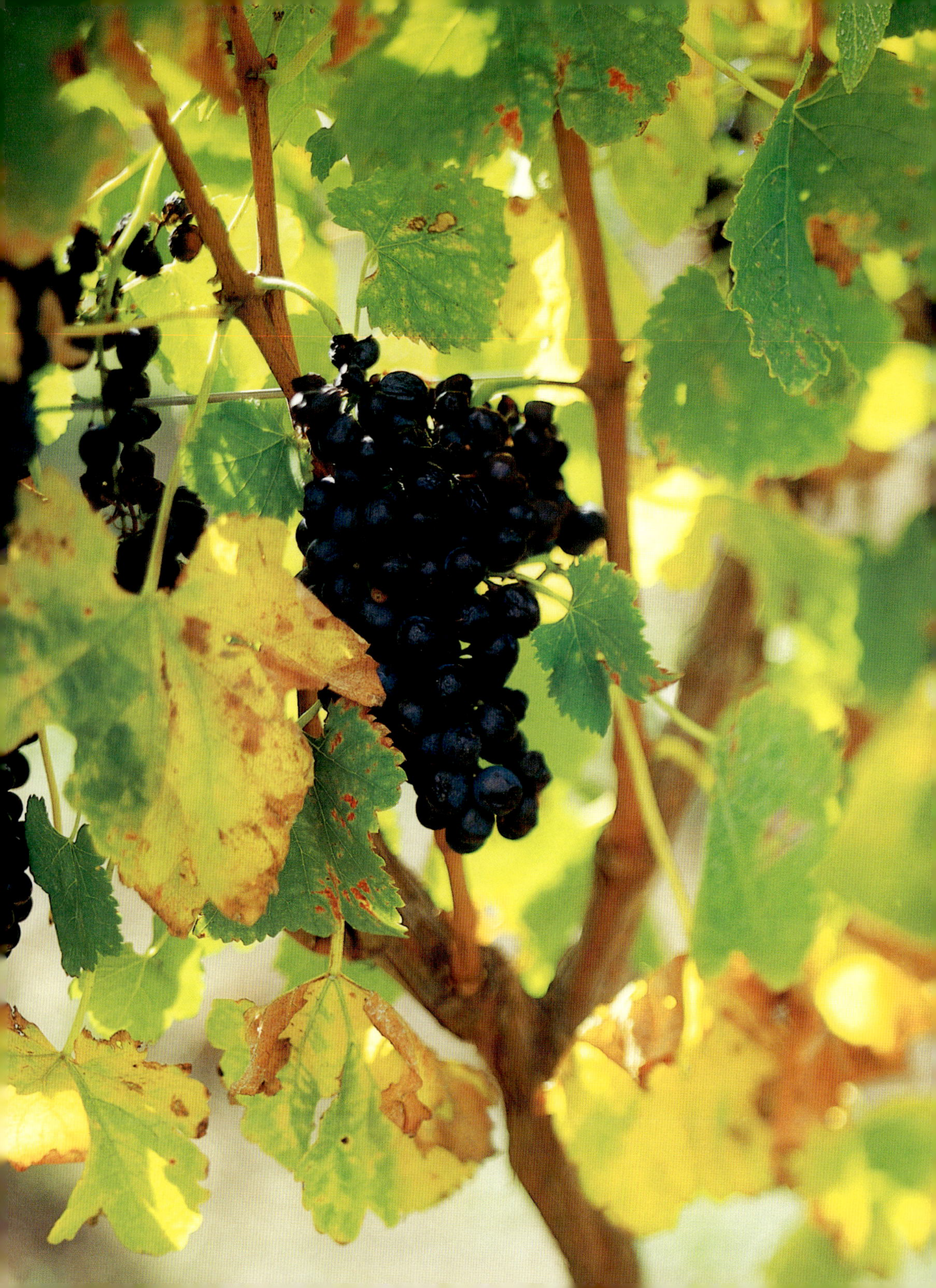

Left and opposite
Grapes at Scotchmans Hill Estate, the largest winery on the Bellarine Peninsula.

Scotchmans Hill

For many wine lovers it was **Scotchmans Hill** that first provided them with an opportunity to try peninsula-made wines. Those initial releases in the mid 1980s set a benchmark for chardonnay and pinot noir in particular that was a world away from what was being offered in those days. **Scotchmans Hill** arrived with wines that were subtle and delicate rather than big and bold.

David and Vivienne Browne first planted vines there in 1982 and the business continues to be family owned and operated. **Scotchmans Hill** is situated on top of Mount Bellarine, an extinct volcano formed over 30 million years ago. It's this hilltop location that provides wonderful views in all directions, with one of the original homes now run as a beautiful tasting room and cellar door for winery visitors.

Robin Brockett has been winemaker here since 1988 and has been instrumental in setting the house style and approach to winemaking. 'It was a very exciting time to get into winemaking as others like Stonier, TarraWarra and Coldstream Hills were also opening and doing really interesting things. **Scotchmans Hill** is by far the biggest winery in the (Bellarine) area.' Brockett says. 'For example in 1990 we produced around 5000 cases of wine. Now we're up around 80,000 cases both for our own labels and contract winemaking for other wineries.'

So what three wines would the winemaker recommend for visitors to start with at the cellar door? 'Well, coming here provides an opportunity for visitors to taste all of our wines side by side and make their own choices. Definitely the Swan Bay Rosé, what I consider the perfect summer drink. It's fragrant and intense with beautiful upfront berry flavours. Perfect to take home and enjoy with a plate of antipasto.'

Next up, Brockett tipped the Scotchmans Hill Estate Chardonnay which is full-on, barrel-fermented style. Creamy and rich, but still restrained, not fatty or over-the-top. His final pick is the Scotchmans Hill Shiraz. He describes it as elegant in the northern Rhone style with peppery spice, rich dark plum

Kilgour Estate

flavours and with soft, silky tannins. 'This shiraz has a very velvety mouth feel, like a pinot noir, which we've found people really like. The aim with all our wines is to make wine to drink and enjoy. For it to be an experience and always over deliver on quality at all levels.'

Kilgour Estate is nestled high on a ridge overlooking Corio Bay, its views stretching from Drysdale and Geelong to the You Yangs. Local mussel farms are clearly visible in the surroundings waters. The Melbourne skyline seems to float far away on the horizon a subtle reminder that you've left the city far behind.

A dirt track winds through the vines to the rustic simplicity of Kilgour Estate's cellar door and restaurant. The vines here weave their way over gently sloping hills with shiraz, cabernet, pinot noir, merlot and chardonnay varieties. Alistair Timms is the young winemaker here and has seen the winery develop from the first plantings in 1989 to the operation it is today complete with restaurant and tasting facilities. He trained at Roseworthy College in Adelaide before spending time at other vineyards around Australia and in Italy.

'I guess I've learned that the very best wines are really made in the vineyard, so if we keep a close eye on our vines we'll have great fruit to work with and I'll be able to make wines that taste of where they are from. We're also keeping our new oak down to around 20 per cent so the fruit flavours, textures of the wine and real character can show through,' explains Timms. 'Because of our north-facing vineyard we find we can ripen cabernet really well here, so in a warm year they're often our best reds. In a cooler year it's probably pinot noir which comes out on top. Our soil drains well so we get great concentration of flavour in our grapes.'

Timms is finding that, being a smaller, family concern they can experiment to produce great wines. The grapes are hand-picked and the wines made in fairly small batches, which gives them an opportunity to really get it right. And his favourite wine at present? 'It would have to be our pinot gris. It has an amazing texture, palate length and wonderful flavours.'

The winery is a real favourite with those who want to enjoy both food and wine, plus spectacular Bellarine views. A spacious deck area ensures diners can actually see the farms where the mussels they are eating were harvested, as well as the vines that produce the estate chardonnay. Most customers are after seafood so – along with the local mussels – scallops, flathead and other fish, often straight from the fishing trawler at Queenscliff, feature strongly on the menu.

Opposite
Shady verandah and tables at Queenscliff Hotel, which overlooks the Queenscliff foreshore.

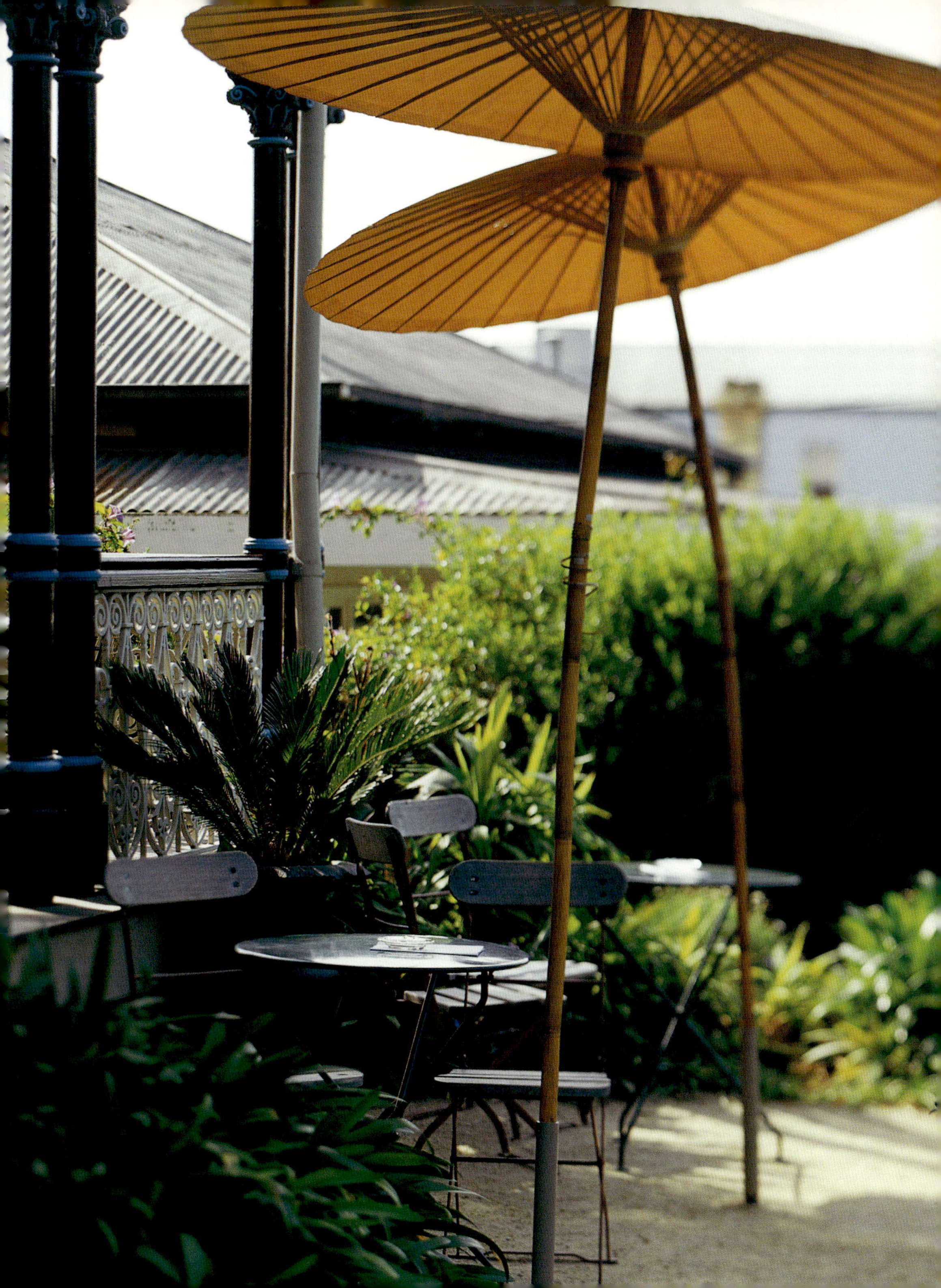

At Harry's, on the balcony of the Esplanade Hotel, guests can enjoy his excellent seafood menu as well as views over the bay to Point Nepean

Eating Out

Queenscliff

Mention staying in Queenscliff for a weekend and most people will think of the **Queenscliff Hotel**. It has a prime position on Gellibrand Street overlooking the harbour with extensive views across Port Phillip Bay. It was built in 1887 in the Victorian style to emulate a grand period home. In 1977 the O'Donnell family, along with Tony Knox, purchased the building and set about restoring it to its former glory. Five years later Patricia O'Donnell bought out her partners and continued to build the hotel's reputation.

Under her meticulous stewardship the Queenscliff Hotel became not just an elegant place to stay but a venue to enjoy fine food with an accent on regional produce. The hotel received many awards and accolades. The building retains a grand tiled entry hall, a host of comfortable lounges and sitting rooms, a conservatory and a splendid dining room. Iron lacework graces the building's façade and grand balconies, creating a shady spot to sit on a hot summer's day. In 2002 the hotel was purchased by Johann and Theresa Schuetz and it retains its period grace and elegance.

Left
Vue Grand Hotel in Queenscliff's main street.

Opposite
Harry's seafood restaurant has moved from Queenscliff foreshore to the balcony of the Esplanade Hotel.

The **Vue Grand Hotel** is another Queenscliff landmark, located in the heart of Hesse Street. It is an imposing example of Victorian architecture, built in 1881, and was one of the key places to stay during the late 1800s and early 1900s.

The Vue Grand was restored in 1983 by Equinox Hotels who still operate the hotel today. A stay here gives a terrific impression of what it would have been like to be a wealthy visitor in the nineteenth century. Everything is gracious, from the tasteful foyer with fresh flowers, tiled floors and beautiful

Opposite
The dining room at Athelstane House, in Queenscliff.

antique furniture through to the sunny courtyard, elegant conservatory and finally the lavish grand dining.

Michael Barrett is a name synonymous with seafood at Queenscliff. He founded the famous **Harry's** at Queenscliff, a restaurant on the foreshore that served the very best seafood available each day. Barrett recently relocated his dining room to the upper balcony of the **Esplanade Hotel**, where guests can enjoy his excellent seafood menu, as well as views over the bay to Point Nepean.

Athelstane House

Athelstane House offers a new approach to accommodation and dining in Queenscliff, far removed from the nineteenth-century hotels of yesteryear. Originally built in 1860 as a guesthouse, in recent years Athelstane has been completely overhauled to contemporary standards, while still retaining its original façade and beautiful wide balconies. Owners Ross Ebbels and Felicity McKenzie have also adapted the food, wine and service to a contemporary level. Guests and visitors have the choice of enjoying breakfast or lunch on the deck or in the courtyard in warmer weather, while the dining room, with paintings by local artists, is used for meals during both the day and evening.

Lighter meals include the mezze plate with garlic Turkish bread, house-made dip and marinated vegetables and the much-loved eye fillet minute steak sandwich topped with caramelised onion and fetta and served with house relish and fries. At dinner, regional ingredients might be represented by locally caught mussels steamed with lemon, garlic and parsley, or free-range Western Plains pork loin on roast vegetables with a spiced apple puree.

A seriously good wine list offers great wines from across Bellarine and Geelong regions and from some of Australia's top vineyards. Ebbels has been collecting wine for many years and offers a generous selection of reserve wines from his cellar to diners – from classic 1980s Coonawarra cabernets to 1990s vintages from wineries such as Petaluma, Bests, Bowen Estate, Henschke and the Bellarine's own Scotchmans Hill.

'We want customers to see us as a small hotel where we can make them welcome and provide a home away from home,' says Ebbles, who trained with Patricia O'Donnell at the Queenscliff Hotel. 'All ten rooms now have ensuite bathrooms and contemporary fittings, while retaining the style of the original building. The front lounge is often used by guests to host a private dinner, or we light the fire in winter and it becomes the perfect place to relax

Athelstane muesli

Ross Ebbles, Athelstane House, Queenscliff

1 cup vegetable oil
¼ cup marmalade
¼ cup pineapple juice
⅓ cup honey
1 kg rolled oats
¼ tbsp flaked almonds
2 tbsp poppy seeds
2 tbsp sesame seeds
2 tbsp hazelnut meal
2 tbsp sunflower seeds
4 tbsp shredded coconut
¾ cup of sultanas
2 cups All-bran

Preheat oven to 170°C. Combine oil, marmalade, pineapple juice and honey in a saucepan and bring to the boil over a medium heat.

Place all dry ingredients except sultanas and All-Bran into a large baking tray. Stir in the liquid and mix. Cook in the preheated oven until golden brown. Stir often.

Add sultanas and All-Bran bran to toasted muesli. Allow to cool and store in airtight containers.

Serves 20–25

Catalan cream

John Salanitri, Port Pier Café, Portarlington

2 tbsp cornflour
1 litre milk
250 g caster sugar
4 eggs
2 cinnamon sticks
2–3 strips lemon peel
pinch saffron powder
caster sugar, extra

Mix cornflour with a little milk in bowl.

Beat sugar and eggs then add cornflour.

Heat remainder of the milk with cinnamon, lemon and saffron. Do not bring to the boil at any stage. When milk is starting to bubble, reduce heat and slowly add sugar and egg mixture. Mix well, stirring until it thickens. Take it off the heat and allow to cool.

Strain to remove the cinnamon and lemon.

To serve, pour into small ceramic bowls. Sprinkle extra caster sugar on top to just cover the surface. Sit under hot grill until sugar caramelises. Enjoy!

Serves 5–6

Opposite
The Ol' Duke at Portarlington, in the original Duke of Edinburgh Hotel.

and read the papers.' Wide balconies on both the lower and upper floors provide perfect spots to sit, relax and watch the world go by.

Ebbels and McKenzie are also involved in organising community events such as wine dinners and book readings, all centred on a meal. 'We feel it's important to be a part of the local community and create events for food and wine lovers. We want people to see Athelstane House as somewhere to stay as well as a dining destination,' he explains. 'For example, we make our own muesli and serve it with fruit compote. Locals are always dropping in with a box of figs or quinces from their tree. So we put them to good use in the kitchen by making our own jams to serve with toasted Irrewarra sourdough bread. Guests can even purchase many of Athelstane's preserves and muesli to take home with them.'

Portarlington

It's fitting that Portarlington's first hotel, the Duke of Edinburgh built in 1855, should also be the first to get a major makeover for the 21st century. Melanie Pitman and her partner Andrew Parker took on the huge task of renovating the run-down pub in 2001. The makeover has been quite extraordinary as the **Ol' Duke**, as it's now known, mixes historic charm with contemporary style to create a modern place to eat, drink or stay. There's a great alfresco area on the front deck overlooking Port Phillip Bay for warmer months and open fires to keep warm in cooler months. They've also transformed a huge former billiard room into a beautiful dining room for weddings and conferences.

'We were aiming to provide a contemporary establishment within an original building,' Pitman explained. 'A place where guests can enjoy top quality service with great food and wine knowledge.' Local produce features heavily on the Ol' Duke menu with fresh herbs, tomatoes and lettuce from hydroponics grower Andrew Pearson at Point Lonsdale, seafood fresh off the boat, local cheeses and meats from western Victoria.

Breakfast is popular here too, especially on weekends. There are a few must-stays on the menu: avocado on toast with coriander and lime, and the Ol' Duke's capsicum and baby corn fritter with smoked salmon, poached egg and aioli, to name just two. Pitman and Parker have brought to Portarlington a talent and passion for their profession, from sourcing egional ingredients and their accessible cooking style, to excellent service and well-chosen wine options.

> The tapas menu runs from spicy grilled chorizo, fish croquettes and panfried sardines to potato tortilla and marinated baby octopus

The **Port Pier Café** is housed in a simple red brick building along the foreshore at Portarlington. Glance at the menu, however, and you'll be transported to the Mediterranean, with a selection of Spanish food not often experienced outside of Spain. The tapas menu runs from spicy grilled chorizo, fish croquettes and panfried sardines with garlic and parsley to potato tortilla and marinated baby octopus. The mains list weaves from half a dozen mussel dishes to seafood hotpot paella.

Port Pier owner John Salanitri attributes much of the café's success to their Spanish chef, who strives to keep the food as authentic as possible, both in flavour and presentation. 'We try hard for a full Spanish experience with imported beers and wines to accompany the dishes. Also, this is food to share which really suits this relaxing, bayside location.'

Another option for easy dining on the peninsula is the bar menu at the **Grand Hotel** in Portarlington, where classics include steak, fish and chips, pasta and soups, plus local mussels of course. The Thai chicken noodle soup is just right if you're after a hearty, well-prepared lunch.

Point Lonsdale and Barwon Heads

The open-plan kitchen at the smart **Kelp**, in Point Lonsdale, serves up what many consider modern Australian food. The menu jumps from Asia to the Mediterranean, with a sharp focus on seafood, as you'd expect from a dining room surrounded by the waters of Port Phillip Bay and Bass Strait.

If you're in a laidback, beachside mood looking for a casual meal then drop into **Barwon Orange** in Barwon Heads and sample their famed wood-fired pizzas. Or make your way to **At the Heads**. This stunning glass-encased dining room is perched right on the water where the Barwon River makes its way into Bass Strait. In winter, warm yourself by the fire and enjoy the beach and water views as far as the eye can see. The macadamia, pear and chocolate chip muffins are particularly good, as is the coffee.

Five feasts with a view

- Portarlington's Port Pier Café for panfried sardines, Spanish Estrella beer and bay views to the Melbourne skyline.
- Kilgour Estate Winery to sample steamed Portarlington mussels with an estate chardonnay, and savour the panoramic bay views.
- At Bellarine Estate, Julian's salad of Radone's Bellarine fig wrapped with prosciutto, a glass of sauvignon blanc and views to the vines.
- At The Heads for an afternoon of muffins, coffee and stunning vistas across the Barwon River to Bass Strait.
- Scorched has excellent views through the pine trees to the waters of Bass Strait. Order up big on seafood, a bottle of riesling and you're set.

Torquay

One of the latest additions to the local dining scene has been **Scorched**, in Torquay. The town stands at the kicking-off point for the Great Ocean Road and is home to wonderful beaches including the world-famous surfers' hangout Bells Beach. Now it can add a contemporary, smart dining room to its list of attractions. The three owners saw the need for a local restaurant with a thoughtful mix of good food and wine – somewhere formal enough for evenings yet casual enough for daytime. Wine dinners have proved to be a resounding success, with the grape variety chosen first, then food selected to show it off at its best. The food here definitely takes a modern approach with dishes such as scallop seviche with avocado, blue swimmer crab and celeriac remoulade. And local wines are a feature on the restaurant's sizeable list.

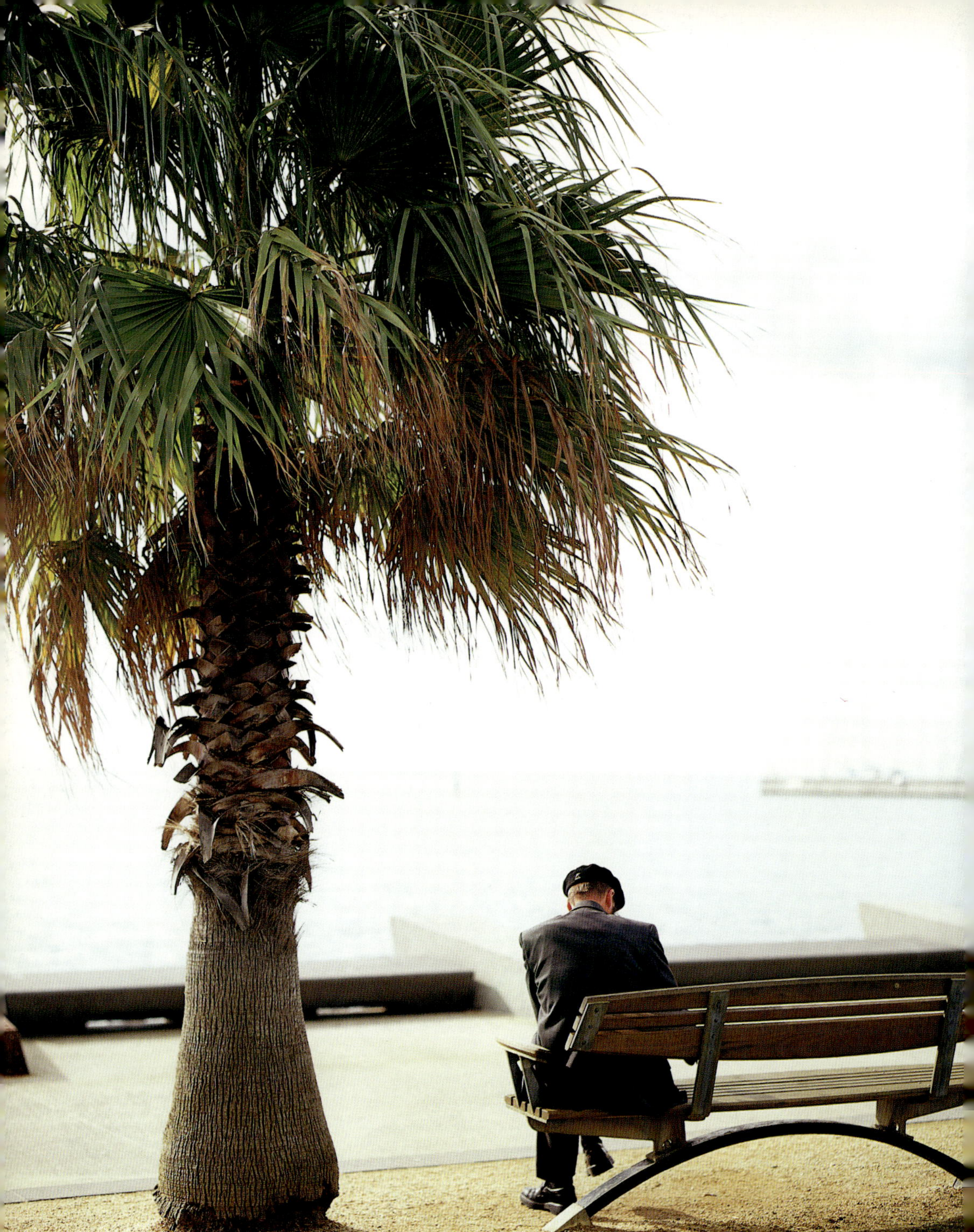

geelong

allan campion

geelong

New foodstores, bakeries, wineries and cafés seem to appear daily, and diners can now enjoy water views from a number of excellent restaurants

Above
Fishermen's Pier on Corio Bay.

Opposite
The Geelong waterfront.

There's a quiet revolution taking place in Geelong that has seen the city regain its position as the state's major regional centre. This bustling town of almost 200,000 people has experienced a makeover in the last decade like you wouldn't believe. To begin with, a review of the city's heritage has seen around 200 buildings receive National Trust classifications. Over $150 million is being spent on beautifying the parks and waterfront area. New food stores, bakeries, wineries and cafés seem to appear daily, and diners can now enjoy water views from a number of excellent restaurants.

All of this activity is bringing Geelong back to its heyday as one of Victoria's premier destinations. After all, this is a place of stunning Victorian homes, wide boulevards, beautiful parks and gardens, and a waterfront setting on Corio Bay that most towns would give their eyeteeth for. Like much of this state it was the discovery of gold that led to Geelong's original boom. As the closest port to the goldfields of Ballarat and Bendigo, Geelong saw hundreds of thousands of miners arrive by ship in the 1850s.

The region's food and wine history started even before gold fever took hold. In fact it was wine that first put Geelong on the map in many ways. In the nineteenth century Geelong was recognised as the largest grape-growing region in Victoria and one of the largest in the country. The first plantings are believed to have been in 1842 and this grew to around 400 hectares within three decades.

Swiss and German migrants in particular brought grape-growing and winemaking skills from Europe to this region. They established over a hundred wineries on the plains around Geelong, making use of the temperate climate and limestone-based soils to create top quality wines. The industry was hit hard by the 1890s recession and was delivered a final blow with the arrival of the disease Phylloxera, and the government's decision to order every vine uprooted and destroyed in an effort to stop the disease spreading to other grape-growing regions.

It wasn't until the 1960s that the first signs of a resurgence appeared, when winemakers began to re-establish vineyards in the Geelong area. Vineyards

Right
The Geelong pier.

Opposite
One of the iconic painted bollards that line the Eastern Beach area along Geelong's foreshore.

such as **Idyll** were planted and led the way for others. **Bannockburn** followed in the early 1970s, planting to the north-west of Geelong and producing some seriously good wines made by Garry Farr. **Scotchmans Hill** Vineyard was planted in the 1980s on nearby Bellarine Peninsula and has gone from strength to strength.

The last ten years have seen Geelong make up lost ground. With a renewed focus on food and wine, from its local farmers' market and well-stocked wine stores to its waterfront restaurants and café life, there's no doubt that Geelong is again the place to be.

Foodstores and producers

As a food-loving visitor I'd expect Geelong to have great fresh seafood on offer fresh from the bay, a couple of top quality sourdough bakeries plus fantastic fruit and vegetables directly from growers in the surrounding area. I'd also be hopeful of coming across a local farmers' market plus a good selection of delicatessens, butchers, and food stores. A few years ago you would have had a 50 per cent success rate on this hit list, now all of this and more is available in this city by the bay. Visit Little Malop Street mall the second Saturday morning of each month and you can experience the **Central Geelong Farmer's Market**.

This market presents the best of the Geelong region, with around forty stallholders at each market. This is a terrific opportunity for consumers to meet producers, taste their wares and find out about how it is grown and produced. Graham Hollis from Origin Speciality Coffee is a regular at the market and loves being in amongst the stallholders and meeting shoppers. 'We can explain the concept of speciality coffee beans. These are the top 7 per cent of the world's crop and are all we will use,' he says. 'We also roast to order so you know you're getting coffee at its very best in terms of flavour and quality. It's also the perfect opportunity for me to discuss people's coffee requirements directly with them.'

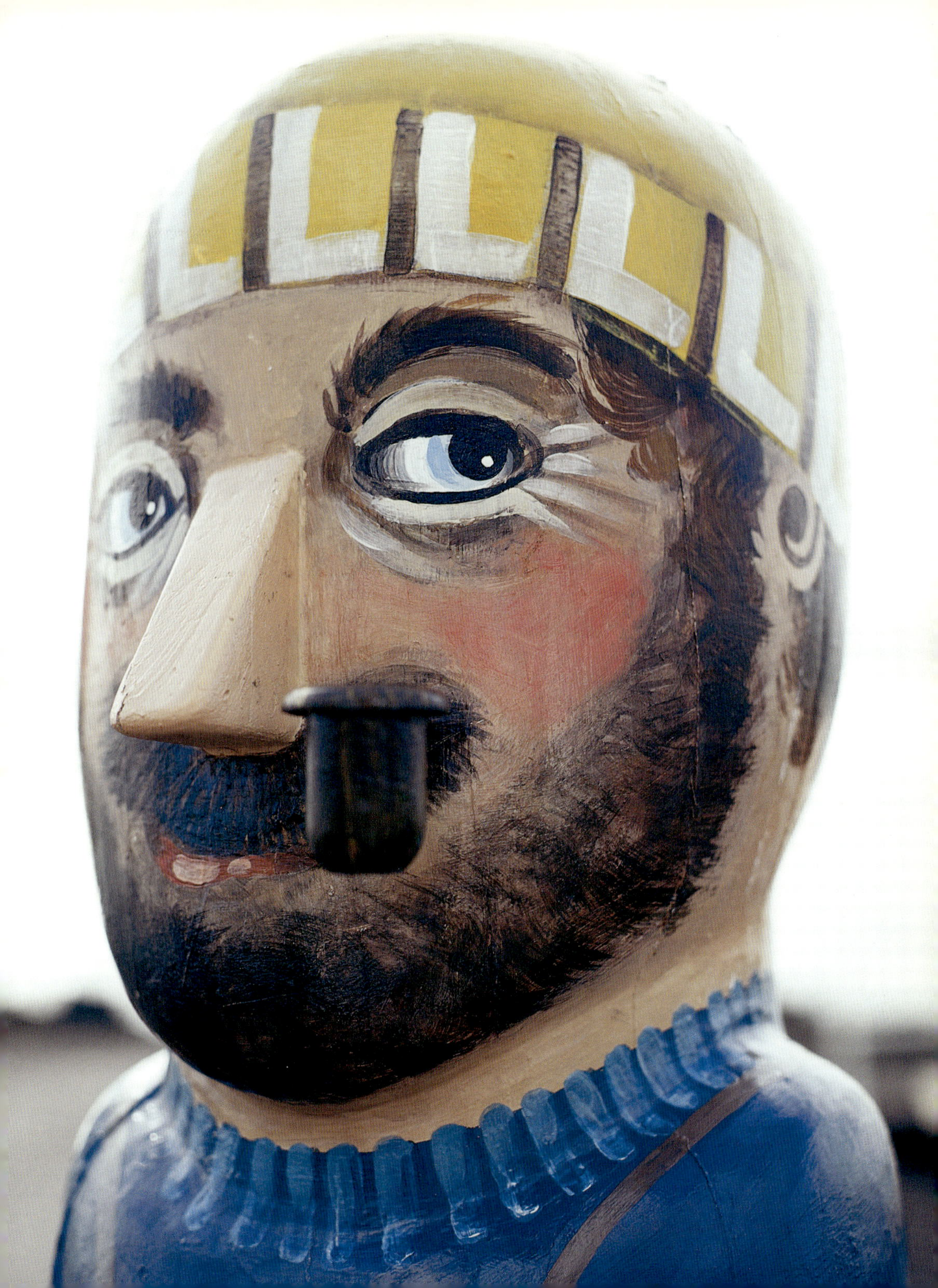

Five foodies' treats around Geelong

- A seeded sourdough loaf hot from the oven at La Madre bakery, sliced and drizzled with Leopold honey

- Thin slices of Cardoso jamon served with a glass of Randall's Geelong Shiraz

- Chocolate panforte and a Genovese coffee from Irrewarra Sourdough Shop and Café

- Fish and chips from Gilligan's on the Geelong waterfront

- Crumbed, panfried chicken with roast red peppers and a glass of sangiovese at Giuseppe's

Opposite top
One of the gourmet sausages from Angel Cardoso's range of Spanish-inspired smallgoods.

Opposite below
Mondo Deli, one of Geelong's well-stocked specialist foodstores, and some of the gourmet fare.

Leaf Tea takes a similar approach with their herbal and green teas by offering tastings and even advice on the health benefits of different teas. Renate Kint from Manzanillo Grove is another regular face at the market with her marinated olives and olive oils. To her way of thinking the market is the perfect way to let people know about the products.

Other stallholders provide local honey, Portarlington mussels, Bellarine Peninsula olives and olive oils, homemade biscuits and fresh seasonal ingredients from apples to artichokes. The overall experience is enhanced by regular activities for children and cooking demonstrations for the rest of the family. A wander along the rest of Little Malop Street mall will bring you to a rejuvenated part of town with a swag of cafés, bars and bookshops as well as galleries and gelato shops.

Geelong producers are also well represented at local delicatessens, the majority of which are spread along Pakington Street. Step into **Mondo Deli**, for example, for some top local fare including Leopold Honey, olive oil from Bellarine Peninsula, Meredith cheeses, La Madre bread, plus pork-and-fennel sausages from a butcher in North Geelong. However, it's the opportunity to get your hands on the wonderful Spanish-inspired smallgoods from local producer **Angel Cardoso** that draws food lovers from far and wide.

Cardoso started creating his Spanish smallgoods in nearby Lara over twenty years ago. When he arrived in Australia there were none of the beautiful hams and sausages he remembered from home, so he set about creating his own. He started out with jamon; the classic air-dried Spanish ham, and perfected a recipe which he still uses today. 'I think to make proper jamon you need country air, lots of trees and nearby mountains,' he explains. 'This is why I established my production facility near the You Yangs.' Spicy chorizo followed once the jamon was perfected and Cardoso now produces chorizo in varying sizes and ages. Mondo Deli regularly stocks the entire range of Cardoso smallgoods.

Newtown Provedore is another top spot in Pakington Street for local goodies. Owner Mark Braley proudly stocks the best the region has to offer. 'We stock a great many local products like the Simply Quince Jelly from Bannockburn, Albie's magical spice mixes from the Great Ocean Road, preserves from Bellbrae Harvest and Manzanillo Olive Groves oil from the Bellarine Peninsula. There's also farmhouse cheeses especially those from Meredith Dairy, north-west of Geelong.' The Meredith marinated feta has become an absolute classic, with delicious soft chunks of goat's milk cheese

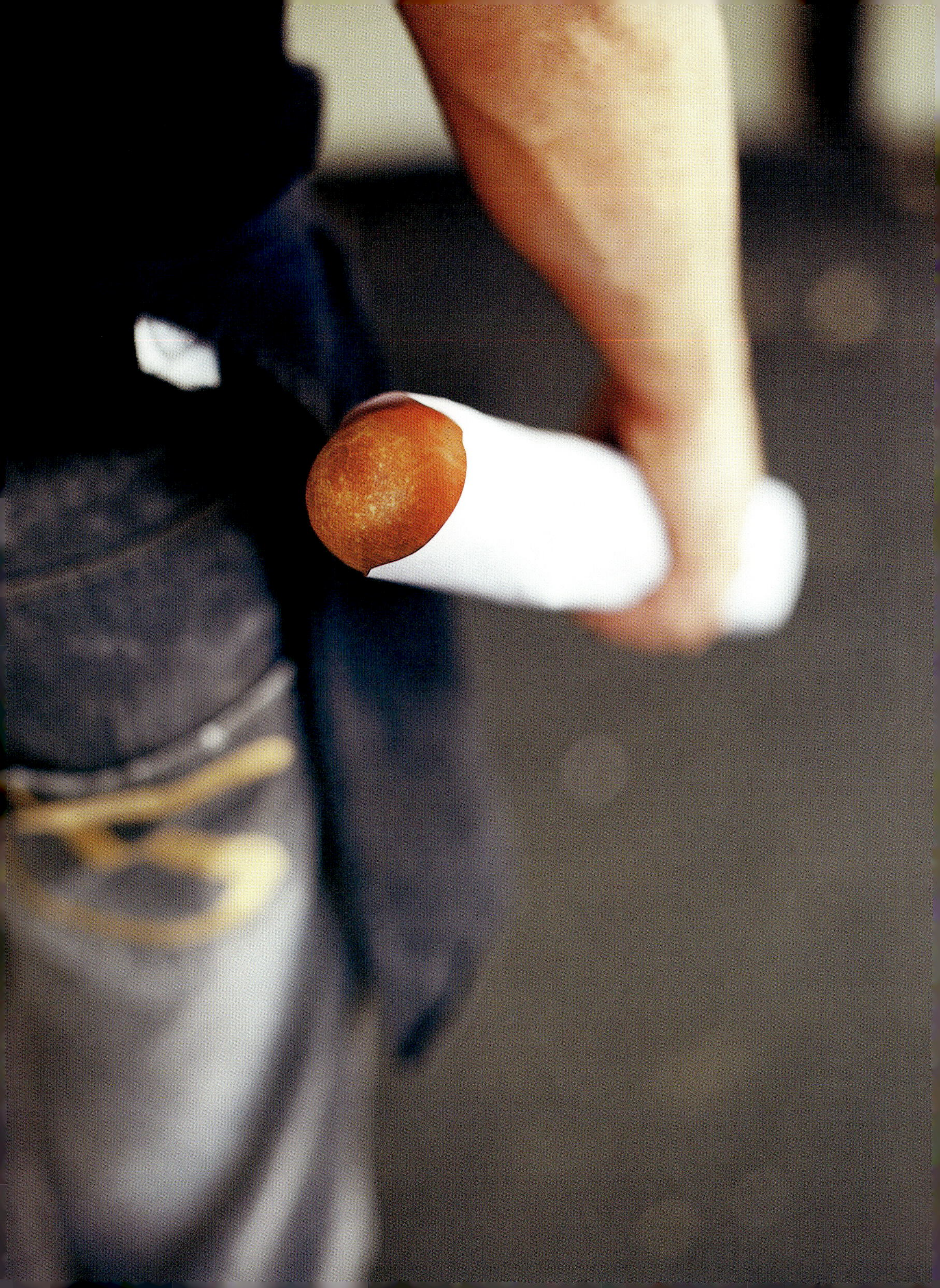

Left
V&R Fruit and Vegetable Market stocks the best and freshest local foods.

Far left and opposite
Specialist foods and fresh breads from Newtown Provedore.

in olive oil. All Meredith products are handmade using French farmhouse methods and the results are there for the tasting.

When it comes to sourcing the best fresh produce **V&R Fruit and Vegetable Market**, is number one. What's on offer is outstanding – the best and freshest of what's in season, and with plenty of tips on how to prepare and cook it. Prices are written up on blackboards behind the generous produce displays. Autumn brings local mushrooms, fennel, quinces and figs, summer sees the arrival of beautiful lettuces, tomatoes and bunches of fragrant basil. During winter local potatoes, root vegetables, pears and apples are piled high, and grapes appear.

Besides being a hit with locals, V&R is a popular stopping-off spot for those wanting to pick up supplies for the beach house. The one-stop shop nature of V&R means the fresh ingredients are supplemented by aromatic spice mixes from Screaming Seeds, beautiful sourdough breads from Irrewarra, and a selection of Victorian cheeses from Holy Goat, Milawa and Meredith.

The back streets of Geelong near the harbour are mostly filled with warehouses and businesses that don't rely on passing trade. Here you get a sense of the old Geelong, back when shipping and trade were the main focus of this city port. Many of the old warehouses have been converted into offices and apartments, but history lingers on in the historic buildings and the impressive streetscape.

It's here on Little Smythe Street you'll find **Katos Fish Supply,** a supplier of local seafood to restaurants and the public. The fish arrive fresh from the boat each morning, are prepared on-site and whisked off to chefs around town. The cabinets are often brimming with flathead, garfish, leather jackets, King George whiting, mussels and pinky snapper. Fresh supplies from the Melbourne fish market supplement the local catch.

Another way of shopping where the chefs do is to visit **Penny's Prime Meats** in Newtown. Mr Penny's top-class selection covers local beef including rib eye, porterhouse and rump, plus ox cheek for slow-braised winter dishes. Lamb, veal, sausages and game meats including kangaroo and even emu round out the offering. **Warren and Hutch** on Pakington Street is another prime spot, especially for meats such as rabbits, beef, lamb and free-range chicken and top quality ducks.

Geelong is a sign to any self-respecting foodie that things are definitely on the up and up. Nip into tiny James Street in the heart of the city to visit the **Irrewarra Sourdough Shop and Café**. Irrewarra is renowned for its range of sourdough breads made using traditional bread-making techniques. Each loaf is hand-shaped then baked on the stone floor of Irrewarra's Colac bakery every morning.

The café creates good, simple food that goes perfectly with the Irrewarra breads, explains co-owner Bronwynne Calvert. 'We take the best local ingredients from Angel Cardoso, Mount Zero olive oil, Meredith cheeses and free-range eggs. We even roast all our own meats and make tapenade and mayonnaise in-house.' This approach has really struck a cord with food lovers and the café is regularly packed to the rafters with locals devouring the fresh sandwiches, muffins, cakes and tarts.

Specialist baked goods at Irrewarra Sourdough Shop and Bakery.

Anton Spoljaric, La Madre Bakery

Anton Spoljaric's earliest memories of eating revolve around his family's farm in Croatia and the great food that appeared from the kitchen. His memory of the big loaves of crusty bread led him from his first career as a chef to his second as a baker. 'I came across a book by the American food author Carol Field called *The Italian Baker* and the photo on the front cover reminded me so much of the bread I remember as a child.'

This spurred him on to start exploring with different bread styles at Kaye's

Each loaf is hand-shaped then baked on the stone floor of the oven at Irrewarra's Colac bakery every morning

Shaw river buffalo mozzarella with lorne tamarillos

Richard Hooper,
Pettavel Winery Restaurant

2 Shaw River mozzarella balls
50 g yellow capsicum, roasted, skinned and deseeded
50 g red capsicum, roasted, skinned and deseeded
75 g picked watercress
30 ml seeded mustard dressing
2 tamarillos
10 ml olive oil
30 ml vincotto
(an Italian vinegar)
flake salt and freshly ground pepper

Cut the mozzarella balls into 16 wedges and set aside.

Mix the capsicum, watercress and seeded mustard dressing.

Cut the tamarillos into 16 wedges and heat in a heavy-bottomed frypan. Add the olive oil and sear the tamarillos (this should only take a minute). The skin can be tough to eat so I remove it now.

Place the tamarillos into the capsicum and watercress salad and mix. The colour will come out of the tamarillos. Arrange the salad in the middle of the plate and add the wedges of mozzarella.

To finish, drizzle with vincotto and sprinkle salt and pepper over the salad.

Serves 4 as an entree

Opposite
Peter Flewellyn, winemaker at Pettavel Winery.

on King restaurant in Melbourne where he was a chef at the time. 'We got a starter happening in the kitchen based on sourdough recipes from John Downes and every day we'd make bread for the restaurant,' explains Spoljaric. 'There was a growing interest in this style of bread and bakeries such as Natural Tucker and Firebrand were really doing great things.'

One thing led to another and another and eventually he decided to set up shop for himself in Bell Park, Geelong. 'Sourdough bread is not something you get right first time, so we found this site which had been a bakery and got to work. All we're working with is organic flour, filtered water, sea salt and our leaven, known as 'the mother'. The first batches were only around 20 kilos each, so very small really. Being away from Melbourne allowed us an opportunity to get the bread just right in our own time.'

News travels fast, however, and it wasn't long before bread lovers from far and wide were making their way to **La Madre**. Soon after a distributor took on the bread and La Madre bread was heading as far as Lorne, Ballarat and Sorrento. Anton's range of breads now includes a beautiful, rustic ciabatta, loaves of full-flavoured rye and a selection of focaccias, some fragrant with rosemary or studded with olives, to name just a few. His fruit breads are also winning high praise. 'Currently we make a fruit loaf in a tin, an apricot and sage sourdough and a currant and walnut rye that is great with cheese.'

The bakery starts dividing the mixes into loaves around midday before proving them through the afternoon. Baking kicks off around 3 pm and continues for twelve hours before the day's orders are ready. From 3 am trucks begin to pick up the loaves and deliver them to bread outlets around the coast and beyond. One of the best things about La Madre is that bread is sold directly from the bakery. 'We have lots of customers who time their visit to get bread hot from the oven, even into the night,' says Spoljaric. 'All the bakers have come to know them by name, and people love nothing more than seeing exactly how their food is made and where it comes from.'

Wineries

Imagine you're sitting in a beautiful, winery restaurant with amazing views across a broad valley. Outside clipped lawns make way for a hillside of grapevines. Waiting-staff glide effortlessly between the linen-covered tables and a long window at the rear allows a peak onto a kitchen filled with the action of a busy lunch service. You glance at the menu trying to decide between braised ox cheek with lemon, garlic, oregano and fennel, or the loin of pork with savoy cabbage, pancetta and cumin.

This imaginary dining room is in fact quite real – it's at **Pettavel Winery and Restaurant**, just 15 kilometres along the Princess Highway from the heart of Geelong. **Pettavel** was named in honour of David Pettavel, one of the original Swiss-born vineyard owners in the Geelong area. His early wines were such a success that he soon expanded with vines across the rolling hills of Geelong. One of the Pettavel ranges is named after the ship he arrived on, the *Platina*, which sailed into Port Phillip Bay in 1842. He planted his first vines in Geelong that same year.

There are twelve wineries with cellar doors open to the public and a host more with restaurants and cafés to entice visitors

For decades there has been just a handful of winery operations in this region, and very few of them open to the public. Now there are twelve wineries with cellar doors open to the public and a host more with restaurants and cafés to entice visitors.

Pettavel chef Richard Hooper is extremely proud of all they've achieved so far. 'The team here are all completely dedicated to producing the best regional food we can. Most of us came from the area originally before travelling and working overseas,' he says. 'It's been great to bring everything we've learned back to Geelong and put it to good use.' And their efforts haven't gone unnoticed. The food here has received a consistent one-hat rating from *The Age Good Food Guide* every year since opening in 2001 as well as numerous awards including best restaurant, best chef and overall winner at the recent Telstra Country Wide Golden Plate competition.

Hooper himself has worked locally with George Biron at Sunnybrae, as well as in Ireland and England before being lured back to Geelong for the Pettavel project. 'I love the fact we can now source so much great regional food and have customers who really appreciate and understand what we're doing.' Regional food can mean anything from heading off on his motorcycle along the Great Ocean Road in search of wild mushrooms to using Angel Cardoso's chorizo, Shaw River and Meredith cheeses, quinces from the bloke in the next property and calamari from Port Phillip Bay. What they cannot source locally they grow themselves in the vegetable patch or make in-house, including bread and ice cream.

Hooper works closely on the menus with Pettavel winemaker Peter Flewellyn and they often discuss which dish to match with a wine from the list. 'The idea is to create a menu of food with big, fat flavours. No pretensions, just a relaxed comfortable food and wine experience.' If the response of the food and wine loving public is anything to go by, these guys are definitely on the right track.

Winemaker Peter Flewellyn operates his state-of-the-art winemaking technology at Pettavel and produces wines under three unique Pettavel brands with each providing a unique variation on the cool-climate fruit flavour of Geelong grown fruit. 'Shiraz is without a doubt our flagship wine. We're finding our sub-climate, soil type and rainfall produce shiraz which has layers of complexity and lots of peppery spice. Also we use French oak which lifts these flavours rather than overpowering it.'

Flewellyn is also having a lot of success with riesling and both vintages have produced gold-medal winning wines. 'We pick our riesling at two stages, so when it comes to blending we can achieve a great mix of minerally acid in the wine as well as the classic citrussy, apple and pear flavours that this variety is famous for,' explains Flewellyn. His chardonnays are also winning fans with their barrel-fermented, complex, rich fruit flavours.

At **Shadowfax**, the impressive contemporary design of the winery gives some hint of the innovative wines available from this Werribee Park winery. Here winemaker Matt Harrop is working with small parcels of fruit from five different vineyards around Geelong and beyond. 'The aim is always to make wines that we really want to drink,' says Harrop. 'In this region we're having great success with shiraz and chardonnay. Our chardonnay, for example, is not too oaky and beautifully balanced. A real Aussie-style wine.' So what would we find in his estate shiraz? 'A fine wine which is concentrated with excellent weight of flavour.'

Each weekend the Shadowfax cellar door stokes up its wood-fired oven and creates fantastic pizzas to match the wines on offer. It's a tough decision – Spanish sausage, roasted peppers, olives, oregano and buffalo mozzarella pizza? Or the pancetta, mushroom and rocket option? Either would be perfect with a glass of the Shadowfax pinot noir. Cheeses, house-made dips and bread are also available on the winery's grazing menu.

The wineries to the north-east of Geelong showcase some of the big changes in play at present. The original **Idyll** vineyard was purchased by brothers Vince and David Littore in the late 1990s and has been substantially

Opposite
The dramatic building at Shadowfax Winery at Werribee Park.

updated to include streamlined winemaking facilities. They bring fruit from their vineyards in Mildura and bottle it under the Jindalee Estate label. The original Idyll vines are bottled under the **Fettlers Rest** label and visitors can enjoy views over these very vines and the Moorabool Valley as they enjoy a tasting in the contemporary ambiance of the cellar door.

As with Shadowfax, there's plenty on offer here outside the classic varieties. In particular the Fettlers Rest gewürztraminer, laden with fruity lychee and turkish delight aromas as well as the estate shiraz, a dark brooding wine with savoury, earthy black fruit flavour and silky tannins. The Fettlers Rest chardonnay won best chardonnay at the Geelong Wine show in 2004. It's a beautiful combination of smoky, integrated oak with full-bodied natural fruit flavours and a crisp finish.

The **del Rios Vineyard and Winery** is located on the Western slopes of Mt Anakie. Here the del Rios family have produced some excellent results from a fairly challenging piece of land. Strong winds from the south-west and hot winds from the north-west mean the vines need a tall trellis system drilled into the volcanic rock. The soil varies from rich, black volcanic to grey alluvial with a granite sand base. Despite these challenges they've managed to snare medals for virtually all of their wines. Their pinot noir, marsanne, cabernet sauvignon, shiraz and chardonnay have picked up awards in wine shows as far afield as Sydney and Melbourne, as well as Ballarat and the local Geelong wine show. 'Our small size allows us to hand prune and hand harvest our fruit at a time which is optimum for the grapes,' explains winery owner Gus del Rios. 'Picking and processing in small batches is not an option for larger vineyards, but it is really paying dividends for us. We can also try new things easily, like different barrels from small parcels of wine, to ensure we're getting the very best results we can.'

Talking with this new breed of winemaker it's easy to get swept up in the excitement of what they're doing. That is, trying new things, new varieties, new ways of making wine, or in some cases going back to classic European winemaking methods. Much like winemaker Gary Farr did for many years at Bannockburn, using wild yeasts and barrel fermenting his chardonnay. He's also renowned for his shiraz, sauvignon blanc and a rosé called saignée.

They've realised that if everyone in the region makes chardonnay and pinot noir the same way, then there's no point of difference between wineries. This is a group of winemakers ready to explore anything to make better and more interesting wine, and their efforts are paying off.

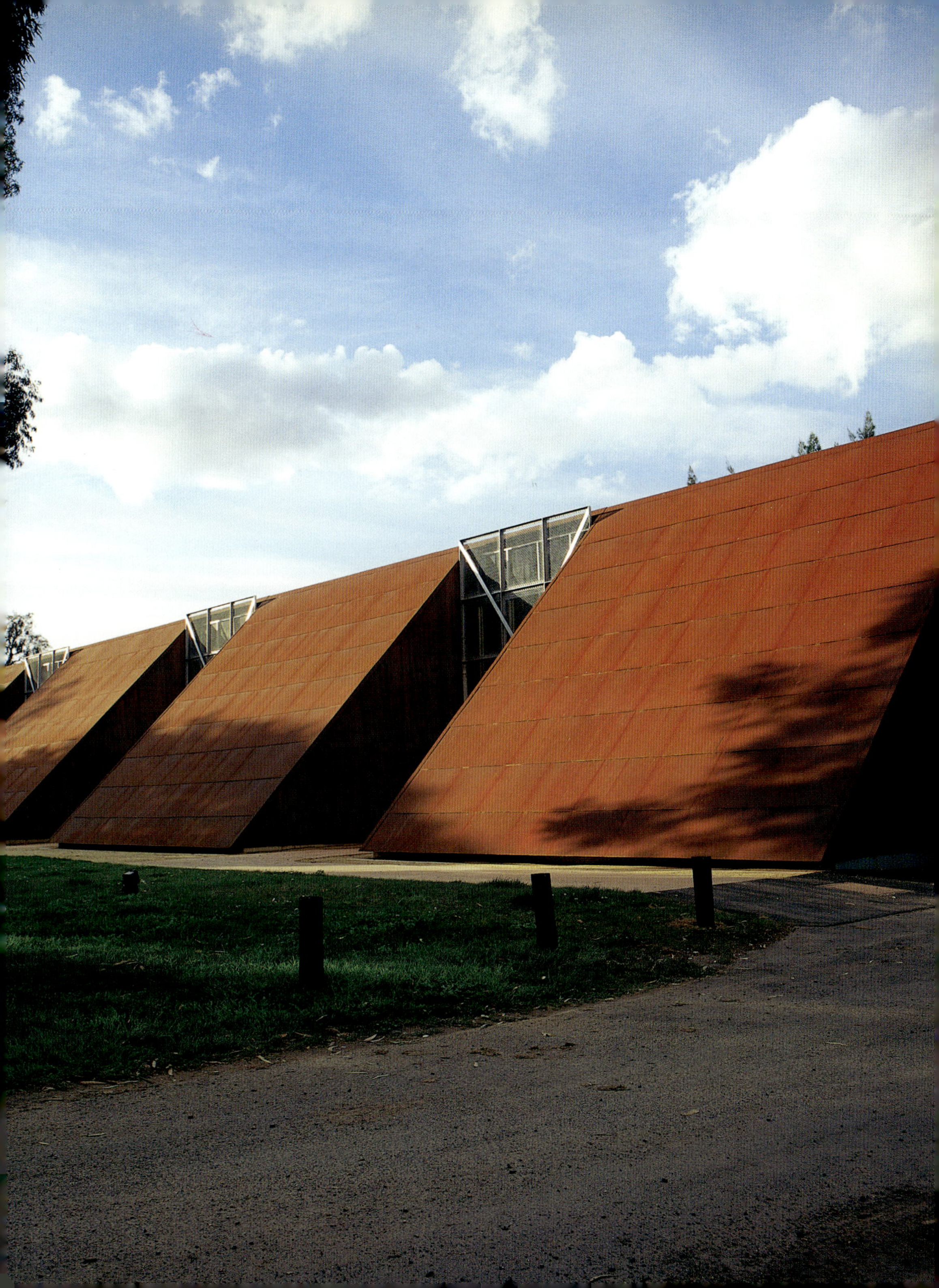

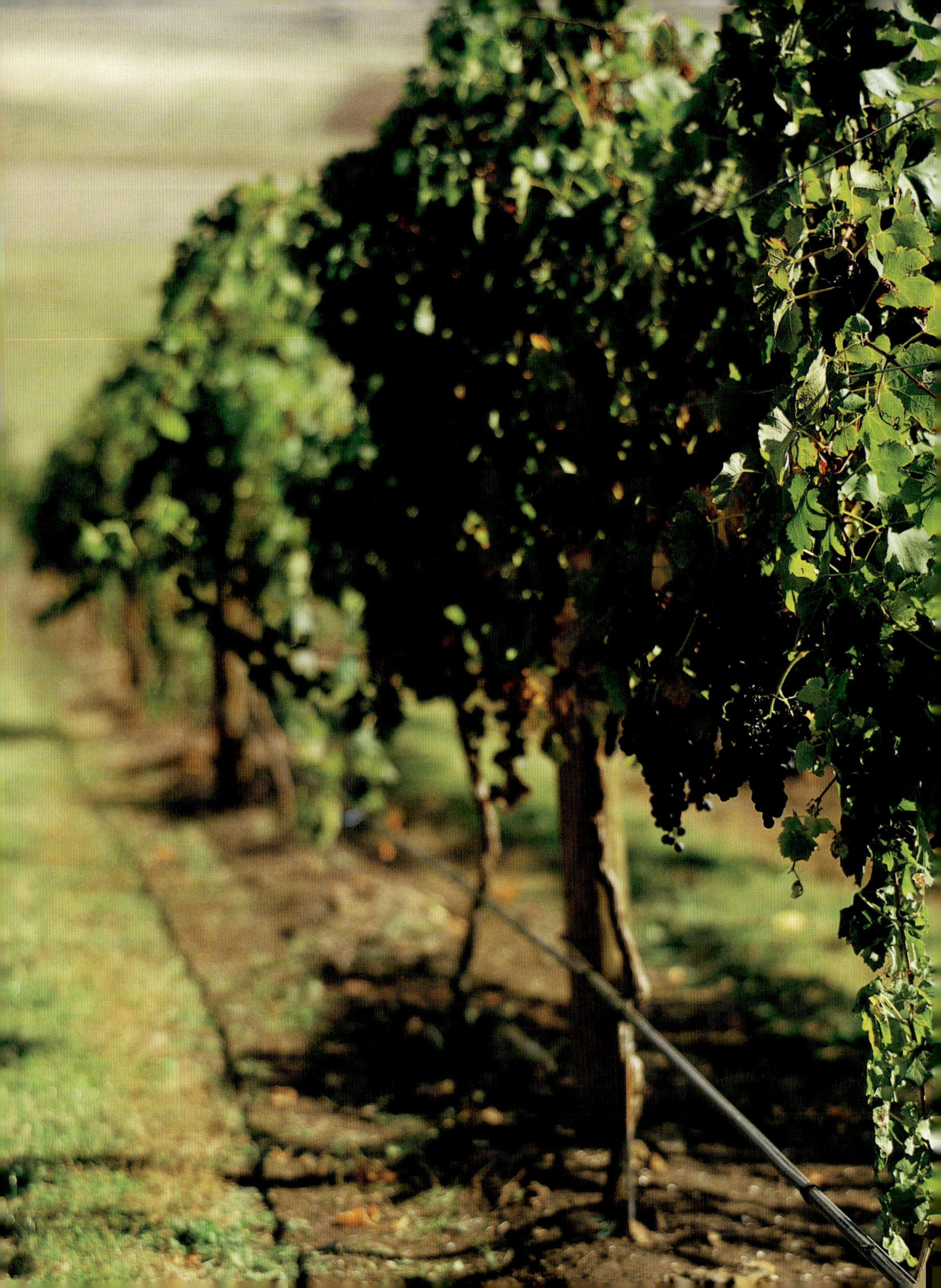

Left
Randall's Wine store, in Geelong's Pakington Street, is a treasure trove of interesting wines.

Another injection of good faith in the region has been the creation of a teaching vineyard and winery at the Geelong Deakin Campus allowing students to study for a degree-level Wine Science course in a cool-climate region for the first time. Incidentally, this flurry of activity has brought the region back to similar levels of plantings as it had in its first heyday in the 1870s, around 400 hectares. It seems as if Geelong finally has the goods to regain its former glory days.

Wine stores

For those travelling through Geelong there's an excellent range of wine stores featuring locally produced wines. We're not talking about the super slick, modern wine store found in shopping strips in the city. Instead, the shelves and aisles of Geelong wine stores are crammed with fantastic choices, the aromas of rich reds and fortified wines linger enticingly in the air, and the staff are passionate about what they sell.

Bannockburn Cellars in central Pakington Street is typical, and without a doubt one of regional Victoria's wine-retailing gems. There's plenty to choose from here, you can browse or be guided by staff if you wish and local winemakers are really well represented. The store also serves as the cellar door for the **Bannockburn Winery**, so this is the best place to pick up current and older vintages of excellent pinot noir, chardonnay, shiraz, sauvignon blanc and saignée.

Geelong shiraz is another feature of Bannockburn Cellars with all the top local names covered. According to marketing manager John Helmer, Geelong shiraz is a classic cool-climate red with rich spicy flavours, hints of white pepper, and a savoury elegance that makes these wines particularly food friendly.

A few kilometres further along the same street is **Randall's**, another treasure trove of local producers. A wander through the huge selection reveals Scotchmans Hill, Long Board, Bellarine Estate, Prince Albert,

'We use as much local seafood as we can get our hands on, so local calamari from Port Phillip Bay, and lobsters from Apollo Bay Fishermen's Co-op'

Bannockburn, Curlewis, Provenance and Wine by Farr, to name just a few. If you were looking to get an overview of the regional wine scene Randall's is definitely a fine starting point.

Randall's owner Randall Pollard has recently begun purchasing batches of prime local fruit and getting involved in the actual winemaking process. His Randall's Shiraz is made from hand-picked fruit from vineyards at Bannockburn and Sutherlands Creek and was made by Matt Harrop at Shadowfax under Randall's directions. According to store manager Rod Long this focus on regional wines is just one of the components of Randall's. 'We aim to ensure that every customer purchases a wine that will be great with the food they have in mind, but more importantly, a wine they'll really enjoy drinking.'

There has been a **Chas Cole Cellars** licence operating in Geelong for over a hundred and fifty years, which is quite a record for any business. Nowadays the Chas Cole retail outlet is on the Princess Highway heading towards the Bellarine Peninsula. Take a step inside the door here and you'll be enticed by rich aromas of gutsy reds and heady, sweet fortified wines. Alongside the varied selection of wines from Geelong are some outstanding

Left to right
The restaurant at Fishermen's Pier; fresh local seafood; Simon Parrott, chef at Fishermen's Pier; Geelong's waterfront.

value-for-money cleanskins, including some ripper sparkling reds. The shop also has an extraordinary range of fortified wines including muscats, ports and sherries available from the huge barrels at the rear of the store.

Eating out

When dining out in Geelong the waterfront is the place to be and be seen. There's nothing quite like sitting at a restaurant table overlooking the water with fishermen unloading the day's catch, yachts scooting across the waves

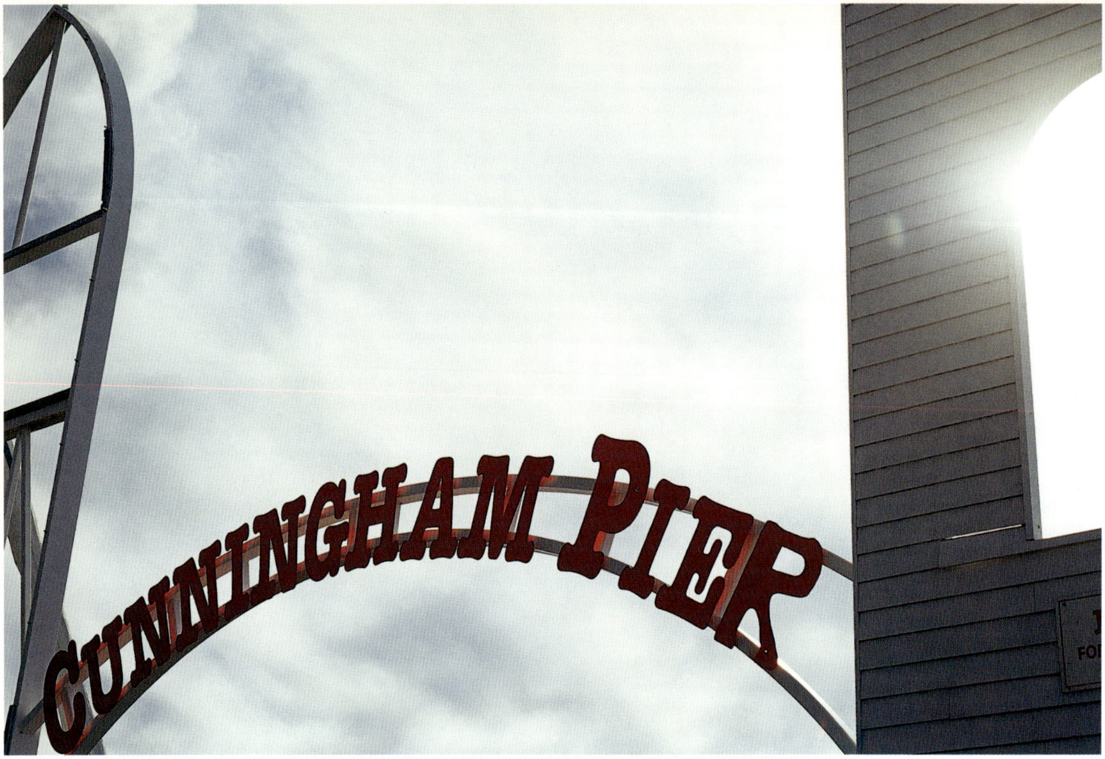

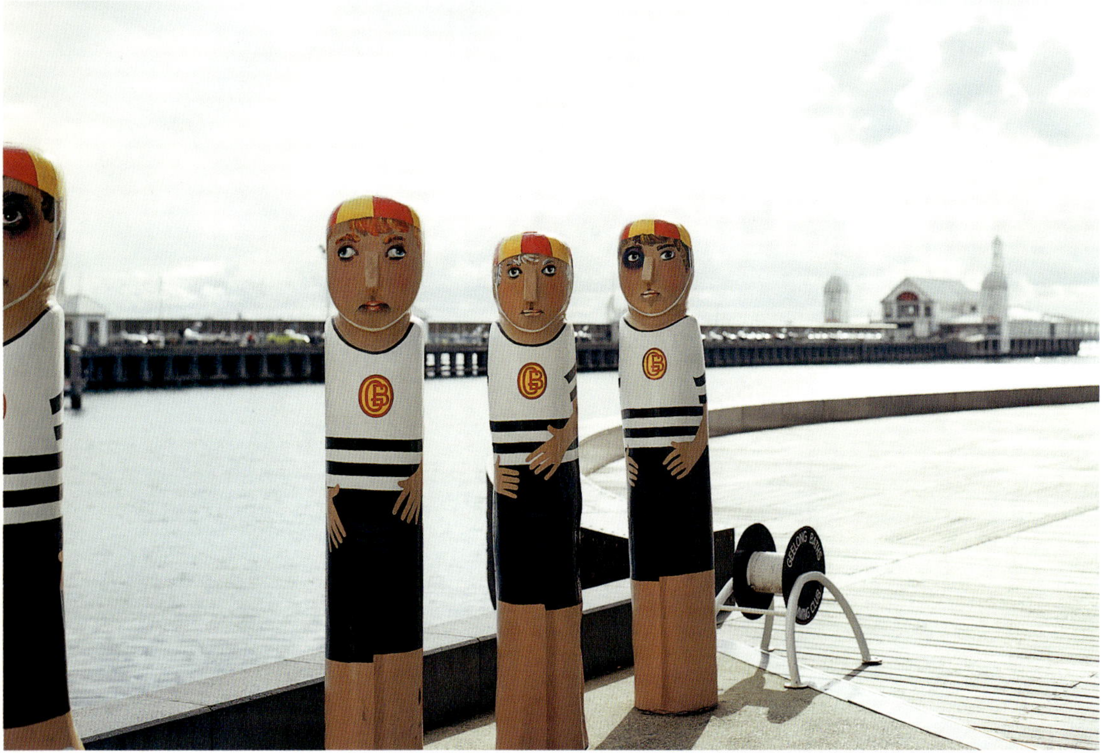

Opposite above
Cunningham Pier.

Opposite below
The quirky bollards that line Geelong's Eastern Beach.

and the You Yangs rising from the plains on the distant horizon. And you can't get much more of a water view in Geelong than from **Fishermen's Pier**. Perched right on the water, the restaurant's enormous front windows allow diners to enjoy every aspect. At night it's a fairytale setting, transformed by the lights glittering on the water.

For more than twenty-five years Fishermen's Pier has been considered 'the big night out' in Geelong – a great location with a fairly classic approach to food. But the arrival of chef Simon Parrott has seen enormous changes with the dining room completely revamped and the creation of a private dining room on the upper floor. Parrott has also brought a contemporary style to the menu and the service.

He comes with an impressive CV starting as an apprentice chef in Geelong, followed by many years at both Mietta's in Queenscliff and Lake House Restaurant in Daylesford. Now he's home, and ready to make his own mark in Geelong. 'We use as much local seafood as we can get our hands, so local calamari from Port Phillip Bay,' says Parrott. 'And lobsters from the Apollo Bay Fishermen's Co-op are grilled as part of the restaurant's famous seafood feast. We also source bay snapper, whiting, mussels and other delicacies as the seasons allow.'

Parrot believes there has been 'absolutely huge change' since his early days. 'The entire waterfront has been beautifully developed, people have moved into the apartments here and the city is becoming more cosmopolitan.' He also sees changes in the dishes people are wanting from the menu. 'Now we can introduce oysters with seaweed, soy and wasabi, deep-fried whitebait on a salad of tomato, cucumber and olives with aioli, and our African fish stew.'

Beyond seafood Parrott also sources lamb, beef, cheese and olive oil from local producers. Each table at Fishermen's Pier features a bottle of the local Manzanillo Grove olive oil for diners to enjoy with bread and drizzle onto grilled seafood. Local wines feature strongly on the restaurant's list with names such as Austin's Barrabool, Bannockburn Vineyards, Innisfail Vineyards, Mount Anakie Wines and Scotchmans Hill. It seems Geelong finally has a contemporary seafood restaurant worthy of its waterfront location.

Virtually alongside Fishermen's Pier is Geelong's other prime waterfront dining room. **Le Parisien** has been run in exemplary fashion by owner-chef Jean-Paul Temple for more than fifteen years. As you would expect with a name such as this the menu offers classic French dishes including onion

Opposite
Handcrafted sourdough bread from La Madre Bakery.

soup, seafood crepes, fillet steak with café de Paris butter, and desserts including profiteroles and chocolate soufflé.

Not all of Geelong's best dining is done by the Bay – just ask Simon Yarham, head chef at **2 Faces** restaurant in the heart of the city. He brings together the heritage of Geelong in an 1850s National Trust-listed building, yet his food is far from old-world. Consider his ever-popular cheese and zucchini soufflé with a blue cheese, spinach and mascarpone cream, a stir-fried blue swimmer crab omelette with green papaya salad and som tam dressing, or Yarham's char-grilled Wagyu beef served sliced with kipfler potato, salsa verde and soft hollandaise. 'After six years in Geelong we're now getting recognised for offering something out of the ordinary,' says Yarham. 'It's taken a few years but our clientele are much more knowledgeable nowadays, and willing to try something different.'

Marilyn Osbourne has been a major player in the Geelong food scene for more than twenty years as both a caterer and restaurateur, and her well-known **Bazil's** restaurant has long been a firm favourite with Geelong diners. So what's her secret? Well according to Osbourne it's about doing things properly, about using seasonal ingredients and not cutting corners. She grew to love food as a child and was encouraged to learn by her mother. 'She used to lay out newspapers on the kitchen bench and allow my brother and I to cook to our hearts' content' she says. This hands-on approach has been her mainstay, as has her love of French Mediterranean and Italian cooking.

'We make our own gnocchi and pasta, source local ingredients and even create our own seasoning and have a butcher make sausages to our directions. This means we can trust everything we put on the menu. Even the Origin coffee we serve has been locally roasted. A typical Bazil's menu may have wild mushroom risotto with fresh thyme, spiced duck breast with grilled apricots and roasted almond pesto or even her Bazil's bouillabaisse packed with local seafood in a herb and tomato ragout. And if you feel like starting the day on a good note, they also offer a popular breakfast menu.

Osbourne recently had to make the move from the city to suburban Highton, so now Bazil's has a bright new look and a contemporary feel to the dining environment. 'I find Geelong of today is so very different from years past. I have customers who have moved here for the lifestyle. They love to live in a small city with Melbourne just an hour away and the beaches of the Great Ocean Road nearby.'

Twice-baked zucchini and cheese soufflés with mascarpone sauce

Simon Yarham,
2 Faces restaurant, Geelong

Soufflés
1 cup milk
70 g butter
50 g self-raising flour
1 tsp baking powder
2 cups chopped spinach
1 zucchini, grated
160 g gruyère cheese, grated
3 eggs, separated
1 clove garlic, minced
pinch of nutmeg
salt, pepper

Preheat the oven to 190ºC.

Place milk in saucepan and bring to the boil.

Melt butter in another saucepan, add flour and baking powder over a medium heat and cook until slightly coloured. Add the milk and beat until smooth. Remove from heat and add spinach, zucchini, cheese, egg yolks, garlic, nutmeg, salt and pepper and mix.

Whip egg whites till stiff peaks and fold into cheese/spinach mixture. Place into small, buttered 1-cup moulds moulds and bake for 20 minutes, or until just golden.

Cool and remove from moulds. Place on a baking tray and bake for 20 minutes, or till starting to colour. Serve surrounded by plenty of sauce (see below).

Mascarpone sauce
500 ml cream
250 g soft blue cheese
250 g mascarpone
1 cup baby spinach leaves

Place cream and crumbled cheese in saucepan. Once melted add mascarpone and stir until mixed well. Add spinach and stir through.

Serves 8–10

Order your Australian fish-and-chip shop classics, then simply cross the road and enjoy your take-away with views along Cunningham Pier and across the blue waters of Corio Bay

All food cities need a good Italian dining room – a place that is casual, but where the food, wine and service is top class. Geelong has such a place with **Giuseppe's Café** in Pakington Street, run for the past nine years by Giuseppe Barbagallo. 'There is a much better awareness of food and wine than when we first opened,' he explains. 'Now locals are very interested in good Italian food and will try something different. Simple dishes like grilled calamari on rocket salad or spaghetti marinara with a glass of sangiovese.'

Other Geelong favourites include **Sticks & Grace**, which is gaining a well-deserved reputation for breakfasts – the corn cakes with mushrooms, asparagus, peppers, poached egg and hollandaise is particularly good. Caffe Smudge is worth a visit if you're in need of a decent coffee, or if it's a classic country pub meal you're searching for then don't miss the **Sawyers Arms Tavern**.

For those times when a freshly cooked serving of fish and chips is the only way to go then **Gilligan's** on the Geelong waterfront is the place to go. Here seafood is the order of the day, including Australian fish-and-chip-shop classics of fried fish, potato cakes and chips, as well as options such as pumpkin fritters and crispy, battered onion rings. From **Gilligan's**, simply cross the road and enjoy your take-away with views along Cunningham Pier and across the blue waters of Corio Bay.

Organic
kipfler
$3/bg

directory

Melbourne

Accommodation

Vibe Savoy Hotel Melbourne

630 Little Collins Street
Melbourne Vic 3000
Tel: 03 9622 8888
Fax: 03 9622 8818
Email: vhsm@vibehotels.com.au
Vibe Savoy Hotel Melbourne offers 162 stylishly appointed guest rooms and suites and is located on the corner of Little Collins and Spencer streets, opposite Telstra Dome. Along with the magnificent location, the hotel offers a fitness centre, restaurants, in-room dining, a business centre as well as flexible conference and event options.

Food stores and producers

Andrew's Choice
03 9687 2419

Babka Bakery Café
03 9416 0091

Baker D. Chirico
03 9534 3777

Boroondara Farmers' Market, East Hawthorn
03 9278 4444

Camberwell Fresh Food Market
03 9539 1361

Canals, The Seafood Appreciation Centre
03 9380 4537

Casa Iberica
03 9419 4420

Collingwood Children's Farm Farmers' Market
03 9417 5806

Dandenong Market
03 9701 3850

Enoteca Sileno
03 9389 7000

Firebrand Bakery
03 9523 0061

Footscray Market
03 9687 1205

Frank's Elsternwick Bakery
03 9528 2380

Gertrude Street Organic Bakery
03 9417 5998

Largo Butchers
03 9417 2689

Organic Gertrude
03 9417 7755

Phillippa's
03 9576 2020

Prahran Continental Butcher
03 9510 3809

Prahran Market
03 8290 8220

Preston Market
03 9478 3130

Queen Victoria Market

Cnr Elizabeth and Victoria Streets
Melbourne Vic 3000
Tel: 03 9320 5822
Web: www.qvm.com.au
Melbourne probably has the most discerning food lovers in the world and if there's one thing they all know, it's that Queen Victoria Market has fantastic value and selection. The best fresh seafood, fruit, vegetables, smallgoods, cheese, meat, wine and a huge range of organic products has made the Queen Vic Market a foodie's paradise for years. So, if you are a foodie, make sure the Market is on your shopping list! Tuesday and Thursday 6am–2pm, Friday 6am–6pm, Saturday 6am–3pm, Sunday 9am–4pm

Richmond Hill Café & Larder
03 9421 2808

Simon Johnson
03 9826 2588

The Essential Ingredient
03 9827 9047

Veg Out St Kilda Farmers' Market
0429 146 627

South Melbourne Market
03 9209 6295

Eating out

Abla's Lebanese Restaurant
03 9347 0006

Ay Oriental Tea House
03 9824 0128

Becco
03 9663 3000

Benito's
03 9670 5347

Café Di Stasio
03 9525 3999

Caffe e Cucina
03 9827 4139

Café Segovia
03 9650 2373

Charcoal Grill on the Hill, Kew
03 9853 7535

Circa, The Prince
03 9536 1122

City Wine Shop
03 9654 6657

Cookie
03 9663 7660

David's Restaurant
03 9529 5199

Degraves Espresso Bar
03 9654 1245

Elements on Lonsdale
192 Lonsdale Street
Melbourne Vic 3000
Tel: 03 9663 3375
Fax: 03 9808 8575
Email: smerc@bigpond.net.au
Located in the heart of the Greek precinct at the newly established QV Melbourne. The restaurant specialises in traditional Greek and modern Mediterranean cuisine, some of the more popular dishes include Moussaka, Gyros and the chef's own seafood Paros pan-fried with crab, prawns, mussels and fish.

European
03 9654 0811

Ezard
03 9639 6811

Flower Drum
03 9662 3655

France-Soir
03 9866 8569

Gertrude Street Enoteca
03 9415 8262

Grossi Florentino
03 9662 1811

il Bacaro
03 9654 6778

Jacques Reymond
03 9525 2178

Journal
03 9650 4399

Ladro
03 9415 7575

Marios Cafe
03 9417 3343

Mecca
03 9682 2999

Mecca Bah
03 9642 1300

Melbourne Supper Club Bar
03 9654 6300

Melbourne Wine Room
03 9525 5599

Mo Vida
03 9663 3038

Mrs Jones
03 9347 3312

Pearl
03 9421 4599

Pelican
03 9525 5847

Supper Inn
03 9663 4759

Syracuse
03 9670 1777

Vue de Monde
03 9691 3888

Yelza
03 9416 2689

Yu-u
03 9639 7073

Zaleti
QV Square
Cnr Lonsdale & Swanston Streets
Melbourne Vic 3000
Tel: 03 9650 7731
Fax: 03 9650 5506
Email: Zaleti_Café@bigpond.com

Located within QV, Zaleti offers a relaxed menu for breakfast, lunch and dinner. Choose from the deli section for a light snack or select from the large range of a la carte meals. Enjoy the excellent, well-priced food and fine service either in the Café or the Square.

Other

Books for Cooks
03 8415 1415

Cloudwine
03 9699 6700

The Prince Wine Store
in South Melbourne
03 9686 3033

The Prince Wine Store
in St Kilda
03 9536 1155

Mornington Peninsula

Accommodation

Lindenderry at Red Hill
142 Arthurs Seat Road
Red Hill Vic 3937
Tel: 03 5989 2933
Fax: 03 5989 2936
www.lindenderry.com.au
Lindenderry at Red Hill is a contemporary boutique hotel situated on 30 picturesque acres in the heart of the Mornington Peninsula. Forty beautiful accommodation rooms are complemented by several superbly furnished lounge areas, an impressive collection of Australian art and a stunning restaurant overlooking the vineyard featuring the best of local produce. With the best of the region within 15 minutes, it is a perfect base for exploring or as a luxurious secluded hideaway.

Foodstores and producers

Ellisfield Farm
03 5989 2008

Flinders Farm
03 5989 0047

Flinders Shellfish
03 5989 0092

Green Olive Gourmet
03 5984 5800

Mirrabella Seafood
03 5979 4277

Montalto Vineyard and Olive Grove
03 5989 8412

Nedlands Lavender Farm
500 Old Moorooduc Road
Tuerong Vic 3933
Tel: 03 5974 4160
Fax: 03 5974 4161
Email: sue@nedlandsfarm.com
Gourmet culinary products

Point Nepean Meats
03 5986 8439

Red Hill Cellars
03 5989 2411

Red Hill Cheese
81 William Road
Red Hill Vic 3937
Tel: 03 5989 2035
Fax: 03 5989 2427
Email: cheesemakers@redhillcheese.com.au
Web: www.redhillcheese.com.au
Family-owned cottage industry in secluded bushland. Hand-made farmhouse cheeses from organic cow or goat milk. View maturing cheeses in the cellars. For discerning epicureans, cheese platters and picnic packs ready to go. Tastings and sales daily 12 noon–5 pm. Groups of more than 8 must pre-book. Home cheese-making classes available.

Red Hill Community Market
03 5974 4710

Red Hill Cool Stores
03 5931 0133

Somerville Village Meats
03 5977 5281

Stringers Stores
03 5984 2010

Sunny Ridge Strawberry Farm

244 Shands Road
Main Ridge Vic 3928
Tel: 03 5989 6273
Fax: 03 5989 6363
Email: info@sunnyridge.com.au
The strawberries at Australia's largest strawberry producer are renowned for their quality, size and flavour. Pick your own fresh from the field (November-April). Try unique, medal-winning fruit wines and liqueurs, artisan-made fresh strawberry ice cream and gourmet food products. Sunny Ridge also has a strawberry café and gift shop.

The Tasting Station
03 5982 0522

Wineries

Crittenden's
03 5981 8322

Dromana Estate
03 5971 8507

Elgee Park
03 5989 7338

Main Ridge Estate
03 5989 2686

Mantons Creek Vineyard
03 5989 6204

Marinda Park Vineyard

238 Myers Road
Balnarring Vic 3926
Tel: 03 5989 7613
Fax: 03 5989 7607
Email: info@marindapark.com
Discover a little piece of France on the Mornington Peninsula! Tour the vineyard, play boule, sample handcrafted wines and sparkling cider. Lunch in the atmospheric barrel-lined café. The blackboard menu changes daily, offering French favourites by the open fire in winter, or al fresco in summer overlooking the vines.

Montalto Vineyard & Olive Grove

33 Shoreham Road
Red Hill South Vic 3937
Tel: 03 5989 8412
Fax: 03 5989 8417
Email: info@montalto.com.au
Web: www.montalto.com.au
Critically acclaimed wine (including one of Victoria's most highly rated chardonnays and award-winning pinot noir), olive oil and a restaurant with three consecutive chefs' hats reflect the 'Estate to Plate' philosophy of this spectacular property. Epicurean picnics, sculptures, wetlands and organic kitchen gardens complete the destination.
Open 7 days.

Montalto
Willow Creek
03 5989 7448

Moorooduc Estate
03 5971 8506

Paringa Estate

44 Paringa Road
Red Hill South Vic 3937
Tel: 03 5989 2669
Fax: 03 5930 0135
Email: info@paringaestate.com.au
Modern European cuisine Spectacular vineyard, cellar and restaurant nestled in the heart of Red Hill. Paringa Estate has the reputation for producing some of the best and most sought after pinot noir and shiraz in Australia. The restaurant offers excellent a la carte dining with equal attention paid to the quality of the food and wine.

Port Phillip Estate
03 5989 2708

Rigel Wines @ Merricks General Store

3458-3460 Frankston Flinders Road Merricks Vic 3916
Tel: 03 5989 8088
Fax: 03 5989 8022
Email: info@rigelwines.com.au
The historic Merricks General Store is home to Rigel Wines featuring a wide range of awarded varieties from the owners' vineyards including local chardonnay, pinot noir and shiraz. Taste them in the cellar door or in the café with fabulous gourmet panini, pizza and wonderfully aromatic espresso coffee.

Stonier Wines

Tel: 03 5989 8300
Fax: 03 5989 8709
Email: stoniers@stoniers.com.au
Celebrating 25 years of winemaking, the striking Stonier Winery is home to ultra-premium chardonnay, pinot noir and sparkling wines of elegance, complexity and length of flavour. Gourmet cheese platters, winery tours and children's playground are available. Winemaker: Geraldine McFaul.

T'Gallant Winery
03 5989 6565

Willow Creek Vineyard

166 Balnarring Road
Merricks North Vic 3926
Tel: 03 5989 7448
Fax: 03 5989 7584
Web: www.willow-creek.com.au
Established 1988 toward the warm northern end of the Peninsula, Willow Creek Vineyard consistently produces chardonnay, pinot noir and cabernet sauvignon of intensity and elegance; complex wines with proven longevity, grown, made and bottled on site. Winemaker, Phil Kerney, has an uncompromising philosophy; low crop levels, wild yeast and minimal intervention winemaking.
- In 2003 Willow Creek Vineyard became the only winery ever to hold the Morning Peninsula Vignerons Association Best White Wine and Best Red Wine trophies in the same year.
- Cellar Door open for sales, tasting and light meals 7 days.
- Salix Restaurant offers fine dining and spectacular views over the vineyard.

Eating Out

Baker Boys Cafe
03 5986 8783

Bittern Cottage
03 5983 9506

Heronswood Café

105 LaTrobe Parade
Dromana Vic 3936
Tel: 03 5984 7318
Fax: 03 5981 4298
Email: info@diggers.com.au
Garden-driven menu

Jill's at Moorooduc Estate
03 5971 8507

Max's at Red Hill Estate
03 5931 0177

Merricks General Store

3458–3460 Frankston Flinders Road Merricks Vic 3916
Tel: 03 5989 8088
Fax: 03 5989 8022
Email: admin@merricksgeneralstore.com.au
Café and produce

Poff's Restaurant
03 5989 2566

Salix at Willow Creek
03 5989 7640

Stillwater at Crittenden

25 Harrisons Road
Dromana Vic 3936
Tel: 03 5981 9555
Fax: 03 5981 9580
Email: manager@stillwateratcrittenden.com.au
Beautiful restaurant set amongst the vines and overlooking manicured lawns and the lake. Indulge your senses with Owner/Chef Zac Poulier's delicious, innovative cuisine using free-range and local produce. With a view from every table, Stillwater offers Peninsula dining at its finest. Crittenden cellar door and vineyard on site. Wedding and events specialists.

The Diggers Club
03 5984 7300

The Long Table
03 5989 2326

Vines of Red Hill
03 5989 2977

Other

Red Hill Brewery
03 5989 2959

Red Hill Regional Shuttle

- Restaurant shuttle

- Winery tours & more
Tel: 03 5989 2929
Email: info@redhillshuttle.com.au
Web: www.redhillshuttle.com.au

Phillip Island

Accommodation

Glen Isla House
230-232 Church Street
Cowes Vic 3922
Tel: 03 5952 1882
Fax: 03 5952 5028
Email: foodandwine@glenisla.com
Award-winning 5-star boutique accommodation offering discerning guests the very finest surroundings, absolute privacy and exceptional personal service. Set in the grounds of the historic Glen Isla Homestead (c1870). Secluded heritage gardens, refined elegance and old-world charm, just 100 metres from the beach. Linger over a chef-prepared breakfast or savour dinner in the licensed restaurant featuring regional produce with extensive wine cellar. Hosts keen members of Slow Food Victoria. The Anderson Suite cottage offers four-poster king-size bed, log fire, spa and period furnishings. Elegant, architecturally designed rooms offer private en suite, sun-drenched deck verandas and superb garden vistas.

The Continental Hotel
The Esplanade
Cowes Vic 3922
Tel: 03 5952 2316
Fax: 03 5952 1878
Email: info@theconti.com.au
Web: www@theconti.com.au
Absolute beachfront views

Foodstores and producers

Churchill Produce Market
03 5664 0096

Freeranger Eggs
03 5678 8483

Island Primary Produce
03 5956 8107

San Remo Fishermen's Co-op
03 5678 5206

Wineries

Bass River Winery
1835 Dalyston-Glen Forbes Road
Glen Forbes Vic 3990
Tel: 03 5678 8252
Fax: 03 9462 2527
Email: info@bassriverwinery.com
Web: www.bassriverwinery.com
Boutique winery

Phillip Island Winery
03 5956 8456

Silverwater Winery
03 5678 5230

The Gurdies Winery
03 5997 6208

Eating out

Chicory Restaurant
115 Thompson Avenue
Cowes Vic 3922
Tel: 03 5952 2655
Fax: 03 5952 6540
Email: info@chicory.com.au
Web: www.chicory.com.au
Enjoy modern Australian food with Asian influences, made from the best seasonal and regional produce. A talented team of young chefs, under Executive Chef Andrew Blackett, produce everything on the premises. The Chicory Cellar has exciting regional wines, with the best from Australia and New Zealand. Chicory brings a Melbourne dining experience to Phillip Island.

Harry's on the Esplanade
03 5952 6226

Jetty Restaurant
03 5952 2060

Taylors Waterfront Restaurant
1215 Phillip Island Tourist Road
Phillip Island Vic 3925
Tel: 03 5956 7371
Fax: 03 5956 6540
Email: restaurant@waterfront.net

Phillip Island's premier seafood restaurant offering spectacular views of Bass Strait. Dine on the famous seafood platter or try the fresh local lobster or one of the international dishes. 'Famous for Seafood'.

The Island Food Store

2/75 Chapel Street
Cowes Vic 3922
Tel: 03 5952 6400
Fax: 03 5956 9447
Email: islandfoodstore@bigpond.com
Located off the main street in Cowes in a courtyard atmosphere, this provisional store, wine shop and café sells regional wine and cleanskins, Australian cheeses and Italian olive oils. The food is modern and full-flavoured. The food store is also open for dinner on Friday nights and caters for any event, large or small.

White Salt Gourmet Fish & Chippery
03 5956 6336

Yarra Valley

Accommodation

Mt Rael Retreat

140 Healesville–Yarra Glen Road
Healesville Vic 3777
Tel: 03 5962 1977
Fax: 03 5962 1577

Email: mtrael@zarliving.com.au
This luxurious mountaintop Retreat and Restaurant '3777' boasts contemporary design and amazing panoramic Yarra Valley views. Stay in one of the modern suites with designer furniture, groovy objets d'art and amazing views to wake up to. Dine in the renowned Restaurant '3777' showcasing the best of regional produce and wine. Enjoy dishes utilising such delights as Yarra Valley salmon, organic game, award-winning Yarra Valley dairy cheeses, Kennedy & Wilson chocolate and Waterwood Farm walnuts.

Foodstores and producers

Cunliffe and Waters
03 9739 0966

Fruition
03 5962 3175

Healesville Harvest Produce and Wine
03 5962 4002

Kennedy and Wilson Chocolates
03 5964 9549

Waterwood Farm
03 5967 3707

Yarra Valley Dairy
03 9739 0023

Yarra Valley Farmers Market
03 9513 0677

Yarra Valley Pasta

325 Maroondah Highway
Healesville Vic 3777
Tel: 03 5962 1888
Fax: 03 5962 2699
Web: www.yarravalleypasta.com.au
Yarra Valley Pasta is made using traditional pasta-making techniques. Only free-range eggs, Australian durum semolina and the highest quality ingredients are used when making this deluxe artisan pasta. Yarra Valley Pasta's retail store showcases the complete, much sought after product range, conveniently packaged for visitors to take home or to enjoy while staying in the many fabulous self-contained accommodation houses in the region. Open Mon–Fri 9am–5.30pm; Sat & Sun 10am–5pm.

Yarra Valley Salmon
03 5773 2466

Wineries

Chateau Yering
03 9237 3333

Coldstream Hills
03 5964 9388

De Bortoli Winery & Restaurant

Pinnacle Lane
Dixons Creek Vic 3775
Tel: 03 5965 2271

Fax: 03 5965 2442
Email: yarra@debortoli.com.au
The family-owned De Bortoli captures the elegance of cool-climate Yarra Valley wines. Discover them for yourself at the friendly Cellar Door or with delicious Italian-inspired food in the restaurant. Cellar Door open daily. Guided tours 11am & 3pm every day. Restaurant open 7 days for lunch, Saturday evening for dinner.

Diamond Valley Vineyard
03 9722 0840

Domaine Chandon
'Green Point'
Maroondah Highway
Coldstream Vic 3770
Tel: 03 9739 1110
Fax: 03 9739 0081
Email: cellardoor@domainechandon.com.au
The Australian winery of Moet & Chandon is nestled in the Yarra Valley just one hour from Melbourne. In the award-winning Green Point Room enjoy a flute of Chandon Sparkling or Green Point still wine accompanied by a Taster's Plate, or settle in for a Light Lunch. Guided winery tours operate daily.

Dominique Portet
03 5962 5760

Kellybrook Winery
03 9722 1304

Punt Road Wines
03 9739 0666

Rochford Wines
03 5962 2119

Roundstone Winery
03 9730 1181

St Huberts
03 9739 1118

TarraWarra Estate
311 Healesville-Yarra Glen Road
Yarra Glen Vic 3775
Tel: 03 5962 3510
Fax: 03 5962 3887
Email: winebar@tarrawarra.com.au
The vineyards of TarraWarra Estate were established in 1983 and produce the premium chardonnay and pinot noir acclaimed both in Australia and internationally. Visitors can taste and savour these exceptional 100% estate- grown wines while looking out over the vineyard and gardens to the incomparable view down Long Gully in the Yarra Valley. Cellar door is open seven days a week for wine tastings and the stunning Wine Bar Café is open from Wednesday to Sunday for delicious food, coffee and, of course, further enjoyment of TarraWarra Estate wine.

Warramate Vineyard
03 5964 9219

Yeringberg
03 9739 1453

Yering Station
03 9730 0100

Eating out

Bella Vedere
03 5962 6161

Cru Restaurant at Outlook Hill Vineyard
03 5962 6966

Healesville Hotel
03 5962 4002

Marylands Country House
Falls Road
Marysville Vic 3779
Tel: 03 5963 3204
Fax: 03 5963 3251
Email: info@marylands.com.au
An award-winning country house hotel ideally located for discovering the wine and food of the Yarra Valley, Marylands Country House restaurant features fresh local produce, and an extensive wine list with over 100 wines from the Yarra Valley alone. Excellent short-break packages include accommodation, a delicious dinner and breakfast.

Other

Tarra Warra Museum of Art
03 5957 3100

Dandenong Ranges

Produce

Australian Rainbow Trout Farm
03 5968 4711

Blue Hills Cherries & Berries
03 9737 9400

Crabapple Bakery
03 9754 5888

Folly Farm Blueberry Growers
03 9751 2184

Herbicious Delicious
03 9751 0026

Montrose Meat Supply
03 9728 201

Olinda Cellars
03 9751 0999

Ruefleur Chestnuts
03 9756 6806

Silvan Estate Raspberries
03 9737 9415

Tea Leaves
03 9755 2222

The Big Berry
03 5967 4413

Eating out

Credo Restaurant
03 9751 1844

Cuckoo Restaurant
03 9751 1003

LadyHawke
1365 Mt Dandenong Tourist Road
Mt Dandenong Vic 3767
Tel: 03 9751 1104
Fax: 03 9751 1104
Email: ladyhawkefleur@optusnet.com.au
Modern Middle Eastern cuisine

Miss Marples Tea Rooms
03 9755 1610

Paperbark Café at Kuranga Native Nursery
03 9760 8100

Pie in the Sky Café
03 9751 2128

Ripe
03 9755 2100

Sky High Mt Dandenong
03 9751 0443

Wild Oak Restaurant & Wine Bar
03 9751 2033

Nagambie and Strathbogie Ranges

Accommodation

Mitchelton Wines
Mitchellstown Road
Nagambie Vic 3608
Melways Map 610 ref M4
Tel: 03 5736 2221
Fax: 03 5736 2266
Email: cds@mitchelton.com.au
Winery Homestead

Foodstores and Producers

Adrian & Valda Martin's Biodynamic Fruit
03 5790 4201

Harvest Home
03 5796 2339

Ruffy's Produce Store
03 5790 4387

Wineries

David Traeger Wines
03 5794 2514

Goulburn Terrace
340 High Street
Nagambie Vic 3608
Tel: 03 5794 2828
Fax: 03 5794 1854
Email: goulburnterrace@bigpond.com
Wine and Food

Mitchelton Wines
Mitchellstown Road
Nagambie Vic 3608
Tel: 03 5736 2221
Fax: 03 5736 2266
Email: cds@mitchelton.com.au
Mitchelton; a world of fine wine, regional food and stunning surrounds.

Whilst visiting enjoy
- Complimentary wine tastings
- Visit our art gallery
- Take in the breathtaking view from the tower
- Enjoy lunch in the Restaurant
- Watch your children in the playground while having a picnic or BBQ
- Treat yourself to a night in our Winery Homestead
- Open Daily 10am–5pm, 7 days.

Murchison Wines
03 5826 2294

Tahbilk Winery & Wetlands Café – Dalfarras Cellar Door

8 km south-west of Nagambie
Tel: 03 5794 2555
Fax: 03 5794 2360
Email: info@tahbilk.com.au
Established in 1860 Tahbilk is one of Australia's most beautiful and historic wineries and offers the visitor a unique opportunity to step back in time with the Cellar Yard and Cellar Door buildings not too unchanged from their original state. Tahbilk's proximity to the Goulburn River and backwaters led to the opening of a Wetlands & Wildlife Reserve and Wetlands Café in August 2005. The Wetlands Café features contemporary café fare with the emphasis on freshness, quality and regionality and also incorporates the Dalfarras Tasting Bar and Gallery. Launched in 1991, Dalfarras is a collaboration between winemaker Alister Purbrick (CEO and chief winemaker at Tahbilk) and his artist wife Rosa Purbrick (nee Dal Farra).

Eating out

Traawool Shed Café
03 5799 1595

Veneto Blu

42 Station Street
Seymour Vic 3660
Tel: 03 5792 2334
Fax: 03 5792 1905
Email: venetoblu@optusnet.com.au
Fully licensed café restaurant. Come and feel the ambience in our beautiful 1876 heritage building. On sunny days experience dining in the courtyard or on cool days, a coffee with our delicious homemade cakes in front of the log fire. Monday closed; Tues–Sun 9.30am–4.00pm; Fri–Sat 6.30pm till late.

Macedon Ranges

Accommodation

Blue Ridge Inn

Cnr Mt Macedon & Falls Roads
Mt Macedon Vic 3441
Tel: 03 5427 0220
Fax: 03 5427 0337
Web: www.blueridgeinn.com.au
As in so many notable eateries, the chef is also the owner of this exceptional establishment. Her comprehensive knowledge of food, use of the finest ingredients, preparation from first principles, and skilful but uncontrived presentation means simply the very best of real food. The dining room windows overlook the Hesket Valley along with mysterious Hanging Rock. Service is unobtrusive and intelligent – reminiscent of the level of care and attention still found in some of the elegant small inns of Europe and America. Dining at Blue Ridge is fixed menu and for resident guests and their guests only.

Foodstores and produces

Emelia's Piquant Sauces
03 5422 2020

Fernleigh Farm
03 5348 5566

Holgate Bar and Brewhouse
03 5427 3522

Kyneton Olive Oil

2090 Kyneton Heathcote Road
Barfold via Kyneton Vic 3444
Tel: 03 9350 5366

Fax: 03 9350 5866
Email: info@kynetonoliveoil.com.au
Web: www.kynetonoliveoil.com.au
Kyneton Olive Oil produce award-winning extra virgin olive oils, infused olive oils, table olives and tapanades, grown and processed within central Victoria. Calling 0419 191 192 (Sam) before visiting is recommended.
10-12 June 2006 'New Season's Product Launch'.
- Cooking demonstrations
- Olive oil tastings
- Local wine tastings
- Café
- Children's activities

Check web page for other open weekend dates.

Lancefield Farmers Market

4th Saturday of Month
(3rd in Dec) 9am–1pm
High Street Lancefield Vic 3435
Contact: Meggs Hannes-Paterson
Tel: 0407 860 320
Email: gingermeggs20@hotmail.com

Macedon Grove Olives
03 5429 1134

Maloa House Gourmet Delights
03 5427 1608

Malmsbury Bakery
03 5423 2369

Michel's Fine Biscuits
03 5472 4274

Mount Gisborne Cherries
03 5428 8044

Pud for all Seasons
03 5473 3363

Wineries

Andreas Brothers
Olde Winilba Vineyard
03 9740 9703

Candlebark Hill
0412 068 777

Chanters Ridge

440 Chanters Lane
Tylden Vic 3444
Tel: 0427 511 341
Fax: 03 5424 8140
Email: chantersridge@nex.net.au
Award-winning Pinot noir

Cleveland Winery
03 5429 1449

Cobaw Ridge
03 5423 5227

Craiglee Vineyard
03 9744 4489

Curly Flat Vineyard
03 5429 1956

Epis & Williams
03 5427 1204

Galli Estate
03 9747 1444

Gisborne Peak Winery
03 5428 2228

Glen Erin Vineyard Retreat
03 5429 1041

Goona Warra Vineyard

790 Sunbury Road
Sunbury Vic 3429
Tel: 03 9740 7766
Fax: 03 9744 7648
Email: goonawarra@goonawarra.com.au
Magnificent 1860s bluestone winery located just 10 minutes past Melbourne airport, set amongst terraced gardens that overlook the picturesque vineyard and distant Macedon Ranges. Goona Warra is noted for its cool-climate red and white table wines, among them the rare roussanne and cabernet franc. It offers wine tastings daily (10–5) and Sunday lunch – good food at reasonable prices, with a seasonal a la carte menu. A new luncheon bistro with garden courtyard is planned to open spring 2006 in the historic bluestone stables. At other times the Cellar and Great Hall are available for weddings and private functions with seating for up to 160 guests.

Granite Hills Winery

1481 Burke & Wills Track
Baynton Vic 3444
Tel: 03 5423 7264
Fax: 03 5423 7288
Email: knights@granitehills.com.au
Arguably one of Victoria's most awarded small wineries, notching up more than 400 awards in its 35-year history. Revered as the birthplace of 'peppery shiraz' and

acclaimed as Victoria's best riesling producer, this maker also has sensational vintage sparkling, chardonnay, pinot noir, merlot and cabernet – a true tasting experience.

Hanging Rock Winery

88 Jim Road
Newham Vic 3442
Tel: 03 5427 0542
Fax: 03 5427 0310
Email: hrw@hangingrock.com.au
Web: www.hangingrock.com.au
John and Ann Ellis established the Hanging Rock Winery in 1983. The range of premium wines made by John Ellis includes the acclaimed sparkling 'Macedon', the 'Jim Jim' Sauvignon Blanc and the multi-award winning Heathcote Shiraz. Cellar door is open 7 days 10am–5pm. Less than one hour from Melbourne.

Kyneton Ridge Estate
03 5422 7377

Longview Creek Vineyard

150 Palmer Road
Sunbury Vic 3429
Tel: 03 9740 2448
Fax: 03 9740 2495
Email: asholm@hotlinks.net.au
Cellar door sales

McWilliams Wines
03 9764 8511

MorganField Vineyard
03 5429 1157

Mount Gisborne Wines
03 5428 2834

Olde Winilba Vineyard
03 9740 9703

Portree Vineyard
03 5429 1422

Wildwood Vineyard
03 9307 1118

Eating out

Annie Smithers Bistrot
03 5422 2039

Avanti at Witchmount
03 9747 1177

Café Adagio

1 Barkly Street
Sunbury Vic 3429
Tel: 03 9740 2111
Modern Australian

Café Colenso
03 5427 2007

Campaspe Country House Hotel & Restaurant

Goldies Lane
Woodend Vic 3442
Tel: 03 5427 2273
Fax: 03 5427 1049
Email: sales@campaspehouse.com.au
Web: www.campaspehouse.com.au
Regional flavour driven food. The exceptional food and wine credentials at the multi award-winning Campaspe Country House ensure a perfect place to dine. The restaurant features an inspired seasonal menu prepared from only the finest local produce and is open every weekend for breakfast, lunch and dinner. With the charm of this 1927 property and *The Age Good Food Guide*-recommended restaurant, it's easy to see why this oasis of country style is a favourite among Melbournians escaping the city. Set on 32 acres of Edna Walling gardens and natural bushland the property also offers a variety of elegant accommodation, open fires crackling, petanque, croquet, tennis court, swimming pool and spa.

Carriage House Restaurant
03 5429 1449

Estelle's
03 9740 4977

Holgate Bar and Restaurant
03 5427 3522

Not Just Fudge Café
03 5427 2210

Rupertswood
03 9740 5020

Sequoia
03 5427 4414

Sitka Foodstore and Café
03 5426 3304

Daylesford

Accommodation

Lake House

On the shores of Lake Daylesford
Vic 3460
Tel: 03 5348 3329
Fax: 03 5348 3995
Email: info@lakehouse.com.au
Renowned for its picturesque waterfront location and outstanding service, Lake House offers stylish, contemporary accommodation. Guests have access to 6 acres of waterfront gardens, the Salus Day Spa, award-winning restaurant and cellar, resort facilities including billiard room, guest lounge with open fires, tennis court and outdoor solar heated plunge pool.

Liberty House
03 5348 2809

Peppers Springs Retreat
03 5348 2202

Foodstores and producers

Chocolate Mill
03 5476 4208

Cliffy's
03 5348 3279

Country Cuisine
03 5348 4141

Fernleigh Farm
03 5348 5566

Gourmet Larder
03 5348 4700

Health Foods Naturally
03 5348 3109

Hepburn General Store
03 5348 2764

Himalaya Bakery
03 5348 1238

Lavandula
03 5476 4393

Meredith Dairy
03 5286 1455

Organic Sunrise Foods
03 5438 6501

Organic Wholefoods and Harvest Café
03 5348 4022

O'Toole's Honey
03 5348 2997

Sausage Corner
03 5422 1074

Stella's Naturally Fine Foods
03 5348 1888

Sweet Decadence
03 5348 3202

Tonna's Fruit & Vegetable Supplies
03 5348 1119

Trewhella Farm
03 5348 5667

Woodend Berry Farm
03 5427 3939

Wineries

Basalt Ridge
03 5423 9108

Big Shed Wines
03 5348 7503

Captains Creek Organic Wines

Kangaroo Hills Road
Blampied Vic 3364
Tel/Fax: 03 5345 7408
Web: www.captainscreek.com
Open: 11 am–5 pm weekends and public holidays.
Captains Creek offers unique handcrafted certified organic wines only 10 minutes from Daylesford. Taste the renowned Sparkling 'Hepburn', chardonnays, pinot noir, pinot gris, rose and verjuice in the old rustic farm cellar by the open fire. Explore old farm relics, organic agriculture and purchase seasonal vegetables, fruit and nuts grown on this family farm.

Ellender Estate

260 Green Gully Road
Glenlyon Vic 3461
Tel: 03 5348 7785
Fax: 03 5348 7784
Email: ellenderestate@netconnect.com.au
Web: www.ellenderwines.com.au

Venture out to Glenlyon to experience our intimate boutique winery and rustic, stylish regional produce from our artisan woodfired oven – open Sundays from 11.00 am to 5.00 pm. Elegant and distinctive Macedon Ranges wines are handcrafted from estate-grown fruit by winemaker, Graham Ellender. Ellender Estate is available for private functions and conference dinners.

Kangaroo Hill Vineyard & Winery
03 5423 9225

Sailors Fall Estate
03 9370 8813

Sandy Farm
03 5348 7610

Zig Zag Winery
03 5423 9390

Eating out

Ambleside on the Lake
03 5348 2691

Bad Habits
03 5348 3211

Boathouse Café
03 5348 1387

Breakfast and Beer
03 5348 1778

Cosmopolitan Hotel
03 5424 1616

Della's on Vincent
03 5348 4458

Farmer's Arms Hotel
03 5348 2091

Frangos & Frangos
03 5348 2363

Garden of St Erth
03 5368 6789

Kouklas
03 5348 4901

Lake House
On the shores of Lake Daylesford
Vic 3460
Tel: 03 5348 3329
Fax: 03 5348 3995
Email: info@lakehouse.com.au
Nestled on the picturesque shores of Lake Daylesford, Lake House is recognised as one of Australia's top restaurants. Visitors can dine on the sun-kissed terraces overlooking the water's edge or by the open fires in the stylish dining room – with spectacular views. A la carte menus change seasonally and multi-course 'tasting menus' offer an opportunity to sample a diverse range of the kitchen's offerings. Winner of numerous awards including Best Restaurant in a Luxury Retreat and a total of 43 chef's hats with *The Age Good Food Guide*, Lake House is a must for people who love food and good living!

Lucinis
03 5348 4345

Mercato at Daylesford
03 5348 4488

Misto Restaurant
03 5348 2843

Not Just Muffins
03 5348 3711

Red Star Café
03 5348 2297

Sault Restaurant & Functions
03 5348 6555

Chimney European Cafe
03 5424 1165

Other

Convent Gallery
03 5348 3211

Tuki Farm Retreat
03 5345 6233

Ballarat

Accommodation

The Ansonia Boutique Hotel
03 5332 4678

Craig's Royal Hotel
03 5331 1377

Foodstores and producers

Decadent Alternatives
03 5341 2367

Darriwill Farm
03 5331 7877

directory 313

Goldfield's Organics
03 5339 5449

Hope Bakery
03 5337 1150

John Harbour Quality Butcher

**615 Lydiard Street
North Ballarat Vic 3350**
Tel: 03 5332 4402
Fax: 03 5331 4907
Prime quality meats and homemade smallgoods. Specialising in
- Locally grown prime beef
- Prime Downs bred lamb
- Western Plains Pork
- Glenloth & Milawa chicken
- Housemade smallgoods
- Harbours ham & bacon and other regional produce.

Springhill Farm
03 5331 2185

Tiggies Puddings & Chocolates
03 5337 6044

Wilson's Fruit & Vegetables
03 5329 1900

Wineries

Dulcinea Winery
03 5334 6440

Eastern Peake Vineyard
03 5343 4245

Mount Beckworth Wines
03 5343 4207

Whitehorse Wines
03 5330 1719

Eating out

Bibo Bistro
03 5331 1255

Boatshed Restaurant
03 5333 5533

Café Companis

**15 Camp Street
Ballarat Vic 3350**
Tel: 03 5320 5798
Web: www.peterfordcatering.com.au
Residing at the Ballarat Fine Art Gallery and providing regionally based food and wine daily to all. Daily specials. Individual cakes. High teas on a weekend. Boardroom for hire. Dinners at night by appointment for groups up to 50.

Glasshouse Restaurant

**The Bell Tower
1845 Sturt Street
Ballarat Vic 3350**
Tel: 03 53341600
Fax: 03 5334 2540
Email: reservations@belltower.com.au
Contemporary Australian cuisine. An outstanding dining experience at realistic prices with local and regional wines in pleasant, comfortable surroundings. The Glasshouse Lounge Bar serves light meals, old favourites and good coffee. Located at the Best Western Bell Tower Motor Inn & Convention Centre on the beautiful Avenue of Honour.

L'espresso
03 5333 1789

Mason's Café & Food Store
03 5333 3895

Mercato
03 5348 4488

Phoenix Brewery Restaurant & Bar

**10 Camp Street
Ballarat Vic 3350**
Tel/Fax: 03 5333 2686
Email: phoenixbrewery@aapt.net.au
Located in historic Camp Street stands a tapas and wine bar with a difference. Graze on the internationally inspired tapas menu or enjoy seasonal dishes from the a la carte blackboard menu. The extensive wine list and European ambience makes the Phoenix Brewery a must visit for lovers of good food and wine.

Piper's on Parade
03 5334 1811

The Potted Pair Pty Ltd

**31 Burnbank Street
Ballarat Vic 3350**
Tel: 03 5339 3445
Fax: 03 5339 3447
Email: pottedpair@bigpond.com
Located just a short stroll from the beautiful Lake Wendouree, the Potted Pair offers sensational coffee, a large range of gourmet cakes and biscuits and a wine list

sourced from the local Pyrenees Wine Region. The Potted Pair also stock an extensive range of unique home and giftwares. Open Mon-Sat 9am–5pm; Sun & public holidays 10 am–5 pm.

Tozer's Restaurant
03 5338 8908

Other

Sovereign Hill
03 5331 1944

Bellarine

Accommodation

Athelstane House
03 5258 1024

Queensliff Hotel
03 5258 1066

The Ol' Duke

40 Newcombe Street
Portarlington Vic 3223
Tel: 03 5259 1250
Fax: 03 5259 1237
Email: theolduke@bigpond.com
Fax: www.theolduke.com.au
Eat, Drink, Sleep

Foodstores and producers

Aussie Blue Mussels
03 5259 3088

Bellarine Golden Olive
03 5253 2399

Lonsdale Hydroponics
03 5258 2665

Manzanillo Grove
03 5251 3621

Starfish Bakery
03 5254 2772

Trident Fish Bar
03 5258 2334

Tuckerberry Hill Blueberry Orchard
03 5251 3468

Wallington Strawberry Farm
03 5250 1541

Wineries

Julian's @ Bellarine Estate

2270 Portarlington Road
Bellarine Vic 3222
Tel: 03 5259 3310
Fax: 03 5259 3393
Email: julians@bellarineestate.com.au
Julian's @ Bellarine offers a picturesque setting overlooking the vineyards of Bellarine Estate, the rolling hills of the peninsula and Corio Bay. This modern dining room offers a wonderful epicurean dining experience where each course is superbly matched to a glass of wine. This is a 'must do' experience for everyone.

Kilgour Estate
03 5251 2223

Scotchmans Hill
03 5251 3176

Eating out

At the Heads
03 5254 1277

Harry's
03 5258 3750

Oakdene Vineyard Restaurant
03 5256 3886

Port Pier Café
03 5259 1080

Scorched
03 5261 6142

The Grand Hotel
03 5259 2260

Vue Grand

46 Hesse Street
Queenscliff Vic 3225
Tel: 03 5258 1544
Fax: 03 5258 3471
Email: info@vuegrand.com.au
A beautifully restored 1881 boutique hotel, the Vue Grand's original ballroom is now the elegant Grand Dining Room

Restaurant and is highly recommended for lunch or dinner. The Terrace and Courtyard offer relaxed style lunches with local estate-grown wines. Short-break packages include accommodation, superb dinner and breakfast.

Other

KYO Pty Ltd
26 Smithton Grove
Ocean Grove Vic 3226
Tel: 03 5255 2444
Trade warehouse open to the public. Discover the most fascinating array of goods in the most unexpected place. Direct importers of antiques, furniture, textiles and interesting and unusual objects from China and Japan. Open every day of the year Mon-Sat 10-5, Sun 1-5. Come to KYO, you won't be disappointed.

Geelong

Accommodation

The Mansion Hotel
K Road
Werribee Vic 3030
Tel: 03 9731 4000
Fax: 03 9731 4001
Email: mansion@bigpond.com
Located in the heart of beautiful Werribee Park, The Mansion Hotel is set among 10 hectares of formal gardens and features 92 guestrooms, acclaimed Joseph's Restaurant with the talents of chef Paul Raynor, Day Spa with indoor pool, indulgent treatments and tennis courts, cosy library, snooker room and nearby Shadowfax winery.

Foodstores and producers

Bannockburn Cellars
03 5229 5358

Chas Cole Cellars
03 5241 1620

Geelong Farmers Market
03 5227 0841

Irrewarra Sourdough Breads
Tel: 03 5233 6219 or 0407 388 219
Web: www.irrewarrasourdough.com.au
Available in Geelong and Bellarine at:
- V&R, Geelong West
- Freshly Doug, Highton
- The Newtown Provedore, Newtown
- Not Just Fruit, Torquay
- Queenscliff Foodworks, Queenscliff
- Elvis Parsley & Grapesland, Ocean Grove
- Annie's Provedore, Barwon Heads
- Purple Duck, Wallington

Katos Fish Supply
03 5229 1265

La Madre Bakery
Shop 1/29 Milton Street
Bell Park Vic 3215
Tel: 03 5272 1727
Fax: 03 5221 2036
Organic sourdough

Mondo Deli
03 5229 1122

Newtown Provedore
03 5221 5654

Penny's Prime Meats
03 5221 1028

Randall's
03 5223 1141

V&R Fruit & Veg market P/L
5 Pakington Street
West Geelong Vic 3215
Tel: 03 5222 2522
Fax: 03 5222 2515
Email: connie@vandrfruit.com.au
V&R stock the best fruit and vegetables and dry goods in a large warehouse-style shop. Visit in any season to find the freshest of seasonal produce, the very best of regional produce, and an outstanding array of olive oils and sweet treats to tempt your taste buds. There's something for all.

Warren and Hutch
03 5229 7720

Wineries

Bannockburn Vineyard
03 5281 1363

Del Rios of Mt Anakie
03 5284 1221

Pettavel Winery & Restaurant

65 Pettavel Road
Geelong Vic 3216
Tel: 03 5266 1120
Fax: 03 5266 1140
Email: pettavel@pettavel.com

Eating out

2 Faces the Restaurant
03 5229 4546
8 Malop Street
Geelong Vic 3200
Tel: 03 5229 4546
Web: www.2faces.com.au
Modern International cuisine

Bazil's Too
03 5241 9311

Fishermen's Pier

Bay end of Yarra Street
Eastern Beach
Geelong Vic 3220
Tel: 03 5222 4100
Fax: 03 5223 2756
Email:
eatfresh@fishermenspier.com.au
Web: www.fishermenspier.com.au
Fishermen's Pier is ideal for any occasion and is open for lunch and dinner 7 days a week. It is fully licensed, with more than 40 varieties of local wines. Chef Simon Parrott and team pride themselves on providing diners the opportunity to try the freshest and best local seafood, while overlooking the stunning Geelong waterfront. Also available is a private dining room. Situated upstairs and offering superb views across the bay, it is perfect for a variety of more intimate functions.

Gilligan's
03 5222 3200

Giuseppe's Cafe
03 5223 2187

Irrewarra Sourdough Bakery

Store & Café
10 James Street
Geelong Vic 3220
Tel: 03 5221 3909
Fax: 03 5221 3989
Open: Mon–Fri, 9am–3pm
Menu is at
Web: www.irrewarrasourdough.com.au

Le Parisien
03 5229 3110

Sawyers Arm Tavern
03 5223 1244

Shadowfax Winery
03 9731 4420

Sticks & Grace Café Catering

4/337 Pakington Street
Geelong Vic 3220
Tel: 03 5224 2900
Fax: 03 5224 2996
Email: amyec@bigpond.com
Contemporary style, award-winning cafe. Located in the boutique shopping and cafe precinct. Serving breakfast, lunch and sweets all day. Tapas-style dinner on Friday and Saturday nights. Enjoy coffee, served in European-style bowls, relaxing in our al fresco area or inside whilst appreciating the local artwork on display.

Summer Sensations Café and Berry Gardens
03 5281 5449

Index

Note: Recipe names are in **bold italic**; foodstuffs are in **bold**. Area names are included in brackets, unless the name makes it clear where that restaurant or other food business is located.

Abla's Lebanese Restaurant (Carlton) 28, 300
Adagio Café (Sunbury) 177
Adrian & Valda Martin's Biodynamic Fruit (Nagambie) 154, 308
Ambleside on the Lake (Daylesford) 206, 313
Andrew's Choice (Melbourne) 300
Annie Smithers Bistrot (Kyneton) 180, 181, 311
Ansonia Boutique Hotel (Ballarat) 232, 313
apples 145, 160, 164, 190, 193, 199
At the Heads (Barwon Heads) 268, 269, 315
Athelstane House (Queenscliff) 247, 264–5, 267, 315
Athelstane muesli 265
Aussie Blue Mussels (Portarlington) 251, 315
Australian Rainbow Trout Farm (Macclesfield) 120, 308
Avanti at Witchmount (Sunbury) 169, 311
Ay Oriental Tea House (South Yarra) 27–8, 301

Babka Bakery Café (Fitzroy) 13, 300
Bad Habits Café (Daylesford) 206, 313
Baker D. Chirico (St Kilda) 13, 300
Baker Boys Cafe (Mornington) 304
bakeries 13, 17–18, 93, 179, 194, 237–9, 252, 254, 280, 283
Ballarat 218–39, 313–15
Bannockburn Cellars (Geelong) 289, 291, 316
Bannockburn Vineyard (Geelong) 274, 286, 289, 317
Barwon Orange (Barwon Heads) 268
Basalt Ridge (Daylesford) 199, 312
Bass River Winery (Glen Forbes) 305
Bazil's (Geelong) 294, 317
Becco (City) 27, 301
beef 44, 60, 74, 142, 193, 220, 222, 251, 279–80
beer 44, 60, 179, 193, 206
Bella Vedere (Coldstream) 111–13, 307
Bellagreen Cattle Farm and Stud (Strathbogie) 142
Bellarine Estate 243, 254–7, 269
Bellarine Golden Olive (Drysdale) 249, 315
Bellarine Peninsula 242–69, 315–16
Benito's (City) 33, 301
berries 118, 121, 122, 125, 164, 190, 197, 247
    pick your own 40, 118, 120, 164
    see also blueberries; cherries; raspberries; strawberries
Bibo Bistro (Ballarat) 235–6, 314
Big Shed Wines (Daylesford) 197, 199, 312
Bindi winery (Gisborne) 169, 171
biscuits, cakes and slices 160, 163, 206, 225–6, 227, 238, 239, 254
Bittern Cottage 59, 304
Blue Hills Cherries and Berries (Silvan) 118, 120, 308
Blue Ridge Inn (Mt Macedon) 309
blueberries 40, 118, 121, 164, 244, 247
Blueberry Farm (Olinda) 121
Boathouse Café (Daylesford) 206, 313
Boatman's (Portarlington) 252
Boatshed Restaurant (Ballarat) 237, 314
Books for Cooks (Fitzroy) 23, 302
Boroondara Farmers' Market (Hawthorn) 300
Braewattie vineyard (Lancefield) 174
Brandon, Jan and Trevor 45–6
Brazo de gitano – gypsy's arm with chocolate olive oil mousse 106
bread 13, 17–18, 93, 179, 194, 237–9, 246, 252, 254, 276, 280, 283
Bread and butter pudding 16
Breakfast and Beer (Daylesford) 206, 313
Bryant's (Rosebud) 40
Bungower Park (Moorooduc) 40
bush flavours 135

Café Adagio (Sunbury) 177, 311
Café Colenso (Woodend) 179, 311
Café Companis (Ballarat) 230, 232, 238, 314
Café di Stasio (St Kilda) 27, 301
Café Segovia (City) 32, 301
Caffe e Cucina (Prahran) 27, 301
cakes, slices and biscuits 160, 163, 206, 225–6, 227, 238, 239, 254
Camberwell Market 9, 300
Campaspe Country House Hotel (Woodend) 177, 178, 311
Canal's (Carlton) 11, 300
Candlebark Farm (Yarra Valley) 93
Candlebark Hill winery (Kyneton) 170, 173, 310
Captains Creek Organic Wines (Blampied) 199, 312
Carriage House Restaurant (Macedon) 311
Casa Iberica (Fitzroy) 11, 300
Catalan cream 266
Chambers, Fiona 210–12
Chanters Ridge winery (Woodend) 173, 310
Charcoal Grill On the Hill (Kew) 20, 301
Chas Cole Cellars (Geelong) 291, 316
Chateau Yarrinya (Yarra Valley) 102, 104–5

Chateau Yering (Yarra Valley) 101, 306
cheese 14, 45–6, 93, 94, 96, 140, 143, 163–4, 193, 220, 277, 279
cherries 40, 118, 120, 140, 145, 164, 190
chestnuts 60, 120, 121, 199, 208
Chicory Restaurant (Cowes) 305
Chilli mud crab 83
Chimney European Café (Trentham) 209, 313
chocolates 93, 97–9, 101, 196–7, 198, 206
Chocolate Mill (Mt Franklin) 196–7, 198, 312
Christopoulos, Con 32–3
Churchill Produce Market 70, 74, 77, 305
Circa, The Prince (St Kilda) 20, 22, 30, 122, 301
City Wine Shop 20, 33, 301
Cleveland Winery (Lancefield) 173, 174, 310
Cliffy's (Daylesford) 190, 194, 196, 198, 206, 312
Cloudwine (South Melbourne) 20, 302
Cobaw Ridge winery (Kyneton) 170, 310
Coldstream Hills vineyard 102, 104, 306
Collingwood Children's Farm 9–10, 300
Coniston winery (Romsey) 173
Convent Gallery (Daylesford) 204, 206, 215, 313
Cookie (City) 20, 301
Cookie Crumbs (Tylden) 160
Coovara Fresh Fish Trawler (Queenscliff) 252
Cope-Williams Winery (Romsey) 166
Cosmopolitan Hotel (Trentham) 209, 313
Country Cuisine (Daylesford) 196, 312
Crabapple Bakery (Dandenongs) 122, 308
Craig's Royal Hotel (Ballarat) 231–2, 313
Craiglee Vineyard (Sunbury) 165, 171, 310
Credo Restaurant (Olinda) 133, 308
Crittenden's winery (Mornington) 52, 303
Cru Restaurant (Yarra Valley) 111, 307
Cuckoo Restaurant (Dandenongs) 129, 308
Cunliffe and Waters (Coldstream) 93, 96–7, 306
Curly Flat Vineyard (Lancefield) 171, 182–3, 310

Damper 238
Dandenong Market 9, 300
Dandenong Ranges 116–35, 306
Darriwill Farm (Ballarat) 226, 313
David's Restaurant (Prahran) 28, 301
David Traeger Wines (Nagambie) 148–9, 308
Daylesford 188–215, 312–13
Daylesford Macedon Produce 190, 193

318

De Bortoli, Leanne 104–5, 111
De Bortoli Winery and Restaurant (Dixons Creek) 102, 104–5, 108, 111, 306–7
Decadent Alternatives (Buninyong) 227, 313
Deco Restaurant (Hepburn Springs) 204
Degraves Espresso Bar (City) 32–3, 301
Del Rios Vineyard and Winery (Mt Anakie) 286, 317
Della's on Vincent (Daylesford) 206, 313
Des O'Toole's Honey (Daylesford) 194, 312
Devonshire teas, Dandenongs 127, 128, 129, 135
Diamond Valley Vineyard (Yarra Valley) 80, 102, 307
Domaine Chandon winery (Coldstream) 102, 104, 307
Dominique Portet winery (Yarra Valley) 103–4, 307
Double baked 'holy goat' cheese souffle 181
Dromana Estate 49, 303
Drum Drum Blueberry Farm (Main Ridge) 40
Dulcinea Winery (Ballarat) 227–8, 314

Eastern Peake Vineyard (Ballarat) 231, 314
eggs 40, 77, 155, 196, 200
Elements on Lonsdale (City) 301
Elgee Park (Mornington) 49, 303
Ellender Estate (Glenlyon) 197, 312–13
Ellis, Ann and John 183–4
Ellisfield Farm (Mornington) 42, 302
Emilia's Piquant Sauces (Kyneton) 165, 309
Emily Hill Farm (Emerald) 120
Enoteca Sileno (Carlton) 20, 23, 300
Epis & Williams winery (Gisborne) 170, 310
Esplanade Hotel (Queenscliff) 264
Estelle's (Sunbury) 166, 169, 311
European (City) 33, 301
ezard (City) 30, 122, 301

Farm Foods (Queenscliff) 249, 251
Farmers Arms Hotel (Daylesford) 200, 201, 203, 313
farmers' markets
  Churchill Is. 70, 74, 77, 305
  Geelong 274, 316
  Lancefield 159–64, 310
  Melbourne 9–10, 25–6, 300
  Mornington 40, 302
  Olinda 120
  Red Hill 40, 302
  Yarra Valley 93, 306
Fernleigh Farm (Bullarto) 160, 193, 210, 212, 309, 312
Firebrand Bakery (Ripponlea) 13, 300
fish and seafood 11, 26, 40, 41, 59, 69, 70–4, 83–5, 251–2, 264, 279, 296
  catching your own 120, 198, 215
Fishermen's Pier (Geelong) 291, 293, 317
Flinders Farm 42, 302

Flinders Shellfish 40, 41, 59, 302
Flippin' Fresh Seafoods (Torquay) 252
Flower Drum (City) 26, 301
Folly Farm Blueberry Growers (Olinda) 121, 308
Footscray Market 6, 300
France-Soir (South Yarra) 20, 301
Frangos & Frangos (Daylesford) 203, 313
Frank's Elsternwick Bakery 13, 300
Freeranger Eggs (Phillip Is.) 77, 305
fruit 155, 190, 193;
  see also particular fruits
Fruition Bread (Yarra Valley) 93, 306
fudge 179

Galli Estate (Sunbury) 169, 310
game 108, 222, 232, 280
Garden of St Erth (Blackwood) 209, 313
Gatehouse Café (Sunbury) 177
Geelong 272–96, 316
Geelong Farmers Market 274, 316
General Store (Merricks) 57
Gertrude Street Enoteca (Fitzroy) 23–4, 301
Gertrude Street Organic Bakery (Fitzroy) 13, 23, 300
Gilligan's (Geelong) 276, 296, 317
Gisborne Peak Winery (Gisborne) 169, 310
Giuseppe's Café (Geelong) 276, 296, 317
Glasshouse Restaurant (Ballarat) 314
Glen Erin Vineyard Retreat (Lancefield) 173, 310
Glen Isla House (Cowes) 74, 305
Glenlyon Fair 197
Goldfields Organics (Ballarat) 222, 225, 314
Goona Warra Vineyard (Sunbury) 165–6, 310
Gorgonzola and dried fig ravioli 95
Goulburn Terrace Winery (Nagambie) 142, 149–50, 153, 154, 308
Gourmet Larder (Daylesford) 196, 312
gourmet shops
  Daylesford 190, 194, 196
  Healesville 93–4
  Melbourne 13–14
  Phillip Is. 77–9
  Queenscliff 248, 251
  Ruffy 154–5
  Yarra Valley 93–4
Granite Hills Winery (Baynton) 170, 171, 310–11
Great Hall of Goona Warra (Sunbury) 166
Green Olive Gourmet (Sorrento) 57, 302
Grogan, Phillippa 16, 17–18
Grossi Florentino (City) 26, 301
Gurdies Winery (Phillip Is.) 79, 305

Hanging Rock Winery 171, 173, 183–4, 311
Harry's (Queenscliff) 264, 315
Harry's on the Esplanade (Phillip Is.) 73, 74, 82, 305
Harry's mussel laksa 41
Harvest Café (Daylesford) 206
Harvest Farm (Yarra Valley) 107

Harvest Home (Avenel) 142–3, 154, 308
Healesville Harvest Produce and Wine 93–4, 306
Healesville Hotel 93, 106, 107–8, 307
Health Foods Naturally (Daylesford) 194, 312
Hepburn General Store 194
herbs 93, 120–1, 190, 244, 247
Herbicious Delicious (Olinda) 120–1, 308
Heronswood Café (Dromana) 57–9, 304
Himalaya Bakery (Daylesford) 312
Holgate Bar and Restaurant (Woodend) 179, 309, 311
Holy Goat cheese 163–4
honey 40, 160, 194, 249, 276, 277
Hope Bakery (Sovereign Hill) 237–9, 314
Idyll Vineyard (Geelong) 273–4, 285–6
Il Bacaro (City) 27, 301
Irrewarra Sourdough Shop and Café (Geelong) 276, 280, 316, 317
Island Food Store (Cowes) 73, 74, 77–9, 306
Island Primary Produce (Cape Woolamai) 69, 74, 305
Issan Thai (Trentham) 209
Istra (Musk) 193
It's Treats Jams and Pickles (Heathcote) 163

Jacques Reymond (Windsor) 26, 301
jams, pickles and preserves 93, 96–7, 140, 155, 163, 164, 165, 196
Jess's fresh fig salad 205
Jetty Restaurant (Cowes) 85, 305
Jill's at Moorooduc Estate 59, 304
John Harbour Quality Butcher (Ballarat) 314
Jones, Jan and Robert 212–15
Journal (City) 33, 301
Julian's @ Bellarine Estate 269, 315

Kangaroo Hill Vineyard and Winery (Daylesford) 199, 313
Katos Fish Supply (Geelong) 279, 316
Keatings Hotel (Woodend) 179
Kellybrook Winery (Yarra Valley) 102, 307
Kelp (Point Lonsdale) 268
Kennedy and Wilson (Yarra Valley) 97–9, 101, 306
Kilgour Estate (Bellarine) 243, 260, 269, 315
Koukla's (Daylesford) 206, 313
Kuranga Native Nursery (Mt Evelyn) 134, 135
Kyneton Olive Oil 160, 164, 309–10
Kyneton Ridge Estate 173, 311
KYO Pty Ltd (Ocean Grove) 316

L'Espresso (Ballarat) 232–3, 234, 238, 314
Ladro (Fitzroy) 23, 27, 301
LadyHawke (Mt Dandenong) 130, 133, 308
Lake House (Daylesford) 189, 190, 193, 198, 200, 208, 209–10, 312, 313

La Madre Bakery (Bell Park) 276, 280, 283, 316
lamb 74, 190, 204, 212–15, 220
Lamb's fry with horseradish yoghurt, potatoes and kaiserfleisch 201
Lancefield Farmers' Market 159–64, 310
laneway restaurants (City) 25, 32–3
Largo Butchers (Fitzroy) 10–11, 300
La Trattoria (Shepherds Flat) 204
Lavandula (Shepherds Flat) 198, 204, 205, 312
Leaf Tea (Geelong) 277
Lemon myrtle tea sorbet 134
Leopold Honey 249
Le Parisien (Geelong) 293–4, 317
Liberty House (Hepburn Springs) 196, 312
Lighthouse Olive Oil 249
Lindenderry at Red Hill 302
Little Saigon Market (Melbourne) 9
Long Table (Mornington) 60, 304
Longleat Vineyard (Murchison) 143, 154
Longview Creek Vineyard (Sunbury) 169, 311
Lonsdale Hydroponics (Bellarine) 315
Lucini's (Hepburn Springs) 204, 313

Macedon Grove Olives (Gisborne) 160, 164, 310
Macedon Ranges 158–85, 309–11
McWilliams Wines (Macedon Ranges) 311
Main Ridge Estate 52, 303
Malmsbury Bakery 179, 310
Maloa House Gourmet Delights (Woodend) 164–5, 310
Mantons Creek Vineyard (Main Ridge) 52, 303
Manzanillo Grove (Drysdale) 246, 249, 315
Marian's Kitchen (Woodend) 165
Marinda Park Vineyard (Balnarring) 302
Mario's Cafe (Fitzroy) 26–7, 301
Martin, Adrian and Valda 143, 145
Marylands County House (Marysville) 307
Masons Café and Foodstore (Ballarat) 236, 238, 314
Max's at Red Hill Estate 60, 304
meat *see* game; particular meats; sausages; smallgoods
Mecca Bah (Docklands) 28
Mecca (Southgate) 301
Melbourne 3–33, 300–2
Melbourne Food and Wine Festival 3
Melbourne Supper Club (City) 20, 33, 301
Melbourne Wine Room (St Kilda) 27, 301
Mercato (Ballarat) 314
Mercato at Daylesford 203, 313
Meredith Dairy (Daylesford) 193, 277, 279, 312
Merricks General Store 304
Michel's Fine Biscuits (Castlemaine) 163, 310
Mirrabella Seafood (Mornington) 302
Miss Marple's Tea Rooms (Sassafras) 129, 308
Misto Restaurant (Hepburn Springs) 204, 313

Mitchelton Winery (Nagambie) 148, 153, 308–9
Mo Vida (City) 25, 301
Mondo Deli (Geelong) 277, 316
Montalto Vineyard and Olive Grove (Red Hill) 62–4, 302, 303
Montalto Willow Creek (Merricks) 303
Montrose Meat Supply 308
Moorooduc Estate 49, 59, 303
Moraghan, Jeni and Phillip 182–3
MorganField Vineyard (Lancefield) 174, 311
Mornington Peninsula 37–64, 302–4
Mount Beckworth Wines (Ballarat) 228, 314
Mount Gisborne Cherries 164
Mount Gisborne Wines 169–70, 310, 311
Mt Macedon Winery 173
Mount Mary winery (Yarra Valley) 102, 121
Mt Rael Retreat (Healesville) 108, 306
Mt William vineyard (Lancefield) 174
Mrs Jones (Carlton) 30, 301
Murchison Wines 143, 309
mushrooms 6, 60, 279

Nagambie region 138–56, 308–9
Nedlands Lavender Farm (Tuerong) 302
Newtown Provedore 277, 279, 316
Nicoise torte 109
Not Just Fudge Café (Woodend) 179, 311
Not Just Muffins (Daylesford) 206, 313

Oakdene Vineyard Restaurant (Bellarine) 247, 315
Olde Winilba Vineyard (Sunbury) 166, 169, 310, 311
Olinda Cellars 121, 308
Olinda Village Produce Market 120
olives and olive oil 40, 62–4, 82, 143, 160, 164, 193, 249
Olive Branch Preserves (Taradale) 163
Olive bread 246
Organic Gertrude (Fitzroy) 23, 300
Organic Sunrise Foods (Daylesford) 194, 312
Organic Wholefoods and Harvest Café (Daylesford) 193, 196, 312
Origin Specialty Coffee (Geelong) 274

Paperbark Café (Mt Evelyn) 135, 308
Paringa Estate (Red Hill) 303
pasta 94, 95, 166, 194
Paternoster Wines (Emerald) 120
Patrick's Vineyard (Macedon) 170
peaches 143, 145, 190
Pearl (Richmond) 30, 301
Pegeric winery (Woodend) 173
Pelican (St Kilda) 33, 301
Penny's Prime Meats (Newtown) 279–80, 316
Peppers Springs Retreat (Daylesford) 215, 312
Pettavel Winery and Restaurant (Geelong) 282, 284–5, 317
Phillip Island 69–85, 305–6

Phillip Island Winery 80–2, 305
Phillippa's (Armadale) 16, 17–18, 300
Phoenix Brewery Restaurant & Bar (Ballarat) 314
pick your own berries 40, 118, 120, 130, 164
Pie in the Sky Café (Olinda) 129, 130, 308
pies 129, 130, 237–9
see also bakeries
Pipers on Parade (Ballarat) 236–7, 314
pizza 23, 50, 166, 169, 206
Poffs Restaurant (Mornington) 60, 304
Point Nepean Meats (Mornington) 302
pork 26, 111, 193, 210, 220
Port Phillip Estate (Mornington) 52, 303
Port Pier Café (Portarlington) 266, 268, 269, 315
Portarlington Bakehouse 252, 254
Portree Vineyard (Lancefield) 174, 311
potatoes 160, 190, 193, 196, 210, 225, 279
Prahran Continental Butcher 10, 300
Prahran Market 9, 14, 26, 300
Preston Market 9, 300
Pud for all Seasons (Elphinstone) 163, 310
puddings 163, 226, 238
Punt Road Wines (Coldstream) 103, 307

Queen Victoria Market (City) 4, 6, 25, 300
Queenscliff Hotel 263, 315

R L Chapman and Sons (Silvan) 118
rabbits 11, 26, 108, 222, 280
Rack of lamb in hunan barbecue sauce 78
Randall's wine store (Geelong) 289, 291, 316
raspberries 122, 125
Red Hill Brewery 44, 60, 304
Red Hill Cellars 40, 302
Red Hill Cheese 45–6, 302
Red Hill Community Market 40, 302
Red Hill Cool Stores 40, 302
Red Hill Regional Shuttle 304–5
Red Star Café (Hepburn Springs) 204
Regional Fare (Yarra Glen) 93
Retreat Café (Hepburn Springs) 204
rhubarb 26, 140, 142
Richmond Hill Café and Larder 14, 300
Rigel Wines @ Merricks General Store 303
Ripe (Sassafras) 125, 126, 127, 308
Risotto with porcini mushrooms, red wine and thyme 233
Rochford Wines (Lancefield) 111, 174, 307
Roundstone Winery (Yarra Glen) 104, 307
Ruefleur Chestnuts (Dandenongs) 120, 308
Ruffy Produce Store 142, 152, 154–5, 308
Rupertswood (Sunbury) 177, 311

Sailors Falls Estate (Daylesford) 199, 313
St Huberts (Yarra Valley) 101, 307

Salad of bellarine figs with prosciutto and dill 256
Salix at Willow Creek (Merricks) 60, 61, 304
Sammy's potato galette thing 152
San Remo Fishermen's Co-op 69, 70, 72, 73, 74, 305
Sandy Farm (Daylesford) 199, 313
Sault (Daylesford) 203–4, 313
sausages 10, 140, 155, 190, 193, 251
Sausage Corner (Kyneton) 193, 312
Sawyers Arms Tavern (Geelong) 296, 317
Schatzi's (Woodend) 179
Scorched (Torquay) 269, 315
Scotchmans Hill (Bellarine) 243, 259–60, 274, 315
seafood and fish 11, 26, 40, 41, 59, 69, 70–4, 83–5, 251–2, 264, 279, 296
 catching your own 120, 198, 215
Seared scallops with stuffed piquillo peppers and almond sauce 61
Sequoia (Woodend) 179, 311
Shadowfax winery (Werribee Park) 285, 317
Shaw river buffalo mozzarella with lorne tamarillos 282
Silvan Estate raspberries 122, 125, 308
Silverwater Winery (San Remo) 82, 305
Simon Johnson (Fitzroy, Toorak) 14, 300
Sitka Foodstore and Café (Macedon) 177, 311
SkyHigh (Mt Dandenong) 130, 308
Slow braise of capretto 178
smallgoods 10–11, 44–5, 155, 190, 193, 220, 222, 276, 277
Smithers, Anne 180–2
Somerville Village Meats 44–5, 302
Soup of daylesford chestnuts 208
South Melbourne Market 9, 25–6, 300
Split Rock Mineral Water 155
Spoljaric, Anton 280, 283
Springhill Farm (Bacchus Marsh) 225–6, 314
Starfish Bakery (Barwon Heads) 254, 315
Stella's Naturally Fine Foods (Daylesford) 194, 312
Sticks & Grace Café Catering (Geelong) 296, 317
Stillwater at Crittenden (Dromana) 304
Stonier Wines (Merricks) 49, 53–4, 303–4
Strathbogie Ranges 138–55, 308–9
strawberries 42, 44, 244, 247
Strawberries with rose cream 44
Stringers Stores (Sorrento) 57, 302
Summer Sensations Café (Geelong) 317
Summerfields (Bittern) 40
Summerhill Farm (Main Ridge) 40
Sunny Ridge Strawberry Farm (Main Ridge) 42, 44, 302–3
Supper Inn (City) 25, 301
Sutton Grange Organic Farm (Daylesford) 193

Sweet Decadence (Daylesford) 206, 312
Syracuse (City) 25, 32–3, 301
Tahbilk Winery (Nagambie) 139, 142, 147–9, 154, 309
Taloumbi Hydroponics (Macedon Ranges) 160
tapas 25, 33, 268
TarraWarra Estate (Yarra Glen) 102, 104, 307
Tasting Station (Rosebud) 40, 303
Taylor's Waterfront Restaurant (Phillip Is.) 73, 83, 84–5, 305–6
Tea Leaves (Sassafras) 121, 308
T'Gallant Winery (Main Ridge) 50, 304
The Big Berry (Dandenongs) 120, 308
The Continental Hotel (Cowes) 305
The Deli (Gisborne) 177
The Diggers Club (Dromana) 57, 304
The Essential Ingredient (Prahran) 14, 300
The Grand Hotel (Portarlington) 268, 315
The Grange Restaurant (Lancefield) 173
The Mansion Hotel (Werribee) 316
The Ol' Duke (Portarlington) 267, 315
The Potted Pair Pty Ltd (Ballarat) 314–15
The Prince Wine Store (St Kilda) 19–20, 302
The Prince Wine Store (South Melbourne) 302
The Springs Retreat (Hepburn Springs) 204
The Wine Hub (Yarra Valley) 96
3777 restaurant (Yarra Valley) 108
Tiggies Puddings & Chocolates (Ballarat) 226, 238, 314
tomatoes 44, 57, 59, 160, 193, 247
Tonna's Fruit and Vegetable Supplies (Daylesford) 196, 312
Tozer's Restaurant (Ballarat) 236, 315
Traawool Shed Café (Nagambie) 153–4, 309
Trewhella Farm (Daylesford) 197, 312
Trident Fish Bar (Queenscliff) 252, 315
Tuckerberry Hill Blueberries (Drysdale) 247, 315
Tuki Farm Retreat (Smeaton) 198, 212–15, 313
Twice-baked zucchini and cheese soufflés with mascarpone sauce 295
2 Faces the Restaurant (Geelong) 294, 295, 317

V&R Fruit and Vegetable Market (Geelong) 279, 316
Veg Out St Kilda Farmer's Market 300
vegetables 40, 107, 142–3, 155, 160, 190, 193, 196, 199, 210, 212, 244, 247, 279
 see also particular vegetables
Veneto Blu (Seymour) 309
Vibe Savoy Hotel (City) 300
Vines of Red Hill 60, 304
Virgin Hills (Macedon) 159
Vue de Monde (City) 25, 30, 301
Vue Grand Hotel (Queenscliff) 247, 263–4, 315–15

Wallington Strawberry Farm 247, 315
walnuts 108, 155, 199, 225, 227
Wantirna Estate (Yarra Valley) 102
Warramate Vineyard (Yarra Valley) 102, 307
Warren and Hutch (Geelong) 280, 316
Waterwood Farm (Yarra Valley) 108, 306
Weber, Steve 104–5
Wellwood Wallace Walnuts (Wallace) 225
Wetlands Café (Nagambie) 154, 309
Whispers from Provence 127
White chocolate and mascarpone tart 230
White Salt Gourmet Fish and Chippery (Cape Woolamai) 69, 73, 85, 306
Whitehorse Wines (Ballarat) 227, 228, 231, 314
Wild Oak Restaurant & Wine Bar (Olinda) 133, 308
Wildwood Vineyard (Sunbury) 166, 311
Willow Creek Vineyard (Merricks) 60, 304
Wilson's Fruit and Vegetables (Ballarat) 226–7, 314
wineries
 Ballarat 227–31, 314
 Bellarine 243–4, 254–60, 315
 Dandenong Ranges 118, 121
 Daylesford 197–200, 312–13
 Geelong district 283–9, 317
 Gisborne 169–70
 Lancefield 173–4
 Macedon Ranges 170–3, 310–11
 Mornington 46–54, 303–4
 Nagambie 145–53, 308–9
 Phillip Is. 79–82, 305
 Sunbury district 165–9
 Yarra Valley 101–7, 306–7
winestores
 Dandenongs 121
 Geelong 289, 291
 Melbourne 18–23
Witchmount winery (Sunbury) 169
Wolf-Tasker, Alla 189, 194, 200, 208, 209–10
Wombat Forest Vineyard (Daylesford) 199
Woodend Berry Farm 164, 312

Yarra Valley 89–113, 306
Yarra Valley Dairy 94, 96, 306
Yarra Valley Farmers Market 93, 306
Yarra Valley Game Meats 108
Yarra Valley Pasta 94, 95, 306
Yarra Valley Regional Food Trail 93, 118
Yarra Valley Salmon 306
Yarra Yering (Yarra Valley) 102, 121
Yellowglen Vineyards (Ballarat) 227
Yelza (Fitzroy) 23, 301
Yering Station Winery (Yarra Glen) 89, 93, 101, 102, 104, 111, 307
Yeringberg (Yarra Valley) 101, 121, 307
Yu-u (City) 25, 301
Zaleti (City) 301–2
Zeppole 126
Zig Zag Winery (Malmesbury) 199, 313
Zucchini flower and anchovy tarts 22

Photography credits

iv Left to right: Simon Griffiths; Adrian Lander; Mark Roper.
ix Simon Griffiths.
x   Left to right: David Hannah; Simon Griffiths; Mark Roper; Simon Griffiths; Mark Roper.

Melbourne: Adrian Lander.
Additional photography: David Hannah – pp. 2, 4, 5, 12 top and centre, p. 25; Simon Griffiths – pp. 14,15.

Mornington Peninsula: Mark Roper.
Additional photography: Simon Griffiths – pp. 38, 42 left, 43, 52, 53, 58.

Phillip Island: Mark Roper.

Yarra Valley: Simon Griffiths.
Additional photography: Courtesy Mt Rael Retreat, pp. 86, 90 left,109.

Dandenong Ranges: Simon Griffiths.
Additional photography: Courtesy Yarra Valley Regional Food Group p. 122.

Nagambie and Strathbogie Ranges: Adrian Lander.

Macedon Ranges: David Hannah.

Daylesford: Simon Griffiths.
Additional photography: Mark Roper – p.198 bottom right, pp. 201, 202.

Ballarat: Adrian Lander.

Bellarine: Mark Roper.
Additional photography: Simon Griffiths – pp. 240, 244, 245, 252, 258, 259, 261, 263, 265, 266, 269).

Geelong: Mark Roper.
Additional photography: Simon Griffiths – p. 276 top, p. 279 right, pp. 282, 287, 288, 295; David Hannah p. 298.

Publisher's note:
Maps are for general illustration only and are not to scale.
Every effort has been made to ensure material is correct but the Publisher and Melbourne & Surrounds Marketing Inc. cannot accept responsibility for any errors or omissions.